FIFTY
KEY LITERARY
THEORISTS

What is it that defines literary theory? Richard J. Lane explores fifty influential figures who have shaped this field over the last century. In one volume theorists from a multitude of disciplines are brought together in order to explore literary theory in all its diversity, covering feminism to postcolonialism, postmodernism to psychoanalysis.

Each entry deals with key concepts and ideas that have informed literary studies in the twentieth and twenty-first centuries. Included in this comprehensive guide are entries on:

- Roland Barthes
- Judith Butler
- Jacques Derrida
- Sigmund Freud
- Edward W. Said.

Richard J. Lane is Professor of English at Malaspina University-College, Canada. His previous publications include *Jean Baudrillard* (Routledge, 2001), *Beckett and Philosophy* (2002), *Contemporary British Fiction* (2003) and *Reading Walter Benjamin* (2005).

Also available from Routledge

Poetry: The Basics
Jeffrey Wainwright
0–415–28764–2

Literary Theory: The Basics
Hans Bertens
0–415–35112–X

Shakespeare: The Basics
Sean McEvoy
0–415–36246–6

Contemporary British Novelists
Nick Rennison
0–415–21709–1

The Routledge Dictionary of Literary Terms
Peter Childs and Roger Fowler
0–415–34017–9

The Routledge Companion to Critical Theory
Simon Malpas and Paul Wake
0–415–33296–6

The Routledge Companion to Feminism and Postfeminism
Edited by Sarah Gamble
0–415–24310–6

The Routledge Companion to Postmodernism
Edited by Stuart Sim
0–415–33359–8

The Routledge Companion to Russian Literature
Edited by Neil Cornwell
0–415–23366–6

FIFTY KEY
LITERARY
THEORISTS

Richard J. Lane

Routledge
Taylor & Francis Group

NEW YORK AND LONDON

First published 2006
by Routledge
270 Madison Ave, New York, NY 10016

Simultaneously published in the UK
by Routledge
2 Park Square, Milton Park, Abingdon, Oxon OX14 4RN

Routledge is an imprint of the Taylor and Francis Group,
an informa business

© 2006 Richard J. Lane

Typeset in Bembo by Florence Production Ltd, Stoodleigh, Devon
Printed and bound in Great Britain by MPG Books Ltd, Bodmin

British Library Cataloguing in Publication Data
A catalogue record for this book is available from the British Library

Library of Congress Cataloging in Publication Data
Lane, Richard J., 1966–
Fify key literary theorists/Richard J. Lane.
p. cm.
Includes bibliographical references and index
1. Criticism – Bio-bibliography. 2. Criticism – History –
20th century.
I. Title.
PN74.L36 2006
801′950922–dc22   2006003837

ISBN10: 0–415–33847–6 (hbk)
ISBN10: 0–415–33848–4 (pbk)
ISBN10: 0–203–44142–7 (ebk)

ISBN13: 9–78–0-415–33847–9 (hbk)
ISBN13: 9–78–0-415–33848–6 (pbk)
ISBN13: 9–78–0-203–44142–8 (ebk)

CONTENTS

PREFACE

This book emerges from a number of intense encounters, over nearly two decades, with what most academics now simply call 'theory', including my doctoral studies with Geoff Bennington, at The University of Sussex, which resulted in my D.Phil. thesis on Jacques Derrida (*Functions of the Derrida Archive: Philosophical Receptions*, 1997, published 2003); time spent at The British Library, London, researching my book on Jean Baudrillard for the Routledge Critical Thinkers Series, edited by Robert Eaglestone (*Jean Baudrillard*, 2000); and my brief period directing the London Network Philosophy and Theory Research Seminar, that met (informally) at The Institute of Contemporary Arts in London between 2000 and 2002. At the ICA meetings, two figures were explored most closely: Samuel Beckett and Walter Benjamin (*Beckett and Philosophy*, 2002 and *Reading Walter Benjamin: Writing Through the Catastrophe*, 2005). This slightly tangled web of interests and connections brought me to the position where I could say 'yes' to Routledge, when they suggested that I might like to tackle fifty key twentieth-century literary theorists. Of course, at that point the debates really began, concerning who the 'fifty' should actually be. Inevitably someone's favourite and important theorist has been left out of this selection, but careful consideration was given to the overall range of critics and/or theorists included here. Some biographical information is given for each thinker, but the bulk of each entry deals with key concepts and ideas that have informed literary studies in the twentieth and twenty-first centuries. The entries are selective, and student readers may wish to follow up particular theorists by turning to the Routledge Critical Thinkers Series. I also strongly recommend to student readers the relevant Gale reference publications, such as the *Dictionary of Literary Biography* and the *Contemporary Literary Criticism* series, where more extensive entries, with competing critical views, can be found. A particularly useful book that I have consulted many times is Patrick Ffrench's *The Time of Theory: A History of Tel Quel (1960–1983)* (Clarendon Press, 1995); Elizabeth Roudinesco's biography of Jacques Lacan (Polity, 1997) provided excellent background information concerning psychoanalysis and theory in France and elsewhere. To these two authors, and many others, I am indebted.

Various people deserve appreciation and thanks for the support that they have given me during the writing of this book. These include David Avital, Andrea Hartill, Rachel Sexton and Rosie Waters at Routledge, Robert Eaglestone at Royal Holloway, University of London, Tamas Benyei, Nora Sellei, Peter Szaffko and Judit Szabó at The University of Debrecen, Hungary, Sherrill Grace at The University of British Columbia, and Terri Doughty, Steve Lane and John Lepage at Malaspina University-College. Deborah Madsen, at The University of Geneva, has been of constant support and I thank her for her intellectual engagement in the areas of postcolonial theory and literature. Joseph Jones, Librarian Emeritus at The University of British Columbia, has continued to support and engage with my research. My research students, Susan Rankin and Bel Birkland, helped with background materials, and the staff at the new Malaspina University-College library provided me with much assistance. I am also indebted to the staff at The British Library, London. However, the bulk of my research support was provided by my wife Sarah, and I dedicate this book to her, with love.

FIFTY KEY LITERARY THEORISTS

HOUSTON A. BAKER, JR (1943–)

Finding common ground between theory and the 'founding condition of Afro-American intellectual history',[1] Houston A. Baker, Jr argues that both seek explanations at a 'metalevel'. Baker comes to this conclusion because of the way in which his intellectual project is always firmly grounded in the history of Afro-American existence, especially an awareness of the uprooting, dispossession and victimization that constituted the African slave trade. Early Afro-Americans maintained their cultural heritage during slavery in ways in which the dispossession of material goods could not touch, leading not just to a privileging of spirituality and spiritual leaders within slave communities, but also the privileging of autobiography as a genre in which Afro-Americans could reinforce and reinvent self-worth in the midst of their debasement. This confluence of theory and intensely personal history is one of the factors that has led to Baker's groundbreaking work in the field of Afro-American literary studies. Born in 1943, in Louisville, Kentucky, Baker was educated at Howard University and the University of California, Los Angeles; his early work on literary criticism involved writing a thesis on Victorian aesthetics, which he achieved in part through his researches at Edinburgh University in Scotland (1967–1968). At Yale University, where Baker initially worked as an instructor, his interests shifted to Afro-American literary studies. In 1970 Baker became a member of the Center for Advanced Studies at the University of Virginia, and in 1974 he became the director of the Afro-American Studies Programme at the University of Pennsylvania. Baker was awarded the prestigious post of Albert M. Greenfield Professor of Human Relations at the University of Pennsylvania in 1982. In his early publications, Baker's focus was on defining, mapping and performing a critique of the 'black aesthetic' in America: major texts from this period include *Long Black Song: Essays in Black American Literature* (1972), *Singers of Daybreak: Studies in Black American Literature* (1974) and the edited collection *Reading Black: Essays in the Criticism of African, Caribbean, and Black American Literature* (1976). In the introduction to *Reading Black*, Baker argues that while it is difficult to precisely date the origins of a black aesthetic, it is possible to offer a basic map that includes:

> The establishment of LeRoi Jones' Black Arts Repertoire Theatre School, the founding of new literary and cultural journals, the widescale repudiation of derogatory white

creative efforts treating the Black experience, [and] the appearance of invaluable anthologies and critical volumes by Black
writers.[2]

Baker also points out that critics have argued for strong links between
the emergence of the Black Power Movement and the black aesthetic.
It was Baker's 1980 book, called *The Journey Back: Issues in Black
Literature and Criticism*, that initiated even more widespread interest
and debate in the black aesthetic in American studies.

In *The Journey Back*, Baker argues for an interdisciplinary approach
to black American literature and culture that analyses the framework that he calls an 'anthropology of art'.[3] The essential critical move
is one of considering context, and this leads to an awareness of the
fact that Afro-American art-works are 'in motion'.[4] Baker's historical
survey also functions as a critique of the early theories of the black
aesthetic; in Chapter 5 of *The Journey Back* he examines the idealistic
desire in the 1960s and 1970s to will 'into being a new art and criticism'[5] using a *conative* mode of utterance, which means one that
expresses a striving towards a goal, in other words as much the *creation*
of a black aesthetic as the *description* of what already exists. Baker refers
to two texts published in 1968: Baraka and Neal's anthology *Black
Fire, An Anthology of Afro-American Writing* and Larry Neal's manifesto
'The Black Arts Movement'; he argues that both texts develop conative utterances through the use of the 'afterimage' defined as 'visual
images that remain after a stimulus has passed'.[6] The stimuli here are
black American urban uprisings and the concomitant equation of
Black Power with the emergent black aesthetic. Why does Baker
critique conative utterances? Because he argues that this is perception
guided by volition, desire and idealism, and that the black aesthetic
gets distorted by its reading and integration into idealism. This is a
crucial point because Baker also argues that white critics create
distorted readings of the black aesthetic by predicating their interpretations on the notion of failure. Instead of this idealism, Baker
advocates a study of black American culture that acknowledges 'a rich
cultural context'[7] rather than predicating that richness as always being
futural, although he does admit the positive, creative potential of the
black aesthetic as a poetic construct. In one of the most dense passages
of *The Journey Back*, Baker describes the existential situation of the
Afro-American artist, suggesting that even though historically white
America has attempted to quell a black collectivity, nonetheless it has
always existed alongside that of a white hegemony in the form of
music, poetry, sacred texts and sculpted images.[8] The suggestion is

that the black artist is no longer working in a void formed by a largely hostile white hegemony, but instead there is an educated Afro-American audience that is an essential part of the creative, productive black collectivity. The 'journey back', then, involves re-affirming the richness and complexity of a culture that the hegemonic society attempted to suppress, oppress and deny; the journey back is not a nostalgia trip, but an engagement with forms that could not always be seen or heard, given limitations of interpretive models and/or previously less-well-educated audiences. Such an engagement and re-affirmation would find powerful expression in Baker's re-examination of the critical reception to the Harlem Renaissance.

Published in 1987, *Modernism and the Harlem Renaissance* is Baker's re-evaluation of an intellectual position that argued that the Harlem Renaissance was a failure. Baker asks who exactly made this powerful value judgement and why Afro-American scholars accepted it. In a series of subversive moves, Baker reorients the critical approach to the Harlem Renaissance, first, by arguing for the importance of '*modern Afro-American sound* as a function of a specifically Afro-American discursive practice',[9] second by reflecting on family history, and the ways in which judgements of success/failure are predicated upon exclusionary forces and different criteria of success, and third by rejecting Eurocentric notions of modernism as inappropriate for understanding Afro-American modernism. Baker's task is to recode the Harlem Renaissance in terms of 'a distinctive, family modernity',[10] the latter phrase being reminiscent of Wittgenstein's concept of 'family resemblance', whereby overlapping shared features group together objects that also have individual differences. Butler utilizes two further terms: the 'discursive constellation' and 'blues geographies'; the combination of the two leads him to replace 'renaissance' with Afro-American 'renaissancism'. The discursive constellation of Afro-American literature, music, art, graphic design and intellectual history, facilitates a shift into new modes of production; what Baker calls 'blues geographies', a unique assemblage of revival and rebirth. Baker is more specific than this, arguing that two key artistic processes are the mastery of form and the deformation of mastery; locating a founding event for Afro-American modernism – Booker T. Washington's opening address to the Negro exhibit of the Atlanta Cotton States and International Exposition on 18 September 1895 – Baker argues that Washington both adopted (discursively and strategically) the minstrel mask and subverted it at the same time. The mask becomes a trope that is simultaneously imprisoning and facilitating. In the employing of such a contentious trope, however, a uniquely Afro–American modernist anxiety

is produced: one that signals a distance from the realm of slavery. Baker
suggests that this 'move up' from slavery is a mode of cultural negotiation. Turning to his essay 'There Is No More Beautiful Way: Theory
and the Poetics of Afro-American Women's Writing', such a negotiation is tied in with 'autobiographical inscription'.[11] Rejecting a need
for an Afro-American liberal humanism, Baker posits instead a notion
of an activist autobiography where there is 'a personal negotiation of
metalevels that foregrounds nuances and resonances of a different
story'.[12] Key here is what Baker calls the 'autobiographical recall of the
auditory', that is to say, a willingness and ability to listen to 'authentic sources of black expressive sound'.[13] The importance of oral cultural forms is conjoined here to the work of contemporary Afro-
American feminists who have created a poetics of African American
women's voices. In his *Blues, Ideology, and Afro-American Literature: A
Vernacular Theory* (1984), Baker expands upon and refines his notion
of orality and blues geographies, developing a theory of an artistic vernacular that is integrated in an economic and socio-political history of
Black America. However, *Blues, Ideology, and Afro-American Literature*
is less a progression, and more a new beginning for Baker, drawing
upon economics *and* poststructuralism, materiality *and* semiotics, symbolic *and* dialectical thought (with emphasis upon Hegel). In a
Hegelian move, Baker sublates (incorporates and lifts up into a new
perspective) his former symbolic-anthropological orientation to argue
that the Afro-American blues is a matrix. What does he mean by this?
Thinking about different definitions of 'matrix' Baker lists: womb,
network, fossil-bearing rock, rocky trace, principal metal in an alloy,
a plate for reproducing media.[14] Using Derridean theory, Baker brings
all of these definitions together in the concept of the *enabling script* of
Afro-American culture. The blues are a code and a force that radically
condition Afro-American cultural significations.[15] Baker lists some key
elements of the synthesis known as the blues: 'work songs, group sec-
ulars, field hollers, sacred harmonies, proverbial wisdom, folk philosophy, political commentary, ribald humor, elegiac lament, and much
more'.[16] As a force, the blues operates as a foundational play of differences: that is to say, an artistic driving force for dynamic production
that respects differences and autonomous artistic expressions; the
implications of such a statement are vast, with the potential for a blues
matrix being 'a vernacular [local, idiomatic] trope for American cultural explanation in general'.[17] A national blues geography emerges
from Baker's reading of: the conclusion to the *Narrative of the Life
of Frederick Douglass*, Zora Neale Hurston's *Their Eyes Were Watching
God*, Richard Wright's *Black Boy*, Ellison's *Invisible Man*, Baruka's *The

System of Dante's Hell and Toni Morrison's *Song of Solomon*. In more recent work, Baker has focused on a concomitant poetics in his *Workings of the Spirit: The Poetics of Afro-American Women's Writing* (1991), which includes a photo essay by Elizabeth Alexander and Patricia Redmond. Once more, there is a Hegelian force identified at work in the mapping of an Afro-American women's poetic, perhaps best revealed by Baker's focus on the radical shift in subjectivity in *Their Eyes Were Watching God*, whereby the protagonist Janie transforms subjectivity via the act of autobiography. As he writes: 'what Janie has done . . . is transform the quotidian rites of a black woman's passage through the world into a series of figures or images that are so resonant that they catapult Pheoby [Janie's friend] into new consciousness.'[18] This fundamental re-telling of the everyday biographical story – i.e. one which black women from this period and beyond may identify with – sublates or 'lifts up' Pheoby so that she grows, changes and has a new sense of dissatisfaction with her lot; the essential point here is that this growth is intersubjective, a shared experience between two women.

Baker's 'blues geographies' – a complex mapping of Afro-American literary, artistic and theoretical culture – incessantly interrogates the black aesthetic in critical and creative ways that rarely lose touch with personal, family history. As such, Baker's synthesis of high theory and the vernacular, which remains focused upon the economic and social conditions of slavery and modern Afro-American history, also provides a pedagogic model for producing readings of indigenous texts, readings that maintain a sensitivity to the everyday conditions of artistic existence and production. In other words, in interrogating and mapping the black aesthetic, Baker has taught critics new ways of reading literature in general.

Notes

1 Houston A. Baker, Jr, 'There Is No More Beautiful Way: Theory and the Poetics of Afro-American Women's Writing', in Houston A. Baker, Jr, and Patricia Redmond, eds, *Afro-American Literary Study in the 1990s*, Chicago and London: The University of Chicago Press, 1989, pp. 135–155; p. 135.
2 Houston A. Baker, Jr, ed., *Reading Black: Essays in the Criticism of African, Caribbean, and Black American Literature*, Ithaca, NY: Africana Studies and Research Center, Cornell University, 1976, p. vi.
3 Houston A. Baker, Jr, *The Journey Back: Issues in Black Literature and Criticism*, Chicago, IL and London: The University of Chicago Press, 1980, p. xvi.
4 Ibid., p. xvii.

5 Ibid., p. 134.
6 Ibid.
7 Ibid., p. 138.
8 Ibid., p. 141.
9 Houston A. Baker, Jr, *Modernism and the Harlem Renaissance*, Chicago, IL and London: The University of Chicago Press, 1987, p. xiv.
10 Ibid., p. xvii.
11 Houston A. Baker, Jr, 'There Is No More Beautiful Way: Theory and the Poetics of Afro-American Women's Writing', p. 136.
12 Ibid., p. 144.
13 Ibid., p. 147.
14 Houston A. Baker, Jr, *Blues, Ideology, and Afro-American Literature: A Vernacular Theory*, Chicago and London: The University of Chicago Press, 1984, p. 3.
15 Ibid., p. 5.
16 Ibid.
17 Ibid., p. 14.
18 Houston A. Baker, Jr, *Workings of the Spirit: The Poetics of Afro-American Women's Writing* (1991), p. 63 with a phototext by Elizabeth Alexander and Patricia Redmond, Chicago, IL: University of Chicago Press.

See also in this book

Gates

Major works

Black Literature in America (ed., 1971). New York: McGraw-Hill.
Long Black Song: Essays in Black American Literature and Culture (1972). Charlottesville, VA: University Press of Virginia.
A Many-Colored Coat of Dreams: The Poetry of Countee Cullen (1974). Detroit, MI: Broadside Press.
Singers of Daybreak: Studies in Black American Literature (1974). Washington, DC: Howard University Press.
Reading Black: Essays in the Criticism of African, Caribbean, and Black American Literature (ed., 1976). Ithaca, NY: Africana Studies and Research Center, Cornell University.
The Journey Back: Issues in Black Literature and Criticism (1980). Chicago, IL and London: The University of Chicago Press.
English Literature: Opening Up the Canon (ed. with Leslie Fiedler, 1981). Baltimore, MD: Johns Hopkins University Press.
Blues, Ideology, and Afro-American Literature: A Vernacular Theory (1984). Chicago, IL and London: The University of Chicago Press.
Modernism and the Harlem Renaissance (1987). Chicago, IL and London: The University of Chicago Press.
Afro-American Poetics: Revisions of Harlem and the Black Aesthetic (1988). Madison, WI: University of Wisconsin Press.
Afro-American Literary Study In The 1990s (ed. with Patricia Redmond, 1989). Chicago, IL and London: The University of Chicago Press.
Workings of the Spirit: The Poetics of Afro-American Women's Writing (1991) with phototext by Elizabeth Alexander and Patricia Redmond, Chicago, IL: University of Chicago Press.

Black Studies, Rap, and the Academy (1993). Chicago, IL and London: The University of Chicago Press.

Further reading

Adell, Sandra, 'The Crisis in Black American Literary Criticism and the Postmodern Cures of Houston A. Baker, Jr., and Henry Louis Gates, Jr.', in Winston Napier, ed., *African American Literary Theory: A Reader*, New York: New York University Press, 2000; pp. 523–539.

Bérubé, Michael, 'Hybridity in the Center: An Interview with Houston A. Baker, Jr.', *African American Review*, 26.4 (1992): 547–564.

Joyce, Joyce A. '"Who the Cap Fit": Unconsciousness and Unconscionableness in the Criticism of Houston A. Baker, Jr., and Henry Louis Gates, Jr.', in Winston Napier, ed., *African American Literary Theory: A Reader*, NY: New York University Press, 2000; pp. 319–330.

Lee, Yu-cheng, 'Houston A. Baker, Jr. and the Archaeology of African American Expressive Culture', *EurAmerica: A Journal of European and American Studies*, 22.1 (1992): 75–93.

Mueller-Hartmann, Andreas, 'Houston A. Baker, Jr.: The Development of a Black Literary Critic', *Literary Griot*, 1.2 (1989): 100–111.

MIKHAIL MIKHAILOVICH BAKHTIN (1895–1975)

One of the most remarkable facts about Bakhtin is that the concepts that he developed in the midst of his obscurity in Soviet Russia so came to dominate Western literary theory towards the end of the twentieth century. Myriad literary-critical papers published in academic journals and books in the humanities utilize Bakhtinian concepts such as: chronotope; dialogism; polyphony; heteroglossia; and most famously, carnival. There has also been much critical disagreement and debate concerning the question of Bakhtin's possible authorship, under two separate names, of three books: *Freudianism: A Marxist Critique* (V.N. Voloshinov, 1927), *The Formal Method in Literary Scholarship* (P.N. Medvedev, 1928) and *Marxism and the Philosophy of Language* (V.N. Voloshinov, 1929). Assessing Bakhtin's contribution to scholarship – and even deciding what books he actually authored – from the perspective of the twenty-first century, is a constant challenge, especially in grasping the powerful ideological forces that disrupted and deformed his life and intellectual development in Soviet Russia. Bakhtin was born in Orel, Russia, in 1895; he studied at Odessa University in 1913, and then progressed in 1914 to Petrograd (St Petersburg) University where he studied classics and philology. Following the disruptions of the Russian Revolution (1917, with the ensuing civil war lasting five years), he moved first to Nevel and then Vitebsk, and was arrested in 1929 for being a member of a Christian movement called Voskresenie.

9

Bakhtin was sentenced to the Solovetsky prison camp, but was spared this fate – which probably would have killed him because of illness – through the intervention of friends; instead, he was exiled to the Kazakh Autonomous Soviet Socialist Republic[1] where he managed to not only maintain his intellectual interests, but research and write some of his key texts while also working as a bookkeeper. In 1936, Bakhtin started to teach at the Mordovia Pedagogical Institute in Saransk, although he was forced to leave the following year because of an imminent Stalinist purge; after the defence of his doctoral thesis on Rabelais at the Gorky Institute of World Literature, Moscow, in 1947, and after changes in the political situation, Bakhtin was once again allowed to teach. In 1957, he became chair of the department of Russian and World Literature at the University of Saransk. How did this relatively obscure academic, who lived through Stalinism and other enormous political and social upheavals, come to dominate the literary theoretical scene in the West at the end of the century? To answer this question, the multiple rediscoveries and recuperations of Bakhtin need to be briefly charted.

Influenced by the work of the neo-Kantian Cohen, and the philosophers Bergson and Buber, Bakhtin's early essays explore the situated subject in a dynamic architectonics of self and other. In his essay 'Art and Answerability',[2] published in *Den'iskusstva* (The Day of Art) in 1919, Bakhtin issues his earliest formulation of a dialogic (or *double-voiced* – see below) relationship between two realms: those of art and life. Suggesting that human beings usually keep these two modes of being separate, Bakhtin asks what will guarantee their connection and 'inner interpenetration' in the unified subject. His answer is his concept of 'answerability' that he posits as a 'unity' based upon guilt: the individual is responsible for each realm, especially the faults of each realm, but once they are interpenetrated in this existential act of ethical responsibility generated through guilt, art and life are unified in the subject. Dialogism is approached again in a manuscript worked upon during 1920 to 1923, called 'Author and Hero in Aesthetic Activity'.[3] In this text Bakhtin introduces some dialogic terminology, such as 'architectonics' (a dynamic mode of construction or building a complex object, such as a literary text), and 'consummation' (the way in which parts of a text get organized into an aesthetic, fictive whole), to reveal the ways in which what appear to be binary oppositions – such as between author/hero – are actually in a dynamic simultaneous relationship of 'an inclusive *also/and*'.[4] Critics have noted that 'Author and Hero' explores analogies between aesthetics and theology: 'Because each *geroj* (character, protagonist, hero) lacks full awareness of its underlying principle, which "is bestowed . . . as a gift," authors create unity, for their godlike knowledge exceeds their characters' by an excess or "surplus" (*ixbytok*).'[5] These early essays by Bakhtin remained untranslated, and in many cases unpublished, until the 1970s because of the repressive political climate in Russia; the publication in 1990 of English translations of key early works, called *Art And Answerability: Early Philosophical Essays by M.M. Bakhtin*, comes *after* the Western reception and adaptation of Bakhtin had already taken place. So what were the major texts that were so eagerly received by twentieth-century Western critics? Bakhtin's dissertation (first published 1965) was translated into English with the title *Rabelais and His World* in 1968 (with a fragment appearing in volume 41 of *Yale French Studies*), *Problems of Dostoevsky's Poetics* (1929) in 1973, *The Dialogic Imagination* (1972) in 1981, and six essays from *Estetika slovesnogo tvorchestva* (Aesthetics of verbal creativity, 1979) as *Speech Genres and Other Late Essays* in 1986. It is through these texts that innovative Bakhtinian terms and concepts entered Western critical discourse.

Carnival is one of Bakhtin's most well-used terms, initially derived from *Rabelais and His World*, which is ostensibly a study of the writings of François Rabelais (1494–1553). Carnival is a subversive force most clearly visible in the laughter and bodily humour of folk culture, in particular the pageants and carnivals of the Middle Ages which, Bakhtin argues, continue in transposed form in literary texts.[6] Carnival is also a lived experience – lived by the people in opposition to authority – with no specific or determinate outcome except for an ambivalent mode of ongoing subversion. In relation to Rabelais, Bakhtin shows how the official pomp and circumstance of the Church and the feudal state are parodied and ridiculed via rituals that foreground low bodily functions, such as excretion and transgressive and grotesque sexuality. Some critics interpret in an allegorical fashion Bakhtin's account of carnival, as being a critique of Stalinism. The literary form that best embodies carnival is that of the grotesque, a parodic and subversive mode of writing exemplified by Cervantes, Rabelais and Shakespeare. Bakhtin's work on carnival continues in his *Problems of Dostoevsky's Poetics*, where he also developed the concept of dialogism, or, double-voicing. Applying to language in general and specific instances of literary expression, dialogism means the co-presence of two voices in one. Awareness of co-present voices may come about through study of rich multiple context – the text's heteroglossia – or, through an awareness of subtle shifts of the presentation of voices drawn from a particular discourse in a literary text. In the latter case, Bakhtin suggests that dialogic language functions as if in quotation marks; in other words, each dialogic expression fore-grounds that it is in a self-aware relationship, or tension, with another voice. A good example is that of irony, where not only does a statement have two competing meanings, but this double-voiced structure is deliberately aimed at a listener or receiver. If a text presents multiple voices, including the author's or the narrator's, without placing them in a hierarchy, then Bakhtin suggests that we experience polyphony. Such a text is perceived as more democratic than those that order speakers or voices according to hierarchical systems or ideologies; Bakhtin's ideal polyphonic writer is Dostoevsky.

In *The Dialogic Imagination*, Bakhtin introduced the concept of the chronotope in his essay 'Forms of Time and of the Chronotope in the Novel: Notes toward a Historical Poetics'. Essentially a way of perceiving the 'intrinsic connectedness'[7] of time and space in litera-ture, Bakhtin argues that the chronotope is also formative for genre. Bakhtin utilizes the chronotope to explain the anachronistic forms that survive in literary genres long after their historical development should have annihilated them; for example, a literary device created in the nineteenth century may still function anachronistically in the twen-tieth century, when society, and its understanding and practice of art and literature, has radically changed. As a constitutive intersection of the temporal and spatial axes that generate texts within a genre, Bakhtin allows for the simultaneous existence of synchronic (actual) and diachronic (developmental) features. As a concrete example he examines the so-called 'Greek romance' and shows how the adven-tures that befall the lovers or protagonists in these narratives do not *influence* them in any way. From a contemporary perspective, we would expect life events to be formative, leading to character devel-opment and maturity; but this is not the case in the Greek romance. Instead, temporality is not progressive but simultaneous, and 'there is a sharp hiatus between . . . moments of biographical time, a hiatus that leaves no *trace* in the life of the heroes or in their personalities'.[8] But what does this adventure-time, extratemporality, or *time axis* of the chronotope, coincide with spatially? It coincides with an 'abstract' expanse of space whereby adventure-time can be played out. Distance and proximity are technical necessities for the functioning of adven-ture-time, the random contingency of meetings suddenly happening (or, just as importantly not occurring), what Bakhtin calls a logic of random disjunctions. Instead of life's normal progression, the Greek romance is punctuated by abnormal catastrophic punctuations in time, whereby powerful superhuman and inhuman forces take control of events. Bakhtin argues that with this chronotope, for all its adventures and mishaps, there is an overall stasis: the characters remain the same throughout, even though they have passed through, and have been tested by, powerful events. In other words, the chronotope of the Greek romance is not developmental, but an affirmation of identity.

Turning briefly to the Rabelaisian chronotope, Bakhtin argues that it is fundamentally an oppositional chronotope, one facilitated by the spatial and temporal expanses of Rabelais' fictional world, in an attempt to purge that world of the symbolism and 'verticality' of the transcendent world view of the Church and the feudal state. The Rabelaisian chronotope attempts to purge itself of the transcendent via the initial destruction of the 'habitual matrices' of the everyday world, followed by the creation of new and unexpected matrices, linguistic connections and logical links.[9] The restorative laughter of Rabelais' folk humour is an anti-idealism that also recovers the 'unmediated connections' between taboo objects and processes; the most unsettling destruction of the religious and feudal hierarchy of values, however, is attained via the 'verbal matrix' or that which collapses idealized time and space into the realm of the body, its presence, its here-and-now, its formation and deformation. The verbal matrix is one that contaminates an idealized, abstract and transcendent linguistic universe to such an extent that it becomes reformed at another scale and in another time and space: that of the human body. With the shift in literary-theoretical attention toward the end of the twentieth century to that of the body, especially via feminist research, Bakhtin's oeuvre retained its importance and influence.

Notes

1 James Whitlark, 'Mikhail Mikhailovich Bakhtin (*16 November 1895–7 March 1975*)', *DLB 242*, p. 53.
2 See M.M. Bakhtin, *Art And Answerability: Early Philosophical Essays by M.M. Bakhtin*, ed., Michael Holquist and Vadim Liapunov, trans. Vadim Liapunov, supplement trans. Kenneth Brostrom, Austin, TX: University of Texas Press, 1990, pp. 1–3.
3 Ibid., pp. 4–256.
4 Ibid., 'Introduction' (Michael Holquist), p. xxiii.
5 James Whitlark, 'Mikhail Mikhailovich Bakhtin (*16 November 1895–7 March 1975*)', p. 51.
6 Sue Vice, *Introducing Bakhtin*, Manchester and New York: Manchester University Press, 1997, p. 150.
7 M.M. Bakhtin, *The Dialogic Imagination: Four Essays by M.M. Bakhtin*, trans. Caryl Emerson and Michael Holquist, ed. Michael Holquist, Austin, TX: University of Texas Press, 1981, p. 84.
8 Ibid., p. 90.
9 Ibid., p. 169.

See also in this book

Kristeva

Major works

Works attributed to Bakhtin

Volosinov, V.N. *Freudianism: A Marxist Critique* (1927). Trans. I.R. Titunik and Neal H. Bruss, New York: Academic Press, 1973.
Medvedev, P.N. *The Formal Method in Literary Scholarship: A Critical Introduction to Sociological Poetics* (1928). Trans. A.J. Wehrle, London and Baltimore, MD: The Johns Hopkins University Press, 1978.
Volosinov, V.N. *Marxism and the Philosophy of Language* (1929). Trans. Ladislav Mateka and Titunik, London and New York: Seminar Press, 1973.

Works by Bakhtin

Problems of Dostoevsky's Poetics (1929). Trans. R.W. Rotsel, Ann Arbor, MI: Ardis, 1973; trans. Caryl Emerson, Minneapolis, MN and London: University of Minnesota Press, 1984.
Rabelais and His World (1965). Trans. Hélène Iswolsky, Cambridge, MA: MIT Press, 1968.
The Dialogic Imagination: Four Essays by M.M. Bakhtin (1972). Trans. Caryl Emerson and Michael Holquist, ed. Michael Holquist, Austin, TX: University of Texas Press, 1981.
Speech Genres and Other Late Essays (1979). Trans. Vern W. McGee, ed. Caryl Emerson and Michael Holquist, Austin, TX: University of Texas Press, 1986.
Art and Answerability: Early Philosophical Essays by M.M. Bakhtin (1990). Trans. Vadim Liapunov, supplement trans. Kenneth Brostrom, eds Michael Holquist and Vadim Liapunov, Austin, TX: University of Texas Press.

Further reading

Bauer, Dale M. and Jaret McKinstrey, S., eds, *Feminism, Bakhtin, and the Dialogic*, Albany, NY: SUNY Press, 1991.
Bernard-Donals, Michael F., *Mikhail Bakhtin: Between Phenomenology and Marxism*, Cambridge: Cambridge University Press, 1994.
Hirschkop, Ken and Shepherd, David, eds, *Bakhtin and Cultural Theory*, Manchester and New York: Manchester University Press, 2002.
Holquist, Michael, *Dialogism: Bakhtin and His World*, London: Methuen, 1990.
Kristeva, Julia, *Desire in Language: A Semiotic Approach to Literature and Art*, ed. Leon Roudiez, trans. Thomas Gora, Alice Jardine, Leon Roudiez, NY: Columbia University Press, 1980.
Todorov, Tzvetan, *Mikhail Bakhtin: The Dialogic Principle*, trans. Wlad Godzich, Manchester and New York: Manchester University Press, 1984.
Vice, Sue, *Introducing Bakhtin*, Manchester and New York: Manchester University Press, 1997.

ROLAND BARTHES (1915–1980)

The elusiveness and brilliance of Roland Barthes can be read in his introduction to a small but significant essay 'The Struggle with the Angel',[1] where in a piece of writing that is primarily about productive and rich narrative repetition in *Genesis* 32, he rejects producing his own 'useless' repetition of a 'preliminary exposition of the principles, perspectives and problems of the structural analysis of narrative', followed by the assertion that his own structural analysis will not be very 'pure'.[2] Instead, his reading will be one contaminated by 'textual analysis' which no longer perceives the literary text as a 'philological object' but rather as a mode of production, of *signifiance*, a term developed by Julia Kristeva meaning a volume or scenic space of meaning-generation, one which is potentially infinite.[3] Barthes' third move in his introduction is to argue that focusing on *text* means perceiving each text's *difference*, not as a fundamental uniqueness or mysterious essence, but rather as an effect of a language network. Crucially, this shift from object to text, from inherent meaning to differential sign, is also a shift away from historical and structural questions of location and formation, towards the noting of the text's dispersal and dissemination along 'coded paths'.[4] Finally, Barthes argues that he will not bring structural and textual analysis into confrontation in his essay, neither will he produce any results or a methodology that can be followed by others: instead, he merely *proceeds*. What follows this series of disclaimers is an exemplary structural and textual analysis that also breaks new ground, not only constantly pushing at the boundaries of the semiological approach (see below), but also resisting the mastery of the text's meanings that would be contra to the work of significance, that which dismantles or deconstructs authorial and interpretive supremacy. In other words, the critic most famous for his often misunderstood phrase 'the death of the author' shows in his 'Struggle with the Angel', written just under a decade before his death, that the real struggle is actually with the text, and the text always, necessarily, 'wins'. How had Barthes arrived at such an assessment, one that has come to dominate contemporary approaches to the study of literature? Born in 1915, in Cherbourg, France, Barthes took an unorthodox route to his position of great eminence of Chair of Semiology at the College de France (awarded in 1976). Suffering from tuberculosis as a child, Barthes underwent treatment in the Pyrenees, instead of cramming for the École Normale Supérieure; his illness would also later lead to a period of intensive private study of Marx and Sartre during the Second World War, while he recuperated in the Alps. After the war, with a degree in languages, Barthes taught French in Romania and then in Alexandria, Egypt, where he met the lexicologist (and later semiotician) A.J. Greimas (1917–1992). Barthes and Greimas would continue to influence one another throughout their careers: Barthes returning to France where he started a thesis on lexicology, and Greimas later abandoning lexicology for semiotics. Barthes gained a teaching post at the École Pratique des Hautes Etudes in 1960, and continued to produce numerous books and articles, dramatically rising in fame with the clash between himself and Sorbonne Professor Raymond Picard, who called the new French theorists – of which Barthes was the main target – 'charlatans'. Barthes died only four years after receiving his prestigious Chair at the College de France, killed by a truck while crossing the road.

The 'Struggle with an Angel' reveals that no canon, image or text was out-of-bounds for Barthes: this was at the heart of Picard's dispute with Barthes, and also one of the reasons for the latter's overall success. The most infamous convergence of image and text is Barthes' *Mythologies* (1957) a collection of previously published essays from *Les Lettres Nouvelles* that critique the 'ideological abuse' created by the media which presents images of society as somehow 'natural' and unhistorical; Barthes, taking a diverse range of subjects – such as wrestling, the face of Garbo, margarine – reveals that the so-called natural meaning is, in fact, a delusional myth.[5] Critics have argued about the results of the approach taken in *Mythologies*: on the one hand, the maintenance of an ideological position, Barthes argues, depends upon the general public accepting societies' myths; on the other hand, revealing their constructed status does not appear to have done Western capitalism much harm. Susan Sontag called the Barthes form of writing in *Mythologies* 'essay-epiphanies'[6] and this phrase neatly recognizes the dilemma in his work: is the analysis of sign–systems a political, scientific or aesthetic gesture? To answer this question – and to ponder Barthes' resistance to such a question – involves an overview of his work.

Barthes' first major publication, *Writing Degree Zero* (1953), attempts to get beyond an account of literature that focuses merely on the division of content and form, aware nonetheless of language as a limit or a horizon. Barthes posits two literary axes: the horizontal dispersal of speech, and the vertical 'depth model' of individual style; in-between these two axes there is the production of writing or *écriture*. Barthes regards language and style as being 'blind' forces, whereas *écriture* is a self-aware act, with a defined set of functions: 'it is a relationship between creation and society, the literary language transformed by its social finality, form considered as a human intention and thus linked to the great crises of history'.[7] Writing, or *écriture*, is thus an ethical and a political act, and in this suggestion, the unnamed target of Barthes' own text becomes clear: Jean-Paul Sartre's *What is Literature?* (1947). Sartre had posited a communicative model of literary intervention; for Barthes, *écriture* is not fundamentally about communication, rather it is counter-cultural, seeking to extend the boundaries of thought and constantly attacking any stasis in literary representation. The exemplary practitioners of the latter are the avant-garde modernist writers such as Mallarmé who achieve 'a degree zero' or self-reflexive 'colourless writing, freed from all bondage to a pre-ordained state of language'.[8] After an extended engagement with Saussurian linguistics, and with Barthes' increasing involvement with the new movements of semiotics and structuralism (key practitioners being Lévi-Strauss, Foucault and Kristeva), a more technical mode of analysis became apparent in his work, especially in the key works of the 1960s: *Elements of Semiology* (1964), *The Fashion System* (1967) and the essay 'Introduction to the Structural Analysis of Narratives' (1966).

The Fashion System was Barthes' doctoral thesis, started in 1957; in his foreword to the published version, Barthes indicates a sense of unease with the rapidity with which his study has dated. However, the text can be read as an historical record of semiology – the science of signs based upon Ferdinand de Saussure's work. Barthes analyses the systems of clothing via the vestimentary code, the latter signifying 'fashion' as an arbitrary, cultural system that attempts to create apparently natural signs, i.e. a particular garment stands in for and signifies a particular time of year. In his foreword, Barthes' use of the word 'potlatch' not only signals his interest in anthropological semiology (e.g. Lévi-Strauss), but the way in which the entire fashion system imposes its own calendar of destruction and excess as a mode of annual renewal and expenditure, rather than being dependent upon clothing's use-value and wear-and-tear. Thus the fashion sign is re-born every year in a gesture of decree; fashion is thus, as Barthes puts it, exempt from time, and this indicates how radically different the semiological approach is: it rejects notions of historical development, evolution, and organic progress, and instead examines encoded ruptures, discontinuities and structural patterns and repetitions (e.g. the annual fashion potlatch) across an entire system. The traversal of such a system need not be as neutral or objective a procedure as the 'science of signs' nomenclature indicated; after the political upheavals of May 1968 in France (and elsewhere), Barthes shifted his approach to encompass not just structuralist but what became known as 'poststructuralist' concerns. Two key works articulated this shift: the book *S/Z* (1970) and the essay that eventually became synonymous with Barthes' name, 'The Death of the Author' (1968). In the latter essay, Barthes argues that writing is not something that is author centred, rather it 'is the destruction of every voice, every origin'. Who, then, speaks in a text? It is language itself, functioning and performing (Barthes once again turns to the example of Mallarmé, although it was the Surrealists, he argues, who desacrilized the 'theological' image of the author). The author is replaced by Barthes with the 'scriptor', that is, someone co-present with the production of writing, not a being who precedes or exceeds the text, which in itself is perceived as a tissue or fabric of quotations. The meaning of a text is no longer anchored in and explained by that point in time called 'author'; now the text is disentangled rather than deciphered, traversed rather than pierced. The multiplicity of writing 'collects' at the site known as 'reader': concomitant, then, with the death of the author is the birth of this reader as site of multiplicities, as the destination (without end) of the text in all of its diversity. What does this reader experience in the process? The reader experiences intensities, the pleasure of the text, an erotics of reading texts that are always coming into being, as Barthes puts it in his work in the early 1970s, *The Pleasure of the Text* (1973). Barthes' shift into poststructuralism opens up not an entirely new, but expanded, realm of creativity for him, including new works on his fictionalized encounter with Japan (*Empire of Signs* (1970)), auto/biography (*Roland Barthes by Roland Barthes* (1975)), love (*A Lover's Discourse: Fragments* (1977)) and photography (*Camera Lucida: Reflections on Photography* (1980)). This move closer to bodily desires, images and processes was signalled in diverse places, as being an attempt to write a 'degree zero' criticism, for example, the fragments on Bataille's 'The Big Toe' arbitrarily placed into alphabetical order in the essay 'Outcomes of the Text', which denies linkages and connections between the fragments precisely to mark them as non-progressive textual outcomes. Readers have generally agreed that there is a more elegiac quality to some of Barthes' final writings, especially his work on photography, although his lifelong attempt to exceed any particular theoretical position has always included an intense appreciation of the past.

Notes

1 Roland Barthes, 'The Struggle with the Angel: Textual Analysis of Genesis 32: 22–32', in, *Image, Music, Text*, pp. 125–141.
2 Ibid., p. 126.

3   Patrick Ffrench, *The Time of Theory: A History of* Tel Quel *(1960–1983)*, Oxford: Clarendon Press, 1995, pp. 167–168.
4   Roland Barthes, 'The Struggle with the Angel: Textual Analysis of Genesis 32: 22–32', p. 127.
5   Jonathan Culler, *Barthes: A Very Short Introduction*, Oxford: Oxford University Press, 2002, p. 23.
6   Preface to *Mythologies*, trans. Annette Lavers, London: Jonathan Cape, 1972, p. viii.
7   Roland Barthes, *Writing Degree Zero*, trans. Annette Lavers and Colin Smith, London: Jonathan Cape, 1967, p. 14.
8   Ibid., p. 76.

See also in this book

Baudrillard, Derrida, Kristeva

Major works

Writing Degree Zero (1953). Trans. Annette Lavers and Colin Smith, London: Jonathan Cape, 1967.
Michelet (1954). Trans. Richard Howard, Oxford: Basil Blackwell, 1987.
Mythologies (1957). Trans. Annette Lavers, London: Jonathan Cape, 1972.
Critical Essays (1964). Trans. Richard Howard, Evanston, IL: Northwestern University Press, 1972.
Elements of Semiology (1964). Trans. Annette Lavers and Colin Smith, London: Jonathan Cape, 1967.
Criticism and Truth (1966). Trans. Katrine Pilcher Keuneman, London: Athlone, 1987.
The Fashion System (1967). Trans. Matthew Ward and Richard Howard, London: Jonathan Cape, 1985.
S/Z (1970). Trans. Richard Miller, London: Jonathan Cape, 1975.
Empire of Signs (1970). Trans. Richard Howard, London: Jonathan Cape, 1983.
Sade, Fourier, Loyola (1971). Trans. Richard Miller, Berkeley, CA: University of California Press, 1976.
The Pleasure of the Text (1973). Trans. Richard Miller, London: Jonathan Cape, 1976.
Roland Barthes by Roland Barthes (1975). Trans. Richard Howard, London: Màcmillan, 1977.
A Lover's Discourse: Fragments (1977). Trans. Richard Howard, London: Jonathan Cape, 1979.
Image, Music, Text (1977). Trans. Stephen Heath, London: Fontana.
Camera Lucida: Reflections on Photography (1980). Trans. Richard Howard, London: Fontana, 1984.
The Grain of the Voice: Interviews 1962–1980 (1981). Trans. Linda Coverdale, New York: Hill and Wang, 1985.
The Rustle of Language (1984). Trans. Richard Howard, Oxford: Blackwell, 1986.

Further reading

Allen, Graham, *Roland Barthes*, London and New York: Routledge, 2003.
Culler, Jonathan, *Barthes: A Very Short Introduction*, Oxford: Oxford University Press, 2002 (first published by Fontana, 1983).
Lavers, Annette, *Roland Barthes: Structuralism and After*, Cambridge, MA: Harvard University Press, 1982.
Moriarty, Michael, *Roland Barthes*, Cambridge: Polity Press, 1991.
Stafford, Andy, *Roland Barthes, Phenomenon and Myth: An Intellectual Biography*, Edinburgh: Edinburgh University Press, 1998.
Trifonas, Peter Pericles, *Barthes and the Empire of Signs*, Cambridge: Icon, 2001.

JEAN BAUDRILLARD (1929–)

Working with hyperbole and taking an argument to its logical limits and beyond, Jean Baudrillard's descriptions and analyses of postmodern culture are vertiginous and at times seemingly ridiculous. As with science fiction, however, what once appeared as mere speculation and fantasy so often turns into everyday reality and generally accepted fact. Baudrillard's prophetic announcements on postmodernism are also grounded in his own serious study of sociological theory and twentieth-century German and French philosophy. Baudrillard was born in Reims, France in 1929, his educational and intellectual trajectory encompassing secondary school teaching (in sociology), translation among others of the German playwrights Bertolt Brecht (1898–1956) and Peter Weiss (1916–1982), publication of articles in Jean-Paul Sartre's journal *Les Temps Modernes* and a Ph.D. thesis called *Le Système des objets* (*The System of Objects*) defended in the year of the student uprisings in France (1968). There are two main intertexts that *The System of Objects* comments upon and in some ways supersedes in relation to commodity culture: Guy Debord's *The Society of the Spectacle* (1967) and Henri Lefebvre's *Critique of Everyday Life* (1947; revised 1958). Lefebvre's book is a Marxist analysis of the alienation central to everyday life under capitalism, while Debord's book argues that a political critique has to account for the ways in which everyday society has been transformed by the shift from material experience to that of representation (the 'spectacles' that now constitute everyday life). Both books posit a type of false consciousness, under which we can attempt to find the real, be it material reality or authentic community. The twist given by Baudrillard to these accounts is to accept that consumer culture is not simply a 'false consciousness' but an alternative reality that may actually be sought after, experienced and enjoyed, and even more radically may eventually be considered 'more real' than 'the real' itself – later, he will utilize the term hyper-reality to make this point. However, to get to the hyperreal, Baudrillard took a long journey that involved critiquing and reworking Marx, re-examining anthropological and sociological theories in the light of Saussurian semiotics and structuralism, and finally exploring the strange new worlds of postmodernism.

The critique of Marx, while ongoing in Baudrillard's work since *The System of Objects*, is most clearly articulated in the *Consumer Society: Myths and Structures* (1970), *For a Critique of the Political Economy of the Sign* (1972) and *The Mirror of Production* (1973). Baudrillard argues that Marx centres his analysis of capitalism on production, whereas in the actual contemporary processes of consumption there are symbolic charges that accrue: in other words, the consumer finds meaning in his or her consumption of a product or object because it can acquire symbolic value, i.e. the creation of social prestige. This symbolic value, while experienced as real, functions in the act of consumption in ways analogous to the Saussurian sign: it is arbitrary and com-mutable (or exchangeable). Baudrillard thus distinguishes between 'Symbolic Exchange Value' and 'Sign Value': the former involves a singularity, say, the act of giving in a moment of ritual, such as the giving of rings in a marriage ceremony, or the destruction of valuable objects at a Native potlatch,[1] where the object is arbitrary *until given*: it is then tied in to *the act* or ritual of giving, the bond, say, between two individuals that is signified via the ritual, and the wider social meanings or rankings generated by the ritual. With 'Sign Value', human or societal relations are, in effect, abolished or dissolved – the consumption of an object may generate or signify social prestige, but it is at the expense of social relations, a decoupling from the com-munity and a foregrounding of individual, solipsistic experience: 'The sign object is neither given nor exchanged: it is appropriated, with-held and manipulated by individual subjects as a sign, that is, as coded difference.'[2] There are the beginnings of a historical analysis here: most of Baudrillard's 'Symbolic Exchange Value' examples come from non-Western, so-called 'primitive' societies, whereas the 'Sign Value' appears to be solely a function of contemporary consumer culture. The reorientation of Marxist theory mapped via Baudrillard's read-ings of Georges Bataille, Marcel Mauss, Lévi-Strauss, Saussurian linguistics and structuralism in general leads Baudrillard to posit what he calls four logics of signification, charted in different ways:

1 A functional logic of use value = practical operations = utility =
   an instrument
2 An economic logic of exchange value = equivalence = the
   market = a commodity
3 A logic of symbolic value = ambivalence = the gift = a symbol
4 A logic of sign value = difference = status = a sign.[3]

Contemporary consumer culture is a liberation of the object of
consumption from the first three positions on Baudrillard's chart, i.e.
a new realm of total commutability where the object is akin to the
signifier, that is, it is arbitrary and differential. But is this a liberated
society? The answer is no: it is a society where meaning is controlled
by 'the code' − that is to say, the political economy of the sign −
where capitalism's main aim is simply to eternally reproduce itself.

The implications of Baudrillard's critique of Marx are phenomenal,
even if at times his project remains sketchy: it is as if once Baudrillard
had glimpsed the connotations of a *detachment* from a political economy based upon production, the political economy of the sign lit
up the skies. An entire new bizarre set of theories emerged after this
revelation in the key publications *Symbolic Exchange and Death* (1976)
and *Simulacra and Simulation* (1981). Baudrillard pits 'the code' − the
overarching term to describe postmodernism − against 'the symbolic',
the only counteracting force now available. For example, dialectical
thought has been overtaken for Baudrillard by 'simulation', so the only
viable counteracting force is 'catastrophe' such as the catastrophic interventions of terrorism. What is 'the code'? It is a self-engendering form,
such as genetic code/DNA, digital code (software/artificial intelligence
systems), and new modes of media (the digital image). Capitalism is
also a code for Baudrillard. What all of these codes share is that they
operate at the 'third level of simulacra': that is, the level of 'simulation'
where there is a negation of Sign Value, and the absorption of the
entire mechanism of 'representation' − 're'-presentation assumes a prior
reality to be copied and refigured; simulation is primary or constitutive. To put this another way, first-order simulation *distinguishes*
between the real and the copy; second-order simulation *blurs the boundaries* between the real and the copy; third-order simulation *replaces*
the entire binary opposition with one state called 'the hyperreal'. In
The Gulf War Did Not Take Place (1991), Baudrillard argues that
the third-order level of simulation was more important for the West's
consumption of the event than any other factor: thus, digital images of
computer-guided missiles, which bore an uncanny resemblance to
computer games, dominated Western media; in the more recent Gulf

War II, 'embedded journalists' were put in place by the Pentagon precisely to ensure that their images had a 'reality effect', but most commentators simply assumed that these journalists were more complex simulacra. To use Marshall McLuhan's phrase to explain this: 'the medium is the message', so control of the medium is, in effect, control of meaning. Baudrillard increasingly turns towards America for examples of hyperreality: from Watergate, Disneyworld, 'reality' television, Death Valley, Silicon Valley, Florida and many other concepts and places explored in books such as *America* (1986) and *Cool Memories* (1987). America appears to function for Baudrillard as the location of the 'global extermination of meaning', a hyperreality that is encompassing the entire world, but is still resisted in other places and by other cultures. But the technologies that have led to the 'implosion' of meaning are themselves transglobal, for example, genetic engineering and cloning, and cannot really be located in any one place. Baudrillard articulates these new technologies using the phrase 'the murder of the real' and in *The Perfect Crime* (1995) he turns detective to try to track down the moment that this crime took place. Detection is a key process for Baudrillard as it offers a way of maintaining a critical perspective within postmodernity: as in *The Truman Show*, where the protagonist gradually finds clues that lead him to believe in the artificiality of his entire world, or the detective work of journalists Woodward and Bernstein who uncovered the Watergate scandal (President Nixon being involved in serious governmental illegalities), the 'total simulation' that is the hyperreal is not without fault-lines or inherent instabilities. In fact, Baudrillard suggests that the more perfect hyperreality becomes, the more liable it is to complete and catastrophic breakdown. An acceleration of this breakdown may be brought about via terrorism, be it sabotage, assassination, the hostage-taking of the 1970s or more violent forms of terrorist attack at the end of the twentieth century and into the beginnings of the twenty-first. The 'twin towers' of the World Trade Center building in New York symbolized for Baudrillard as early as 1976 the potential closure of the postmodern system: no longer the binary opposition of original and copy, now just the endless production of hyperreality embodied architecturally by these monuments to capitalism. In *The Spirit of Terrorism* (2002) and *Requiem for the Twin Towers* (2002) Baudrillard revisits this territory after the terrorist attacks of 11 September 2001 to explore the violent imposition of an 'irreducible singularity' on a world that is predicated upon endless general exchange.

Circularity is one of the major aspects of Baudrillard's thought: a constant covering of the same critical territory, a turning again and again to the same subjects (the media, death, sex, advertising, cloning, terrorism and so on). In some ways this circularity is mimetic of the claustrophobic repetition of the same that is a central feature of postmodernity, i.e. the *illusion* of choice, the *apparent* proliferation of options, and the flattening out of differences. Baudrillard has been remarkably prescient in charting this territory: in *Simulacra and Simulation* (1981) he analysed American reality television from 1971 (following the lives of the aptly named Loud family), the apparently imperceptible difference between American warfare and film (in relation to the Vietnam War and *Apocalypse Now*), the mutation of human space with the development of 'hypermarkets', and the mutation of the human body with the use of prostheses and cloning. These early examples of postmodern society from the US are now familiar territory across the Western world and beyond. Baudrillard's role has in some ways switched from that of being a prophet of postmodernism to being a commentator who reminds us of the radical changes in human society that have been rapidly normalized and neutralized. Theorists continue to turn to Baudrillard not just for his critical tools developed in his media and other analyses, but also for his urgent sense that something radical is under way and perhaps needs to be resisted from within.

Notes

1 Richard J. Lane, *Jean Baudrillard*, chapter 3, New York and London: Routledge, 2000.
2 Jean Baudrillard, *For a Critique of the Political Economy of the Sign*, trans. Charles Levin, St Louis, MO: Telos, 1981, p. 65.
3 Ibid., p. 67 (modified by Lane).

See also in this book

Barthes, Jameson

Major works

The System of Objects (1968). Trans. James Benedict, London: Verso, 1997.
The Consumer Society: Myths and Structures (1970). London: Sage, 1998.
For a Critique of the Political Economy of the Sign (1972). Trans. Charles Levin, St Louis, MO: Telos, 1981.
The Mirror of Production (1973). Trans. Mark Poster, St Louis, MO: Telos, 1975.
Symbolic Exchange and Death (1976). Trans. Iain Hamilton Grant, London: Sage, 1998.
Simulations (1981). Trans. Paul Foss, Paul Patton and Philip Beitchman, New York: Semiotext(e), 1983.

Simulacra and Simulation (1981). Trans. Sheila Faria Glaser, Ann Arbor, MI: University of Michigan Press, 1994.
Fatal Strategies (1983). Trans. Philip Beitchman and W.G.J. Niesluchowski, New York and London: Semiotext(e)/Pluto, 1990.
America (1986). Trans. Chris Turner, London and New York: Verso, 1988.
The Gulf War Did Not Take Place (1991). Trans. Paul Patton, Sydney: Power, 1995.
The Illusion of the End (1992). Trans. Chris Turner, Cambridge: Polity, 1994.
The Vital Illusion (2000). New York: Columbia University Press.
The Spirit of Terrorism (2002). London and New York: Verso.

Further reading

Bataille, Georges, *Visions of Excess: Selected Writings, 1927–1939*, trans. Allan Stoekl, Carl R. Lovitt and Donald M. Leslie, Jr, Minneapolis, MN: University of Minnesota Press, 1985.
Butler, Rex, *Jean Baudrillard: The Defence of the Real*, London: Sage, 1999.
Debord, Guy, *The Society of the Spectacle*, trans. Donald Nicholson-Smith, New York: Zone Books, 1998.
Gane, Mike, ed., *Baudrillard Live: Selected Interviews*, London and New York: Routledge, 1993.
Genosko, Gary, *Baudrillard and Signs: Signification Ablaze*, London and New York: Routledge, 1994.
Lane, Richard J., *Jean Baudrillard*, London and New York: Routledge, 2000.
Lefebvre, Henri, *Critique of Everyday Life*, trans. John Moore, London and New York: Verso, 1991.
Levin, Charles, *Jean Baudrillard: A Study in Cultural Metaphysics*, London: Prentice Hall, 1996.
Mauss, Marcel, *The Gift: The Form and Reason for Exchange in Archaic Societies*, London and New York: Routledge, 1990.

WALTER BENJAMIN (1892–1940)

Best known for a text called 'The Work of Art in the Age of Mechanical Reproduction' where the world of mass produced artworks, in particular those of photography and film, are explored, Benjamin is also regarded as an iconic intellectual of the twentieth century, who blurred the boundaries of many traditionally isolated subject areas, from the impact of modernity to the meaning of Mickey Mouse. Benjamin was born on 15 July 1892 in Berlin; he was educated at Kaiser Friedrich Schule in Berlin, and at the Landerziehungsheim Haubinda in Thuringia where, significantly, he came into contact with the charismatic school reformer Gustav Wyneken, an important figure in Benjamin's youth. The German youth movements – via Wyneken's mediation – inspired Benjamin, and he became a member of the radical 'group for school reform' at Albert Ludwig

University in Freiburg im Breisgau, also joining the committee of the Free Students Union during his time at the Royal Freidrich Wilhelm University in Berlin. While the youth movements led him to some passionate early publications in journals such as *Der Anfang* (*The Beginning*), Benjamin's academic career did not lead to the expected result of a professorial position: he completed his doctoral dissertation in 1919 (published the following year as *The Concept of Criticism in German Romanticism*) and worked on his post-doctoral dissertation, or *Habilitation*, on the German Baroque mourning play, which he completed in 1925, eventually withdrawing it from the University of Frankfurt after an extremely negative reception. The *Habilitation* called the *Ursprung des deutschen Trauerspiels* (*The Origin of German Tragic Drama*) was eventually published in 1928, alongside a radically different text, the *Einbahnstrasse* (*One Way Street*), which is virtually the opposite of a university dissertation, utilizing playful montage techniques and linguistic games. During this period Benjamin was mixing with exciting new German thinkers, such as his philosopher friends Ernst Bloch and Gershom Scholem (Bloch's *The Spirit of Utopia* was published in 1923, the same year as an important new Marxist text, Georg Lukács's *History and Class Consciousness: Studies in Marxist Dialectics*). Other new intellectual developments were occurring at this time: the German Judaic thinkers Franz Rosenzweig (1886–1929) and Martin Buber (1876–1965) were producing challenging works. Buber's journal, *Der Jude*, explored literary, critical and political issues of the day, while Rosenzweig published his *Star of Redemption* in 1921, a book which attempted a 'new thinking' bringing together ethics, philosophy and theology; both men worked on a translation of the Hebrew Bible into German, which had a mixed reception. While Benjamin did not ally himself with Zionist thought or a particularly 'Judaic' sensibility, he also kept at a distance from other intellectual and cultural movements and charismatic leaders, such as the *Georgekreis*, a literary and spiritual movement that aimed at a German cultural renewal under the leadership of Stefan Anton George (1868–1933). Benjamin followed an independent path: it took him on complex intellectual and physical journeys, to Paris, Capri, Naples, Rome, Florence, Ibiza, Moscow, Lourdes, Marseille and Port Bou, on the Spanish border, where he committed suicide on 25 September 1940, fleeing Nazi Germany.

Benjamin's early writings are deeply metaphysical and theological, and are renowned for their philosophical density. In essays such as 'On Language as Such and on the Language of Man' (1916), 'On the Program of the Coming Philosophy' (1918) and the substantial

'The Concept of Criticism in German Romanticism' (1920), Benjamin presents interlinked concepts of language, sacred text, a projected re-working of Kant's limited concept of experience, and a new approach to criticism and Romanticism as a tracing of the absolute in early Romantic writing. Benjamin argued for an 'immanent criticism' which would engage in some ways quite mystically with a text's internal structures and divine traces. This very early work can be compared with the popular English translation of Benjamin's *selected* essays, collected under the title *Illuminations*, which show Benjamin theorizing modernity by bringing together, among other things, Marxist dialectics, Surrealism, snippets of theology, Baudelaire's poetry (and, most importantly, his theories of the *flâneur*), Kafka's novels, the image of Proust, a Klee painting called the *Angelus Novus*, book-collecting, translation, story-telling, photography and film. In this heterogeneous world, old and new collide, the material and the spiritual intersect, industrial modes of production have an impact upon, and transform irrevocably, the making and reception of art, and philosophical grand narratives are broken into small pieces: essays, radio shows, images and fragments. *Illuminations* shows how though starting with deep metaphysical and theological perspectives, Benjamin's thinking was radically modified by his own encounters with Marxism and Surrealism, leading to a hybrid approach to the analysis of contemporary culture. The *flâneur* – the bourgeois subject strolling idly through the new city-spaces of modernity – is more than a mobile spectator: his very identity is constituted by the physiological charges and shocks of the city, and his enjoyment of the commodification of all subjects. The fast-paced, ever-changing experiences of the city are reflected in new artistic production processes and forms, those of photography and film. Where once the unique high art forms dominated, now, for Benjamin, the mass-produced realm of the copy had come into its own, neutralizing the traditional concepts of individual creativity, genius, eternal value and mystery. Where once the work of art had a unique aura, in part generated by the venerating approach of the subject to the work, fixed in its unique location, now the mass-produced work comes to the subject, meeting her halfway. For example, radio, television and now the internet come directly into the home, and mass-produced works are available and consumed much of the time through ubiquitous advertising. Both 'high' and 'low' art forms are treated by Benjamin as viable objects of collecting and critical study, but new mass-produced works are not secondary to previous forms: the new techniques can achieve things that the old could not, e.g. slow-motion photography or digital images. The 'copy' thus outperforms the 'original' and does away with this outmoded binary opposition. New technologies of image (re)production de-couple or detach mass-produced art from the sphere of tradition, and from the ritualistic practices in which 'high' art is embedded. Instead of achieving significance through sacred ritual, art becomes a political practice. Benjamin adds to this argument his study of history, Marxism and Surrealism, to develop the concept of the 'dialectical image' that, as with Surrealist images, substitutes a political for a historical view of the past. Surrealist 'profane illumination' is a process whereby all human experiences are revealed to have revolutionary potential: this is revealed via a dialectics of shock, intoxication, the blurring of real and dream worlds, and linguistic experimentation, combined with a radical concept of freedom. Inspired by the 'profane illumination', which Benjamin thought exceeded the Surrealist's grasp, Benjamin went on to develop his 'dialectical image' or 'dialectics at a standstill' in a massive work of collecting called *The Arcades Project*. This history of the nineteenth-century Paris arcades, creatively triggered by Louis Aragon's (1897–1982) *Le Paysan de Paris* or *Paris Peasant* (1926), collects thousands of quotations strategically arranged with snippets of critical commentary in chapters or bundles called 'convolutes'. The materials in each convolute form a critical constellation – or esoteric pattern – whereby the collective dreamworlds of nineteenth-century commodity capitalism are given form and are explosively shattered: the collective can thereby awaken from its non-dialectical slumbers (at least, that is the theory).

Benjamin's last work – his essay 'On the Concept of History' (known previously in English as the 'Theses on the Philosophy of History') brings together many strands in his oeuvre: a critique of the Enlightenment (and subsequently capitalist) concept of 'history as progress', a melancholic analysis of the crisis-bound twentieth century, and the persistence of the theological and the messianic in the midst of the Marxist attempts to develop historical materialism (a rejection of universal truths, and the notion that such truths are teleological, that is to say, moving towards a pre-determined endpoint or goal). For oppressed peoples, Benjamin argues, the 'state of emergency' (say, the oppression of a particular ethnic group) is *not* a lived exception but the rule: adapting this lesson to historical materialism means constantly reassessing the present via past events and emergencies. The past is not something that is hermetically sealed and contained, it must constantly be re-addressed and re-conceptualized as it is dangerously appropriated by the ruling classes at any moment; thus Benjamin argues that: 'Each age must strive to wrest tradition away from the conformism that is working to overpower it.' The most infamous image from this final work is the angel in Klee's *Angelus Novus* (a painting that Benjamin owned); Benjamin calls this image 'the angel of history' and imagines history here as a series of catastrophic events piling wreckage at this angel's feet as he is blown into the future by the storm that human beings call 'progress'.

Benjamin is one of the key thinkers of modernity, and an important figure on the margins of the Frankfurt School and other schools of Marxist criticism. While his experimental techniques, and essays on film and popular culture have been the most influential in the West, recent new English translations of a wider range of his work, in particular *The Arcades Project*, have led to considerable new interest in Benjamin in the English-speaking world. Much of Benjamin's work is firmly rooted in metaphysics, however, and this aspect of his work continues to be troubling in the post-metaphysical humanities and, in some cases, is simply ignored.

Major works

Illuminations (1955). Trans. Harry Zohn, London: Fontana, 1992.

The Origin of Tragic Drama (1963). Trans. John Osborne, London and New York: Verso, 1998.

One-Way Street and Other Writings (1974–1976). Trans. Edmund Jephcott and Kingsley Shorter, London and New York: Verso, 1985.

The Correspondence of Walter Benjamin: 1910–1940 (1978). Edited and annotated by Gershom Scholem and Theodor W. Adorno, trans. Manfred R. Jacobson and Evelyn M. Jacobson, London and Chicago, IL: The University of Chicago Press, 1994.

The Arcades Project (1999). Trans. Howard Eiland and Kevin McLaughlin, Cambridge, MA and London: Belknap Press of Harvard University Press, 1999.

Selected writings

Selected Writings, Volume 1: 1913–1926. Edited by Marcus Bullock and Michael W. Jennings, Cambridge, MA and London: Belknap Press of Harvard University Press, 1996.

Selected Writings, Volume 2: 1927–1934. Edited by Michael W. Jennings, Howard Eiland and Gary Smith, trans. Rodney Livingstone and others, Cambridge, MA and London: Belknap Press of Harvard University Press, 1999.

Selected Writings, Volume 3: 1935–1938. Edited by Howard Eiland and Michael W. Jennings, trans. Edmund Jephcott, Howard Eiland and others, Cambridge, MA and London: Belknap Press of Harvard University Press, 2002.

Selected Writings, Volume 4: 1938–1940. Edited by Howard Eiland and Michael W. Jennings, trans. Edmund Jephcott and others, Cambridge, MA and London: Belknap Press of Harvard University Press, 2003.

Further reading

Britt, Brian, *Walter Benjamin and the Bible*, New York: Continuum, 1996.

Buck-Morss, Susan, *The Dialectics of Seeing: Walter Benjamin and the Arcades Project*, London and Cambridge, MA: MIT Press, 1991.

Caygill, Howard, *Walter Benjamin: The Colour of Experience*, London and New York: Routledge, 1998.

Ferris, David S., ed., *The Cambridge Companion to Walter Benjamin*, Cambridge: Cambridge University Press, 2004.

Gilloch, Graeme, *Walter Benjamin: Critical Constellations*, Cambridge: Polity, 2002.

Jacobs, Carol, *In the Language of Walter Benjamin*, Baltimore, MD and London: The Johns Hopkins University Press, 1999.

Lane, Richard J., *Reading Walter Benjamin: Writing through the Catastrophe*, Manchester: Manchester University Press, 2005.

Pensky, Max, *Melancholy Dialectics: Walter Benjamin and the Play of Mourning*, Amherst, MA: University of Massachusetts Press, 2001.

Smith, Gary, ed., *Benjamin: Philosophy, Aesthetics, History*, Chicago, IL and London: University of Chicago Press, 1989.

HOMI K. BHABHA (1949–)

The discourse of postcolonial theory has been indelibly marked by the work of Homi K. Bhabha, especially with his development of critical terms such as 'hybridity', 'interstitial' and the 'third space'. Born in Bombay, India, Bhabha grew up in a Parsi community, a religion that is of Zoroastrian origin. The diasporic history of the Parsis – the etymology of the word meaning 'a Persian', with a major migration to India in the eighth century – is matched by their modern-day dispersal throughout the world, while still maintaining an important core community within India. Bhabha comments, in an interview with W.J.T. Mitchell, that the Parsis are 'a hybridized community: often their rituals pay formal respect to Hindu customs and rituals while articulating their own religious and ethnic identity. Then what is interesting about Parsis is their own sense of a negotiated cultural identity.'[1] In these comments Bhabha articulates some recurring themes and questions about identity, which he also applies to the literatures that emerge from complex intersections of people and place. Bhabha's own intellectual trajectory involved studying for his undergraduate degree at Elphinstone College, Bombay University, India (1970), and then gaining an M.Phil. (1974), MA (1977) and D.Phil. (1990, on the author V.S. Naipaul) from Christ Church College, Oxford. While Bhabha was influenced in his studies by poststructuralist theory, particularly the works of Jacques Derrida, Michel Foucault and Jacques Lacan, he

also cites the German-Jewish critic Walter Benjamin as being important to the development of his ideas. Other major figures for Bhabha
include theorist and political activist Frantz Fanon, the postcolonial
critic Edward Said, and the writers Toni Morrison, Salman Rushdie
and Derek Walcott. After teaching at a number of British universities,
including The University of Sussex and Warwick University, Bhabha
moved to the US where he became a professor at The University of
Chicago in 1994; he went on to hold visiting fellowships at Princeton
University where he was the Senior Fellow and Visiting Professor, the
University of Pennsylvania where he was the Steinberg Visiting
Professor and Dartmouth College where he served as Faculty Fellow
in the School of Criticism and Theory. Key lectures include the
Richard Wright lecture series at the Center for Black Literature and
Culture at the University of Pennsylvania (1991), the Annual Inter-
disciplinary Lecture at the School of Oriental and African Studies,
University of London (1995), the W.E.B. Du Bois Lectures at Harvard
(1999), the Presidential Lecture at Stanford University (2000), and the
Clarendon Lectures at the University of London (2001–2002).[2] In
2001 Bhabha became Professor of English and American Literature and
Chair of the Committee of Degrees on History and Literature in the
Faculty of Arts and Science, Harvard University.

In 1986 Bhabha published a foreword to Frantz Fanon's *Black Skin,
White Masks*, in the new Pluto edition. In this short essay, much of
Bhabha's own theoretical approach is mapped out. In comparing Fanon with 'English socialism' Bhabha articulates the demands
of 'the "autonomous" struggles of the politics of race and gender'
and the 'questions of race and sexuality [that] make their own organ-
izational and theoretical demands on the primacy of "class", "state"
and "party"'.[3] In other words, instead of regarding, from a traditional
socialist perspective, the configurations of race/gender and race/
sexuality as 'petty-bourgeois deviation' these are instead vital to an
understanding of colonialism's impact upon humanity. While Bhabha
charts Fanon's intellectual background in a conventional way, he also
articulates Fanon's approach using some now familiar Bhabhaesque
terminology:

> he [Fanon] speaks most effectively from the uncertain inter-
> stices of historical change: from the area of ambivalence
> between race and sexuality; out of an unresolved contradic-
> tion between culture and class; from deep within the struggle
> of psychic representation and social reality.[4]

31

The rejection of binary thinking in this passage is clear: not 'either/or' but *in-between, interstitial* spaces of thought and representation are of importance; contradictions are perceived as, and remain, unresolved in Bhabha's analysis and political struggles are articulated via and through the psychological mechanisms of individuals and societies. Fanon's debt to existentialism, especially Jaspers and Sartre, is clear in this sketch of his work, a debt that is given a fresh batch of coordinates by Bhabha: instead of drawing upon Freud and the existential-psychoanalytic approaches of Jaspers and Sartre, Bhabha explores colonialist and postcolonial aesthetics and theory via Jacques Lacan (although it should be noted here that Fanon was familiar with some aspects of Lacan). Fanon's shift of focus from 'the politics of nationalism to the politics of narcissism'[5] is one that Bhabha observes closely.

While Bhabha's important and traumatic 're-membering'[6] of *Black Skin, White Masks* remains a key contemporary essay on Fanon, especially for readers encountering Fanon for the first time, it was the edited collection of essays *Nation and Narration* (1990), that brought Bhabha's work to a much wider audience. Bhabha argues that the concept of the nation, read 'as a system of cultural signification' is one that involves recognizing the instability and ambivalences of its knowledge-production and representations; conceiving of nation 'as' narration is to introduce an entire field of poststructuralist terms, or 'strategies' as Bhabha calls them, into the equation: 'textuality, discourse, enunciation, *écriture*, "the unconscious as a language" to name only a few'.[7] These 'disjunctive forms of representation' that produce the discourse of the nation are explored in more detail in Bhabha's own essay in his edited collection 'DissemiNation: Time, Narrative, and the Margins of the Modern Nation'. The central category of the essay – *ambivalence* – is utilized to re-think, from a postcolonial perspective, the temporality of nation-formation and existence. Bhabha theorizes a double-writing or 'dissemi-*nation*' which reveals 'the internal contradictions of the modern liberal nation'[8] in its ongoing maintenance and resistances via a performative discursive production. Towards the end of his essay, Bhabha shifts from his analysis of nationhood and diaspora to the 'gathering' of diasporic peoples in the city, the space where the repetition/return of the migrant occurs, undermining and haunting nationalist narratives that have tried to ignore the fact that nation-formation has always taken place, during the colonial era, elsewhere, on the 'margins' of empire. This shift in Bhabha's closing lines (drawn in part from the importance of London in his reading of Salman Rushdie's *The Satanic Verses*), is mimetic of an intellectual shift across Bhabha's work as a whole, from colonial discourse analysis in an early phase, to a preoccupation as Bart Moore-Gilbert puts it: 'with the issues raised by the cultural consequences of neo-colonialism in the contemporary era and the complex and often conflictual relationship of postcolonial discourse to postmodernism'.[9] *Nation and Narration* was followed four years later by the work that established Bhabha as a major intellectual force in the contemporary humanities: a revised collection of previously published essays called *The Location of Culture* (1994).

Bart Moore-Gilbert has commented that Bhabha's essays in *The Location of Culture* 'considered as a developing body of work, rather than as a series of discrete articles published in journals which are widely dispersed in different disciplinary and geographical locations' enable the reader 'to appreciate the degree to which Bhabha challenges the vision of his predecessors in the postcolonial field and those of Fanon and Said in particular'.[10] In *The Location of Culture* Bhabha develops a critical discourse that has become de rigueur in postcolonial literary studies, a dense and at times difficult-to-follow way of articulating readings of texts and situations. Such a critical discourse emerges from a project that seeks always to engage with heterogeneous communities and voices: 'women, the colonized, minority groups, the bearers of policed sexualities'.[11] In Bhabha's writing, there is a convergence of patterns of minority, migratory and diasporic existence with that of the ambivalences of contemporary 'high' theory. In other words, the multiple allegiances and hybrid identities of minority and migratory ethnic groups reveals not just a borderland or in-between existence but, more profoundly, these allegiances can lead to a deconstruction of previously rigid and static concepts of community, nation, identity and history. As John McLeod puts it:

> living at the border, at the edge, requires a new 'art of the present'. This depends upon embracing the contrary logic of the border and using it to rethink the dominant ways we represent things . . . The space of the 'beyond' is often described in terms which emphasise this transitory, in-between sense: such as 'liminal', 'interstitial' or 'hybrid'.[12]

The potential problems involved in expressing the experiences of often substantially marginalized groups through the vehicle of Eurocentric high theory are addressed in Bhabha's first essay in *The Location of Culture*: 'The Commitment to Theory'. Apart from his rejection, however, of a simplistic equation of high theory with the Western production of the Other (potentially a new form of Orientalism),

Bhabha reveals how in working with the concept of the postcolonial, binary oppositions start to break down; as an example, he explores the support for 'Third [World] Cinema' in the West, where at the same time as Western cinema dominates world-wide production and consumption, the West also provides alternative viewing spaces, funding streams and a critical capacity to support film producers from the Third World. *Postcolonial existence*, then, is already resistant to the sorts of binaries that would oppose theory to politics. Theory is produced in-between the polarities of binary thinking – in other words, Bhabha regards it as emerging not just through, but *as*, an expression of postcolonial existence. In many respects, Bhabha is simply rejecting the traditional Marxist Base-Superstructure model, whereby cultural production is relegated to an after-effect of economic activity. Instead, Bhabha argues that: 'Forms of popular rebellion and mobilization are often most subversive and transgressive when they are created through oppositional *cultural* practices.'[13] But how does this answer the criticism that high theory attempts to speak for the Other? First, the suggestion is that postcolonial theory *emerges from* the interstices, not some hegemonic Eurocentric position; second, theory has the 'conceptual potential for change and innovation';[14] and third, recognition of 'the tension within critical theory between its institutional containment and its revisionary force'[15] leads to an ongoing translation or relocation of theory itself, one that foregrounds cultural difference. *The Location of Culture* is an exemplary set of essays embodying the successes and difficulties of such a project, while constantly resisting the move to produce a new hegemonic theory. This resistance mimics the hybrid identities under discussion, which as McLeod notes 'are never total and complete in themselves, like orderly pathways built from crazy-paving. Instead, they remain perpetually in motion, pursuing errant and unpredictable routes, open to change and reinscription.'[16] Colonial discourses are still analysed in *The Location of Culture*, however, such as the essay 'Signs Taken for Wonders', which examines the irruption of the 'English book' into colonial India. Bhabha's essay starts with the tripartite discovery of the English book among indigenous peoples: first the Bible, 'discovered' in India in multiple copies by Messeh in 1817, then Conrad's Marlow 'discovering' Towson's *Inquiry into Some Points of Seamanship* in the Congo, in *Heart of Darkness* and finally V.S. Naipaul coming across the same Conradian scene himself, the same discovery of Towson's book but recontextualized. The 'discovery' of the English book in a colonial situation is precisely a moment where the 'privileged position of a standard code' and a 'monocentric view of human experience' is foregrounded, leading to a Eurocentric re-coding of the indigenous. What exactly does the appearance of the English book signify? Why is Bhabha so concerned with it here? There are at least two things going on with the irruption of the English book into a colonial context. Bhabha argues that the 'discovery of the English book establishes both a measure of mimesis and a mode of civil authority and order'.[17] What does this mean? First, the English book tells people how to behave by providing a model, an exemplar, be it religious or social, in other words, to do with matters of taste and etiquette. Second, the English book functions like the law, or, it *is* the law: it presents an ideology, a political machine, and a measure of not just civility but what Bhabha calls 'civil authority and order'. The English book cannot exist in a vacuum: there can be no purist positions with cultural hybridity. So, the colonial context of the irruption of the English book affects *how* the book signifies, and further, *how* the book is constituted. Bhabha says: 'For it is in-between the edict of Englishness and the assault of the dark unruly spaces of the earth, through an act of repetition, that the colonial text emerged uncertainly.'[18] The colonial text, be it by Messeh, Conrad or Naipaul, is constructed in the space of in-betweenness. But, in turn, it is in this space that the English book is constituted. Bhabha wants to understand the role of the English book in colonial texts because if the English book is constituted at the moment of colonial construction – or put more simply, if the English book is written into its meanings through the colonial experience – then the colonial text is itself attempting to transfer a body of power and knowledge – the English book – to itself, at the point which that body is shown to be less than whole and stable. Bhabha calls this process of transference and ownership 'the colonial presence' and it is a disjunction because, as he puts it, it is 'split between its appearance as original and authoritative and its articulation as repetition and difference'.[19]

Notes

1 W.J.T. Mitchell, 'Interview with Homi Bhabha', *Artforum*, 33.7 (March 1995): 80–84, http://prelectur.stanford.edu/lecturers/bhabha/interview. html, accessed 8 June 2005.
2 Ken Gewertz, 'Telling tales out of, and in, class: *Bhabha studies culture and genre with a moral squint*', *Harvard Gazette Archives*, www.news.harvard. edu/gazette/2002/01.31/03-bhabha.html, accessed 8 June 2005.
3 Homi Bhabha, foreword to Frantz Fanon, *Black Skin, White Masks*, trans Charles Lam Markmann, p. vii.
4 Ibid., p. ix.
5 Ibid., p. xxiv.

6 Ibid., p. xxiii.
7 Homi Bhabha, *Nation and Narration*, London and New York: Routledge, 1990, p. 4.
8 Ibid., p. 299.
9 Bart Moore-Gilbert, *Postcolonial Theory: Contexts, Practices, Politics*, London and New York: Verso, 2000, p. 114.
10 Ibid.
11 Homi Bhabha, *The Location of Culture*, London and New York: Routledge, 1994, p. 5.
12 John McLeod, *Beginning Postcolonialism*, Manchester and New York: Manchester University Press, 2000, p. 217.
13 Homi Bhabha, *The Location of Culture*, p. 20.
14 Ibid., p. 31.
15 Ibid., p. 32.
16 Ibid., p. 219.
17 Ibid., p. 107.
18 Ibid.
19 Ibid.

See also in this book

Fanon, Said, Spivak

Major works

Nation and Narration (1990). London and New York: Routledge.
The Location of Culture (1994). London and New York: Routledge.
Anish Kapoor (1998). California: University of California Press.

Further reading

Byrne, Eleanor, *Homi Bhabha*, London and New York: Macmillan, 2002.
Huddart, David, *Homi Bhabha*, London and New York: Routledge, 2005.
Moore-Gilbert, Bart, *Postcolonial Theory: Contexts, Practices, Politics*, London and New York: Verso, 2000.
Parry, Benita, 'Signs of Our Times: A Discussion of Homi Bhabha's *The Location of Culture*', in Masao, Miyoshi and H.D. Harootunian, eds, *Learning Places: The Afterlives of Area Studies*, Durham, NC: Duke University Press, 2002; pp. 119–149.
Yao, Steven G., 'Taxonomizing Hybridity', *Textual Practice* 17.2 (2003): 357–378.

HAROLD BLOOM (1930–)

A controversial and dynamic figure throughout his academic career, Harold Bloom has more recently portrayed himself as a bastion of humanism in the midst of anti-humanist literary theorists. It would be a mistake following this to think that he is a theoretical naïf, even given recent best-sellers such as his *Shakespeare: The Invention of the Human* (1998), which is clearly articulated in passionate non-theoretical prose. Ever since publication of *The Anxiety of Influence: A Theory of Poetry* (1973), Bloom has been engaged in highly charged theoretical issues and in the late 1970s he was aligned with the Yale School of Deconstruction. To begin to understand Bloom, however, the reader must be aware that Bloom has decried the constraining labels of 'humanist' and/or 'deconstructionist' and regards himself instead as someone who has an aesthetic, rather than ideological, appreciation of literature. Born in New York, Bloom was educated at Cornell University where he gained his BA in 1951, and at Yale University, gaining his doctorate in 1955. His academic career has been based at Yale since 1955, when he started as an instructor; by 1974 he was awarded the prestigious post of DeVane Professor of the Humanities, and in 1977, that of Sterling Professor of Humanities. He has had numerous visiting professorships, including in the late 1980s the Charles Eliot Norton Professor of Poetry at Harvard and the Berg Visiting Professor of English at New York University; he has also won numerous awards for his many academic works. Bloom may have come to the attention of the wider critical world with publication of *The Anxiety of Influence*, but he is also regarded as having developed a sophisticated approach to Romanticism paralleled only by the work of Geoffrey Hartman. Key texts were his doctoral dissertation published in 1959 as *Shelley's Mythmaking*, and the subsequent studies *The Visionary Company: A Reading of English Romantic Poetry* (1961), *Blake's Apocalypse: A Study in Poetic Argument* (1963), *Yeats* (1970) and his essay collection *The Ringers in the Tower* (1971). Taken as a whole, these critical writings critique the notion of the Romantics as being mere nature poets, asserting instead the 'triumph' of their imaginative vision.[1] In each work, Bloom reveals a dialectical, redemptive relationship between nature and the imagination. Bloom has been attacked for 'misreading' his six members of his 'visionary company' – Blake, Wordsworth, Coleridge, Byron, Shelley and Keats – but his response has been to develop a strong theory of misreading, in the company of other Yale School critics such as Paul de Man. His study of Yeats is a case in point: countering the accepted traditional reception of Yeats as a Romantic who progressed into modernism, Bloom argues instead that his best work was produced in his Romantic period, and that the later works are hollowed out precisely by Yeats' inability to sustain a Romantic vision. David Fite sketches Bloom's four central characteristics of the visionary imagination:

First, the visionary imagination represents a complex triumph over all that is merely 'given,' especially over . . . [the] natural world . . . Second, the visionary impulse, in struggling to achieve expression, characteristically enacts a quest . . . Third, the moments of pure vision or pure mythmaking in a Romantic poem . . . are evanescent, because the visionary imagination . . . necessarily lapses from sublimity back into the constrictions of mere language. Fourth, this sublimity, since it exists by virtue of its passage beyond all context to an absolute purity of vision, in some sense has no referent and is always focused on the problematics of pure visionary desire.[2]

With Bloom's emphasis upon the visionary imagination, it is clear that psychoanalytical models of the human subject would be not only useful but highly relevant to the overarching theoretical approach that Bloom was developing in his extended readings of Romanticism. In *The Anxiety of Influence*, Bloom synthesized some of his most powerful arguments about literature and subjectivity to date.

Bloom's thesis is delivered on the first page of *The Anxiety of Influence*: 'Poetic history . . . is held to be indistinguishable from poetic influence, since strong poets make that history by misreading one another, so as to clear imaginative space for themselves.'[3] The problem that develops in this process is one of the psychological charge or anxiety generated by the subsequent indebtedness and relationship to one's literary predecessors. Bloom wittily examines his own influences to his theory of influence: he regards them as being the Nietzsche of the *Genealogy of Morals* and the works of Sigmund Freud, especially his Oedipal theory of the rivalry between fathers and sons. So how does this anxiety-inducing rivalry with one's literary 'forefathers' work in poetic terms? Bloom breaks down the process into six 'revisionary ratios' or tropes: Clinamen (misreading/misprision); Tessera (completion and antithesis); Kenosis (breaking with a previous state); Daemonization (moving towards a counter-sublime); Askesis (self-purgation); and Apophrades (return of the dead). Each of these tropes describes a reaction to the forefather or poetic precursor. In Clinamen, the new poet regards the precursor as being correct in his or her poetic vision up to a certain point, but then should have 'swerved' in a new direction, the one provided by the new poet (in other words, the process is one of wilfully finding fault in the precursor, *that was never there in the first place*). In Tessera, the new poet goes further than the precursor to 'complete' him or her. In Kenosis, there is a combined 'humbling' of poet and precursor, whereby the new poet simulates his or her 'deflation'. The uniqueness of the precursor's work is displaced by Daemonization, whereby an intermediary in the form of the 'counter-sublime' is discovered in the precursor's poem, which is also perceived to be the true force of the work. With Askesis, there is a combined truncation of human and imaginative power, while in Apophrades, the openness to the precursor has the uncanny effect of the new poet appearing to be the author of the precursor's works. Bloom's theory, however, should not be read as a mere schematic approach: he ponders both the pleasures of the text, when it is engaged with critically, and the suppressed anxieties that are generated by the poet within each reader. He calls the anxiety of influence 'the dark and daemonic ground', which he enters through his critical question: 'How do men [sic] become poets?'[4] The answer, in part, is that of the dialectic of influence: 'the sense — amazing, agonizing, delighting — of *other poets* . . . the poet is condemned to learn his profoundest yearnings through an awareness of *other selves*'.[5] Freud's 'family romance' is key: Bloom mentions 'birth trauma', separation anxiety (from the child's parent) and anxiety concerning castration, as well as the 'death anxiety' whereby the ego fears the superego. Bloom regards the poet's anxiety as both one of separation anxiety and compulsion neurosis, engaged not just with his or her precursor but also with his or her Muse in a relationship that parallels the two 'late phases' of the family romance, whereby 'the notion of a higher origin [in the child/poet] and thwarted destiny yields to images of erotic degradation'.[6] Feminist critics have argued that Bloom's apparent theoretical dependence on Freud's patriarchal models of human sexuality and development is problematic, although notable critics such as Gilbert and Gubar have gone on to develop feminist versions of the anxiety of influence. But Bloom's model of 'antithetical criticism' that emerged from this text, goes beyond its patriarchal roots, and needs to be read in relation not only to its wide-ranging companion volume *A Map of Misreading* (1975), but also to the Yale School of critics, each of whom was developing a counter-humanist, counter-'New Criticism' approach to literary studies. Bloom's own position within the Yale School is thus complex: his antithetical criticism also places him at odds with the overall project of deconstruction, even though the Yale School's 'deconstructive' readings are now perhaps what it is most famous for.

In which directions did Bloom direct his critical powers after *The Anxiety of Influence*? Bloom's critical vision, if anything, deepened and broadened, to include a wide range of philosophers, authors and theological perspectives, in his texts *Kabbalah and Criticism* (1975), *Poetry and Repression* (1976), *Agon: Towards a Theory of Revisionism* (1982) and *The Breaking of the Vessels* (1982). Bloom delights in the fact that for deconstructionists, his writing appears traditionalist, whereas for traditionalists, his writing appears deconstructive. He opposes these labels with the notion of an American pragmatic, derived from James, whereby any particular theory is a mere instrument, not a moment of answer or closure; as Bloom thus argues in *Agon*:

> Poetry and criticism are useful not for what they really are, but for whatever poetic and critical use you can usurp them to, which means that interpretive poems and poetic interpretations are concepts you make happen, rather than concepts of being.[7]

In more recent years, Bloom has continued to infuriate academics and delight the book-reading public, with a series of texts that defend the canon and the literary 'greats' at a time when within humanities departments such concepts have been accused of being oppressive components of Eurocentric 'grand narratives'. The most notable of these more recent works is *The Western Canon: The Books and School of the Ages* (1994) and *Shakespeare: The Invention of the Human* (1998). The former, controversially, studies twenty-six authors, selected by Bloom for their 'sublimity' and 'representative nature'. What makes these authors canonical? For Bloom, it is their 'strangeness', the sense in reading them for the first time of an uncanny 'startlement' rather than a fulfilment of predicted and expected ideas. In other words, as readers we may bring a whole series of expectations to a text: what it will do, or say, what it should and should not express, and so on. For Bloom, a canonical text will always exceed our own expectations and critical limitations, in the sense that we will never be able to entirely 'assimilate' a canonical work. Part of Bloom's book is a diatribe against ideological readings of texts and the concomitant expansion of the canon (he calls it 'the destruction' of the canon); he also defends his theory of the anxiety of influence from detractors, arguing that it should be read as a series of tropes, not a patriarchal application of Freud, thus aligning the creative 'will to figuration' that is literature with the creation of new language via figures of speech. For Bloom, the 'flight from the aesthetic' in contemporary ideological theories of reading is the most reductive moment of what he terms the 'School of Resentment'. In his *Shakespeare: The Invention of the Human*, Bloom explores what he would like to maintain is the 'fixed center of the Western canon'[8] and he agrees with Johnson, that it was Shakespeare who taught us how to understand human nature: Bloom takes this a step further, and argues that Shakespeare invented the concept of the human per se, and therefore invented *us*. In fact, Shakespeare goes beyond being the centre, he becomes 'the universal canon' to survive the onslaughts of 'the current debasement of our teaching institutions'.[9] When Bloom asks where shall wisdom be found?, in the book with that title, Shakespeare is there in the thick of things: 'Shakespeare is so large a form of thought and language, of persons in spiritual turmoil, and of intimations of transcendence blocked by realities that we scarcely have begun to understand and absorb him.'[10] From the anxiety of influence, Bloom has proceeded to an anxiety that the humanities will not be influenced enough by Shakespeare and other canonical writers. In the general public, Bloom has found a large, receptive audience for these ideas, even if within the university system, he is kicking against the pricks, to use the biblical phrase. Bloom's own influence on literary criticism has been immense, whether it has been regarded as a positive or negative phenomenon, and in other related areas of service to literary studies, such as in his several-hundred-long list of edited books and essay collections, Bloom has performed constantly and admirably.

Notes

1 Harold Bloom, *Blake's Apocalypse: A Study in Poetic Argument*, Ithaca and New York: Cornell University Press, 1970, p. 145.
2 David Fite, *Harold Bloom: The Rhetoric of Romantic Vision*, Amherst, MA: The University of Massachusetts Press, 1985, p. 17, ellipses and slight modifications to punctuation by Lane.
3 Harold Bloom, *The Anxiety of Influence: A Theory of Poetry*, New York: Oxford University Press, 1973, p. 5.
4 Ibid., p. 25.
5 Ibid., p. 26.
6 Ibid., p. 62.
7 Harold Bloom, *Agon: Towards a Theory of Revisionism*, New York and Oxford: Oxford University Press, 1982, p. 39.
8 Harold Bloom, *Shakespeare: The Invention of the Human*, New York: Riverhead, 1998, p. 3.
9 Ibid., p. 17.
10 Harold Bloom, *Where Shall Wisdom Be Found?*, New York: Riverhead, 2004, p. 115.

See also in this book

Gilbert and Gubar

Major works

Shelley's Mythmaking (1959). New Haven, CT: Yale University Press.
The Visionary Company: A Reading of English Romantic Poetry (1961). Garden City, NY: Doubleday; revised and enlarged edition, Ithaca, NY: Cornell University Press, 1971.
Blake's Apocalypse: A Study in Poetic Argument (1963). Garden City, NY: Doubleday.
Yeats (1970). New York: Oxford University Press.
The Ringers in the Tower: Studies in Romantic Tradition (1971). Chicago, IL and London: University of Chicago Press.
The Anxiety of Influence: A Theory of Poetry (1973). New York: Oxford University Press.
A Map of Misreading (1975). New York: Oxford University Press.
Kabbalah and Criticism (1975). New York: Seabury Press.
Poetry and Repression: Revisionism from Blake to Stevens (1976). New Haven, CT and London: Yale University Press.
Figures of Capable Imagination (1976). New York: Seabury Press.
Wallace Stevens: The Poems of our Climate (1976). Ithaca, NY and London: Cornell University Press.
Agon: Towards a Theory of Revisionism (1982). New York and Oxford: Oxford University Press.
The Breaking of the Vessels (1982). Chicago, IL and London: University of Chicago Press.
The Western Canon: The Books and School of the Ages (1994). New York: Harcourt Brace.
Shakespeare: The Invention of the Human (1998). New York: Riverhead.
Where Shall Wisdom Be Found? (2004). New York: Riverhead.

Further reading

Baumlin, James S., 'Reading Bloom (Or: Lessons Concerning the "Reformation" of the Western Literary Canon)', College Literature 27.3 (2000): 22–46.
Desmet, Christy and Sawyer, Robert, eds, Harold Bloom's Shakespeare, New York: Palgrave, 2001.
Fite, David Joseph, Harold Bloom: The Rhetoric of Romantic Vision, Massachusetts: University of Massachusetts Press, 1985.
Gallop, Jane, 'Precursor Critics and the Anxiety of Influence', Profession (2003): 105–109.
Redfield, Marc, 'Literature, Incorporated: Harold Bloom, Theory and the Canon', in Peter C. Herman, ed., Historicizing Theory, Albany, NY: SUNY Press, 2004; pp. 209–233.

WAYNE C. BOOTH (1921–)

Writing just over two decades after the publication of Booth's *The Rhetoric of Fiction* (1961), Shlomith Rimmon-Kenan ponders the relationship between the actual author of a text and its 'implied author' as described by Booth;[1] writing about narrative and film four decades after the initial publication of Booth's text, Jakob Lothe theorizes the implied author, as a construct assembled by the reader, or viewer, of a written or visual narrative.[2] These examples reveal just two ways in which one of the terms either invented or developed by Booth, has become common literary theoretical currency. Born in 1921, Wayne C. Booth was the George M. Pullman Professor of English and Distinguished Service Professor at The University of Chicago, where he had come under the influence of R.S. Crane (1886–1967) as a graduate student. Crane was leader of the Neo-Aristotelian School of criticism, an approach that was sceptical of New Criticism's interest in language. The Neo-Aristotelian approach is based upon Aristotle's four causes of literary works: 1, the poet (efficient cause); 2, the effect on the reader (final cause); 3, the language (material cause); and 4, the mimetic content (formal cause). This holistic approach to literature acted as a counterbalance to New Criticism; however, the focus on language continued in later movements such as Deconstruction, Semiotics or Structuralism, whereas the Neo-Aristotelian School is now defunct.

The Rhetoric of Fiction, republished in 1983 with an expanded second edition, combines the holistic approach of the Neo-Aristotelians with the precision of the New Critics; the resulting text has been widely influential, and even as the book has also more recently gone out of fashion, the analytical tools developed therein have simply become part of an everyday critical or narratological discourse. Booth's mission in *The Rhetoric of Fiction* is a defence of the author (either 'real' or 'implied'), that is to say, the author as an interplay of judgements and observations that give 'ironic complexity', 'intensity of illusion', 'portrayal of moral ambiguities', 'revelation of truth' and 'prophetic vision'. Critics and modern writers such as Jean Paul Sartre had argued that literature should be autonomous, that all traces of authorial intervention should be removed; Booth responded by revealing what is gained, and what is lost, when authorial intervention is minimized or effaced. Overall, any choice that has been made in a text, argues Booth, is a sign of authorial judgement: 'though the author can to some extent choose his disguises, he can never choose to disappear'. Important literary devices theorized by Booth are the showing/telling binary opposition, and the notion of the unreliable narrator. Percy Lubbock (1879–1965) in his influential *The Craft of Fiction* (1921) argues that there is aesthetic value in 'showing' whereas direct 'telling' is a crude narrative device: in effect, Lubbock is saying that 'showing'

is an autonomous and subtle mode of 'telling'. Think of time passing in a novel: the statement 'ten years went by' is an example of
telling; to *show* ten years passing by would involve describing changes,
the aging of people or their belongings, shifts in fashion, and so on.
Booth, in effect, deconstructs the showing/telling opposition: he
argues that all showing reveals interpretive choice and critical judgement, and that, at times, 'telling' can be more successful and interesting than showing. In other words, the boundary between showing
and telling is arbitrary and highly permeable. The 'unreliable narrator'
is another important literary device: a reliable narrator is a relatively
trustworthy source of information about the fictional world and its
characters as depicted, whereas the unreliable narrator is, to put it
mildly, 'economical with the truth'. The latter may be deliberate, or
because of some factor outside of the narrator's control, such as
restricted vision, ideological intensity or mental incapacity. Booth's
classic example of unreliability is the Governess in Henry James's *The
Turn of the Screw*; a more recent example is Margaret Atwood's narrator in her popular novel *Surfacing*. In James's novella, the reader
never knows if the narrator is deceived or deceiving; in Atwood's
novel, the unreliable narrator gradually reveals 'the truth' about her
own unreliability (although ambiguities remain). Booth runs through
the arguments for and against the reliability of the narrator in *The Turn
of the Screw*, i.e. those arguments that attempt to analyse the psychic
'deficiencies' of the narrator, and those that take her judgements at
face value; the resulting 'unintentional ambiguity of effect' found in
such modern novels is seen as endlessly proliferating. An examination
of 'confusions of distance' created in earlier eighteenth-century fiction
enables Booth to prepare the way for his analysis of modern fiction.
He argues that there are a number of causes that problematize the
question of distance, these are: 'lack of adequate warning that irony
is at work'; 'extreme complexity, subtlety, or privacy of the norms to
be inferred'; and 'vivid psychological realism'.[3] In relation to *The Turn
of the Screw*, the latter cause is of most interest, because it appears
from this perspective to diminish the capacity for sound judgement
in the reader, and it is the one that Booth argues creates sympathy for
protagonists who may not morally deserve it:

> The deep plunges of modern inside views, the various streams-
> of-consciousness that attempt to give the reader an effect of
> living thought and sensation, are capable of blinding us to the
> possibility of our making judgements not shared by the
> narrator or reflector himself.[4]

The pre-eminent form for such a 'deep plunge', according to Booth, is autobiography:

> let us finally bind the reader so tightly to the consciousness of the ambiguously misguided protagonist that nothing will interfere with his delight in inferring the precise though varying degrees of distance that operate from point to point throughout the book.[5]

Resisting the relativism of infinite co-present interpretations of any one text, with especial reference to Joyce's work, Booth is reminding the critic that certain 'factual' bases must exist in a text for judgements to be grounded; while this appears immensely outmoded after postmodernism, it is not outmoded in relation to a general theory of functional perception, for example, as developed by Edward Pols in his *Radical Realism: Direct Knowing in Science and Philosophy* (1992).

The pedagogic aspects of *The Rhetoric of Fiction* point towards Booth's wider concern with teaching, ethics and the impact of literature (Booth was president of the Modern Languages Association in 1982, reflecting his standing in the field and interests in teaching, and was one of the founding members of the influential journal *Critical Inquiry*). The ethics of literary ambiguities are explored by Booth in *Modern Dogma and the Rhetoric of Assent* (1974) and the conflictual nature of the heterogeneous literary theoretical field comes under attack in *Critical Understanding* (1979). But it is the more recent *The Company We Keep: An Ethics of Fiction* (1988) that develops more rigorous theoretical tools, in particular Booth's concept of 'coduction', which is a process of evaluation and ongoing conversation based upon previous experience of texts. Coduction also attempts to explain the process of encountering the Other in a literary context, and the ways in which the reader's value system is affected and even transformed by this encounter. Booth also engages with Reader Response Theory (see Stanley Fish, 1938–) in *The Company We Keep*, arguing that coduction implies a set of values embedded in a text regardless of the need for a reader to respond to them. It is this notion of 'a set of values' in literary texts that Booth has explored in various ways throughout his career and via all of his publications.

Notes

1 Shlomith Rimmon-Kenan, *Narrative Fiction: Contemporary Poetics*, London and New York: Methuen, 1983.

2 Jakob Lothe, *Narrative in Fiction and Film: An Introduction*, Oxford: Oxford
    University Press, 2000.
3 Wayne C. Booth, *The Rhetoric of Fiction*, Chicago, IL: The University of
    Chicago Press, 1983, pp. 316–322.
4 Ibid., p. 324.
5 Ibid.

See also in this book

Genette

Major works

The Rhetoric of Fiction (1961). Chicago, IL: The University of Chicago Press.
Second, expanded edition, 1983.
Now Don't Try to Reason with Me: Essays and Ironies for a Credulous Age (1970).
Chicago, IL: The University of Chicago Press.
A Rhetoric of Irony (1974). Chicago, IL: The University of Chicago Press.
Modern Dogma and the Rhetoric Of Assent (1974). Notre Dame: Notre Dame
University Press.
'Metaphor as Rhetoric: The Problem of Evaluation' (1978). *Critical Inquiry*
5 (Autumn): 49–72.
Critical Understanding: The Powers and Limits of Pluralism (1979). Chicago, IL:
The University of Chicago Press.
'Freedom of Interpretation: Bakhtin and the Challenge of Feminist Criticism'
(1982). *Critical Inquiry*, 9 (September): 45–76.
The Company We Keep: An Ethics of Fiction (1988). Berkeley, CA: University
of California Press.
The Vocation of a Teacher: Rhetorical Occasions (1989). Chicago, IL: The
University of Chicago Press.

Further reading

Antczak, Frederick J., ed., *Rhetoric and Pluralism: Legacies of Wayne Booth*,
    Ohio State University, 1995.
Crane, R.S., *The Idea of the Humanities and Other Essays*, Chicago, IL: The
    University of Chicago Press, 1967.
Fowler, Roger, *Linguistics & the Novel*, London and New York: Methuen,
    1977.
Lothe, Jakob, *Narrative in Fiction and Film: An Introduction*, Oxford: Oxford
    University Press, 2000.
Pols, Edward, *Radical Realism: Direct Knowing in Science and Philosophy*, Ithaca,
    NY and London: Cornell University Press, 1992.
Rimmon-Kenan, Shlomith, *Narrative Fiction: Contemporary Poetics*, London
    and New York: Methuen, 1983.
Wellek, René, *A History of Modern Criticism 1750–1950. Vol. VI: American
    Criticism, 1900–1950*, New Haven, CT and London: Yale University
    Press, 1986.

JUDITH BUTLER (1956–)

When critics discuss the concept of 'performing gender', they inevitably refer to, or base their work upon, the groundbreaking study by Judith Butler called *Gender Trouble* (1990). While 'Queer Theorists' – especially those who work in feminism and literary studies – are most likely to repeatedly turn to this book, Butler's academic background is actually in philosophy, which she studied at Yale University. Between undergraduate and graduate studies, Butler won a Fulbright Scholarship to the University of Heidelberg, where she studied with the German philosophers Hans Georg Gadamer and Dieter Henrich. After academic appointments at Wesleyan University, George Washington University and Johns Hopkins University, she was awarded in 1993 the prestigious post of Maxine Elliot Professor in the Departments of Rhetoric and Comparative Literature at the University of California. But this still begs the question: how did Butler's academic study of philosophy lead her to produce such a groundbreaking text for gender studies, one that still resonates and informs theory today? Answering this question involves turning to Butler's doctoral thesis on 'Recovery and Invention: The Projects of Desire in Hegel, Kojève, Hyppolite, and Sartre', which was published in 1987 with the title *Subjects of Desire: Hegelian Reflections in Twentieth-Century France*.

Butler finds the logic and grammar of Hegel's work, especially his *Phenomenology of Spirit*, to be dynamic and subject to the very process being defined in the latter text: the process of negation. Each time that a stable position of identity is reached, it is undermined via negation; but more compelling is Butler's observation that any definition of negation is, in itself, subject to negation. In other words, negation is in itself always in process. This links closely with the overall subject of her thesis: the relationship between philosophy (especially German Idealism) and desire. In her preface to the paperback edition of *Subjects of Desire*, Butler writes:

> all of my work remains within the orbit of a certain set of Hegelian questions: What is the relation between desire and recognition, and how is it that the constitution of the subject entails a radical and constitutive relation to alterity [otherness]?[1]

Desire is perceived to be something that philosophers cannot 'obliterate' from their conceptual systems of thought; they must maintain a distance that is uncontaminated by the appetites, by the arbitrary nature of desire's object(s), and by the constant slippage of desire (it is never to be found at a single site); Butler argues that philosophers formulate integrative strategies to 'silence or control' desire: the philosopher becomes the exemplary figure of a rational, desiring being. The definition of desire being critiqued – at this stage in Butler's work – is Hegelian; desire is the overriding human need for self-sufficiency via the recognition that all apparent differences in the external world are in fact 'immanent features' of the subject (in other words, differences are internal to the subject whose self-consciousness is all important). To understand this statement is to involve oneself in Hegel's dialectic, whereby the desiring/knowing subject has to step outside of *itself* to gain a perspective known as 'self-reflection'; the subject attempts to understand the relations between itself and some other being or object. Once it understands this *relation* (which is called more technically, *mediation*), it has expanded its consciousness to such an extent that the subject cannot go back to the very position of identity it was exploring in the first place; the Hegelian subject, desiring self-consciousness, is thus always on the move. Another way of thinking this process is via a series of ever-expanding circles: each time that the subject steps outside of itself to perceive the mediated relationship between itself and its other, its new level of awareness contains the entire resolved relationship with the additional shift to a new position of self-consciousness that starts the process all over again at a higher level; the first circle now has a relationship with another object or subject, which will, in turn, encompass all of the prior relationships. It is important to remember this movement of the Hegelian subject when reading Butler's *Gender Trouble*, because although she is, in effect, deconstructing Hegel, the subject-in-formation, or permanently on the move, in *The Phenomenology of Spirit* is, in a sense, constantly re-performing identity relations between itself and some other being or object. Butler's deconstruction of Hegel proceeds via a study of the contemporary reception of Hegel via the readings of Kojève, Hyppolite, Sartre and the now more familiar theorists Deleuze, Derrida, Foucault, Kristeva and Lacan. Each of these readers of Hegel were highly influential in relation to a dismantling of different aspects of the Hegelian dialectic: Kojève and Hyppolite introduced the notion of becoming as of priority in Hegel (a shift from more static notions of being); Sartre reads Hegelian desire 'as a vain metaphysical striving'[2] which is best directed toward the construction of identity through writing; the poststructuralists attack Hegel's apparent dynamism as being a masked metaphysics of presence (Derrida) and a narrative of dialectical progress (Foucault), and the subject's desire, rather than being a unifying force, is now read as multiplicity and discontinuity (Deleuze, Lacan, Kristeva).

Desire is the subject of Butler's most famous work: *Gender Trouble: Feminism and the Subversion of Identity*. Moving beyond binary thinking, Butler performs a sophisticated deconstruction of patriarchal *and* a number of feminist foundational accounts of gender; her constant move is to attack any theory that argues for a 'natural' or normative notion of what she argues is a social construct. The latter also requires a shift away from the notion of an originary heterosexuality, and a secondary homosexuality; in other words, utilizing the deconstructive rejection of binary hierarchy, Butler rejects the possibility of there being an 'authentic' expression of gender followed by its deficient or aberrant copy. Many literary critics have been inspired by Butler's work here, especially her notion that gender is a performance, but it is essential to gain a sense of Butler's wider impact, which can be seen through brief analysis of section two of *Gender Trouble*: 'Prohibition, Psychoanalysis, and the Production of the Heterosexual Matrix'. One of Butler's goals in this section is to reject the feminist move of re-instituting a natural bodily 'sex' before the law of patriarchy and hierarchical gender differences, and instead to pinpoint the law's cultural displacement within and through its very processes of power. Examining key concepts or events in gender formation – such as structuralist anthropologist Lévi-Strauss's reading of incest taboo leading to exogamic heterosexuality – Butler foregrounds the possibility that the law's generativity and performativity can be turned against itself in a series of subversive moves. Thus, Butler calls naturalization processes – for example, the incest taboo regarded as a 'universal truth' – 'discursive constructions' rather than natural laws. A powerful re-reading of Freud's work on mourning and melancholia leads Butler to argue that preceding the incest taboo is the prohibition of homosexual desire; in the process of prohibition, there is a renunciation of the desire, and the object, which then 'become subject to the internalizing strategies of melancholia' according to Butler.[3] For Freud, melancholia is a mechanism essential to the formation of the ego and of character; thus, Butler theorizes that melancholic heterosexual gender formation, which involves an internalization and incorporation of the Other, is not only founded upon the prohibition of homosexual desire, but functions *because of* that desire. The key shift into performativity is the realization that prohibition and internalization is not a singular event: 'this identity is constructed and maintained by the consistent application of this taboo, not only in the stylization of the body in compliance with discrete categories of sex, but in the production and "disposition" of sexual desire'.[4] In other words, the prohibition is not a static fixing of gender identity once and for all, but an ongoing productivity: it continues to produce the signs of sexuality – the 'stylization of the body' – just as it works to efface the constructedness of gender (the societal law of prohibition or taboo). The need to constantly re-perform heterosexuality reveals a fundamental anxiety: that if gender is constructed, and there is an internalized, prohibited same-sex desire, then this situation may be dismantled or at the least destabilized. It is Butler's work on 'drag' that reveals gender performance in all of its complexities and undoes the 'false stabilization of gender'[5] prevalent in the production of heterosexuality. For Butler, 'drag' creates a 'dissonance' between what she calls the 'three contingent dimensions' of anatomical sex, gender identity and gender performance.[6] Through this dissonance, the apparently naturalized, stabilized heterosexuality is parodied and revealed to be merely another style, or, another performance in and of itself. Thus, instead of there being an 'originary' or first heterosexuality, now theorists perceive there to be nothing but gender 'imitation'; instead of there being a natural heterosexuality, there is the contingency of gender – i.e. the chance of developing in a certain social context, one in which a set of prohibitions may differ from another social context. In *Bodies that Matter: On the Discursive Limits of 'Sex'* (1993), Butler extends and amplifies her arguments on the repetitious, continual re-performance of gender (with interest in the places where this performance breaks down) as well as the constructedness of gender and the body itself (i.e. the ways in which we know and represent the body through language).

Butler continues her exploration of gender performance in two books that were published in 1997: *The Psychic Life of Power: Theories in Subjection* and *Excitable Speech: A Politics of the Performative*. Chapter five of *The Psychic Life of Power*, 'Melancholy Gender/Refused Identification', is a return to and expansion of Butler's re-reading of Freud, and should be read in conjunction with section two of *Gender Trouble*. In chapter four, '"Conscience Doth Make Subject of Us All": Althusser's Subjection', Butler investigates the concept of interpellation, which is the two-way process of hailing or calling a subject into being through his or her accepting the call, and making of a response. Butler is intrigued by the ways in which subjects accept the guilt involved in the call, as well as the parallels between interpellation and divine naming (as in baptism). Her critique is aimed at the notion that the subject precedes the call; she argues that the subject (and his or her subjection via guilt or the law) comes into being through the power of interpellation; it is a founding, and potentially imprisoning, gesture. Being constituted by naming is expanded in *Excitable Speech* to being constituted by language; Butler asks: 'Does the power of language to injure follow from its interpellative power?'[7] The 'problem of injurious speech' expands in a network that forms the book, to include not just linguistic vulnerability, but also speech acts, the regulation of hate speech, pornography, the 'zone of partial citizenship' in the military, especially as it pertains to the naming of homosexuality, and censorship. Drawing upon legal discourse, Butler notes how 'excitable' utterances are those that have been made under duress, and are therefore considered to be beyond the subject's control (thus, for example, a confession made under duress is not admissible in the law); she theorizes from this position to argue that all speech acts are in some ways 'excitable' because the subject is constituted in and through language. Butler's aim here is to think through the ways in which certain types of speech can 'break with context'[8] to produce new contexts and, potentially, new identities.

Notes

1 Judith Butler, *Subjects of Desire: Hegelian Reflections in Twentieth-Century France*, New York: Columbia University Press, 1987, p. xiv.
2 Ibid., p. 15.
3 Judith Butler, *Gender Trouble: Feminism and the Subversion of Identity*, London and New York: Routledge, 1999, p. 75.
4 Ibid., p. 81.
5 Ibid., p. 172.
6 Ibid., p. 175.
7 Judith Butler, *Excitable Speech: A Politics of the Performative*, London and New York, Routledge, 1997, p. 2.
8 Ibid., p. 40.

See also in this book

Foucault, Freud

Major works

Subjects of Desire: Hegelian Reflections in Twentieth-Century France (1987). New York: Columbia University Press.
Gender Trouble: Feminism and the Subversion of Identity (1990). London and New York: Routledge. Anniversary Edition, 1999.
Bodies that Matter: On the Discursive Limits of 'Sex' (1993). London and New York: Routledge.
Excitable Speech: A Politics of the Performative (1997). London and New York, Routledge.

The Psychic Life of Power: Theories in Subjection (1997). Stanford, CA: Stanford University Press.
Antigone's Claim: Kinship Between Life and Death (2000). New York: Columbia University Press.

Further reading

Breen, Margaret Sonser and Blumenfeld, Warren J., eds, *Butler Matters: Judith Butler's Impact on Feminist and Queer Studies*, Ashgate, 2005.
Jagger, Gill, *Judith Butler: Sexual Politics, Social Change and the Power of the Performative*, London and New York: Routledge, 2005.
Robbins, Bruce, '"I Couldn't Possibly Love Such a Person": Judith Butler on Hegel', *Minnesota Review*, 52–54 (2001): 263–269.
Salih, Sara, *Judith Butler*, London and New York: Routledge, 2002.

HÉLÈNE CIXOUS (1937–)

While Hélène Cixous is a theorist most well known for the concept of *écriture féminine*, she is also a highly prolific playwright and author. Born in Oran, Algeria, Cixous grew up in a polyvocal and ethnically diverse family situated in the midst of French colonialism: her mother had an Austro-German background, and her father's background was Sephardic Jewish. Many languages were spoken in Cixous' youth – including Spanish, Arabic, German and French[1] – and this led to a personal love of language that she would continue to explore and express later in her academic life. Her father's death, when she was eleven years old, was a profound and moving event, one that Cixous later articulated as 'the essential primitive experience' which gives 'access to the other world';[2] the experience of loss leading to a gain becomes a central trope[3] in her work. But what is it that Cixous gained? Some would argue that it was writing: 'Writing is learning to die. It's learning not to be afraid, in other words to live at the extremity of life, which is what the dead, death, gives us.'[4] Further, writing is perceived as a complex activity *originating* in the 'relationship' between the living and the dead. This sense of loss as a central trope goes beyond the death of Cixous' father, and manifests itself in many ways throughout her work. After moving to France, Cixous passed her *aggrégation d'anglais* degree in 1959, and began to work as an *assistante* at The University of Bordeaux in 1962; she became *maître de conference* at Nanterre in 1967, followed by an outstanding year in which she gained her *docteur dès letters*, and was appointed *chargé de mission* to found the new Université de Paris VIII at Vincennes where she was also appointed as Professor of English Literature. In 1970 Cixous was co-founder with Gérard Genette, Tzvetan Todorov, and J.-P. Richard, of the journal and literary collection *Poétique* at Editions du Seuil; she inaugurated the Centre de recherches en etudes féminines in 1974, and became involved in the theatre in 1976. Her fiction and writings for theatre have won many accolades and awards, and some critics argue that to understand Cixous the reader has to immerse herself in all of Cixous' diverse modes of writing. Given that her writing output is so immense, this overview will focus on her critical work.

Cixous' first publication was a collection of short stories (*Le prénom de Dieu*, 1967), but her first academic book was her doctoral thesis *L'exil de James Joyce ou l'art du remplacement* (1968, translated as *The Exile of James Joyce*, 1972). Cixous' Joyce is a Hegelian figure, passing through various stages of artistic self–portrayal and unhappy consciousness; for Cixous, the subject in/of Joyce is distanced or exiled from the strangeness of objective reality, and the subject's progression is towards a coincidence between outer and inner worlds. Instead of achieving Hegel's Absolute Knowledge, Joyce instead discovered language and 'the magic power possessed by words'.[5] For Cixous, the 'Circe' episode in Joyce's *Ulysses* is the achievement of a coincidence between subject and object, an immediacy attained via language. This notion represents the shift in French theory under way at the time that Cixous wrote her thesis, from structuralism to a more radical poststructuralism. For example, the character of Bloom, in *Ulysses*, exists in the infinitive, having no power over others, his history or destiny, or even 'the organs of his own body'.[6] Bloom exists via the 'counter-presence' of others, but not in a hierarchical or transcendent position: like the critic, Bloom is immersed in the linguistic world of the novel where 'there is no more separation between the inside and the outside, spirit and matter, reality and the self, no more guarantee of what Jaspers calls *Meinigkeit* or the feeling of the self to be distinct and not alienated'.[7] As Cixous argues, several years before an analogous point was made by Deleuze and Guattari, all that exists in this stage of being is movement, that 'which animates simultaneously objects, one's body, society, and the self'.[8] For Cixous, a departure must be made from this point, that of gender and the relationship between the subject and the Other; in her newly established Centre de recherches en etudes féminines, and in her creative writing, Cixous began to rethink the poststructuralist subject via a re-reading of Freud, especially Freud's theory of castration ('Le Rire de la Méduse', (1975)) and his problematic relationship with the patient known as Dora. Working with Catherine Clément, Cixous published this work in her 1975 volume *La Jeune Née*, translated in 1986 as *The Newly Born Woman*.

The route taken by Cixous and Clément to reveal the form and force of *écriture féminine* is in itself an enactment of the term as an inter-weaving of critical and conceptual writing. Starting with the French title of the book, there is a play on words/sounds that more than hints at the subversive power of 'an/other writing' as Susan Sellers trans-lates *écriture féminine*.[9] *La Jeune Née* can be heard as, or signifies: *La Genêt* (the French author Jean Genet, who wrote texts that subverted bourgeois norms of gender and race), *Là je n'est* (There I, a subject, is not), or *Là je une nais* (There I, a subject, a feminine one, am born).[10] What is the subject resisting in this intertextual, rich play on words? She is resisting the patriarchal order in a way that gives her 'a dan-gerous symbolic mobility' as Clément puts it.[11] Cixous opens her section of the book, called 'Sorties: Out and Out: Attacks/Ways Out/Forays', with a question – 'Where is she?' – answered at first by a hierarchical list of binary oppositions that privilege masculine over feminine traits, subordinating questions of sexual difference to the overarching binary opposition activity/passivity. From her aphoristic opening, Cixous' argument powerfully develops, especially with her critique of the effacement of the mother from philosophy and literary history, as part of their 'phallocentric' foundations. *Écriture féminine* is the concept that is proposed as not just a replacement, but a sup-planting of 'phallogocentrism', or, systems of thought that are patri-archal and rely on a 'logocentric', that is to say, Judeo–Christian, notion of the power of the word. Cixous also situates her concept in the injustices of colonialism and racism; she produces an autobio-graphical sketch of her childhood in French-occupied Algeria, wit-nessing the repression of 'invisible' peoples: 'proletarians, immigrant workers, minorities who are not the right "color," Women'.[12] She rejects the implicit racism and sexism in the metaphor of woman as the 'dark continent', an interiority that has not been adequately 'explored' because of the prejudices of patriarchy. What emerges from this frame, is a concept that is akin to Derrida's neologism *différance*, that is, a process of thought and writing that cannot be totalized or contained by binary thinking. The mode of writing called *écriture fémi-nine* is described as 'a place [that] exists which is not economically or politically indebted to all the vileness and compromise. That is not obliged to reproduce the system. That is writing.'[13] This may sound utopian, but it is grounded in writing-the-body, a recovery of mater-nal tropes and identity, a rejection of the Oedipal drama and castra-tion theories of Freud and the privileging of the phallus in Lacan, and a celebration of the pleasure-of-the-text, the text's *jouissance*. Thinking back to the Hegelian journey of Joyce mapped out in *The Exile of*

James Joyce, we can now see that Molly Bloom, for all her agency, is ultimately constrained by phallocentrism, becoming the 'nonsocial, nonpolitical, nonhuman half of the living structure'[14] that organizes that text. Cixous argues that *écriture féminine* involves recognizing the Other in a process that is *not* dependent upon the negativity of the Hegelian dialectic, in other words 'a type of exchange in which one would keep the *other* alive and different'.[15] In Joyce's *Ulysses*, there is a Hegelian 'schema of recognition' which retains 'no place for the other, for an equal other, for a whole and living woman'.[16] Yet, Molly Bloom's final orgasmic 'yes', a kind of infinite *jouissance* that keeps the novel open, carries *Ulysses*, according to Cixous, 'in the direction of a new writing'.[17] In gender terms, the positive recognition of the Other leads to a mode of writing that celebrates bisexuality, expressed also as an entirely open love of the Other. As Susan Sellers puts it: '*écriture féminine* is the endeavour to write the other in ways which refuse to appropriate or annihilate the other's difference in order to create and glorify the self in a masculine position of mastery'.[18] If the negativity of Hegel is rejected, what does *écriture féminine*, following the deconstructive logic of Derrida's *différance*, put in its place? Cixous turns to the processes of indigenous and other excessive/transgressive gift-giving economies described and analysed by Marcel Mauss, Claude Lévi-Strauss, and radically re-theorized by Georges Bataille as an anti-Hegelian tool (i.e. Bataille's work on the potlatch). Cixous notes that it 'is men who have inscribed, described, theorized the para- doxical logic of an economy without reserve'.[19] So why turn to this concept of an extreme expenditure, or gift-giving, that threatens cap- italism, and overturns in its excessiveness Western hierarchy? Cixous clearly regards the dangerous writing-without-return as 'feminine' whereas 'masculine' writing or investment in the Other, continually demands more signs of 'masculinity' (the 'profit' of virility, authority, power, money, pleasure to use Cixous' words); *écriture féminine*, on the other hand, is a gift-giving *for* the Other, without return, a giving 'without self-interest'.[20] In this argument, Cixous recognizes that there are some men, although they are 'rare', who can write *écriture féminine*; as Susan Sellers notes:

> In *The Newly Born Woman* . . . [Cixous] cites as illustrations of *écriture féminine* the works of William Shakespeare, the French playwright Jean Genet and the German dramatist Heinrich von Kleist: 'beings who are complex, mobile, open' . . . and in whose writings there is 'an abundance of the other' . . . The incessant movement in Genet's writing, Cixous argues, means

55

that his plays constantly change shape so that they are never arbitrarily fixed to represent (only) one viewpoint.[21]

Cixous also reads a diverse range of authors to explore *écriture féminine*, in particular the Brazilian writer Clarice Lispector, in her study *Reading With Clarice Lispector* (1989, trans. 1990), and critics regard Cixous' own mature creative works as embodying this central concept, for example, her fiction *Vivre l'orange/To Live the Orange* (1979), *Illa* (1980), *(With) Ou l'art de l'innocence* (1981), *Limonade tout était si infini* (1982) and *Le Livre de Promethea* (1983),[22] and plays such as *L'Histoire terrible mais inachevée de Norodom Sihanouk, roi du Cambodge* (Théâtre du Soleil, 1985) and *L'Indiade ou l'Inde de leurs rêves* (Théâtre du Soleil, 1987). In her work for the theatre, Cixous deals most insistently with the issue of resisting speaking-for-another, i.e. *écriture féminine* as a way of not claiming to entirely know the Other, but a letting-others-speak; in 'The Scene of the Unconscious' Cixous describes her personal journey as an author through an ego-centred stage, descending and re-emerging from the unconscious, not with the goal of self-enlightenment, but rather self emerging oriented 'towards the Other'. Theatre, Cixous claims, allows the Other to speak in her writing. In her critical work, the preoccupations briefly sketched above recur in multiple, fluid, dynamic and different ways; Cixous' critical texts are a joy to read, attuned always to the other voice of the authors she studies and learns from, and the incidents from their biographies that strike her, particularly with the figures of Kafka and Lispector. While Cixous' at times elusive concept of *écriture féminine* has come under criticism for its apparent essentialist basis, her resistance to phallocentrism, critique of key patriarchal thinkers, and above all her exploration and creation of multiple genres, continues to resonate with each new generation of feminists who turn to her work.

Notes

1 Hélène Cixous, 'From the Scene of the Unconscious to the Scene of History', trans. Deborah W. Carpenter, in Ralph Cohen, ed., *The Future Of Literary Theory*, London and New York: Routledge, 1989, pp. 1–18; p. 2.

2 Hélène Cixous, *Three Steps on the Ladder of Writing*, trans. Sarah Cornell and Susan Sellers, Chichester, West Sussex and New York: Columbia University Press, 1993, p. 10.

3 Julia Dobson, 'Hélène Cixous (1937–)', in Jon Simons, ed., *Contemporary Critical Theorists: From Lacan to Said*, Edinburgh: Edinburgh University Press, 2004, pp. 118–134; p. 119.

4 Hélène Cixous, *Three Steps on the Ladder of Writing*, p. 10.

5 Hélène Cixous, *The Exile of James Joyce*, trans. Sally A.J. Purcell, New York: David Lewis, 1972, p. 359.
6 Ibid., p. 708.
7 Ibid., p. 727.
8 Ibid.
9 Susan Sellers, *Hélène Cixous: Authorship, Autobiography and Love*, Cambridge: Polity, 1996, p. xi.
10 Betsy Wing, 'Glossary', in Hélène Cixous and Catherine Clément, *The Newly Born Woman*, trans. Betsy Wing, Minneapolis, MN and London: University of Minnesota Press, 1986, p. 166.
11 Hélène Cixous and Catherine Clément, *The Newly Born Woman*, p. 7.
12 Ibid., p. 70.
13 Ibid., p. 72.
14 Hélène Cixous, *The Exile of James Joyce*, p. 66.
15 Ibid., p. 79.
16 Ibid.
17 Ibid., p. 85.
18 Susan Sellers, *Hélène Cixous: Authorship, Autobiography and Love*, pp. 11–12.
19 Hélène Cixous and Catherine Clément, *The Newly Born Woman*, p. 86.
20 Ibid., p. 87.
21 Ibid., p. 11.
22 I agree with Helen Sellers that this group of texts represent a significant shift from the more conventional format of Cixous' earlier writings. See Susan Sellers, *Hélène Cixous: Authorship, Autobiography and Love*, p. 55.

See also in this book

Derrida, Kristeva

Major works (excluding fiction/drama)

The Exile of James Joyce (1968). Trans. Sally A.J. Purcell, New York: David Lewis, 1972.
The Newly Born Woman (with Catherine Clément, 1975). Trans. Betsy Wing, Minneapolis, MN and London: University of Minnesota Press, 1986.
Reading With Clarice Lispector (1989). Trans. Verena A. Conley, Minneapolis, MN: University of Minnesota Press, 1990.
Coming to Writing and Other Essays (title essay 1977). Trans. Deborah Jenson, Sarah Cornell, Ann Liddle and Susan Sellers, Cambridge, MA: Harvard University Press, 1991.
Readings: The Poetics of Blanchot, Joyce, Kafka, Kleist, Lispector, and Tsvetayeva (1991). Trans. Verena A. Conley, Minneapolis, MN: University of Minnesota Press.
Three Steps on the Ladder of Writing (1993). Trans. Sarah Cornell and Susan Sellers, Chichester, West Sussex and New York: Columbia University Press, The Wellek Library Lectures at the University of California, Irvine.
The Hélène Cixous Reader (1994) ed. Susan Sellers, London and New York: Routledge.

Selected fiction/drama

Le prénom de Dieu (1967). Paris: Grasset.
Dedans (1969). Paris: Grasset.
Les commencements (1970; part 1 of trilogy). Paris: Grasset.
Le troisième corps (1970; part 2 of trilogy). Paris: Grasset.
Neutre (1972; part 3 of trilogy). Paris: Grasset.
Vivre l'orange/To Live the Orange (1979). Bilingual edition, trans. Ann Liddle and Sarah Cornell, Paris: Des Femmes.
Illa (1980). Paris: Des Femmes.
With, Ou l'art de l'innocence (1981). Paris: Des Femmes.
Limonade tout était si infini (1982). Paris: Des Femmes.
Le Livre de Promethea (1983). Paris: Gallimard.
L'Histoire terrible mais inachevée de Norodom Sihanouk, roi du Cambodge (1985). Paris: Editions Théâtre du Soleil.
L'Indiade ou l'Inde de leurs rêves (1987). Paris: Editions Théâtre du Soleil.
Manne aux Mandelstams aux Mandelas (1988). Paris: Des Femmes.
On ne part pas, on ne revient pas (1991). Paris: Des Femmes.

Further reading

Bray, Abigail, *Hélène Cixous: Writing and Sexual Differences*, London and New York: Palgrave, 2004.
Conley, Verena Andermatt, *Hélène Cixous*, Toronto: University of Toronto Press, 1992.
Sellers, Susan, *Hélène Cixous: Authorship, Autobiography, and Love*, Cambridge: Polity Press, 1996.
Shiach, Morag, *Hélène Cixous: A Politics of Writing*, London and New York: Routledge, 1991.

SIMONE DE BEAUVOIR (1908–1986)

The shock effect for contemporary readers in reading Beauvoir has multiple causes, with perhaps two being the most important: the fact that Beauvoir was an existentialist, and the fact that she writes at a time when patriarchal values were the norm. As with many founding figures, it is sometimes difficult for readers to place themselves into the historical milieu, which then reveals the radical and controversial brilliance of the founding figure in question. Born in Paris, Beauvoir studied for her *licenses* in literature, philosophy and mathematics, progressing to her *aggregation de philosophie* at the Sorbonne in 1928, with a thesis on 'freedom and contingency', a topic that she studied with another student, the future existentialist and her lifelong friend and partner Jean-Paul Sartre. Awarded her *aggregation* in 1929, Beauvoir went on to teach philosophy at a lycée, holding various posts until 1943, when she left teaching for a writing career. Having already written one unpublished novel called *When Things of the Spirit Come First*, she went on to publish the existentialist novels *She Came to Stay* (1943), *Blood of Others* (1945) and *All Men Are Mortal* (1946), the play *Who Shall Die* (1945) and a number of significant essays, collections and philosophical studies including *Pyrrhus et Cinéas* (1944) and *Ethics of Ambiguity* (1947). However, it was publication of the highly controversial and subsequently best-selling *The Second Sex* (1949) that brought Beauvoir notoriety as well as wider fame. *The Second Sex* – which opens with a single-word question, 'Woman?' – is a remarkable and powerful pioneering study of sexual difference, examining woman as Other. Published over half-a-century ago, the book still manages to provoke readers, not always it must be said in a positive or constructive fashion, although since the publication of Toril Moi's essay *Feminist Theory and Simone de Beauvoir* (1990), there has been a marked change in the reception of *The Second Sex* among contemporary feminists.

Beauvoir began gathering her thoughts about the role of women in society in preparation for writing her book *Ethics of Ambiguity*; she notes how:

> I wanted to draw up perhaps an essay on myself, not exactly my memoirs. It was in thinking of that, that it seemed necessary first of all to situate myself as a woman and to understand what it meant to be a woman.[1]

The Second Sex was the resulting study: part history of women's oppression, part insightful social and existentialist analysis, and part autobiographical treatise, this finely structured but wide-ranging text draws a painful picture of patriarchal injustice and domination. Condemned upon publication by conservatives and communists alike for its frank and explicit exploration of female sexuality, contemporary critics are just as likely to condemn this side of the book for being 'too phallic'. Toril Moi notes that the continued negative reception to the book is indicative of a deeper social and ideological problem: 'To have to insist on women's right to speak today . . . is disappointing to say the least.'[2] Moi is implying that there has not been as much progress within society from a feminist perspective as might otherwise be assumed, and this is made clear with the ongoing critical onslaught, the hostile effect, of reading and writing about Beauvoir: 'What is it about Beauvoir that produces this effect? Why do so many readers find themselves stirred to the point of irritation or even rage? How does one account for such *reading-effects* as these, regularly produced by Beauvoir's texts?'[3] Ironically, given the subject matter of *The Second Sex*, Moi's first major category that she explores in answer of her questions, is that Beauvoir's books are reduced to her personality, her *philosophy* thus also being reduced to her personality. Questioning patriarchy, Beauvoir is therefore responded to with a questioning of her authority to speak of intellectual and aesthetic matters *as woman*. This short-circuiting of her complex discourse must be borne in mind when thinking about Beauvoir's relationship with Jean-Paul Sartre and the 'grounding' of her work in his *Being and Nothingness*. More recent scholarship has argued convincingly that not only was Beauvoir's personal life more complex than was previously made apparent in the first wave of biographical and autobiographical writings, but that the existential implications of her novel *She Came to Stay* inspired and gave new direction to Sartre's writing of *Being and Nothingness*.[4] The existential language of the opening pages of *The Second Sex*, however, also refers to a Hegelian master/slave dialectic at work.[5] Beauvoir argues that woman is Other to man: 'She is defined and differentiated with reference to man and not he with reference to her; she is the incidental, the inessential as opposed to the essential. He is the subject, he is the Absolute – she is the Other.'[6] In other words, the male subject can only define himself through his relation with, and opposition to, woman. It is the 'reciprocal claim' of woman that Beauvoir argues has not been heard or accepted, which is where she diverges from the Hegelian narrative (the 'slave' is, in fact, the creator of value through work, and *the* constitutive factor in the dialectical relationship) and she suggests instead that as a question of sexual difference, the role of the Other is one of relentless oppression and indifference. Beauvoir asks: 'How is it, then, that this reciprocity has not been recognized between the sexes?'[7] In many respects, *The Second Sex* is an extended answer to this question, one that pleases no one, and annoys virtually everyone. It is in this annoyance, however, that the unsettling nature of the book becomes not only apparent, but indicative of Beauvoir's strong critique of social and sexual norms. In other words, there are still lessons to be learnt from Beauvoir's account, as theorists such as Judith Butler have argued, drawing for example upon her notion that 'one is not born, but rather becomes, a woman' translated as the notion that this 'formulation distinguishes sex from gender and suggests that gender is an aspect of identity gradually acquired'.[8]

The exposure of self-identity that Beauvoir had courageously undergone in *The Second Sex*, also led to much pain when she came under a barrage of criticism following publication of the book. Critics have recently turned to the strategic rewriting of self that Beauvoir undertook with the publication of her memoirs following *The Second Sex*: *Memoirs of a Dutiful Daughter* (1958), *Prime of Life* (1960), *Force of Circumstance* (1963), in relation to the death of her mother, *A Very Easy Death* (1964), and concerning her feminist role, *All Said and Done* (1972). Beauvoir continued to write novels and other non-fictional and critical materials, including a study of aging, called *The Coming of Age* (1970), and she contributed greatly to women's rights in France and beyond. Her relationship with Jean-Paul Sartre was explored in *Adieux: A Farewell to Sartre* (1981) and in the edited letters called *Lettres au Castor* (1983). The last word – and manifesto – should remain here to Beauvoir:

> We must not believe . . . that a change in woman's economic condition alone is enough to transform her . . . but until it has brought about the moral, social, cultural, and other conse-quences that it promises and requires, the new woman cannot appear.[9]

Notes

1 Simone de Beauvoir, quoted in Carol Ascher, *Simone de Beauvoir: A Life of Freedom*, Boston, MA: Beacon, 1981, p. 128.
2 Toril Moi, *Feminist Theory & Simone de Beauvoir*, Oxford: Basil Blackwell, 1990, p. 24.
3 Ibid., pp. 26–27.
4 See Kate Fullbrook and Edward Fullbrook, 'Sartre's Secret Key', in Margaret A. Simons, ed., *Feminist Interpretations of Simone de Beauvoir*, Pennsylvania, PA: The State University of Pennsylvania Press, 1995, pp. 97–111.
5 Judith Okely, 'Rereading *The Second Sex*', in Elizabeth Fallaize, ed., *Simone de Beauvoir: A Critical Reader*, London and New York: Routledge, 1998, pp. 19–28; p. 22.
6 Simone de Beauvoir, *The Second Sex*, trans. H.M. Parshley, New York: Alfred A. Knopf, 1968, p. xvi.
7 Ibid., pp. xvii–xviii.
8 Judith Butler, 'Sex and Gender in Simone De Beauvoir's *Second Sex*', in Elizabeth Fallaize, ed., *Simone de Beauvoir: A Critical Reader*, pp. 29–42; p. 30.
9 Simone de Beauvoir, *The Second Sex*, Paris: Gallimard; two volumes, trans. H.M. Parshley, New York: Knopf, 1952, p. 725.

Major works

She Came to Stay (1943). Paris: Gallimard.
Pyrrhus et Cinéas (1944). Paris: Gallimard.

Blood of Others (1945). Paris: Gallimard.
Who Shall Die (1945). Paris: Gallimard.
All Men are Mortal (1946). Paris: Gallimard.
Ethics of Ambiguity (1947). Paris: Gallimard.
The Second Sex (1949). Paris: Gallimard; two volumes. Trans. H.M. Parshley, New York: Knopf, 1952.
Memoirs of a Dutiful Daughter (1958). Paris: Gallimard.
Prime of Life (1960). Paris: Gallimard.
Force of Circumstance (1963). Paris: Gallimard.
A Very Easy Death (1964). Paris: Gallimard.
The Coming of Age (1970). Paris: Gallimard.
All Said and Done (1972). Paris: Gallimard.
Adieux: A Farewell to Sartre (1981). Paris: Gallimard.
Lettres au Castor (1983). Paris: Gallimard.

Further reading

Bair, Deirdre, *Simone De Beauvoir: A Biography*, New York: Summit Books, 1990.
Moi, Toril, *Simone De Beauvoir: The Making of an Intellectual Woman*, Oxford: Blackwell, 1994.
Tidd, Ursula, *Simone De Beauvoir*, London and New York: Routledge, 2004.

GILLES DELEUZE (1925–1995) AND PIERRE FÉLIX GUATTARI (1930–1992)

The title to one of Deleuze's later books, *Essays Critical and Clinical*, describes well the transdisciplinary interests of Deleuze and Guattari, leading to their shared projects and infamous publications. Both men had training in philosophy at the Sorbonne, but Guattari did not complete his degree, and also abandoned his training in pharmacy in favour of psychoanalysis. Both men rapidly developed a desire to cross disciplinary boundaries, and transform accepted pedagogical conventions and ideas. Under the shadow of orthodox Hegelianism and Marxist dialectics, Deleuze engaged in a radical re-reading of philosophy, and wrote studies of Hume (*Empiricism and Subjectivity: An Essay on Hume's Theory of Human Nature* [1953] 1991), Nietzsche (*Nietzsche and Philosophy* [1962] 1983), Kant (*Kant's Critical Philosophy: The Doctrine of the Faculties* [1963] 1984), Bergson (*Bergsonism* [1966] 1988), and Spinoza (*Expressionism in Philosophy: Spinoza* [1968] 1990) as well as a literary-oriented study that utilizes Bergson, called *Proust and Signs* ([1964 and 1970] 1972). This first wave of publications had a two-fold effect: first, having an impact upon the philosophy curriculum in France (especially with the return to Nietzsche), second, leading to Deleuze's more radical poststructuralist assault upon metaphysics.

Guattari's intellectual trajectory took place via extreme left thinking and practice: in the communist-based youth hostelling system and other related groups, and via his involvement with the antipsychiatric movement at La Borde where he became an analyst in 1953. In their education, Deleuze and Guattari experienced the thought of some of France's leading pedagogues and innovators; Deleuze studying initially with Georges Canguilhem and Jean Hyppolite among others, and Guattari studying with Jacques Lacan, undergoing analysis with him between 1962 and 1969, leading to his membership of the École Freudienne de Paris. It was in 1969 that Deleuze and Guattari met, leading eventually to an intensity of intellectual production, and the joint-publications for which they are now so well known in literary-theoretical circles: *Anti-Oedipus: Capitalism and Schizophrenia* ([1972] 1977), *Kafka: Toward a Minor Literature* ([1975] 1986), *A Thousand Plateaus: Capitalism and Schizophrenia* ([1980] 1987), and *What is Philosophy?* ([1991] 1994).

Guattari's early writings are theoretical interventions in the formation and creative deformation of psychoanalytical groups and institutions. As Gary Genosko points out, during this period the innovative thought of Fernand and Jean Oury was decisive for Guattari; Fernand's work on analysing pedagogic institutions and Jean's analogous work at La Borde, led Guattari to profound insights into the 'processual creativity' needed to generate open and fluid group/institutional formations.[1] Guattari's publications from this period were collected and published in 1972 as *Psychanalyse et transversalité*. Deleuze's key pedagogical intervention was his work *Nietzsche and Philosophy* originally published in 1962 (with a second book on Nietzsche published in 1965). *Nietzsche and Philosophy* had a powerful and explosive effect. Why is this? What were the key elements of Deleuze's re-reading? Treated as an antidote to Hegelian dialectics, Deleuze's Nietzsche passes from the world of negative *ressentiment* to that of a positive affirmation. Two key Nietzschean concepts are foregrounded and interpreted by Deleuze: will to power and eternal return. Simply put, Deleuze, via Nietzsche, *replaces* the dialectic with a play of forces; he thus calls Nietzsche's anti-Hegelian theory of forces a 'cutting edge'. What do forces 'want'? No longer (the representation of) power, as in dialectics, but now the affirmation of difference; this Deleuzian rejection of negative power is found in his other texts from this early phase. The play of forces is not just perceived to be affirmative: it is also active and creative, compared with the rejected reactive and essentially exhausted 'slave' morality of dialectics (the 'bad conscience'). Will to power becomes a will to chance, an acceptance of the 'dicethrow' and its results. But what about Nietzsche's eternal return? To affirm the eternal return is to affirm *becoming* and the endless generation of difference. It is not, therefore, the repetition of the same, but a repetition of diversity: the openness of forces to reform in a different assemblage, and the openness of an assemblage to the passing of static forms. We can see here in this summary parallels with Guattari's task to remain open to radical new group or institutional assemblages; for Guattari, the task is to discover what closes a group formation, to discover the forces that turn it into a static entity, what Genosko calls 'complexifying componential heterogeneity' and 'respecting singular (automodeling) and collective (general modeling) assemblages'.[2] If there are parallels between two highly individual thinkers prior to their meeting, the convergence of their thought in *Anti-Oedipus: Capitalism and Schizophrenia*, or that which Didier Eribon calls 'the strange alchemy of writing done in duet', is explosive.[3]

Starting with the 'schizo's stroll', Deleuze and Guattari preface their entire attack upon the Oedipal Myth with the schizophrenic as a 'universal producer'. Meaning is not to be reduced to Freudian-Oedipal analysis or interpretation, e.g. the concept of repression, or, the representation of the Other via Freudian discourse, rather, meaning is produced by the human subject now figured as a desiring-machine. The task of *Anti-Oedipus*, drawing here upon Antonin Artaud, is to chart radical 'flows' and 'couplings' of the machinic 'body without organs' as part of an explosive attack on Freudian analysis and capitalism. But what is the essential problem with the Oedipal Myth in the first place? For Deleuze and Guattari, the very productivity of 'desiring-machines' cannot be divided into the functional/non-functional, or, the whole versus the part(s). In other words, desiring-machines function via hiatuses, ruptures, breakdowns, failures, stalling, short circuits, distances and fragmentations.[4] In Freudian analysis, the parts are subsumed into the whole, and the subject is perceived as either dysfunctional or functional. The latter division depends upon the notion of a primary trauma, repression, and the subsequent generation of neurosis; for Freud, the Oedipal Myth is his founding structure for explaining human (mis)behaviour.

In Greek mythology, Oedipus was the son of the King and Queen of Thebes, who unknowingly killed his father, and married his mother, fulfilling a prophecy; once he discovered the truth of his situation, he blinded himself, and his mother/wife committed suicide. Freud, in his development of the *Oedipus complex*, becomes like the Sphinx: prophesying that all neuroses originate in some version of the Oedipal process, whereby sexual maturation involves for boys an

initial rivalry with the castrating father, eventually leading to identification with him, and for girls, the perceived lack of the phallus
leading to desire for the father (she becomes the mother's rival). The
important point for understanding *Anti-Oedipus* is that this entire
process is perceived as a drama that Freudian psychoanalysis believes
can be re-staged, leading to a healed subject. Deleuze and Guattari
call this drama a totalization in Oedipus, reducing the logic of partial
objects, of parts of the desiring machines (which are, themselves,
autonomous and capable of coupling with other parts), to nothing
whatsoever. Under the totalizing narrative of Oedipus, parts must
represent some absent whole – say the parental figures of the Oedipal
drama or originary trauma – but for Deleuze and Guattari, parts are
not representative, they are merely relations of production that are
irreducible and prior to Oedipus;[5] as they ask themselves, and their
readers: why revert to myth?[6] To reject representation is to maintain
the importance of the machinic couplings and flows that exist, and
in their existence, produce more couplings and flows; this immanent
world of production is affirmative in the Nietzschean sense, and is
perceived by Deleuze and Guattari to be radically uncontainable by
the State. The scale of their project becomes apparent here, as it
traverses their books *Kafka: Toward a Minor Literature* and *A Thousand
Plateaus: Capitalism and Schizophrenia*. The infinite debt of closed territories of power is explored through a historical narrative that owes
its own debt to Nietzsche's *On The Genealogy of Morals*; flows of desire
are contained by *overcoding*, a process constitutive of the repressive
State which becomes 'a new deterritorialized full body'.[7] Put another
way, previous territories of power are subsumed by the State, allowed
a surface inscription, and even a dispersed organization, but are
thereby overcoded or transcended. The new deterritorialized full
body of capitalism is inhabited by the forces of antiproduction: the
repressive State apparatus (to use Althusser's different terminology),
or, the State-sanctioned repression of desire. This regulative force is
the target of Deleuze and Guattari who take the logic of capitalist
deterritorialization to its extreme, i.e. its ultimate openness, or free-
flow, with their schizo-analysis.

Literature plays a continual role in the thought of Deleuze and
Guattari: from Artaud's aesthetics of a theatre of cruelty, and the body
without organs, through the assemblages of Proust's *In Search of Lost
Time*, and in the machinations of Beckett's characters, plays and
film. The 'minor' literature of Kafka – that is, a literature that is non-
representational, one that is a creative play of intensities and affects,
one that 'disrupts and dislocates the tradition'[8] – irrupts throughout

the work of Deleuze and Guattari. References to Henry Miller, D.H. Lawrence, L.-F. Céline, Lewis Carroll and Malcolm Lowry, to name just a few, charge *Anti-Oedipus*. 'Minor peoples' – people of becoming-revolutionary and permanent incompletion – are exemplified in the works of Melville and Kafka, as Deleuze says in 'Literature and Life'. In Beckett's work language is divided into three categories, and Deleuze is the most intrigued by 'language III', the language of spatiality and images, of potentialities, events, detonation, combustion and dissipation – the language that irrupts in the event, and then dismantles itself in its exhaustion of the idea. Deleuze continues his analysis of aesthetics shared with Guattari in their three joint works, in observations concerning film, exemplified once again by his comments on Beckett's film, which 'traversed the three great elementary images of the cinema, those of action, perception, and affection'.[9] In two groundbreaking books, *Cinema 1: The Movement-Image* (1983) and *Cinema 2: The Time-Image* (1985) Deleuze had embarked on a Bergsonian project, which came to more radical conclusions than Bergson could have imagined. The machine assemblage of movement-images explored in *Cinema 1* posits a plane of immanence on which the movement-image exists in and for itself; similarly, in *Cinema 2*, the immanent montage-time is initially perceived as constitutive of the time-image, not a representation of, say, time passing, leading in modern cinema to the *direct* time-image, or, the dissociation between image and logical sensory movement. Gazing at time 'itself' in modern cinema, is also to experience the endless, Nietzschean becoming, endlessly celebrated or affirmed in the machine-like thought of Deleuze and Guattari.

Notes

1   Gary Genosko, 'Félix Guattari: Towards a Transdisciplinary Meta-methodology', *Angelaki*, 8.1 (April 2003): 129–140; 130.
2   Ibid.
3   Didier Eribon, 'Obituary of Gilles Deleuze', *Artforum International*, (March 1996): 35–36.
4   Gilles Deleuze and Pierre Félix Guattari, *Anti-Oedipus: Capitalism and Schizophrenia*, trans. Robert Hurley, M. Seem and Helen R. Lane, 1977, p. 42.
5   Ibid., p. 46.
6   Ibid., p. 298.
7   Ibid., p. 198.
8   Claire Colebrook, *Gilles Deleuze*, London and New York: Routledge, 2002, p. 103.
9   Gilles Deleuze, *Essays Critical and Clinical*, trans. Daniel W. Smith and Michael A. Greco, London and New York: Verso, 1998, p. 26.

See also in this book

Freud

Major works by Deleuze and Guattari

Anti-Oedipus: Capitalism and Schizophrenia (1972). Trans. Robert Hurley, M. Seem and Helen R. Lane, New York: Viking Press, 1977.
Kafka: Toward a Minor Literature (1975). Trans. Dana Polan, Minneapolis, MN: University of Minnesota Press, 1986.
A Thousand Plateaus: Capitalism and Schizophrenia (1980). Trans. Brian Massumi, Minneapolis, MN: University of Minnesota Press, 1987.

Major works by Deleuze

Empiricism and Subjectivity: An Essay on Hume's Theory of Human Nature (1953). Trans. Constantin V. Boundas, New York: Columbia University Press, 1991.
Nietzsche and Philosophy (1962). Trans. Hugh Tomlinson, New York: Columbia University Press, 1983.
Kant's Critical Philosophy: The Doctrine of the Faculties (1963). Trans. Hugh Tomlinson and Barbara Habberjam, Minneapolis, MN: University of Minnesota Press, 1984.
Proust and Signs (1964 and 1970). Trans. Richard Howard, New York: G. Braziller, 1972.
Bergsonism (1966). Trans. Hugh Tomlinson and Barbara Habberjam, New York: Zone Books, 1988.
Expressionism in Philosophy: Spinoza (1968). Trans. Martin Joughin, New York: Zone Books, 1990.
Difference and Repetition (1969). Trans. Paul Patton, London: Athlone Press, 1994.
The Logic of Sense (1969). Trans. Mark Lester, New York: Columbia University Press, 1990.
Dialogues (With Claire Parnet, 1977). Trans. Hugh Tomlinson and Barbara Habberjam, New York: Columbia University Press, 1987.
Francis Bacon: The Logic of Sensation (1981). Trans. Daniel Smith, Cambridge, MA: MIT Press, 1992.
Spinoza: Practical Philosophy (1981). Trans. Robert Hurley, San Francisco, CA: City Lights Books, 1988.
Cinema 1: The Movement-Image (1983). Trans. Hugh Tomlinson and Barbara Habberjam, Minneapolis, MN: University of Minnesota Press, 1986.
Cinema 2: The Time-Image (1985). Trans. Hugh Tomlinson and Robert Galeta, Minneapolis, MN: University of Minnesota Press, 1989.
Foucault (1986). Trans. Seán Hand, Minneapolis, MN: University of Minnesota Press, 1988.
The Fold: Leibniz and the Baroque (1988). Trans. Tom Conley, Minneapolis, MN: University of Minnesota Press, 1992.
Essays Critical and Clinical (1993). Trans. Daniel W. Smith and Michael A. Greco, London and New York: Verso, 1998.

Major works by Guattari

Psychanalyse et transversalité (1972). Paris: François Maspero.

Molecular Revolution: Psychiatry and Politics (1977). Trans. Rosemary Sheed, New York: Penguin, 1984.
L'Inconscient machinique: Essais de schizo-analyse (1979). Fontenay-sous-Bois: Encres/Recherches.
Communists Like Us: New Spaces of Liberty, New Lines of Alliance (with Toni Negri, 1985). Trans. Michael Ryan, New York: Semiotext(e), 1990.
Cartographies schizoanalytiques (1989). Paris: Galilée.
Chaosmosis (1995). Trans. Paul Bains and Julian Pefanis, Bloomington, IN: Indiana University Press.
Chaosophy (1995). New York: Semiotext(e).

Further reading

Badiou, Alain, *Deleuze: The Clamor of Being*, trans. Louise Burchill, Minneapolis, MN: University of Minnesota Press, 1999.
Bogue, Ronald, *Deleuze and Guattari*, London and New York: Routledge, 1989.
Buchanan, Ian, *Deleuzism: A Metacommentary*, Edinburgh: Edinburgh University Press, 2000.
Colebrook, Claire, *Gilles Deleuze*, London and New York: Routledge, 2002.
Genosko, Gary, *Félix Guattari: An Aberrant Introduction*, London: Continuum, 2002.
Williams, James, *Gilles Deleuze's Difference and Repetition: A Critical Introduction and Guide*, Edinburgh: Edinburgh University Press, 2003.
Žižek, Slavoj, *Organs without Bodies: Deleuze and Consequences*, London and New York, Routledge, 2004.

PAUL (ADOLPH MICHEL) DE MAN (1919–1983)

When the wartime newspaper publications of de Man were discovered, the critical reception of his work underwent a rapid sea change: one of the leading proponents of deconstruction and a key figure in the Yale School, de Man had written for a Belgian paper called *Le Soir*, that followed the Nazi line, and this act of collaboration virtually destroyed his subsequent reputation in North America. De Man was born in Antwerp, Belgium, and studied for his first degree (called a *Candidature*), at The University of Brussels. During the Second World War, de Man worked as a journalist and translator, and then moved into the book world, working for the publisher Agence Dechenne, before setting up his own publishing house called Editions Hermès, after the war had ended. A number of factors, including the difficulties of the book trade in a depressed post-war Europe, meant that the publishing venture failed, and de Man moved to the US where he again worked in the book trade and taught at Bard College (1949–1951) and the Berlitz School, Boston. In 1952 de Man joined the graduate programme at Harvard University (1952–1960) where he was awarded his MA (1958) and his Ph.D. on 'Mallarmé, Yeats, and the Post-Romantic Predicament' (1960). De Man taught at Harvard and Cornell before moving to the Johns Hopkins University where he became Professor of Humanistic Studies (1967–1970); subsequently he moved to Yale University where he was awarded the Sterling Professor of Comparative Literature and French (1970–1983). How did de Man become known as a major force in the introduction of deconstruction into the humanities? Very early essays are available in translation in de Man's first collection of essays: *Blindness and Insight: Essays in the Rhetoric of Contemporary Criticism* (1971, revised 1983). In one of these early works, 'Heidegger's Exegeses of Hölderlin' (1952), de Man compares Heidegger's literary-critical approach with that of philology. Where the latter takes an approach that leads to the production of more reliable and complete primary texts (a desire for editorial objectivity), de Man notices that Heidegger is content to work without the 'restrictions' of philology:

> He relies upon a text whose unreliability must have been known to him, and engages in detailed analyses, referring to manuscript corrections, marginal notes, and the like, without verifying for accuracy . . . He comments on the poems independently of one another and draws analogies only in support of his own thesis. [. . .] He ignores the context, isolates lines or words . . . without any regard for their specific function in a poem . . . [and he] bases an entire, and fundamental, study . . . upon a text [which is] probably apocryphal.[1]

And yet, Heidegger produces a powerful, compelling reading of Hölderlin. De Man notices that Heidegger works through reversal to reveal the Hölderlin who can speak the presence of Being; what is important here is that in perceiving how Heidegger produces his powerful reading working with fragments of text and philologically 'suspect' materials, Heidegger creates a deeply insightful reading, one that philology cannot in itself reach. The lesson foreshadows the later playful and disruptive methodology of deconstruction, which in turn develops via an encounter with and a critique of Heidegger; in other words, it is precisely in the gaps, the playful linkages, the close reading of a word, and the reversals in a text, that a new mode and level of signification will be found. De Man, therefore, is reading texts in a highly original and 'deconstructive' way before his own meeting with Jacques Derrida. Another example of this process can be seen in de Man's early essay on romanticism, which opens *The Rhetoric of Romanticism* (1984) where the relationship within romanticism between imagination and nature is deconstructed, or, to use de Man's phrase, 'never ceases to be problematic'.[2]

De Man first met Jacques Derrida in 1966 at a conference held in Baltimore, at the Johns Hopkins University ('The Structuralist Debate'). As Martin McQuillan notes: 'This conference opened the door in North America to a growing interest in certain French philosophers and theorists.'[3] De Man and Derrida not only shared an interest in the French writer and philosopher Jean-Jacques Rousseau, but they also shared an interest in the same text: Rousseau's 'Essay on the Origins of Language'. Derrida's work on Rousseau appeared in his book *Of Grammatology* (1967) and de Man would follow with a key essay written in 1977, called 'The Rhetoric of Blindness: Jacques Derrida's Reading of Rousseau'. What is it that links de Man and Derrida beyond this shared interest? Both work with the notion that a reading of a text involves working with textual insight, and moments of textual 'blindness' (what Derrida calls a text's aporia). So for Derrida, Rousseau writes within the metaphysical tradition where speech is privileged over writing, and this 'logocentrism' or privileging of the spoken Word (a transcendental word or signifier) is the aporia at the heart of Rousseau. De Man, however, locates the moment of 'blindness' in Derrida's reading of Rousseau, which is the fact that for de Man, Rousseau asserts the importance of speech *and* writing in his essay on language. This is not a criticism as such of Derrida or deconstruction, rather it is in agreement with the deconstructive notion that there will always be an aporia at work in a text. This has further implications for criticism, since it means that a text cannot be closed off by the interpretive act, because the completeness or totality of interpretation can never be verified, and, a text will always prefigure its 'misunderstanding' via its rhetorical status. McQuillan summarizes the four consequences for de Man's theory of reading here: (1) texts are figurative, and are aware of that figurative nature and will always thus be misread; (2) cognitive insight occurs in the text, not the reader; (3) the speech/writing opposition has already been deconstructed by literature; and (4) there is therefore no need to deconstruct Rousseau because his (figurative) text already deconstructs itself.[4] In de Man's most important critical work called *Allegories of Reading: Figural Language in Rousseau, Nietzsche, Rilke, and Proust* (1979), these consequences are brilliantly illuminated.

As de Man notes in the preface to *Allegories of Reading*, what started as a historical study ended as a theory of reading: 'What emerges is a process of reading in which rhetoric is a disruptive intertwining of trope and persuasion or – which is not quite the same thing – of cognitive and performative language.'[5] De Man endorses the structuralist and semiotic turn in criticism, but he anxiously notes the subsequent conflation of grammar and rhetoric: for de Man, the rhetorical 'radically suspends logic and opens up vertiginous possibilities of referential aberration'.[6] In other words, the logical impetus of structuralism and semiotics, for all its advances over hermeneutics or philology, must be countered with the *illogical* work of rhetoric or tropes, that 'potentiality' of all figural language that de Man equates with literature itself. But what of literary criticism? A recognition of 'vertiginous possibilities' in a literary text occurs with deconstruction, and because a literary text both asserts and denies its own rhetorical workings in a complex self-reflexive interplay, de Man concludes that literature is, in itself, deconstructive. The self-awareness of the rhetorical nature of language can be transposed into the philosophical realm; the deconstructive lesson here is that traditional modes of philosophy – metaphysics – effaces its own reliance upon rhetorical language. Thus philosophical concepts are considered outside of the play of literature, whereas the deconstructive move is to show that this is a self-delusion. Why does de Man use the term 'allegories' of reading, rather than 'deconstructive' reading? It must be noted that while de Man uses the word 'deconstruction' that does not mean that he has a critical project identical with that of Derrida, or even the other 'members' of the Yale School (also bearing in mind that some of the key thinkers at Yale at this time, such as Shoshona Felman, were not even included in this grouping). De Man uses 'allegories' to refer to the structure of narrative, which always refers to something other than itself; again, this is a textual movement that will always displace itself, and any attempt to stabilize or solidify a particular reading will be in vain because of this very movement. Similarly, stabilizing or solidifying a particular definition of 'theory' is a misguided task, as de Man notes in the opening pages of *The Resistance to Theory* (1986), where the hostility to theory reveals its threatening nature regarding traditional or conservative critical and pedagogic models. Such a threat occurs with the shift from non-linguistic to linguistic approaches to literature: 'The assumption that there can be a science of language which is not necessarily a logic leads to the development of a terminology which is not necessarily aesthetic.'[7] Such a terminology, that roots out the modalities of a text's production and its ideological framework, competes powerfully with other discourses, such as philosophy, philology and aesthetics. The resistance to theory, argues de

Man, may simply be reduced to the resistance to language itself, to the 'possibility' that language conveys or is structured by 'factors or functions that cannot be reduced to intuition'.[8] Ironically, the 'ideological framework' of de Man's wartime writings, would return to haunt him in 1987, when the *New York Times* revealed the existence and extent of his apparently collaborationist journalism. The final word here should probably go to Jacques Derrida, whose *Memoires for Paul de Man* is one of the most thoughtful responses to the impact of this discovery, asking always the question: 'to read him, that is the task. [Yet] How shall one do that from now on?'[9]

Notes

1 Paul de Man, *Blindness and Insight: Essays in the Rhetoric of Contemporary Criticism*, London: Routledge, 1989, p. 250.
2 Paul de Man, *The Rhetoric of Romanticism*, New York: Columbia University Press, 1984, p. 2.
3 Martin McQuillan, *Paul de Man*, London and New York: Routledge, 2001, p. 8.
4 Ibid., p. 28.
5 Paul de Man, *Allegories of Reading: Figural Language in Rousseau, Nietzsche, Rilke, and Proust*, New Haven, CT and London: Yale University Press, 1979, p. ix.
6 Ibid., p. 10.
7 Paul de Man, *The Resistance to Theory*, Minneapolis, MN: University of Minnesota Press, 1986, p. 8.
8 Ibid., p. 13.
9 Jacques Derrida, *Memoires for Paul de Man*, New York: Columbia University Press, 1989, p. 230.

See also in this book

Derrida

Major works

Blindness and Insight: Essays in the Rhetoric of Contemporary Criticism (1971). New York: Oxford University Press.
Allegories of Reading: Figural Language in Rousseau, Nietzsche, Rilke, and Proust (1979). New Haven, CT and London: Yale University Press.
The Rhetoric of Romanticism (1984). New York: Columbia University Press.
The Resistance to Theory (1986). Minneapolis, MN: University of Minnesota Press.
Aesthetic Ideology (1988). Minneapolis, MN: University of Minnesota Press.
Wartime Journalism, 1939–1943 (1988). Lincoln, NE: University of Nebraska Press.

Further reading

Derrida, Jacques, *Memoires for Paul de Man*, New York: Columbia University Press, 1989.

Lehman, David, *Signs of the Times: Deconstruction and the Fall of Paul De Man*, New York: Poseidon Press, 1991.

McQuillan, Martin, *Paul de Man*, London and New York: Routledge, 2001.

JACQUES DERRIDA (1930–2004)

'Deconstruction' is by now a familiar word within literary theory (naming a critical process and/or a movement), but it is also a word that has a deeply *philosophical* heritage. The word deconstruction is firmly attached to the name Jacques Derrida, although he in turn derived it from the work of philosophers Martin Heidegger and Edmund Husserl. Derrida was born in 1930 in Algeria, and moved to France in 1959; he lectured at the Sorbonne (1960–1964) and was made a professor of philosophy at the École Normale Supérieure in 1965. His career has been largely transatlantic, with major posts in France and visiting professorships in America, at Yale University, University of California at Irvine and Cornell University. In the UK, Derrida has worked closely with the critic Geoffrey Bennington, contributing to numerous conferences, seminars and research organizations, culminating in a joint publication called, perhaps unsurprisingly, *Jacques Derrida* (1991, trans. 1993), a book widely considered one of the best surveys of Derridean thought.

Many modes of critical thought coincide or intersect in deconstruction: two in particular, philosophy and Saussurian linguistics, are of particular interest to literary theory. This can be explained via one of Derrida's key terms – *différance* – a neologism that contains two overlayered meanings: *différence* (to differ) and *différer* (to delay, to defer). There are a number of points being brought together with this neologism, two of the most important being, (1) that meaning itself, following Saussure, is perceived not as something immediately present, but as something that is produced via an open, never-ending system of differences, deferrals and delay; and (2) that the production of meaning is involved in what Bennington calls the 'witticism' of the neologism: that the difference between the normal word '*différence*' (in French) and the abnormal word '*différance*' can only be registered in writing not speech. Writing is thus not only foregrounded in Derrida's work, but eventually leads to a questioning of the speech/writing binary opposition, where traditionally, speech, or presence, was given priority over writing, or absence. Derrida's strange new word *différance*, called 'linguistic abuse' by the critic Rodolphe Gasché, reveals a deep concern not only with radicalizing Saussurian linguistics – literally taking Saussure to his limits – but also with philosophical issues. *Différance* describes the production of meaning in a way that is radically different (no pun intended) from that of traditional philosophical systems of thought. For example, the notion of deferral embedded in *différance* is derived in part from the importance of time in Heidegger's monumental critique of metaphysics, *Being and Time*. The endless deferral involved in the production of meaning is also a spacing: that is to say, the graphic mark depends as much upon spacing as does the *time* of meaning, which is always elsewhere (in the future, or retroactively concluded, but never simply in the present or now). The turn to time has radical implications: when Derrida 'goes back' to earlier philosophical positions, he is not attempting to replace those positions with a new origin or foundation (this is the non-reflective part of deconstruction, based on Husserl's process of dismantling or *Abbau*). So what is the point of 'going back'? This is where the relationship to Heidegger is revealing; as Gasché points out, Heidegger's term 'destruction' or *Destruktion* is a shaking loose of the philosophical tradition, a way of uncovering what has been concealed by philosophy as it asked the wrong questions, or a way of recovering the forgotten answers that were themselves once thought to be of great importance. This is not to say that Derrida simply adopts Husserl's or Heidegger's positions, rather, he develops their work, taking over the key terms *Abbau* and *Destruktion*, and developing them in new directions. Just as deconstruction shakes loose the philosophical tradition, so does it perform a similar service to traditional modes of literary theory.

The idea of a 'new' approach (to philosophy or literature) via deconstruction has led to many misunderstandings; while Derrida has been hugely influential as regards deconstruction – in philosophy, literary criticism, as well as other fields, such as architecture and the visual arts – the process does *not* lead to an eventual abandonment or replacement of the philosophical or literary text with something entirely different or other. Deconstruction works upon, with and through texts, be they canonical or counter-canonical. One of Derrida's earliest examples is *Of Grammatology* (1967; trans. 1977) where the work of Rousseau is deconstructed via the speech/writing opposition. *Of Grammatology* reveals the systematic side of deconstruction: Rousseau's prioritizing of speech over writing is located via his negative views concerning the supplement. That is to say, the ideal self-present or immediate originary point of meaning falls away in speech, and falls even further, or is degraded, in the supplementarity of writing. Derrida doesn't simply overturn Rousseau, but, rather, takes the concept of the supplement and occupies it from the 'inside': he utilizes the notion of the supplement to argue that all language functions as supplement, be it speech or writing. It is the *way* that Derrida produces this argument that is as fascinating as what he ultimately says: he locates a set of statements in Rousseau's texts that are not only contradictory but actually undermine Rousseau's fundamental arguments. This set of statements constitutes a series of aporias, whereby Derrida can appropriate and re-work, in a positive way, the concept of the supplement. In other words, this is not an *overturning* of the concept of the supplement, because Derrida has shown how it always already functions in its deconstructive sense, i.e. it functions deconstructively from the beginning. *Of Grammatology* quite seriously argues for a science of writing; this 'science' has been interpreted as a highly creative replacement for conventional modes of literary and theoretical production, most notably by Gregory Ulmer. The overall methodological implications of deconstruction, however, are revealed by Derrida in a long list of essays and books, many of which develop particular terms such as *différance* or the supplement – terms that are called 'undecidables' because of the way they resist becoming *fixed* foundations of thought in the traditional philosophical sense. Another key undecidable revealed in *Dissemination* (1972; trans. 1981) is that of the *pharmakon* a term from Plato's *Phaedrus*, meaning 'poison' or 'medicine/cure'. *Pharmakon* is an undecidable precisely because it can mean opposing or contradictory things: a translation in one direction or another, would radically change the meaning of Plato's text. But there is another side revealed to Derrida's work by the play of contradictions in the word *pharmakon*, and that is the play of polysemia in multiple directions, the 'catachrestic violence' whereby Derrida follows and sometimes creates, complex interwoven and interrelated forcefields of signification. Often, in reading a densely philosophical text, Derrida will show how such a polysemic forcefield is responsible for the core components of a system of thought that would otherwise like to clear away connotation in favour of denotation, or, the arts in favour of certainty, be it of the scientific or speculative variety. That is not to say that because systems are shown to be produced via polysemic forcefields they are simply reduced to polysemia; as with Nietzsche's overturning of Platonism, metaphysics still goes marching on.

The deconstruction of Western metaphysics can thus be seen as a revealing of inherent polysemic play, and this revealing in turn depends upon a number of key literary or artistic producers in Derrida's work, such as Antonin Artaud ('La parole soufflée' and 'The Theater of Cruelty and the Closure of Representation'), Jean Genet (*Glas*, 1974; trans. 1986), and Van Gogh ('Restitutions') among many others. The works of Freud have also played a significant part in deconstructive thought (see 'Freud and the Scene of Writing' and *The Postcard*, 1980; trans. 1987). From a literary-theoretical standpoint, it is Derrida's interventions in the arts, psychoanalysis and feminism, that have had a major impact. Examples include *Glas*, the essays in *The Truth in Painting* (1978; trans. 1987), *Spurs: Nietzsche's Styles* (English and French, 1978), and *The Post Card: From Socrates to Freud and Beyond*. Each of these texts is a hybrid production, examining the interpenetration of aesthetics and philosophy. *The Truth in Painting* begins with a major essay on Kant's sublime from his *Critique of Judgement*, called 'The Parergon'; the parergon is an undecidable, a framing device, or aesthetic boundary which, in Derrida's hands, is revealed to be simultaneously permeable and sub-divided.

There are many followers of deconstruction, across a wide range of literary theoretical fields. Notable critics in North America include Jonathan Culler, Geoffrey Hartman, Barbara Johnson, Paul de Man, J. Hillis Miller and the early work of Gayatri Spivak; in the UK, notable critics are Geoffrey Bennington and Nicholas Royle. Bennington, Johnson and Spivak have all translated major works by Derrida, for example *Of Grammatology* (Spivak), *Dissemination* (Johnson), *The Truth in Painting* (Bennington and McLeod), *Of Spirit: Heidegger and the Question* (Bennington and Bowlby). Literary-theoretical deconstruction is most prevalent in the US, with the Yale School being widely accepted as the precursor to a wider interest. It is important to note that literary-theoretical deconstruction is a heterogeneous body of work, at times simply involved in a process of finding aporias within literary structures and tropes.

See also in this book

De Man, Foucault, Kristeva

Major works

Edmund Husserl's Origin of Geometry: An Introduction (1962). Trans. John P. Leavey, Jr, Lincoln, NE and London: University of Nebraska Press/Bison, 1989.
Of Grammatology (1967). Trans. Gayatri Chakravorty Spivak, Baltimore, MD and London: Johns Hopkins University Press, 1976.

Speech and Phenomena and Other Essays on Husserl's Theory of Signs (1967). Trans. David B. Allison, Evanston, IL: Northwestern University Press, 1973.

Writing and Difference (1967). Trans. Alan Bass, Chicago, IL and London: University of Chicago Press, 1978.

Dissemination (1972). Trans. Barbara Johnson, Chicago, IL and London: University of Chicago Press, 1981.

Margins of Philosophy (1972). Trans. Alan Bass, Chicago, IL and London: University of Chicago Press, 1982.

Positions (1972). Trans. Alan Bass, Chicago, IL and London: University of Chicago Press, 1982.

The Archaeology of the Frivolous: Reading Condillac (1973). Trans. John P. Leavey, Jr, Lincoln, NE and London: University of Nebraska Press/Bison, 1987.

Glas (1974). Trans. John P. Leavey Jr and Richard Rand, Lincoln, NE: University of Nebraska Press, 1986.

The Truth in Painting (1978). Trans. Geoff Bennington and Ian McLeod, Chicago, IL and London: University of Chicago Press, 1987.

Spurs: Nietzsche's Styles = *Eperons, Les styles de Nietzsche* (1978; English and French). Trans. Barbara Harlow, Chicago, IL and London: University of Chicago Press, 1979.

The Post Card: From Socrates to Freud and Beyond (1980). Trans. Alan Bass, Chicago, IL and London: University of Chicago Press, 1987.

Signéponge = *Signsponge* (1984; English and French). Trans. Richard Rand, New York: Columbia University Press, 1984.

Of Spirit: Heidegger and the Question (1987). Trans. Geoffrey Bennington and Rachel Bowlby, Chicago, IL and London: University of Chicago Press, 1989.

Given Time: I. Counterfeit Money (1991). Trans. Peggy Kamuf, Chicago, IL and London: University of Chicago Press, 1992.

The Other Heading: Reflections of Today's Europe (1991). Trans. Pascale-Anne Brault and Michael B. Naas, Bloomington and Indianapolis, IN: Indiana University Press, 1992.

Specters of Marx: The State of the Debt, the Work of Mourning, and the New International (1993). Trans. Peggy Kamuf, London and New York: Routledge, 1994.

The Gift of Death (1996). Trans. David Wills, Chicago, IL and London: University of Chicago Press, 1996.

Further reading

Bennington, Geoffrey (with Jacques Derrida), *Jacques Derrida*, Paris: Seuil, 1991; English version trans. Geoffrey Bennington, Chicago, IL: Chicago University Press, 1993.

Critchley, Simon, *The Ethics of Deconstruction: Derrida & Levinas*, Oxford: Basil Blackwell, 1992.

Gasché, Rodolphe, *The Tain of the Mirror: Derrida and the Philosophy of Reflection*, Chicago, IL: Chicago University Press, 1993.

Johnson, Barbara, *A World of Difference*, Baltimore, MD and London: Johns Hopkins University Press, 1987.

Norris, Christopher, *Deconstruction: Theory & Practice*, London and New York: Methuen, 1982.

Royle, Nicholas, *After Derrida*, Manchester and New York: Manchester University Press, 1995.

Ulmer, Gregory, *Applied Grammatology: Post(e)-Pedagogy from Jacques Derrida to Joseph Beuys*, Baltimore, MD and London: Johns Hopkins University Press, 1985.

TERRY (TERRENCE FRANCIS) EAGLETON

(1943–)

Writing about the impossibility of filming philosophy, Eagleton suggests a dialectical solution: find a scriptwriter interested in ideas (Eagleton) and a director with visual imagination (Derek Jarmen); the resulting unhappy consciousness soon resolves itself with an outstanding film about Ludwig Wittgenstein. Eagleton, the man known by students for writing one book, called *Literary Theory* (1983), is in reality a critic and reviewer of prodigious output, whose books occupy just about every call-number in the humanities library catalogue. Born in Salford, England, Eagleton studied at Cambridge University, where he studied with the Marxist critic Raymond Williams. Eagleton received his BA in 1964 and his Ph.D. in 1968. After working as a Fellow at Cambridge, Eagleton moved to Wadham College, Oxford in 1969, where he was a Fellow and poetry tutor, becoming Lecturer in Critical Theory in 1989, and Thomas Wharton Professor of English in 1992. Eagleton is now Professor of Cultural Theory and John Rylands Fellow at the University of Manchester.

Writing about the 'contradictions' of Eagleton, Roger Kimball traces the origins of his criticism, arguing that it is 'a compound of [Raymond] Williams's socialist organicism, F. R. Leavis's meticulously autocratic practical criticism, and left-wing, liberationist Catholicism'.[1] Eagleton's first book, *The New Left Church* (1966) is a synthesis of Catholic theology and Marxist criticism, while *Shakespeare and Society* (1967) is in some senses a less radical text, given not just its canonical subject, but its contextualization of Shakespeare in historical and political terms. Eagleton returned to the subject of Catholicism in *The Body as Language* (1970), again attempting a Marxist and Christian synthesis, leaving this subject for good with another book published the same year, *Exiles and Émigrés: Studies in Modern Literature* (1970). *Exiles and Émigrés* ponders the question of the internationalization of 'English' modernist literature long before postcolonial critics got in on the act of defining British fiction through its Others. Arguing that the nineteenth-century realist novelists could grasp society as a totality (and draw creative energies and modes of expression from this act),

Eagleton compares their fiction with that of the 'foreigners' such as Conrad, James, Eliot, Pound, Yeats and Joyce. This enables him to have the dialectical insight that the 'controlled evaluations' of the exiles and émigrés was brought about by 'an awareness that the declining culture they confronted was in no full sense their own'.[2] Thus, the 'felt presence of alternative traditions' is the enabling factor in the production of literary expression. Eagleton utilizes this insight to produce readings of what he terms 'upper' and 'lower middle-class' novels, Conrad's *Under Western Eyes*, and the works of Greene, Eliot, Auden and Lawrence.

The more familiar Eagleton emerges with his next three books: *Myths of Power: A Marxist Study of the Brontës* (1975), *Criticism and Ideology: A Study in Marxist Literary Theory* (1976), and *Marxism and Literary Criticism* (1976). In his introduction to the second edition of *Myths of Power*, Eagleton notes how the book was published 'on the very threshold of a major resurgence of Marxist criticism in Britain'.[3] This is a key statement in situating the intellectual and political contexts of Eagleton's work and his place in the institutional study of literature:

> Since the radical political events of the late 1960s, Marxist criticism had been much in the air; but when *Myths of Power* first appeared, the chief theoretical formulations of this critical current were still to emerge. My own work of Marxist literary theory, *Criticism and Ideology*, appeared one year later in 1976; the following year witnessed the publication of Raymond Williams' important *Marxism and Literature*, and 1978 saw the English translation of Pierre Macherey's influential *A Theory of Literary Production*. From 1976 onwards, a series of annual conferences on Marxist literary and cultural theory were held at the University of Essex, bringing physically together for the first time a large number of young radical critics whose work and political allegiances had been shaped in the aftermath of Paris 1968.[4]

Eagleton also sketches the failures and successes of *Myths of Power*, with the interesting observation that he did not feel that the book achieved the goals of its 'relatively' sophisticated Marxist theory compared with what he calls its 'fairly conventional critical *practice*' suggesting further that only the chapter on *Wuthering Heights* came near to achieving his aims. However, Eagleton does see *Criticism and Ideology* as a genuine shift from regarding the literary text as ' "expressive" of an underlying ideology or historical situation' to one whereby the text is a ' "production" or transformation of these elements into a quite new configuration'.[5] Following this Marxist trio, Eagleton's more sophisticated Marxist approach was brought to bear on the subject of Walter Benjamin in *Walter Benjamin, or, Towards a Revolutionary Criticism* (1981) and Richardson in *The Rape of Clarissa* (1982).

Students the world over are often introduced to the subject of literary theory with a book that bears that title; published in 1983, *Literary Theory: An Introduction* has become Eagleton's best-known text. Critic David Alderson notes that 'its publication was nothing short of an event in the history of English studies' yet this has also 'served to obscure Eagleton's achievements up to that point and has overshadowed subsequent work'.[6] It is ironic that an introductory work on theory, written from a Marxist perspective, should have become so subject to capitalist market forces by becoming what can only be called a 'best-seller'. *Literary Theory* remains popular with academics teaching the subject, however, because of its underlying commitment to social and political contexts. Read in conjunction with *The Function of Criticism: From* The Spectator *to Poststructuralism* (1984) and *Against the Grain: Selected Essays* (1986), Eagleton's early 1980s trio provides some of the most insightful analyses of the development of literary theory. Eagleton returned to Shakespeare in 1986 with his *William Shakespeare*, and brought together some of his most compelling essays in his key text, *The Ideology of the Aesthetic*, in 1990, with analysis of Shaftesbury, Hume, Burke, German Romanticism and German Idealism, Schopenhauer, Kierkegaard, Marx, Nietzsche, Freud, Heidegger, Benjamin and Adorno, with a final essay on postmodernism. The accessibility of the essays therein must surely be one of the reasons for Eagleton's popularity, and indeed in a later collection, *Figures of Dissent: Critical Essays on Fish, Spivak, Žižek and Others* (2003), Eagleton makes a point of mildly parodying theorists who produce overly dense and unreadable texts. With Gayatri Spivak, for example, Eagleton argues that she writes an 'overstuffed, excessively elliptical prose' where 'the ellipses, the heavy-handed jargon, the cavalier assumption that you know what she means, or that if you don't she doesn't much care, are as much the overcodings of an academic coterie as a smack in the face for conventional scholarship'.[7] Summarizing Žižek from a perspective that is slightly more in awe of his (no doubt repetitive) command of Hegelian and Lacanian discourse, Eagleton produces one of the most amusing parodies of his writing:

At first glance it would seem that the sausage in the hot dog wedges apart the two pieces of roll. But the roll itself is nothing but a 'space' which the sausage creates around it, the phantasmal 'frame' or support of the sausage without which it would vanish to nothing . . . This is my parody rather than Žižek's own words, but much odder passages are to be found in his work.[8]

Undoubtedly the recognition of the 'much odder passages' is what moves Eagleton's own parody from the ridiculous to the sublime.

Eagleton continues to support the book industry with his prodigious output; focused accounts of theoretical and ideological concepts following *The Ideology of the Aesthetic* include *The Significance of Theory* (1990), *Ideology: An Introduction* (1991), *The Illusions of Postmodernism* (1996) and *The Idea of Culture* (2000). In 2001 Eagleton published *The Gatekeeper: A Memoir*, a critical reflection upon key figures and institutions in his life. In the concluding lines of a key essay on nationalism, irony and commitment, Eagleton summarizes in some ways his entire enterprise:

It is only ambiguously, precariously, that any of us can experience at once the necessary absolutism of a particular demand – to be freed, for example, from an immediate, intolerable oppression – and the more general truth that no one such demand, however just and urgent, can finally exhaust or preprogram a political future in which the content will have gone beyond the phrase. As Kierkegaard might have said, it is a matter of trying to live that dialectic passionately, ironically, in all of its elusive impossibility, rather than merely providing an elegant theoretical formulation of it.[9]

Notes

1   Roger Kimball, 'The Contradictions of Terry Eagleton', *The New Criterion*, 9.1 (September 1990), www.newcriterion.com/archive/09/sep 90/eagleton.htm.
2   Terry Eagleton, *Exiles and Émigrés: Studies in Modern Literature*, London: Chatto & Windus, 1970, p. 18.
3   Terry Eagleton, *Myths of Power: A Marxist Study of the Brontës*, Basingstoke and London: Macmillan, 1988, p. xi.
4   Ibid.
5   Ibid., p. xiii.
6   David Alderson, *Terry Eagleton*, Basingstoke and New York: Palgrave Macmillan, 2004, p. 1.

7   Terry Eagleton, *Figures of Dissent: Critical Essays on Fish, Spivak, Žižek and Others*, London and New York: Verso, 2003, p. 160.
8   Ibid., p. 204.
9   Terry Eagleton, 'Nationalism: Irony and Commitment', in *Nationalism, Colonialism, and Literature: Terry Eagleton, Fredric Jameson, Edward W. Said*, introduced by Seamus Deane, Minneapolis, MN: University of Minnesota Press, 1990, pp. 23–39; p. 38.

See also in this book

Lukács

Major works

The New Left Church: Studies in Literature, Politics and Theology (1966). London and Melbourne: Sheed & Ward..

Shakespeare and Society (1967). London: Chatto & Windus.

The Body as Language (1970). London: Sheed & Ward.

Exiles and Émigrés: Studies in Modern Literature (1970). London: Chatto & Windus.

Myths of Power: A Marxist Study of the Brontës (1975). London: Macmillan.

Criticism and Ideology: A Study in Marxist Literary Theory (1976). London: Verso.

Marxism and Literary Criticism (1976). London: Methuen.

Walter Benjamin, or, Towards a Revolutionary Criticism (1981). London: Verso.

The Rape of Clarissa (1982). Oxford: Blackwell.

Literary Theory: An Introduction (1983). Oxford: Blackwell.

The Function of Criticism: From The Spectator *to Poststructuralism* (1984). London and New York: Verso.

Against the Grain: Selected Essays (1986). London and New York: Verso.

William Shakespeare (1986). Oxford: Blackwell.

The Ideology of the Aesthetic (1990). Oxford: Blackwell.

The Significance of Theory (1990). Oxford: Blackwell.

Ideology: An Introduction (1991). London and New York: Verso.

Heathcliff and the Great Hunger (1995). London and New York: Verso.

The Illusions of Postmodernism (1996). Oxford: Blackwell.

Marx and Freedom (1997). London: Phoenix.

Crazy John and the Bishop and Other Essays on Irish Culture (1998). Cork: Cork University Press.

The Idea of Culture (2000). Oxford: Blackwell.

The Gatekeeper: A Memoir (2001). London: Allen Lane.

Figures of Dissent: Critical Essays on Fish, Spivak, Žižek and Others (2003). London and New York: Verso.

Sweet Violence: The Idea of the Tragic (2003). Oxford: Blackwell.

Further reading

Alderson, David, *Terry Eagleton*, Basingstoke and New York: Palgrave Macmillan, 2004.
Dienst, Richard, 'Action in the Present: An Interview with Terry Eagleton', *Polygraph*, 2–3 (1989): 30–36.

McQuillan, Martin, 'Irish Eagleton: Of Ontological Imperialism and Colonial Mimicry', *Irish Studies Review*, 10.1 (2002): 29–38.

Wood, James, 'Terry Eagleton in Conversation', *Poetry Review*, 82.1 (1992): 2–7.

Wright, Colin, 'Centrifugal Logics: Eagleton and Spivak on the Place of "Place" in Postcolonial Theory', *Culture, Theory and Critique*, 43.1 (2002): 67–82.

(SIR) WILLIAM EMPSON (1906–1984)

Reading a poem by Wordsworth, Empson once wrote that 'It is not sufficient to say that these lines convey with great beauty the mood intended'.[1] This opening phrase – 'It is not sufficient to say' – reveals the historical shift that was taking place in Cambridge's English School, with the rejection of haphazard interpretive and mystical approaches to literature, to be replaced by more rigorous techniques, such as I.A. Richards' practical criticism, or the analysis of 'ambiguity' that his best student, Empson, would produce after being banished from the University (and Cambridge town) for owning contraceptives. Empson's exile would lead to a number of interesting overseas posts, after his rapid educational rise through Winchester and then Magdalene College, Cambridge, where he briefly held the Charles Kingsley Bye Fellowship. At Magdalene Empson studied mathematics and English, as well as being an active writer of poetry and drama. He received his BA from Cambridge in 1929, and his MA in 1935, by which time he had already worked as Professor of English Literature at Tokyo University of Literature and Science, Japan. Empson went on to become Professor of English Literature at Peking National University, China (1937–1939 and 1947–1952), with a wartime interruption whereupon he worked for the BBC's Far Eastern Section as an editor (1940–1946). After Peking, Empson moved to Sheffield University, where he was Professor of English (1953–1971) and Professor Emeritus during his retirement. Awards include honorary doctorates from the University of East Anglia, the University of Bristol and the University of Sheffield, and in 1979 he was knighted.

Working on an essay for I.A. Richards at Cambridge, Empson's book on ambiguity soon emerged, with his definition of ambiguity undergoing some refinement during his lifetime. In the third edition of *Seven Types of Ambiguity* (first edition, 1930; third edition 1953), Empson argues that:

An ambiguity, in ordinary speech, means something very pro-
nounced, and as a rule witty or deceitful. I propose to use the
word in an extended sense, and shall think relevant to my
subject any verbal nuance, however slight, which gives room
for alternative reactions to the same piece of language.[2]

The seven types of ambiguity that Empson posits and explores are:
(1) where 'a detail is effective in several ways at once'; (2) where 'two
or more alternative meanings are fully resolved into one'; (3) where
'two apparently unconnected meanings are given simultaneously'; (4)
where 'alternative meanings combine to make clear a complicated
state of mind in the author'; (5) where there is 'fortunate confusion'
when an 'author is discovering his idea in the act of writing . . . or
not holding it all in mind at once'; (6) where 'what is said is contradictory or irrelevant and the reader is forced to invent interpretations';
and (7) where there is 'full contradiction, marking a division in the
author's mind'.[3] Empson's achievement with his *Seven Types of
Ambiguity* are manifold: not only a series of insightful and creative
readings of canonical poetic texts, but also the diverse ways in which
his critical methodology would become key for the close reading
approach, including some recognition of a shared enterprise by the
New Critics. Indeed, Empson had defended the need for new analytical approaches in reply to John Sparrow, who had attacked I.A.
Richards' *Practical Criticism* in an article published in 1930 in the
Oxford journal *Farrago*; Empson replied to this attack the same
year in the *Oxford Outlook*, arguing that from a poet's perspective
'some form of intelligible process of interpretation is urgently needed'
and that Richards' experiment and collecting of the responses (the
'protocols') was a valid exercise in revealing the general lack of interpretive knowledge in the public.[4] In response to Sparrow's attack on
him, following this exchange, Empson provides a neat summary of
Richards' approach:

> The essential objection of Mr Sparrow to Mr Richards . . .
> seems to reside in this: Mr Richards considers that there is
> no one certainly 'right' way of reading a given piece of
> poetry; that poetry is important because of the way it acts
> on people; that it does not only act valuably on the best
> critics; that it would be useful both for the critics and the
> educator to know how it acts on people; and that this can be
> found out (in a sufficient degree to be useful) by a process
> of inquiry.[5]

Following the highly successful *Seven Types of Ambiguity*, Empson published substantial numbers of his poems, including *Poems* (1934), *The Gathering Storm* (1940) and *Collected Poems of William Empson* (1949). Critic Paul Dean argues that: 'At his death, Empson was counted, along with Richards, Eliot, and Leavis, as one of the great twentieth-century critics.'[6] But what of his poetry? Dean suggests that: 'we read his poetry because it is by Empson the critic, just as, perhaps, we read Eliot's criticism because it is by Eliot the poet'.[7] M.C. Bradbrook argues that the poems collected in *The Gathering Storm* 'showed Empson truly engaged, but with a cool sardonic wit, of the kind that fighting men develop in the face of the enemy'.[8] Empson's critical development included a Marxist and Freudian shift with *Some Versions of Pastoral* (1935), and in 1951 he returned to more familiar territory with the publication of *The Structure of Complex Words*. Some of Empson's most powerful writing is found in his critique of Christian modes of thought, published as *Milton's God* (1961); Empson's hunt for Christian and neo-Christian criticism would be long and sustained, and he would root out such work like an animal snuffling for truffles. In a response to such a reading of Orwell's *1984*, Empson argued that: 'I think literary criticism has got into a very corrupt frame of mind when it can regard a sustained denunciation of the Christian God as an unwitting testimonial for him',[9] and in a review article called 'Literary Criticism and the Christian Revival' he suggested that 'the neo-Christian method of literary criticism leads frequently to large and unpleasant misinterpretations'.[10] Significant volumes that appeared posthumously include *Using Biography* (1984), *Essays on William Shakespeare* (1986), *Argufying: Essays on Literature and Culture* (1987) and the two-volume *Essays on Renaissance Literature* (1993 and 1994). Paul Dean summarizes this complex and contradictory man, and his wealth of critical and cultural insights; Empson was:

> a Voltairean rationalist with a strong sense of mystery, an anti-Christian with a highly developed capacity for religious awe, a utilitarian with a compassionate heart, a forensic thinker in a casual style, a defender of the use of biography in criticism who was willing to conjecture or even invent episodes in the lives of his subjects, and a man who insisted on the importance of story in literature and harbored a suspicion of symbolism, whose first instinct was nonetheless to look below the literal surface of a work.[11]

Notes

1 William Empson, *Seven Types of Ambiguity* (first edition, 1930), London and New York: Penguin, 1995, p. 181.
2 Ibid., p. 19.
3 Ibid., contents pages.
4 William Empson, *Argufying: Essays on Literature and Culture*, Iowa City, IA: University of Iowa Press, 1987, p. 195.
5 Ibid., p. 202.
6 Paul Dean, 'The Critic as Poet: Empson's Contradictions', *The New Criterion*, (October 2001): 23–30; p. 25.
7 Ibid.
8 M.C. Bradbrook, 'Sir William Empson (1906–1984): A Memoir', *The Kenyan Review*, p. 110.
9 William Empson, *Argufying: Essays on Literature and Culture*, p. 602.
10 Ibid., p. 637.
11 Paul Dean, 'The Critic as Poet: Empson's Contradictions', p. 24.

See also in this book

Richards

Major works

Seven Types of Ambiguity (1930). London and New York: Penguin, 1995.
Poems (1934). London: Chatto & Windus.
Some Versions of Pastoral (1935). London: Chatto & Windus.
The Gathering Storm (1940). London: Faber & Faber.
Collected Poems of William Empson (1949). London: Chatto & Windus.
The Structure of Complex Words (1951). London: Chatto & Windus.
Milton's God (1961). London: Chatto & Windus.
Using Biography (1984). London: Chatto & Windus.
Essays on William Shakespeare (1986). Cambridge: Cambridge University Press.
Argufying: Essays on Literature and Culture (1987). Iowa City, IA: University of Iowa Press.
Essays on Renaissance Literature (1993 and 1994). Cambridge: Cambridge University Press.

Further reading

Day, Frank, *Sir William Empson: An Annotated Bibliography*, London: Taylor & Francis, 1984.
Fry, Paul H., *William Empson: Prophet Against Sacrifice*, London and New York: Routledge, 1991.
MacCabe, Colin, 'The Cambridge Heritage: Richards, Empson and Leavis', *Southern Review*, 19.3 (1986): 242–249.
Norris, Christopher, *William Empson and the Philosophy of Literary Criticism*, London: Athlone, 1978.
Rodensky, Lisa, 'Empson's Seven Types of Ambiguity', *Essays in Criticism*, 53.1 (2003): 54–67.

FRANTZ OMAR FANON (1925–1961)

Three powerful critical modes of thought intersect in the work of Frantz Fanon: dialectics, existentialism and psychoanalysis, all in the service of his searing critique of colonialism and racism. Born in Martinique in 1925, Fanon went on to fight in the Free French Forces in the Second World War, and was awarded the Croix de Guerre. Fanon studied medicine and psychiatry in France, and went on to work in the Psychiatric Department at Blida-Joinville Hospital in French Algeria, where he became Head of Department. This progress through service and excellence – from the French Antilles, decoration for patriotic heroism, education in the 'mother' country of France, to a senior position in colonial Algeria as doctor, administrator and *evolué* – was ended and overturned by Fanon's resignation from his post in 1956 in favour of serving the FLN, the National Liberation Front, a guerrilla organization at war with the French occupiers. This spectacular rejection and reversal of his colonial career gave Fanon unique insight into both sides of the colonial situation – as a representative of the French educated elite, and, through his work for the FLN, his editorial duties at the FLN's newspaper *El Mondjahid*, and above all, as an intellectual who mapped the socio-psychic complexes of colonial rule. Fanon's role as spokesman for the oppressed gained a world-wide reception, although ironically, given his commitment to revolutionary thought and action, Fanon is most likely to be encountered or studied on university courses in postcolonial theory and literature.

Starting with existential situations, drawing extensively on the work of Karl Jaspers and Jean-Paul Sartre, Fanon engages in his first book, *Peau noire, masques blancs* (*Black Skin, White Masks*, 1952), with the question of how and why black colonial subjects are alienated at individual and social levels. *Black Skin, White Masks* performs a double task: analysis of racism *and* colonialism. The existentialist approach starts with the concrete, experiencing subject, the first-person singular 'I', identified and located via Fanon's key question 'what does the black man want?'. The question of gender is crucial as Fanon uses 'man' at times to mean 'the subject' in general and at other times to distinguish between men and women's experiences of race and sexuality. While this terminology is problematic for feminist readings of Fanon, it does allow for analysis of what Fanon calls (in Chapter 5 of *Black Skin, White Masks*) 'the fact of blackness', where the individual is interpellated (hailed and identified) by racist epithets and situated as an 'object'. Fanon, continuing the existentialist recording of the experience, feels crushed; he first turns to the black community around him but finds that their customs and cultural sources of meaning have been effaced by colonialism; he turns to the white community and finds himself reflected in a chain of stereotypes, racist narratives, categories and myths. The resulting fragmented subjectivity allows for an exploration of the multiple narratives of blackness via a range of discursive fields: 'the texts of history, literature, science, myth' as Homi Bhabha puts it in his foreword to the English translation.[1] But this fluidity is forever in danger of solidifying back into objecthood. Fanon's use of Hegelian dialectics is constantly undermined by his analysis of desire: oppositional categories such as black/white, subject/object, self/Other and so on, are never stable in Fanon's view, because of the disruptive, excessive nature of desire, fantasy and neurosis. In asking what the subject 'wants' Fanon is also asking what the subject 'desires'; he also realizes that much of the racism that interpellates the colonial subject is generated through sexual fantasy, examined in detail in the second and third chapters of *Black Skin, White Masks* ('The Woman of Color and the White Man' and 'The Man of Color and the White Woman') and throughout much of the book. Discourses of desire intersect with Hegelian phenomenology to reveal that the subject defined via his or her relation with the Other bears the heavy load of external imposed (mis)identities: the European *imago* of the 'over-sexualized' black man. While Fanon has been criticized for a lack of historical perspective in *Black Skin, White Masks*, by starting with the existential subject, implicated and subjugated within a colonialist field of desire (necessitating a psychoanalytical response), Fanon reveals the fundamental human impact of racism and colonial rule.

The extended complex interplay of aesthetic, psychoanalytical and philosophical (mainly existential) discourses of *Black Skin, White Masks* provided Fanon with an intellectual matrix that would undergo another level of transformation: through his experiences with the FLN, Hegel is replaced by Marx, and the burning issue of the day becomes 'decolonization' *without* transposing colonial rule to the new indigenous elites. The anti-colonial force of Fanon's FLN activities finds direct expression in *Les Damnés de la terre* (*The Wretched of the Earth*) published in the year of Fanon's death (1961). Along with his *L'An V de la révolution algérienne* (*Studies in a Dying Colonialism*, 1959), *The Wretched of the Earth* is a powerful addition to the texts of the Marxist national liberation movements found in this period in countries such as Algeria, Cuba and Vietnam. The processes of decolonization, argues Fanon, are necessarily violent, leading to 'a murderous and decisive struggle' between the colonialists and nationalists. Fanon is careful to analyse the period immediately following the withdrawal of colonial rule, that is to say, the potential move to a neocolonial society ruled by the 'comprador' class, the new elite who adopt the ideology and some of the methods of their previous foreign masters. The most problematic functionaries are the 'national middle class' – the educated and the merchants – portrayed by Fanon as a catastrophic group with neither the creative nor productive abilities of their predecessors or the 'heroic' desire to be schooled by the people, to maintain Fanon's Marxist terminology. The national middle class exist merely to perpetuate the status quo and this leads, in part, to their failure when they are left to manage affairs on their own. Fanon argues that this group simply becomes a new type of intermediary – the 'business agent' – who continues to manage the State's resources for another power – such as the wealthy Western tourists in search of overseas game reserves, casinos and brothels. The solution put forward appears in retrospect simplistic: the replacement of the comprador class with the rule of the workers, with shared ownership and state-controlled economic production.

From the beginning of Fanon's research into race and colonialism the question of culture is central. The first chapter of *Black Skin, White Masks* examines the role of language in the formation of the divided black subject; Fanon argues that to speak a particular language involves taking on an entire worldview, that of another culture. In this case, it is the indigenous subject taking upon himself the burden of the colonizer: the French. Mastery of the French language in the colonial situation appears to offer power to the colonized subject, but it is power predicated upon an internalized alienation: never quite French enough because the 'white mask' of language does not entirely hide the sign of difference, to use Fanon's phrase, the 'black skin' that the new language cannot entirely efface, and additionally there is the problem of being too French to friends and family back home, who also suffer alienation. For colonized peoples, the language of the colonizer is a burden with which they are constantly confronted; adopting that language confers temporary citizenship, one that can be taken away in the blink of an eye. In a paper given to the Second Congress of Black Artists and Writers in Rome in 1959 (published as the chapter 'On National Culture' in *The Wretched of the Earth*), Fanon expands upon his ideas of cultural burden. He performs a critique of the 'Negritude' movement, which, he argues, ignores indigenous cultural specificities; in other words, the unified effort to promote 'African' culture as counter to 'European' culture (and the conjoining

of African with American cultures) is regarded by Fanon as a necessary and productive stage in rejecting the notion of Eurocentric
'universalist' values, but at the risk of ignoring national differences. Is
the alternative to the 'Negritude' movement a return to indigenous
cultural artefacts? And if so, in a neocolonial or postcolonial society,
where are those cultural artefacts to be found? Have they been transformed by the colonial experience? Fanon addresses these questions
from the perspective of the 'native intellectual' and maps out three
main phases of cultural reception and production: (1) the period of
unqualified assimilation, (2) the literature of just-before-the-battle, (3)
the fighting phase. What does he mean by these three phases? The
first phase is where the native intellectual has entirely gone over to
the cultural values of the colonizers: he rejects indigenous artefacts as
being 'primitive' and naive because he has completely assimilated the
value-system of the colonizers. The second phase involves remembering and recovering the indigenous cultures: the native intellectual
has been triggered into a desire for cultural recovery but, crucially,
has lost touch both with his heritage and with the current struggles
of the people, so all he can do is misinterpret his own past. The third
phase is a creative accord with the political struggles of the people: it
generates a literature that is both in touch with the people and inspires
them to further action. In the third phase, indigenous culture is no
longer seen as being permanently located in a primitive past, but
neither is it appropriated and misinterpreted by neocolonial intellectuals: now there is a new creativity that catches up with the fact that
indigenous culture is being produced on the battlefields of resistance.
Fanon describes this phase in almost mystical terms:

> It is not enough to try to get back to the people in that past
> out of which they have already emerged; rather we must join
> them in that fluctuating movement which they are just giving
> shape to, and which, as soon as it has started, will be the signal
> for everything to be called in question. . . . it is to this zone
> of occult instability where the people dwell that we must
> come; and it is there that our souls are crystallized and that
> our perceptions and our lives are transfused with light.[2]

This Marxist model of aesthetics may once more appear crude in
retrospect, but it had widespread influence in its time, and still feeds
in to debates about neocolonial and postcolonial aesthetic production.
Should a postcolonial author write in the languages of the global
marketplace – English and French – when these were the languages

of colonial rule? Should postcolonial artefacts represent ongoing political struggles? Fanon's analyses of subjectivity, indigenous and 'colonizing' languages, 'Negritude', Islam, national consciousness and neocolonial/postcolonial aesthetics still resonate in many cultures, countries and political situations today.

Notes

1   Homi Bhabha, foreword to Frantz Fanon, *Black Skin, White Masks*, trans. Charles Lam Markmann, London: Pluto, 1986, p. xiii.
2   Frantz Fanon, *The Wretched of the Earth* (1961). Trans. Constance Farrington, New York: Grove, First Evergreen Black Cat Edition, 1968, p. 227.

See also in this book

Bhabha

Major works

Black Skin, White Masks (1952). Trans. Charles Lam Markmann, London: Pluto, 1986.
Studies in a Dying Colonialism (1959). Trans. Haakon Chevalier, New York: Grove, 1965.
The Wretched of the Earth (1961). Trans. Constance Farrington, New York: Grove, First Evergreen Black Cat Edition, 1968.
Towards the African Revolution (1964). Trans. Haakon Chevalier, Harmondsworth: Penguin, 1967.

Further reading

Bhabha, Homi, *The Location of Culture*, London and New York: Routledge, 1994.
Christian, Laura, 'Fanon and the Trauma of the Cultural Message', *Textual Practice*, 19.3 (2005): 219–241.
Gendzier, Irene L., *Frantz Fanon: A Critical Study*, New York: Pantheon/Random House, 1973.
McLeod, John, *Beginning Postcolonialism*, Manchester and New York: Manchester University Press, 2000.
Penney, James, 'Passing into the Universal: Fanon, Sartre and the Colonial Dialectic', *Paragraph*, 27.3 (2004): 49–67.
Said, Edward, *Culture and Imperialism*, London: Vintage, 1994.

SHOSHANA FELMAN (1942–)

The rise to power of psychoanalytical modes of thought created, for some critics, an unnecessarily hierarchical relationship with literary texts; Felman's deconstruction of this hierarchy, exemplified by the essays she edited for *Yale French Studies* (1977), collected in book form as *Literature and Psychoanalysis, The Question of Reading: Otherwise* (1982), also marks the emergence of an increasingly sophisticated theoretical discourse in North America. Well-known American contributors to *Literature and Psychoanalysis* include Fredric Jameson, Barbara Johnson and Gayatri Chakravorty Spivak, and Felman's foreword and essay on James's *The Turn of the Screw* have become key documents in the history of literary-psychoanalytical engagement. Felman was born in France, and studied for her BA (1964) and MA (1966) at The Hebrew University of Jerusalem. She studied at The University of Geneva (1969–1970) and The University of Grenoble (1970), where she received her Ph.D., moving in the same year to Yale University's department of French and Comparative Literature. In 1982 Felman received recognition from the French government for her services to French culture, with the awarding of the *Chevalier de l'ordre des palmes academiques*, and in 1986 she was awarded the prestigious post of Thomas E. Donnelly Professor of French and Comparative Literature at Yale.

In addressing the subject and societal juxtaposition of 'women and madness' in an early essay from 1975, Felman begins to interrogate and disturb the discursive formations of feminism, psychoanalysis and literary criticism. In 'Women and Madness: The Critical Phallacy', Felman opens with reference to two apparently complementary feminist texts: Phyllis Chesler's *Women and Madness* (1973) and Luce Irigaray's *Speculum of the Other Woman* (1974). Chesler counteracts the sociological, statistical juxtaposition of women and madness by letting women speak about their psychiatric experiences for themselves, although Felman does not regard such 'cries for help' as leading to political action. Irigaray addresses not the empirical voices of women, but rather the patriarchal theoretical discourses that speak for, and define, women. Thus, she examines the 'fundamental' philosophical and psychoanalytical texts that construct from a patriarchal perspective the notion of femininity. In exploring Irigaray's debt to Derrida, Felman clarifies the role of deconstruction in French feminist theory and simultaneously performs a critique of Irigaray, arguing that the question of how woman as Other can then speak, even from a deconstructive feminist position, has not been clarified. Why does Felman juxtapose Chesler and Irigaray? Because in the apparent complementarity and incompatibility of these two perspectives, she suggests that a third perspective is needed: that of the literary critical (in the form here of a reading of a short story by Balzac called 'Adieu'). Felman uses a feminist and psychoanalytical approach to 'Adieu' to suggest that women can escape from being defined by madness not simply by 'taking up' critical and therapeutic methodologies and perspectives, but by re-learning how to speak oppositionally and outside of the binary structures of patriarchal thought. Thus, Felman advocates the construction of an entirely new discourse that is in no way defined by phallic and logocentric thinking. The implications of such a statement are far-reaching, as such a discourse involves the reconstruction of Western culture from a feminist perspective. This reconstruction now has many different aspects, but for Felman, one key approach was the development of a reading 'otherwise' in the special issue of *Yale French Studies* in 1977, the volume republished as *Literature and Psychoanalysis, The Question of Reading: Otherwise*. In the foreword to the republished version, Felman ponders how the new French theoretical approach, based mainly on Lacanian and deconstructive re-readings of Freud, could function as a model for thinking and critically arguing 'otherwise': not just a new approach to literary and feminist theory, but also an abandonment of the hierarchical relationship of literature and psychoanalysis. While the *Yale French Studies* version was seen as a way of familiarizing the 'American public' (*sic*) with Lacanian psychoanalysis and initiating a dialogue between French and American theorists, the later reprint, Felman notes, was even more appealing and timely for those academics inspired by Lacan and his variants. However, why is it necessary, for thinking 'otherwise', to dismantle the hierarchical relationship between literature and psychoanalysis? Felman suggests that literature has been considered a discourse in need of interpretation, while psychoanalysis has been considered a methodology and knowledge-base that enables interpretation. Literature is thus the 'object' that psychoanalysis as 'subject' works upon. Felman compares this relationship to the master/slave passage in Hegel's *Phenomenology of Spirit*, where there is a 'fight for recognition' between the two, resulting, Felman suggests, in recognition of the master. This is highly problematic for literary critics, who perceive literature – or the literary – as elusive subject, precisely that which escapes the master and is therefore misrecognized. Felman argues that what is needed is a truly open dialogue between literature and psychoanalysis, and this can be achieved by reversing the usual relationship: 'in much the same way as literature falls within the realm of psychoanalysis (within its competence and its knowledge), psychoanalysis itself falls within the realm of literature, and its specific logic and rhetoric'.[1] But would this not simply reverse the positions of master and slave, subject and object? Felman suggests not, because the strategy is disruptive of binary thinking and hierarchy, in much the same way that the first move or reversal of deconstruction functions: mastery, as a function of constituting the hierarchy, is displaced and avoided:

> Psychoanalysis tells us that the fantasy [of authority] is a fiction, and that consciousness is itself, in a sense, a fantasy-effect. In the same way, literature tells us that authority is a *language effect*, the product or the creation of its own *rhetorical* power: that authority is the *power of fiction*; that authority, therefore, is likewise a fiction.[2]

Further, for Felman, literature is constitutive of the discourse of psychoanalysis, for example, the reliance of proper names, such as Oedipus, Narcissus, Masochism and Sadism: narrative is at the heart, defines the founding moments and concepts, of psychoanalysis. Felman illustrates these relationships between literature and psycho-analysis in her reading of James's *The Turn of the Screw* in the same volume. She asks what, precisely, is it in a literary text that invites or authorizes psychoanalytical reading, and what resists or disqualifies such an approach? In the chiasmus between the two, Felman begins to sketch a practical response to how the critic might think, and write, 'otherwise', whereas in a much lengthier publication, Felman's *Jacques Lacan and the Adventure of Insight: Psychoanalysis in Contemporary Culture* (1987), a personal journey into and through Lacanian analysis reveals the self-reflexive project of thinking 'otherwise'. Felman's most widely read book, however, is her collection of essays called *Writing and Madness (Literature/Philosophy/Psychoanalysis)*, which was published in French in 1978 and appeared in translation in 1985.

Writing and Madness, Felman notes in the reprint of 2003, is her most literary theoretical book, which still maintains its popularity even though she has worked in many other related areas, such as her key feminist text *What Does a Woman Want? Writing and Sexual Difference* (1993), and her work on testimony with Dori Laub in *Testimony: Crises of Witnessing in Literature, Psychoanalysis and History* (1992). Once more, in *Writing and Madness* Felman returns to and expands upon 'the specificity of literature by exploring literature's constitutive relation to what culture has excluded under the label "madness" (nonsense, alienating strangeness, a transgressive excess, an illusion, a delusion, a disease)'.[3] In exploring these relations, Felman is able to interrogate modernity as the age of psychiatry, and its power-knowledge base, where literature functions at the margins, reclaiming and critiquing structures of dominance and exclusion.

Notes

1 Shoshana Felman, ed., *Literature and Psychoanalysis, The Question of Reading: Otherwise*, Baltimore, MD and London: The Johns Hopkins University Press, 1982, pp. 6–7.
2 Ibid., p. 8.
3 Shoshana Felman, *Writing and Madness (Literature/Philosophy/Psychoanalysis)*, trans. Martha Noel Evans and Shoshana Felman, with Brian Massumi, and appendices trans. Barbara Johnson, Palo Alto, CA: Stanford University Press, 2003, p. 2.

See also in this book

Freud, Lacan

Major works

La 'folie' dans l'oeuvre romanesque de Stendhal (1971). Paris: Corti.
Literature and Psychoanalysis, The Question of Reading: Otherwise (ed., 1977). First published in Yale French Studies, nos. 55 and 56; Baltimore, MD and London: The Johns Hopkins University Press, 1982.
Writing and Madness (Literature/Philosophy/Psychoanalysis) (1978). Paris: Seuil; trans. Martha Noel Evans and Shoshana Felman, with Brian Massumi, Ithaca, NY: Cornell University Press, 1985; new edition, appendices trans. Barbara Johnson, Palo Alto, CA: Stanford University Press, 2003.
The Literary Speech Act: Don Juan with J. L. Austin, or Seduction in Two Languages (1980). Paris: Seuil. Translated edition Ithaca, NY: Cornell University Press, 1984; reissued as *The Scandal of the Speaking Body: Don Juan with Austin, or Seduction in Two Languages*, Palo Alto, CA: Stanford University Press, 2003.
Jacques Lacan and the Adventure of Insight: Psychoanalysis in Contemporary Culture (1987). Cambridge, MA: Harvard University Press.
Testimony: Crises of Witnessing in Literature, Psychoanalysis and History (with Dori Laub, 1992). New York and London: Routledge.
What Does a Woman Want? Writing and Sexual Difference (1993). Baltimore, MD: Johns Hopkins University Press.
The Juridical Unconscious: Trials and Traumas in the Twentieth Century (2002). Cambridge, MA: Harvard University Press.

Further reading

Johnston, Georgia, 'Virginia Woolf's Autobiographers: Sidonie Smith, Shoshana Felman, and Shari Benstock', in Beth Rigel Daugherty and Eileen Barrett, eds, *Virginia Woolf: Texts and Contexts*, New York: Pace University Press, 1996; pp. 40–44.
Moore, Michelle E., 'Teaching Ambiguity: *The Turn of the Screw* and Shoshana Felman's "Turning the Screw of Interpretation"', in Kimberley C. Reed and Peter G. Beidler, eds, *Approaches to Teaching Henry James's Daisy Miller and The Turn of the Screw*, New York: MLA, 2005; pp. 127–131.

Mucci, Clara, 'The Blank Page as a Lacanian "Object a": Silence, Women's Words, Desire, and Interpretation between Literature and Psychoanalysis', *Literature and Psychology*, 38.4 (1992): 23–35.

Young, Robert, 'Psychoanalytic Criticism: Has It got beyond a Joke?', *Paragraph* 4 (1984): 87–114.

STANLEY EUGENE FISH (1938–)

Renowned for asking 'is there a text in this class?', Fish, in the process of answering, reveals how he believes that language is embedded and perceived within a social system of norms where social situations are open to change, and thus our interpretations are similarly open. As a leading exponent of reader-response criticism, having developed his earlier theory of 'affective stylistics', Fish shares many of the concerns of poststructuralism, while occupying a parallel hermeneutic universe, one that is anchored by the lifelong study of what readers do – i.e. in terms of utilizing a competency – rather than what they 'should' do (the demands of contemporary theory) when they interpret texts. Fish should, therefore, be infamous not for asking if there is a text in 'this' room, but for stating that 'theory is an impossible project which will never succeed'.[1] Fish was born in Providence, Rhode Island, and studied for his BA at the University of Pennsylvania (awarded 1959), moving to Yale University for graduate study, where he was awarded his MA in 1960 and his Ph.D. in 1962. After spending just over a decade at the University of California, Berkeley (1962–1974), Fish became the Kenan Professor of English at Johns Hopkins University (1974–1985), the Arts and Sciences Distinguished Professor of English and Law at Duke University (1985–1998), and Dean of the College of Liberal Arts and Sciences at the University of Illinois, Chicago (1999–). Awards include an American Council of Learned Societies Fellowship (1966), a Guggenheim Fellowship (1969) and a Humanities Research Institute Fellowship at University of California, Irvine (1989).

Fish's first book, *John Skelton's Poetry* (1965) asks why readers of his work have failed to see that at the heart of his poetry there is a 'psychological' or 'spiritual' history of each protagonist. In reading Skelton for 'psychological conflict', Fish also reads the readers of Skelton, to understand why it is that they miss this structuring force. The seeds of reader-response criticism are thus sown. In Fish's following books – *Surprised by Sin: The Reader in* Paradise Lost (1967) and *Self-Consuming Artifacts: The Experience of Seventeenth-Century Literature* (1972), Fish developed the concept of 'affective stylistics', whereby the meaning of a text is found in the reader's experience of that text.

The reader of *Paradise Lost* is not only subject to its rhetorical complexities, but is the subject *of* the text: 'while in most poems effects are achieved through the manipulation of reader response, this poet is telling the story that *created* and still creates the responses of its reader and of all readers'.[2] The reader's difficulties in the encounter with Milton are thus embedded in the narrative that created difficulties – and Christian subjectivity – in the first place: the Fall. As Fish argues:

> The reader who falls before the lures of Satanic rhetoric displays again the weakness of Adam, and his inability to avoid repeating that fall throughout indicates the extent to which Adam's lapse has made the reassertion of right reason impossible. Rhetoric is thus simultaneously the sign of the reader's infirmity and the means by which he is brought first to self-knowledge, and then to contrition, and finally, perhaps, to grace and everlasting bliss.[3]

But what of the text in this process? Fish's term for what happens as such to the text neatly describes its dialectical sublation: he thus calls texts 'self-consuming artifacts'. In the opening chapter to *Self-Consuming Artifacts* Fish explains his overall approach with four theses that the book utilizes: (1) the opposition of dialectical to rhetorical readings (where the former disturbs, and the latter satisfies, the reader); (2) the opposition of the discursive/rational and the antidiscursive/antirational (where there is a dialectical transition from the former to the latter in the process of reading texts); (3) that a dialectical reading will necessarily lead to an abandonment of the textual 'vehicle' through which it points to the non–discursive (the self-consuming process); and (4) that the proper site of analysis is not the text but 'the' reader. With the fourth thesis Fish responds to the charge of the 'affective fallacy': the critical confusion between a text and its 'results', where the psychological effects of the latter are the grounds for creating a critical methodology, the text 'itself' disappearing in the process. Fish responds by saying that this is not an erroneous procedure but precisely what *does* happen in the reading process: 'when we read – the work as an object tends to disappear . . . any method of analysis which ignores the affective reality of the reading experience cuts itself off from the source of literary power and meaning'.[4] Fish had explored these issues in a key essay published in *New Literary History* in 1970, called 'Literature in the Reader: Affective Stylistics', where the reading process is described as an event, something that is participated in and experienced. Signification, in this case, is the experience or event itself, not an abstracted version of it. Searching for the actual 'message' embedded in a text becomes an erroneous and futile procedure, since according to Fish (and philosophers such as Wittgenstein), that is to misunderstand that the meaning is in the use, and that a text is 'kinetic' not stable and solidified into a unified set of meanings.

'Literature in the Reader: Affective Stylistics', has gained the status of a reader-response manifesto, reprinted and published in many locations. The essay also opens one of Fish's best-known books, *Is There a Text in this Class? The Authority of Interpretive Communities* (1980). As a collection of essays, *Is There a Text in this Class?* is a superb mapping of Fish's intellectual engagement in literary-critical and theoretical debates. But the book does more than this: it teases out many of the consequences and contradictions of the reader-response method. In the fifteenth chapter, 'What Makes an Interpretation Acceptable?', Fish examines the institutions within which reader responses are made. In attempting to understand why there are observable limits to acceptable textual readings, Fish turns to the communities within which interpreters function, and the interdictions and dynamic schemas that both close certain readings in the present, yet remain open to future methodologies where what is now unacceptable, becomes *the* acceptable or even cutting-edge way of interpreting. Fish's point is that these interdictions and schemas are not present in the text, but in the interpretive communities themselves. Fish's humorous example of a future possibility is the 'discovery' of a non-ironic Jane Austen. Fish's notion of 'canons of acceptability' is worth bearing in mind as theory becomes more interdictive and concerned with 'ethical' readings, whereby certain values *should* be found, and if not the texts or authors are themselves to be condemned; as Fish notes, 'canons of acceptability' have the potential to change.

Fish's manifesto writing became far more wide-ranging in the publications that followed *Is There a Text in this Class?* In his *Doing What Comes Naturally: Change, Rhetoric, and the Practice of Theory in Literary and Legal Studies* (1989), Fish engages with poststructuralism and with issues in legal studies. Once more Fish explores the interpretive communities within which these practitioners are embedded and via which they make interpretive decisions. Fish continues to explore these communities in debate with the conservative critic Dinesh D'Souza in *There's No Such Thing as Free Speech, and It's a Good Thing, Too* (1994) and his study of the pervasiveness of political structures of meaning in *Professional Correctness: Literary Studies and Political Change* (1995).

Notes

1   Stanley Fish, *Doing What Comes Naturally: Change, Rhetoric, and the Practice of Theory in Literary and Legal Studies*, Durham, NC and London: Duke University Press, 1989, p. 320. Note: 'theory' refers to a more complex discussion of foundationalist and anti–foundationalist theory and Fish's belief in the lack of consequences of either.
2   Stanley Eugene Fish, *Surprised by Sin: The Reader in* Paradise Lost, Berkeley, CA: University of California Press, 1971, p. 38.
3   Ibid.
4   Stanley E. Fish, *Self-Consuming Artifacts: The Experience of Seventeenth-Century Literature*, Berkeley, CA: University of California Press, 1972, p. 4.

Major works

John Skelton's Poetry (1965). New Haven, CT and London: Yale University Press.
Surprised by Sin: The Reader in Paradise Lost (1971). New York: St Martin's Press.
Self-Consuming Artifacts: The Experience of Seventeenth-Century Literature (1972). Berkeley, CA: University of California Press.
Is There a Text in this Class? The Authority of Interpretive Communities (1980). Cambridge, MA and London: Harvard University Press.
Doing What Comes Naturally: Change, Rhetoric, and the Practice of Theory in Literary and Legal Studies (1989). Durham and London: Duke University Press.
There's No Such Thing as Free Speech, and It's a Good Thing, Too (1994). Oxford: Oxford University Press.
Professional Correctness: Literary Studies and Political Change (1995). Oxford and New York: Clarendon.
The Stanley Fish Reader (1999). Oxford: Blackwell.
The Trouble with Principle (1999). Cambridge, MA and London: Harvard University Press.

Further reading

Bezeczky, Gábor, 'Self-Consuming Arguments', *Hungarian Journal of English and American Studies*, 3.1 (1997): 75–82.
Donnelly, Phillip J., *Rhetorical Faith: The Literary Hermeneutics of Stanley Fish*, Victoria: University of Victoria Press, 2000.
Leonard, John, 'Reading with Stanley Fish', *Milton Quarterly*, 30.4 (1996): 173–176.
Olson, Gary A., *Justifying Belief: Stanley Fish and the Work of Rhetoric*, Albany, NY: SUNY Press, 2002.
Williams, Jeffrey J., 'Stanley Agonistes: An Interview with Stanley Fish', in Jeffrey J. Williams, ed., *Critics at Work: Interviews 1993–2003*, New York: New York University Press, 2003; pp. 15–27.

(PAUL-)MICHEL FOUCAULT (1920–1984)

Over two decades after his death, Foucault's legacy continues to impact upon the humanities.[1] Key phrases and concepts drawn from Foucault's historical work now form part of the everyday language of criticism and analysis. Foucault's texts continue to resonate with contemporary readers, and this resonance can be misunderstood in a chronological survey of his key ideas and works, since the man who rejected notions of historical progress – preferring to work with the notion of what he called the *epistemic break* – produced works that cannot be neatly fitted into a condensed and orderly summary that appears to move smoothly from one text to another. In other words, it is important when reading any summary of Foucault's life and work, to think of his theories as forming a critical constellation, rather than a developmental, logical system. Born in Poitiers, France, Foucault studied at school with the great commentator on Hegel, Jean Hyppolite, who was one of the teachers preparing Foucault for entry into the École Normale Supérieure, in Paris, which he achieved in 1946. During his time at the ENS, Foucault studied with the philosophers Maurice Merleau-Ponty and Louis Althusser; in 1948 he gained his *licence* in philosophy, and he progressed to his *licence* in psychology in 1949, as well as receiving a diploma in pathological psychology from the Institut de Psychologie de Paris in 1952.[2] Alongside teaching at the ENS, Foucault was involved with analyst and researcher Jacqueline Verdeaux in translating Ludwig Binswanger's work of existential psychology, *Traum und Existenz* (published in France in 1954 as *Le Rêve et l'existence*); Foucault helped with the translation, and wrote a lengthy introduction that revealed his predilection for a creative synthesis of philosophy, psychology and psychoanalysis.[3] However, it would be a mistake to locate Foucault's ideas solely in his intellectual pursuits: he also worked during this period in the psychiatric Hôpital Sainte-Anne and at a laboratory in the Fresnes prison, doing investigative experiments on the prisoners. Foucault's first book came out in 1954, called *Maladie mentale et personnalité*, where he sketches his first attempt at locating illness beyond the subject's responsibility, by arguing from a Marxist perspective that *society* has alienated – and thus made ill – the subject.[4] Leaving Paris for a cultural post in Uppsala, Sweden, moving next to Warsaw, Poland, and then Hamburg, Germany, Foucault was all the time working on his thesis, *Folie et déraison: Histoire de la folie à l'âge classique*, translated into English as *Madness and Civilization: A History of Insanity in the Age of Reason* (1961). Returning to France, Foucault took up a post at the University of Clermont-Ferrand, eventually becoming Head of Philosophy at the Université de Paris, Vincennes, becoming an elected member of the Collège de France.

Madness and Civilization was a huge tome in its manuscript form, published in French at over six hundred pages, and in much abbreviated form in its English translation; regardless of which version is read, it is a powerful and moving account of different historical perspectives on defining and confining 'madness'. Foucault's central thesis is that of epochal shifts, or alignments, between those subjects deemed mad, and those who are part of the 'unreason' of the human world: the subjects who have transgressive and excessive sexualities, ideas and modes of behaviour. In charting these alignments throughout history, Foucault arrives at the birth of the asylum, the constitution of the 'insane' subject, placed in confinement and under scientific surveillance. Rather than seeing this as progress, Foucault projects such a procedure as being repressive and punishing. Foucault's companion text to this study was his next book, *Naissance de la clinique: Une Archéologie du regard medical* (1963) translated in 1973 as *The Birth of the Clinic: An Archeology of Medical Perception*. While the leading semiotician Roland Barthes praised *Madness and Civilization* as 'a cathartic question asked about madness',[5] it was Jacques Derrida's critique – 'Cogito and the History of Madness' – that received the most explosive reply from Foucault, in the form of an angry essay published nine years later as 'My Body, This Paper, This Fire'. Foucault would receive a much more widespread response from the public to his third major historical study *Les Mots et les choses: Une Archéologie des sciences humaines* (1966) translated in 1970 as *The Order of Things: An Archaeology of the Human Sciences*.

The 'archaeological' method utilized by Foucault owed a great debt to the philosopher Friedrich Nietzsche: where historians had once looked for connections and developmental continuity through time, Foucault, following Nietzsche, now looked for historical breaks and ruptures. In *The Order of Things*, he sketches out the a priori discourses that constitute knowledge of the world and of being, discourses that create the 'episteme' of any particular period. For example, in what Foucault calls 'Classical' thought, metaphysics is possible because of the concept of human finitude (in relation to forces that transcend humanity); for Foucault, an epistemic shift occurs when human finitude is measured not in relation to something else (say, God), but when it is measured in its own terms (say, physiology or the sciences of the body). In other words, modernity is constituted by the epistemic break whereby metaphysics is replaced with self-reflexive knowledge of actual human existence (the human sciences, the humanities, etc.). But modernity, in turn, gives way to another violent epistemic break: that of the period in which Foucault ends his book (the late 1960s), with its political and intellectual upheavals in France, and the rise of structuralist and poststructuralist thought. Now the a priori or paradigm of existence becomes, for Foucault, language – the rise of the language philosophies, communication models, Saussurian linguistics, semiotics, and so on. These are what constitute 'the subject' and in the process thereby begin to erase and efface prior notions of self-centred subjectivity, humanity and that historically located entity known as 'man'. Foucault's controversial thesis in *The Order of Things* triggered much enthusiastic debate, but in retrospect it is intriguing to note how in an interview Foucault called this enthusiasm a 'passion for concepts and for what I will call "system"'.[6] *The Order of Things* was, for Foucault, more than simply another way of doing history: it was a revolution in thought. To explain his methodology and its full implications, Foucault went to work on a highly abstract work called *L'Archéologie du savoir* (1969), translated in 1972 as *The Archaeology of Knowledge*. The poststructuralist theorist Gilles Deleuze sketches Foucault's approach:

> there is nothing prior to knowledge, because knowledge, in Foucault's new concept of it, is defined by the combinations of visible and articulable that are unique to each stratum or historical formulation. Knowledge is a practical assemblage, a 'mechanism' of statements and visibilities.[7]

The other important statement that needs to be added here is that the various permutations of knowledge do not proceed towards some final grand goal; thus Foucault's archaeological method is resistant to Hegelian thought:

> one can see to what extent it has freed itself from what constituted, not so long ago, the philosophy of history, and from the questions that it posed (on the rationality or teleology of historical development (*devenir*), on the relativity of historical knowledge, and on the possibility of discovering or constituting a meaning in the inertia of the past and in the unfinished totality of the present).[8]

Apart from being an attack upon a generalized notion of more traditional historical studies, this is an implicit critique of Hegel's *Philosophy of History* and *Phenomenology of Spirit*. Thus, Foucault says that in the traditional approach, by making the history of thought the 'locus of uninterrupted continuities', the subject is constructed in advance in a highly abstract manner, simultaneously providing 'a privileged shelter for the sovereignty of consciousness'.[9] Such an analysis suggests that the philosophy of history invests in the discontinuous only to gain a secure return: the discontinuous is thereby placed in a series controlled by the forces of a progressive development/evolution. Foucault's focus on a *methodological* level of analysis is an attempt to question generalized teleological categories and 'totalizations', exemplified by Hegel's 'Absolute Spirit', as well as being an attempt at providing a non-subject-centred account of the intersecting fields of study that surround and construct the sciences *of* the subject.

In the shift away from what Foucault calls the 'unities' of discourse exemplified by classical notions of: the book; the *oeuvre*; authorial intention; the recovery of self-presence and the return to origins, all of these humanist notions are rejected with a consequent re-focus away from interpretation to functional description. Thus, as critic Gary Gutting notes, the 'archaeological' method formulated in the *Archaeology* is 'a historical method of inquiry, concerned not with structural possibilities but with actual occurences and their effects'.[10] Foucault delimitates what he calls the *discursive formation* which has four basic elements. As Gutting notes, these are: the *objects* its statements are about, the kinds of cognitive stature and authority they have [*enunciative modality*], the *concepts* in terms of which they are formulated, and the *themes* or theoretical viewpoints they develop.[11] Gutting stresses that the same discursive formation may be used as

> a vehicle for discourse about different systems of objects, categorized in terms of different conceptual frameworks, and its statements will have a variety of enunciative modalities and may develop very diverse theoretical viewpoints . . . Foucault does not regard a discursive formation as distinguished by unity (of, e.g., objects, concepts, method) provided by its elements. Rather, a discursive formation is a 'system of dispersion' for its elements: It defines a field within which a variety of different, even conflicting, sets of elements can be deployed.[12]

The 'unity' of any particular discursive formation is defined by the rules of its operation. Foucault argues there are four 'types' of rules governing the formation: (1) rules for the *formation of objects*; (2) rules for the *formation of concepts*; (3) rules specifying various *procedures of intervention*; (4) rules governing the *formation of strategies*.[13] There is a certain degree of post-theorizing here, in that Foucault is re-articulating the methodology of his earlier works, thus there is more stress on the 'unity' of the earlier discursive formations, than upon their status as systems of dispersion. This can also be seen in the extent that certain 'rules' are given priority over others. However, Deleuze regards this as Foucault laying 'the foundations for a new pragmatics',[14] in that the 'rules' define ways in which the elements of the system operate in relation to one another; there is no transcendental set of rules that rises above the discursive formation to order and describe all others.

While all of Foucault's texts rapidly impacted upon the worlds of literary theory and other methodologies within the humanities – especially once he started to visit the US in the early 1970s – it is perhaps his *Surveiller et punir: Naissance de la prison* (1975), translated in 1977 as *Discipline and Punish: The Birth of the Prison*, that has continued to inspire literary critics. This is not so much for the subject matter of the book, but for the metaphor of internalized surveillance, embodied most memorably in Jeremy Bentham's prison design called the panopticon. Foucault's concept of the 'microphysics of power' suggests that modern disciplinary methods are internalized and produce subjects that are constituted via a network of relations. The traditional 'top down' notion of power is thus replaced with one that is horizontal, not vertical. The panopticon, a prison where the prisoners believe themselves to be under total surveillance, functions as a metaphor explaining how and why subjects thereby modify their own behaviour. Applied to countless literary texts, the panopticon lives on in myriad works of literary theory. Self-regulation is explored from another perspective in Foucault's final works, a series of studies called *A History of Sexuality*. In many respects, this apparent shift of focus, from disciplinary discourses and institutions that have radically transformed and reinvented themselves, to that of the body and *sexualities*, may indeed be the major continuity in Foucault's work, since bodily regimes have always been a subtext, be they overt or covert, textual or autobiographical, in his approach; Foucault's impact remains high as the contemporary humanities follows the trajectories of his thought, and the discontinuous, but traceable, contours of his map of knowledge production and being.

Notes

1 This entry is partly based upon chapter one of my study of Derrida and Foucault, *Functions of the Derrida Archive: Philosophical Receptions*, Budapest: Akademiai Kiado Rt, 2003, Ph.D. thesis series, pp. 10–26.

2 Didier Eribon, *Michel Foucault*, trans. Betsy Wing, Cambridge, MA: Harvard University Press, 1991, p. 42.
3 Ibid., pp. 44–46.
4 Ibid., p. 69.
5 Ibid., p. 118.
6 Ibid., p. 161.
7 Gilles Deleuze, *Foucault*, trans. Sean Hand, Minneapolis, MN: University of Minnesota Press, 1988, p. 51.
8 Michel Foucault, *The Archaeology of Knowledge*, Trans. A.M. Sheridan Smith, New York: Pantheon, 1972, p. 11.
9 Ibid., p. 12.
10 Gary Gutting, *Michel Foucault's Archaeology of Scientific Reason*, Cambridge and New York: University of Cambridge Press, 1991, p. 228.
11 Ibid., p. 232.
12 Ibid.
13 Ibid., p. 234.
14 Gilles Deleuze, *Foucault*, p. 9.

See also in this book

Butler, Deleuze and Guattari, Derrida, Kristeva

Major works

Madness and Civilization: A History of Insanity in the Age of Reason (1971). Trans. Richard Howard, London: Tavistock.
The Archaeology of Knowledge and The Discourse on Language (1972). Trans. A.M. Sheridan Smith, New York: Pantheon.
The Order of Things: An Archaeology of the Human Sciences (1974). London and New York: Tavistock.
Language, Counter-Memory, Practice: Selected Essays and Interviews by Michel Foucault (1977). Trans. Donald F. Bouchard and Sherry Simon, Ithaca, NY: Cornell University Press.
Discipline & Punish: The Birth of the Prison (1979). Trans. Alan Sheridan, New York: Vintage.
'My Body, This Paper, This Fire' (1979). Trans. Geoff Bennington, *The Oxford Literary Review*, 4 (1).
The Birth of the Clinic (1989). London and New York: Tavistock.
The History of Sexuality: Volume 1, An Introduction (1990). Trans. Robert Hurley, New York: Vintage.
The Use of Pleasure: Volume 2, The History of Sexuality (1990). Trans. Robert Hurley, New York: Vintage.
The Care of the Self: Volume 3, The History of Sexuality (1990). Trans. Robert Hurley, New York: Vintage.

Further reading

Deleuze, Gilles, *Foucault*, trans. Sean Hand, Minneapolis, MN: University of Minnesota Press, 1988.
Eribon, Didier, *Michel Foucault*, trans. Betsy Wing, Cambridge, MA: Harvard University Press, 1991.

Gutting, Gary, *Michel Foucault's Archaeology of Scientific Reason*, Cambridge and New York: University of Cambridge Press, 1991.
Mills, Sara, *Michel Foucault*, London and New York, 2003.

SIGMUND FREUD (1856–1939)

Introducing his essay on the 'uncanny', Freud says that it is only rarely that he feels 'impelled' to turn to the subject of aesthetics; this statement is replete with irony, since Freudian psychoanalysis has been responsible for countless new readings of aesthetic texts and artefacts, as well as influencing or triggering more contemporary approaches to art and related expressions or representations of the psyche. While Freud wrote a number of influential essays and books on art and literature, such as *Leonardo Da Vinci and a Memory of his Childhood* (1910) and 'The Moses of Michelangelo' (1914), it is his more general theories of subjectivity that have arguably had the greatest impact upon literary criticism. Born in Freiberg, in Austro-Hungarian Moravia, Freud initially studied Medicine at The University of Vienna, enrolling in 1873. He worked for six years in the Physiological Laboratory of Ernst Brücke, primarily researching the anatomy of the central nervous system, and he eventually gained his degree and a post at the Vienna General Hospital. The desire to marry initiated Freud's next career moves: he studied under Jean-Martin Charcot in Paris at the Salpêtrière (1885–1886), and he set up a private practice upon his return to Vienna. Freud became dissatisfied with Charcot's approach to 'nervous diseases' which was to treat patients using hypnosis, so he turned to the methodology of Josef Breuer, involving the recollection of forgotten trauma to achieve the 'talking cure', Breuer's most famous patient being 'Anna O' (Bertha Pappenheim). Freud was to make Breuer's methodology his own, significantly modifying and developing it from the early notion of 'hysterical conversion' whereby mental trauma was repressed and transformed into physiological symptoms, into the complex field of psychoanalysis, with its competing maps of the psyche and powerful models of interpretation. Of course, while philosophers, artists and others had long explored aspects of the human mind, it was Freud who synthesized and formulated a scientific and interpretive approach, speculating upon various models of the psyche with research rooted in the ongoing encounter of analyst and analysand, research that was first jointly published with Breuer in their *Studies on Hysteria* (1895), but was soon to be followed by a series of publications written alone by Freud. In *The Interpretation of Dreams* (1900), the sheer brilliance of Freud's approach was forcefully revealed, not least in the sheer range of neurotic situations and experiences that he encountered, revealed and explained to his peers. This study was soon followed by *The Psychopathology of Everyday Life* (1901), *Three Essays on the Theory of Sexuality* (1905) and *Jokes and their Relation to the Unconscious* (1905). The break with Breuer occurred with Freud's turn to the importance of sexuality, and sexual drives (as well as Freud's rejection of Breuer's use of hypnosis). In this early period, Freud developed: the unconscious/conscious or dualistic model of mind; the notion of childhood sexuality and the importance of sexual drives, or libido, in the establishment and ongoing processes of subjectivity; and methods of accessing repressed trauma (such as free association) that would replace the faulty methodology of hypnosis. In *The Interpretation of Dreams*, Freud's theory that a dream is a disguised fulfilment of a suppressed or repressed wish found a powerful interpretive formulation in the notion of latent (hidden) and manifest (as remembered) dreams.[1] Freud formulated five 'dream work' mechanisms that explain the transition from latent to manifest dream: symbolization, dramatization, displacement, condensation and secondary revision. Freud also expands here upon his concept of the Oedipus complex, one of his most influential theories.

Why, asks Freud, does the play *Oedipus Rex* – which is about a man who in attempting to avoid the oracle's predictions fulfils them by inadvertently murdering his father and marrying his mother – still move us today? Why does a 'tragedy of destiny' affect us more in this form than any other modern version? Freud answers, in *The Interpretation of Dreams*, that: 'His destiny moves us only because it might have been ours – because the oracle laid the same curse upon us before birth as upon him.'[2] In other words: 'It is the fate of all of us, perhaps, to direct our first sexual impulse towards our mother and our first hatred and our first murderous wish against our father.'[3] The shock that occurs in reading or seeing the play is that of recognizing a shared experience, with the difference that Oedipus went unwittingly through with his primal desires, whereas the contemporary reader or audience member successfully 'detaches' and suppresses them. In *The Ego and the Id* (1923), Freud summarizes the Oedipus complex from the perspective of a male child, arguing that the child develops an 'object-cathexis' for his mother and initially identifies with his father; as the desire for the mother intensifies, the father begins to be perceived as an obstacle to the fulfilment of that desire, an obstacle that needs to be removed. In a paper written in 1924, called 'The Dissolution of the Oedipus Complex', Freud further argued that the Oedipus complex is the 'central phenomenon' of childhood sexuality and maturation. Pondering how the complex is brought to an end, however, Freud introduces an even more radical complex: that of the threat of castration (in boys) and 'penis envy' (in girls). The initial threat of castration is not entirely believed in; for Freud, the radical shock that generates this belief is 'sight of the female genitals'.[4] In other words, it is a perceived absence, or lack, that makes the threat real, and this triggers the end of the Oedipus complex, whereby the child has been forced to choose between castration or 'the libidinal cathexis of his parental objects'.[5] Freud argues that the female Oedipal complex (named the 'Electra complex' by Jung), functions 'after' castration, i.e. with the belief that castration has already taken place. Freud argues that the desire in girls to compensate this perceived lack, becomes the desire for a child, and that the unfulfilled desire eventually terminates the complex. While much subsequent research has critiqued (if not parodied) Freud's Oedipus complex, especially his patriarchal interpretation of female sexuality, there is no doubt that his formulation and assertion of childhood sexuality and trauma facilitated much needed research that has led in turn to the recognition of a more complex childhood identity and experience.

The fact that Freud's exploration of Oedipus originates in an aesthetic text, Sophocles' *Oedipus Rex*, may go some way to explaining the success of the concept in its other literary applications. In *The Interpretation of Dreams*, Freud suggests that while Shakespeare's *Hamlet* is rooted in the same soil, an epochal shift has occurred between the time of the Greeks and the Elizabethans: 'the changed treatment of the same material reveals the whole difference in the mental life of these two widely separated epochs of civilization: the secular advance of repression in the emotional life of mankind'.[6] Instead of the realization of the child's desire that is portrayed in Sophocles' *Oedipus Rex*, the play *Hamlet* reveals only the *consequences* of the repression of that same desire. While such a crude psychoanalysis of the character Hamlet, and indeed of Shakespeare, is now seen as overly simplistic, what is more important than the interpretation is Freud's awareness that human subjectivity has in itself developed historically, and that epochal shifts in psychic structure occur. Freud's own shift from the dualistic model of mind to the tripartite model – that of ego, id, and superego – is reflective of the dynamic thinking that Freud remained committed to, although as critics point out, the new theory of the mind does not entirely do away with the dualism of the previous model.[7] However, Freud also points out that while historical change can account for developments of the ego and superego, the id drives remain the same across time and place, as Freud suggests in his book *Das Unbehagen in der Kultur/Man's Fundamental Unease Within Civilization*, translated into English as *Civilization and Its Discontents* (1930). With this book, Freud launched most thoroughly into the issue that was the main focus of his later research: the relationship between the individual and society, explored previously with the groundbreaking works *Totem and Taboo* (1913), 'Thoughts for the Times on War and Death' (1915), *Group Psychology and the Analysis of the Ego* (1921) and *The Future of an Illusion* (1927), to be explored further with *Moses and Monotheism: Three Essays* (1939).

In *Group Psychology and the Analysis of the Ego*, Freud is careful to point out that psychoanalytical research into the individual reveals relationships that are *primarily* social phenomena; as Mikkel Borch-Jacobsen points out, this observation

> does not aim at extending or 'applying' 'individual psychology'
> to the study of 'social phenomena,' but rather at *reducing* the
> latter to the former: psychoanalysis . . . is already a 'social psy-
> chology,' the analysis of the ego is already a mass psychology.[8]

The aporia at the heart of this assertion, as Borch-Jacobsen notes, is that in his work on narcissism, Freud had posited a self-centred ego divorced from the Other, thus *severing* all social relations. This aporia, however, is what drives Freud to go beyond the reasoning of social psychologists such as Tarde, Le Bon, McDougall and Trotter. Freud's writings here span two world wars, with the unremitting rise of Fascism and Nazism towards the end of his life, culminating in his own fleeing of Germany for self-imposed exile and safety in England. At the end of his life, and at the beginning of the Second World War, Freud's ideas had been disseminated widely across Europe and, in some ways more importantly, the US, where many German Jewish intellectuals would settle to escape the Shoah, and where psychoanalysis had gained a foothold. By 1950, a history of American psychology would assert that Freud's ideas had 'pervaded all thinking about human motivation both among the psychologists and among the lay public';[9] in the decades that followed, psychoanalytical terminology would enter popular culture, and become part of the common discourse of Western culture, to such an extent, that we no longer notice the Freudian roots of our everyday expressions.

Notes

1 Henk De Berg, *Freud's Theory and Its Use in Literary and Cultural Studies*, Rochester, NY: Camden House, 2003, p. 18.
2 Sigmund Freud, *The Interpretation of Dreams*, Harmondsworth: Penguin, 1986, p. 364.
3 Ibid.
4 Sigmund Freud, *On Sexuality*, Harmondsworth: Penguin, 1987, p. 318.
5 Ibid.
6 Sigmund Freud, *The Interpretation of Dreams*, p. 366.
7 Ibid., p. 52.
8 Mikkel Borch-Jacobsen, *The Freudian Subject*, trans. Catherine Porter, Houndmills and London: Macmillan, 1989, p. 129.
9 Quoted in Marius G. Schneider, 'Sigmund Freud and the Development of Psychoanalysis', in John K. Ryan, *Twentieth-Century Thinkers: Studies in the Work of Seventeen Modern Philosophers*, Staten Island, NY: Alba House, 1967, pp. 239–265; p. 239.

See also in this book

Butler, Lacan

Major works

The following works can be found in *The Standard Edition of Complete Psychological Works* (24 volumes) (1940–1968), London: The Hogarth Press and the Institute of Psychoanalysis, translated from Gesammelte Works, vols I–XVIII, London and Frankfurt.
Studies on Hysteria (1895).
The Interpretation of Dreams (1900).
The Psychopathology of Everyday Life (1901).
Jokes and their Relation to the Unconscious (1905).
Three Essays on the Theory of Sexuality (1905).
Leonardo Da Vinci and a Memory of his Childhood (1910).
Totem and Taboo (1913).
'The Moses of Michelangelo' (1914).
'Thoughts for the Times on War and Death' (1915).
Group Psychology and the Analysis of the Ego (1921).
The Future of an Illusion (1927).
Civilization and Its Discontents (1930).
Moses and Monotheism: Three Essays (1939).

Further reading

Borch-Jacobsen, Mikkel, *The Freudian Subject*, trans. Catherine Porter, Houndmills and London: Macmillan, 1989.
De Berg, Henk, *Freud's Theory and Its Use in Literary and Cultural Studies*, Rochester, NY: Camden House, 2003.
Gay, Peter, ed., *The Freud Reader*, NY: W.W. Norton, 1989.
Gilman, Sander L., *Freud, Race and Gender*, Princeton, NJ: Princeton University Press, 1993.
Noland, Richard W., *Sigmund Freud Revisited*, NY: Twayne, 1999.

Wright, Elizabeth, *Psychoanalytic Criticism: Theory in Practice*, London and New York: Methuen, 1984.

NORTHROP FRYE (1912–1991)

One of Canada's most successful critical exports, Northrop Frye produced visionary literary criticism in a morphological or taxonomical mode that is currently out of vogue. While morphological precursors such as Goethe and Spengler explored cultural and philosophical patterns and developments, Frye became known for his deep understanding of literature, mythological and Biblical narrative, symbol, ritual, and archetypal literary criticism. Born in Sherbrooke, Quebec, Frye came from humble origins, and as a young man he was initially torn between his love of literary study, and a desire to serve his religious beliefs; subsequently, while he gained a BA in philosophy and English from the University of Toronto, he also studied at Emmanuel College where he was ordained as a United Church minister in 1936. His initial work as a trainee pastor did not go well, and he realized that he was a fish out of water when it came to attempting to serve a remote farming community in Saskatchewan. Back at the University of Toronto, he worked as a lecturer in English at Victoria College, and gained his MA from Merton College, Oxford, in 1940; he rose rapidly through the ranks at Victoria College, becoming Professor of English in 1948, Head of Department in 1952, Principal in 1959 and Chancellor in 1978. Frye held many visiting professorships, and major international scholarships; he served as President of the MLA in 1976, one of many prestigious appointments. Even given the international nature of the literature that he studied and wrote about, and the world-wide renown that developed during his lifetime, Frye argued that his work remained essentially 'rooted in Canada and has drawn its essential characteristics from there'.[1] The publication that first brought Frye to the world's attention was his *Fearful Symmetry: A Study of William Blake* (1947); Frye called this book a 'necessary step' in the art of reading poetry and writing criticism:

> if poetic thought is inherently schematic, criticism must be so too. I began to notice that as soon as a critic confined himself to talking seriously about literature his criticism tightened up and took on a systematic, even a schematic form.[2]

In other words, what Frye found in his reading of Blake, provided him with a schema that he believed could be applied to all literature. But what exactly did he find? Unlike previous readers and readings of Blake, Frye perceived a unified corpus in Blake's poetry; applying an allegorical method immanent to the poems, Frye expands this to build a general theory of poetry.[3] In the process of elucidating Blake's 'iconography' – the myth, symbolism, images and archetypes of his visionary work – Frye discovered 'that there is such a thing as an iconography of the imagination';[4] in other words, poets draw upon a wider imaginative 'grammar'. Could Frye prove this beyond his at times difficult reading of Blake, difficult because of his methodology of interpretive paraphrase? The answer is yes, he would prove his case, in a book that changed the face of literary criticism for several decades: the *Anatomy of Criticism: Four Essays* (1957).

The overarching project of the *Anatomy of Criticism* reveals why Frye's approach is now out of favour: he attempts to account for the entire field of literary criticism in a totalizing gesture that is now read as deluded. However, it would be a mistake to regard his book as merely totalizing: rather, it presents a complex and diverse schema that maps the terrain, charts its structure, its divisions, its shared processes. Where contemporary critics may now perceive fundamental differences and divisions in literary culture, Frye perceived coherence; where contemporary notions of literary theory are often based upon a decentred network (of signs, ideologies, ethnicities, etc.), Frye argued for a centred schema. Frye's first section of his book, 'Historical Criticism: A Theory of Modes', declares that there are five modes of literature: myth, romance, high mimetic, low mimetic and irony. Historically, narrative has moved through these modes to our current time and place of irony. In the second section, 'Ethical Criticism: Theory of Symbols', Frye argues that there are four fundamental types of symbol: sign (motif), image, archetype and monad. In the third, longest, and most popular section, 'Archetypal Criticism: Theory of Myths', Frye comes into his own, developing a core theory of criticism: 'the theory of myths and *mythoi* becomes a method by which to organize literary works into an order of words, not through their history or sequence of meanings but through their larger generic forms'.[5] The narrative forms of romance, comedy, tragedy and satire/irony are examined via archetypal imagery. The final section, 'Rhetorical Criticism: Theory of Genres', brings into play the relational aspects of literature, between poet and public, the rhetorical presentation or performance of four genres: drama, *epos* ('extended poetry in meter'), fiction and lyric.[6] Why did the *Anatomy of Criticism* have such an impact upon the study of literature? Frye was advocating literature as an autonomous realm of fundamental imaginative archetypes, with vast interlocking schemas that shifted historically like geological tectonic plates; the dominant methodology of New Criticism, with its close focus on particular texts, came under challenge from this cosmic critical visionary. The original title of the work, *Structural Poetics*, changed by the publishers, is more suggestive of the contemporaneity of Frye's thought with new directions in criticism elsewhere; in other words, Frye's challenge to New Criticism, while unique, was just one of several fronts that the New Critics would have to deal with in the ensuing years. As Adamson argues: 'It is important . . . to stress the heuristic quality of Frye's exposition. Like any useful diagram or scheme, the system is there for the purposes of demonstration and insight, and is not an end in itself.'[7] In this statement lies a clue to the ongoing relevance of the *Anatomy of Criticism* several decades after its publication: rather than reducing the unique experience of a literary work to abstracted principles, the *Anatomy of Criticism* offered instead a framework via which the unique experience could not only be appreciated, but understood. In other areas of literary study, such as the newly emerging worlds of structuralism and semiotics, as well as narrative theory, literary works were similarly 'rediscovered' by larger schemas of reading.

Much of Frye's thought is self-consciously traced back to Biblical text, in part through his study of Blake, but also through his theological education and teaching. While Frye was publishing a significant series of academic books – such as his work on Shakespeare, which appeared as *A Natural Perspective: The Development of Shakespearian Comedy and Romance* (1965) and *Fools of Time: Studies in Shakespearian Tragedy* (1967), on Milton in *The Return of Eden: Five Essays on Milton's Epics* (1965), his work on Romance, in *The Secular Scripture: A Study of the Structure of Romance* (1976), and Canadian literature, published as *The Bush Garden: Essays on the Canadian Imagination* (1971) – the question of the Bible remained key. As Frye's biographer, John Ayre writes, from the late 1960s the 'Bible now became more firmly tied to . . . [Frye's] quest to reveal a symbolic universe animated by concern.'[8] The long and at times torturous path to formulate his thoughts eventually resulted in another best-selling work: *The Great Code: The Bible and Literature* (1982).

Written for a general audience, Frye's secular reading of the Bible as literature still makes many demands on the reader, not the least being his opening engagement with the philosopher Vico, and a theory of translation. Vico had posited three cyclical historical ages that he called the mythical age (the age of the gods), the heroic age (the age of the aristocracy) and the age of the people; each of these ages produces a general language (*langage*), the poetic, the heroic/noble and the vulgar. Utilizing this model, Frye posits three historical language phases which are equated with the preceding types: the hieroglyphic, the hieratic and the demotic. This is Frye's starting point, which enables him to start thinking about the Bible, itself a text that spans historical time in terms of its literary production (and of course in its presentation of Biblical time) and reception. For example, if we as contemporaries are in the demotic, descriptive phase of *langage*, how can we understand a text that was produced in the hieratic phase, with echoes and embedded memories of an earlier phase? Frye's answer involves analysis of Biblical stories, the commanding linguistic processes of the text, with metaphor occupying pride of place (metaphor is the vehicle for expressing a 'faith beyond reason' to use Frye's phrase), and typology (the 'mirroring' of Old and New Testaments). In some ways today Frye's *The Great Code* runs the danger of pleasing no one and annoying everyone: his secular approach is perfect for an audience that is in steep decline, and his separation of faith and reason (writing the book through the latter perspective), will potentially annoy just about every sect still in existence. Nonetheless, upon its publication in 1982, *The Great Code* was an instant best-seller, receiving more than one hundred and fifty review articles. Frye would complete his Biblical musings with another powerful book: *Words with Power, Being a Second Study of the Bible and Literature* (1990).

While Frye's best-known works had a considerable impact upon international critical trends, generating intense debate among his supporters and those who were not interested in the morphological or schematic approach, there are myriad other aspects of his work that resonate with scholars of Canadian literature. His contributions to the rise of Canadian literature as an academic mode of study were immense, including his ongoing reviews of Canadian poetry for the *University of Toronto Quarterly*, and his editorial work on the *Literary History of Canada* (1965), within which his own conclusion has been called by critic E.D. Blodgett 'a brilliant summa of the English-Canadian understanding of the relation of literature to history'.[9] Frye's work in Canada, on Canadian culture and literature, remained integral to his mythopoeic vision throughout his working life; scholars are still grappling with his ideas as they have impacted Canadian studies and other international perspectives.[10]

Notes

1 Northrop Frye, opening remarks in *The Bush Garden*, cited in A.C. Hamilton, *Northrop Frye: Anatomy of his Criticism*, Toronto: University of Toronto Press, 1990, p. xii.

2 Northrop Frye, *The Stubborn Structure: Essays on Criticism and Society*, p. 176, cited in A.C. Hamilton, *Northrop Frye: Anatomy of his Criticism*, p. 39.
3 Ian Balfour, *Northrop Frye*, Twayne's World Author Series, Boston, MA: Twayne, 1988, pp. 4–7.
4 Northrop Frye, *Fearful Symmetry: A Study of William Blake*, quoted in Ian Balfour, *Northrop Frye*, p. 16.
5 A.C. Hamilton, *Northrop Frye: Anatomy of his Criticism*, p. 123.
6 Ian Balfour, *Northrop Frye*, p. 44.
7 Joseph Adamson, *Northrop Frye: A Visionary Life*, Toronto: ECW Press, 2003, p. 61.
8 John Ayre, *Northrop Frye: A Biography*, p. 326.
9 E.D. Blodgett, *Five Part Invention: A History of Literary History in Canada*, Toronto: University of Toronto Press, 2003, p. 122.
10 See Jean O'Grady and Wang Ning, eds, *Northrop Frye: Eastern and Western Perspective*, Toronto: University of Toronto Press, 2003.

See also in this book

Bloom, Empson

Major works

Fearful Symmetry: A Study of William Blake (1947). Princeton, NJ: Princeton University Press.
Anatomy of Criticism: Four Essays (1957). Princeton, NJ: Princeton University Press.
Fables of Identity: Studies in Poetic Mythology (1963). New York: Harcourt, Brace and World.
T.S. Eliot (1963). Edinburgh: Oliver and Boyd.
The Well-Tempered Critic (1963). Bloomington, IN: Indiana University Press.
A Natural Perspective: The Development of Shakespearian Comedy and Romance (1965). New York: Columbia University Press.
The Return of Eden: Five Essays on Milton's Epics (1965). Toronto: University of Toronto Press.
Fools of Time: Studies in Shakespearian Tragedy (1967). Toronto: University of Toronto Press.
A Study of English Romanticism (1968). New York: Random House.
The Stubborn Structure: Essays on Criticism and Society (1970). Ithaca, NY: Cornell University Press.
The Bush Garden: Essays on the Canadian Imagination (1971). Toronto: Anansi.
The Secular Scripture: A Study of the Structure of Romance (1976). Cambridge, MA: Harvard University Press.
Spiritus Mundi: Essays on Literature, Myth, and Society (1976). Bloomington, IN: Indiana University Press.
Creation and Recreation (1980). Toronto: University of Toronto Press.
The Great Code: The Bible and Literature (1982). New York: Harcourt Brace Jovanovich.
The Myth of Deliverance: Reflections on Shakespeare's Problem Comedies (1983). Toronto: University of Toronto Press.

Words with Power, Being a Second Study of the Bible and Literature (1990). New York: Harcourt Brace Jovanovich.
The Double Vision: An Essay on the Social Context of Literary Criticism (1991). Toronto: University of Toronto Press.

Further reading

Cotrupi, Caterina Nella, *Northrop Frye and the Poetics of Process*, Toronto: University of Toronto Press, 2000.

Denham, Robert D., *Northrop Frye: A Bibliography of His Published Writings, 1931–2004*, Emory, VA: Iron Mountain, 2004.

Denham, Robert D., *Northrop Frye: Religious Visionary and Architect of the Spiritual World*, Virginia: University of Virginia Press, 2005.

Donaldson, Jeffery and Mendelson, Alan, eds, *Frye and the Word: Religious Contexts in the Writings of Northrop Frye*, Toronto: University of Toronto Press, 2003.

Ford, Russell, *Northrop Frye on Myth: An Introduction*, New York: Garland, 1988.

Halmi, Nicholas, 'Northrop Frye's *Fearful Symmetry*', *Essays in Criticism*, 55.2 (2005): 159–172.

Perkin, J. Russell, 'Northrop Frye and Matthew Arnold', *University of Toronto Quarterly*, 74.3 (2005): 793–815.

HANS-GEORG GADAMER (1900–2003)

The dream of recovering the *complete* or total meaning of a literary text, by re-imagining the author's intentions, comes to an end with the work of Hans-Georg Gadamer; instead of this hermeneutic or interpretive circle (circling back from the text to the author, and back again, closing off, or finishing the job of interpretation), Gadamer's hermeneutical approach involves understanding the historical situations of text and reader, and the ways in which these interact to create a temporarily shared meaning. The mystical divination of a text is thus replaced by Heidegger's notion that the hermeneutical circle is actually 'part of the structure of understanding itself'.[1] Gadamer's insights into a hermeneutics for the twentieth century thus draw not only from some of the great phenomenological thinkers such as Husserl and Heidegger, but also partake of the paradigm shift of the observer being part of the equation when it comes to measuring or assessing the observed, a shift that many thinkers argue paved the way for postmodernism. Gadamer was born in Marburg, Germany and was educated at Breslau University where he studied art and music history, German literature and neo-Kantian philosophy, receiving his doctorate for a thesis on Plato in 1922. An early publication called 'On the Idea of System in Philosophy' (1924) reveals the influence of Martin Heidegger, with whom Gadamer had studied the previous year; Gadamer described the experience of first reading Heidegger as affecting him 'like an electric shock' and his lectures as revealing 'the energy of a revolutionary thinker'.[2] Heidegger continued to impact upon Gadamer throughout his early years as an academic, and this can be seen in his first book, a phenomenological reading of Plato published in 1931. By that time Gadamer had passed his higher doctorate, called a *habilitation* (1928) and was lecturing at Marburg. During the early Nazi period, through which he lived, Gadamer turned his attentions to the study of mathematics, and published a book on Johann Gottfried Herder (1942). In 1937 Gadamer was promoted to the position of professor, followed by a professorship in classical philology at Halle, and then a professorship at Leipzig (1938–1947), where he became the rector. Gadamer returned to scholarship with a move to Frankfurt (1947–1949), being awarded in 1949 Karl Jaspers' Chair at Heidelberg (1949–1968). It was during this period that Gadamer produced his major work *Wahrheit und Methode: Grundzüge einer philosophischen Hermeneutik* (1960) translated in 1975 (without the important subtitle) as *Truth and Method*.

How is the reader new to Gadamer going to approach the more than five hundred pages of critical and philosophical analysis of his *Truth and Method*? One of the leading commentators on Gadamer (and hermeneutics), Richard E. Palmer, suggests that a list of twenty key terms from *Truth and Method* are essential for understanding the relevance of Gadamer's approach. Taking just five of these terms – understanding, play, event, experience and conversation[3] – one can at least get a sense of the dynamic process that Gadamer advocates in releasing the reader from the traditional closed hermeneutic circle where a total or complete truth is to be recreated and recovered. For Gadamer, interpretation is fundamentally dialogic: the metaphor of an ongoing conversation is therefore extremely important. This dialogue or conversation also implies an openness to the text's 'alterity' or otherness. How does the interpreter achieve this? Not through neutrality or effacing one's own identity, but through foregrounding what one brings to the text, those attitudes that Heidegger, in section forty-five of *Being and Time* calls the 'fore-having', 'fore-sight' and 'fore-conception' of interpretation. In other words, the recognition of the 'prejudice' that readers bring to the text, is also a way of clearing a space to recognize the otherness of the text, or, as Gadamer puts it, allowing the text to 'assert its own truth'.[4] The reader, however, is not an entirely autonomous agent: she is situated historically, which means that her identity has been formed in part by the tradition, and she carries on, in participation and understanding, to contribute to the production of the tradition. Gadamer thus argues that understanding is not something miraculous, but a 'sharing in a common meaning' between text and reader, tradition and interpreter.[5] Where traditional hermeneutics regarded the interpretive act as a recovery of a text's full meaning (an act of closure), Gadamer argues that the correct stance is one of a disrupted 'fore-conception of completeness' where we *assume* that a text is 'full' or complete in its meaning, but reality (the encounter with the object) reveals that this assumption is incorrect and the text is *unintelligible*. Gadamer distinguishes here between the attempt to understand the content of a text versus the attempt to recover another's meaning embodied via the writing of a text. While there is a bond between the interpreter and the text as transmitted by tradition, it is not necessarily a mystical union between the two; rather, Gadamer suggests that hermeneutics is affected by the polarity of 'familiarity and strangeness'. It is the play between the two, the crossing 'between' belonging and alienation, that is the space of hermeneutics. Temporal distance here is not a problem to be overcome, but a constitutive factor. In other words, the traditional hermeneutic approach whereby the past authorial position needed to be *reproduced*, crossing the vast gulf of time (transposing 'ourselves into the spirit of the age'),[6] is replaced by a notion of interpretive *production*, achieved through temporal distance, and the falling away of the cares and concerns of 'the present' in relation to the object in question. Poststructuralist theorists are deeply suspicious of this move, because it suggests that there is an underlying authenticity or universality that such hermeneutic inquiry uncovers, for example, that Shakespeare's plays are expressive of aesthetic genius regardless of the age in which they are read or performed. In fact, the hermeneutics being described here would have to argue that it is *only* across time that such a recognition could occur, not in the sense of 'historicism' (the object is now isolated and stable because of the passing of time) but in the sense of 'historicity' (the foregrounding of the reader's situated prejudices). The reader thus has an awareness of her hermeneutical situation, a limited standpoint which has a finite *horizon*, yet, and this is essential, Gadamer argues that human beings are never limited by a single horizon: horizons shift and change as life itself moves on. Further, understanding is the fusion of historical and present horizons, with the understanding that this is not a permanent arrival at truth. Again, we can see how this notion of understanding prefigures postmodernism, because here 'the knower's present situation loses its status as a privileged position and becomes instead a fluid and relative moment'.[7]

As Palmer notes, since the publication of *Truth and Method*, everything in Gadamer's life 'has been a series of articulations, explanations, further developments, even changes, in this masterwork'.[8] Published in 1960 at the age of sixty, Gadamer spent the next four decades exploring the implications of his work to an international audience. Why was there such an audience for Gadamer when high theory was taking over the academy, even given his importance for followers of a more specialist phenomenological hermeneutics? The clue lies in the third section of *Truth and Method*, titled 'The ontological shift of hermeneutics guided by language'. As the academy went through the linguistic turn, there was Gadamer's outstanding critique of philosophy and interpretation making an analogous move:

> only in the third part of Gadamer's major work does it become clear that the deconstruction of all privileged positions is a bold and unconditioned move to language. Language is not a 'tool' that the privileged consciousness may use to 'express' its positions. It is rather a phenomenon that speaks us before we speak it, and this means that we can never step outside of it and stand over against it.[9]

It is worth considering how the horizon of poststructuralism here fuses with that of Gadamer's hermeneutics.

Notes

1 John M. Connolly, 'Gadamer and the Author's Authority: a Language-Game Approach', *The Journal of Aesthetics and Art Criticism*, 44.3 (Spring 1986): 271–277; p. 271.
2 Hans-Georg Gadamer, *Philosophical Apprenticeships* (1985), trans. Robert R. Sullivan, Cambridge, MA and London: MIT Press, pp. 46–47 and p. 48.
3 Richard E. Palmer, 'The Relevance of Gadamer's Philosophical Hermeneutics to Thirty-Six Topics or Fields of Human Activity.' A lecture delivered at the Department of Philosophy Southern Illinois University at Carbondale, 1 April 1999. www.mac.edu/faculty/richard-palmer/relevance.html.
4 Hans-Georg Gadamer, *Truth and Method*, second, revised edition, trans. Joel Weinsheimer and Donald G. Marshall, London and New York: Continuum, 2004, p. 272.
5 Ibid., pp. 192–193.
6 Ibid., p. 297.
7 David E. Linge, 'Editor's Introduction' to Hans-Georg Gadamer, *Philosophical Hermeneutics*, trans. David E. Linge, Berkeley, CA: University of California Press, 1976, p. xix.
8 Richard E. Palmer, 'The Relevance of Gadamer's Philosophical Hermeneutics to Thirty-Six Topics or Fields of Human Activity.' A Lecture

Delivered at the Department of Philosophy Southern Illinois University at Carbondale, 1 April 1999. www.mac.edu/faculty/richardpalmer/relevance.html.
9 Robert R. Sullivan, 'Translator's Introduction' to Hans-Georg Gadamer, *Philosophical Apprenticeships*, Cambridge, MA and London: MIT Press, 1985, p. xvii.

See also in this book

Ricoeur

Major works

Truth and Method (1960). Trans. revised by Joel Weinsheimer and Donald G. Marshall, Second Revised Edition, London and New York: Continuum, 2004.
Hegel's Dialectic: Five Hermeneutical Studies (1976). New Haven, CT: Yale University Press.
Philosophical Hermeneutics (1976). Berkeley, CA: University of California Press.
Dialogue and Dialectic: Eight Hermeneutical Studies on Plato (1980). New Haven, CT: Yale University Press.
Heidegger Memorial Lectures (with Hans Georg, Werner Marx, Steven W. Davis and Carl Friedrich Weizsäcker, 1982). Pittsburgh, PA: Duquesne University Press.
Philosophical Apprenticeships, Studies in Contemporary German Social Thought (1985). Cambridge, MA: MIT Press.
The Idea of the Good in Platonic-Aristotelian Philosophy (1986). New Haven, CT: Yale University Press.
The Relevance of the Beautiful and Other Essays (with Robert Bernasconi, 1986). Cambridge: Cambridge University Press.

Further reading

Code, Lorraine, ed., *Feminist Interpretations of Hans-Georg Gadamer*, University Park, PA: Pennsylvania State University Press: 2003.
Dostal, Robert J., ed., *The Cambridge Companion to Gadamer* (Cambridge Companions to Philosophy), Cambridge: Cambridge University Press, 2002.
Krajewski, Bruce, ed., *Gadamer's Repercussions: Reconsidering Philosophical Hermeneutics*, Berkeley, CA: University of California Press, 2003.
Levi, Neil, 'The Subject of History: Gadamer, Lacoue-Labarthe, and Lyotard', *Textual Practice*, 5.1 (1991): 40–54.
Malpas, Jeff, Arnswald, Ulrich and Kertscher, Jens, eds, *Gadamer's Century: Essays in Honor of Hans-Georg Gadamer*, Cambridge, MA: MIT Press, 2002.

HENRY LOUIS GATES, JR (1950–)

Advocating an end to the Eurocentric and North American bias in literary criticism and the study of literary canons, Henry Louis Gates, Jr offers a visionary alternative that draws upon traditional Afro–American aesthetic forms and what he evocatively calls 'black structures of meaning'.[1] The historical range of Gates' criticism is necessarily immense, reinscribing as he does black authors and signifying structures into the orthodox narratives of the Enlightenment, modernity and the contemporary, covering at the very least the two centuries that, as he writes in the preface to *The Norton Anthology of African American Literature* (1997) 'separate the publication of Phillis Wheatley's curious book of poems and Toni Morrison's reception of the Nobel Prize for literature in 1993'.[2] Born in Keyser, West Virginia, Gates studied for his BA in history at Yale University (1973) and his MA and Ph.D. at Clare College, University of Cambridge, awarded in 1979. At Cambridge Gates met and was mentored by Wole Soyinka, the leading Nigerian author and Nobel laureate, who steered Gates in the direction of literary critical studies. Gates would later write admiringly of Soyinka that his 'vast corpus of works is perhaps the most sustained and challenging in the African canon'.[3] After completing his Ph.D., Gates taught at Yale, where he also received a major five-year grant from the MacArthur Foundation that enabled him to move ahead with his Black Periodical Literature Project, one that aimed to recover nineteenth-century Afro-American writings from the obscurity of periodical publication. This project received an immense boost with Gates' rediscovery and republication of the first novel by an Afro-American woman, *Our Nig* (1859), by Harriet E. Wilson (1828?-1863?). Gates was awarded the W.E.B. Du Bois Professorship of Literature which was created for him at Cornell University in 1988, and the John Spencer Bassett Professorship of English and Literature at Duke University in 1990. The following year Gates was awarded the W.E.B. Du Bois Professorship of the Humanities, at Harvard University, where he also became the Chair of Afro-American Studies, and Director of the W.E.B. Du Bois Institute for Afro-American Research. Other awards and prizes are almost too numerous to list, ranging from the Yale Afro-American Cultural Centre Faculty Prize (1983), the Zora Neale Hurston Society Award for Cultural Scholarship (1986), the African American Students Faculty Award (1993), and in 1997 being recognized by *Time* magazine for being one of the '25 most influential Americans'.

Gates' first decade of criticism is collected in his *Figures in Black: Words, Signs, and the 'Racial' Self* (1987), which also includes the important 'introduction' to *Our Nig*, where Gates states that 'it is difficult to imagine how such a seminal contribution to black letters could have been ignored or lost'.[4] In many respects, Gates' major contribution to literary criticism is an ongoing reply to the implied frustration in this statement; the effacement and ignoring of Harriet E. Wilson's hybrid text – part fiction, autobiography and exposé[5] – as well as the wider black canon, demands a theory of reading that Gates develops not only in *Figures in Black* but also his groundbreaking work *The Signifying Monkey: A Theory of African-American Literary Criticism* (1988). Gates calls *Figures in Black* 'a book of hypothesis and experimentation'.[6] What does he mean by this? In an autobiographical sketch that opens the introduction to the book, Gates discusses his shift at Cambridge – from the study of history to the study of literature – as a dialogue between Afro-American literature and literary theory, where the latter was never localized in one overarching theoretical approach functioning as 'divine revelation', to use Gates' parodic phrase, but rather is regarded as a prism that can be looked through and turned to reveal different colours (or meanings in texts). The image of the prism serves to explain how maintaining a critical distance from theoretical movements led Gates to become suspicious of Eurocentric and North American theory per se: 'For the black critic, the languages of contemporary criticism are imaginative constructs or white fictions to be analyzed and explicated just as any other literary text.'[7] Gates' 'experiment' then, is precisely in taking different theoretical approaches to a range of Afro-American authors, bearing in mind his assertion that the Eurocentric canon from which theoretical discourses are derived, has created black subjects as 'signs of absence'.[8] For Gates, the 'return of the repressed' in this entire process occurs with close readings of Afro-American literature: the languages or deep structures of the 'black text' are not to be merely explicated by a largely Euro-American discourse, but, if fully acknowledged, will instead transform Euro-American literary criticism itself. The dialogue becomes dialectic, where the hegemonic white dis-course is eventually sublated by the black tradition. Gates regards this as a process of enrichment:

> by learning to read a black text within a black formal cultural matrix and explicating it with the principles of criticism at work in both the Euro-American and the African-American traditions, I believe that we critics can identify and produce richer structures of meaning than are possible otherwise.[9]

Literary theory thus becomes transformed by the 'black idiom' found in noncanonical literature, and even though Gates thinks of his initial approach as one with uneven results, he follows this 'experiment' with a highly structured and powerful mode of Afro-American theory in *The Signifying Monkey*.

The black vernacular tradition, asserts Gates in the opening pages of *The Signifying Monkey*, is one that has gone from strength to strength. Inscribed 'within' the black vernacular tradition is, for Gates, a theory of criticism or reading that he shows 'informs the shape of the Afro-American literary tradition'.[10] This tradition does not become subsumed by Euro-American theory: instead, it *confounds* high theory. Gates utilizes two key trickster figures in his book – Esu-Elegbara and the Signifying Monkey – who embody a self-reflexive awareness, and consciously articulate, formal language or black rhetorical tropes. Gates' wider argument is that the two seemingly disparate trickster figures – one from the Yoruba cultures and one from Afro-American cultures – are actually not just historically related, but expressive of an underlying 'unified phenomenon': 'Together the two tricksters articulate the black tradition's theory of its literature.'[11] But how does 'the vernacular' relate to 'the formal'? Gates explains that these two appear to create a parallel 'discursive' universe, but on closer examination, the vernacular actually creates the conditions of possibility for the formal. In other words, if Gates wants to seek an authentic indigenous black literary criticism, the vernacular is the place to find it, with the important reminder that the black vernacular is outside of the Euro-American tradition. Even where Afro-American authors are working with the Euro-American tradition, then, for Gates this means that they always create new texts with a difference: 'a compelling sense of difference based on the black vernacular.'[12] The reworking of the Western tradition from a black perspective creates double-voiced texts (Gates gives the examples of Ralph Ellison and Ishmael Reed); such texts create a simultaneity of vision, and a two-toned history. For Gates, the 'unifying metaphor' reflecting this schema is the trope of the 'Talking Book' which first appeared in James Gronniosaw's slave narrative of 1770.[13] From this unifying metaphor, Gates derives four double-voiced textual relations: (1) Tropological Revision; (2) The Speakerly Text; (3) Talking Texts; and (4) Rewriting the Speakerly. Tropological Revision is repetition with a difference, an 'ur-trope' for Gates; The Speakerly Text creates a new perspective through the use of free indirect discourse and the emergence of a 'speaking black voice in writing'; Talking Texts describes a black form of intertextuality; and Rewriting the Speakerly denotes instances where the creation of a virtual black dialect is registered and revised through a direct production of black dialect (Gates uses the example of Walker producing texts that realize the virtual idiom in Hurston). Gates precedes his extended literary analyses in *The Signifying Monkey* with the tropology of Signifyin(g), the 'trope of tropes' which is both a familiar rhetorical practice for those who use the black American vernacular, and a powerful new way of thinking about double-voiced texts (oral *and* written) and textual revision. Gates' contributions to a more nuanced understanding of Afro-American aesthetics and criticism are immense, at the levels of interpretation *and* editorial intervention. The return to African and Afro-American discourses in *The Signifying Monkey* is one in a wider series of interventions in literary history, including important textual and pedagogical projects such as the *Oxford-Schomburg Library of Nineteenth Century Black Women Writers* (1991), the co-edited *Norton Anthology of African American Literature* (1996) and the co-edited *Encarta Africana* (CD-ROM, 1999) published in book form as *Africana: The Encyclopedia of the African and African American Experience* (1999). These, and other extensive projects and publications, have contributed not just to the study of black aesthetics, but also to that of black identity and subjectivity.

Notes

1 Henry Louis Gates, Jr, *The Signifying Monkey: A Theory of African-American Literary Criticism*, Oxford and New York: Oxford University Press, 1989, p. xiv.
2 Henry Louis Gates, Jr and Nellie Y. McKay, general editors, *The Norton Anthology of African American Literature*, London and New York: W.W. Norton, 1997, p. xxxiii.
3 Henry Louis Gates, Jr, ed., *Black Literature & Literary Theory*, London and New York: Routledge, 1990, p. 4.
4 Henry Louis Gates, Jr, *Figures in Black: Words, Signs, and the 'Racial' Self*, Oxford and New York: Oxford University Press, 1987, p. 129.
5 Henry Louis Gates, Jr and Nellie Y. McKay, eds, *The Norton Anthology of African American Literature*, p. 439.
6 Henry Louis Gates, Jr, *Figures in Black: Words, Signs, and the 'Racial' Self*, p. xviii.
7 Ibid.
8 Ibid.
9 Ibid., p. xxi.
10 Henry Louis Gates, Jr, *The Signifying Monkey: A Theory of African-American Literary Criticism*, p. xiv.
11 Ibid., p. xxi.
12 Ibid., p. xxii.
13 Ibid., p. xxv.

See also in this book

Baker

Major works

Wole Soyinka: A Bibliography of Primary and Secondary Sources (co-ed., with James Gibbs and Ketu H. Katrak; 1986). Westport, CT: Greenwood Press.

The Classic Slave Narratives (ed., 1987). New York: New American Library.
Figures in Black: Words, Signs, and the 'Racial' Self (1987). Oxford and New York: Oxford University Press.
The Signifying Monkey: A Theory of African-American Literary Criticism (1989). Oxford and New York: Oxford University Press.
Black Literature & Literary Theory (ed., 1990). London and New York: Routledge.
Reading Black, Reading Feminist: A Critical Anthology (ed., 1990). New York: Meridian Books.
Oxford-Schomburg Library of Nineteenth Century Black Women Writers (1991). Oxford and New York: Oxford University Press.
Bearing Witness: Selections from African-American Autobiography in the Twentieth Century (ed., 1991). New York: Pantheon Books.
Black Biography, 1790–1950: A Cumulative Index (co-ed., with Randall K. Burkett and Nancy Hall Burkett, 1991). Alexandria: Chadwyck-Healey, three volumes.
Loose Canons: Notes on the Culture Wars (1992). New York: Oxford University Press.
Colored People: A Memoir (1994). New York: Knopf.
Speaking of Race, Speaking of Sex: Hate Speech, Civil Rights, and Civil Liberties (ed., et al. 1994). New York: New York University Press.
Identities (co-ed., with Kwame A. Appiah, 1995). Chicago, IL: University of Chicago Press.
The Future of the Race (with Cornel West, 1996). New York: Knopf.
The Norton Anthology of African American Literature (general editors Gates and Nellie Y. McKay, 1997). New York: W.W. Norton.
Thirteen Ways of Looking at a Black Man (1997). New York: Random House.
The Dictionary of Global Culture (co-ed., with Kwame A. Appiah, 1997). New York: Knopf.
Africana: The Encyclopedia of the African and African American Experience (1999). Basic Civitas Books.
Encarta Africana (CD-ROM, 1999). Microsoft.

Further reading

Bucknall, Brad, 'Henry Louis Gates, Jr. and the Theory of "Signifyin(g)"', *Ariel*, 21.1 (1990): 65–84.
Johnson, Thomas C., 'Interview with Henry Louis Gates, Jr.', *Worcester Review*, 19.1–2 (1998): 61–67.
Joyce, Joyce A. '"Who the Cap Fit": Unconsciousness and Unconscionableness in the Criticism of Houston A. Baker, Jr., and Henry Louis Gates, Jr.', in Winston Napier, ed., *African American Literary Theory: A Reader*, New York: New York University Press, 2000; pp. 319–330.
Kjelle, Marylou Morano, *Henry Louis Gates, Jr.*, New York: Chelsea House Publications, 2003.
Naden, Corinne J. and Rose Blue, *Henry Louis Gates Jr.*, Chicago, IL: Raintree, 2005.
Osinubi, Viktor, 'African American Writers and the Use of Dialect in Literature: The Foregrounding of Ethnicity', *Journal of Commonwealth and Postcolonial Studies*, 4.1 (1996): 65–77.

Steele, Meili, 'Language and African-American Culture: The Need for Meta-Philosophical Reflection', *Philosophy Today*, 40.1–4 (1996): 179–187.

Ward, Jerry W. Jr, 'Interview with Henry Louis Gates, Jr.', *New Literary History*, 22.4 (1991): 927–935.

GÉRARD GENETTE (1930–)

Genette's readings of Marcel Proust's *Remembrance of Things Past* have long been recognized as the touchstone of his entire theoretical enterprise: the brilliance of these readings epitomizes a lifetime spent reading, mapping and categorizing narrative fiction in an illuminating and rewarding way. In the hands of lesser practitioners systematic, structural analysis can turn a text into the driest of basic or architectonic elements; Genette does the opposite, elucidating complex spatial and temporal patterns produced by narrative, observing interesting functions and categories that may otherwise go unnoticed. His best-known work in English, *Narrative Discourse*, generated an entire field of narrative theory (called *narratology*, a term coined by Tzvetan Todorov in 1969),[1] one that continues to be immensely useful for literary and media studies. The origins of narrative theory can be traced on virtually every page of *Narrative Discourse*: for example, discussing the ways in which narrative disengages 'its arrangement from all dependence' on chronological sequence,[2] Genette separates the syntagmatic from the temporal order in *Remembrance of Things Past*, and reveals a textual grouping that 'hurried readers' might otherwise miss, one bound together by spatial proximity, climatic identity and thematic kinship; while the conclusion is that narrative has a capacity for 'temporal autonomy', Genette, like Roland Barthes, also warns against 'drawing definitive conclusions' from his reading.[3] The discourse of structuralism and semiotics pervades Genette's approach, but he rarely, if ever, reduces a text in the process of analysing it (he calls textual analysis a 'radioscopic penetration');[4] Genette's debt – and contribution to – poststructuralism is thus observable. The structuralist-poststructuralist connections in Genette's work can be traced to his peer-group; educated at the École Normale Supérieure in Paris, Genette went on to teach at various *lycées*, and then lectured at the Sorbonne (1963–1967); in 1967 he was awarded the post of Director of Studies in poetics and aesthetics at the École des Hautes Études en Sciences Sociales. In 1970, Genette, with Tzvetan Todorov, Hélène Cixous and J.-P. Richard founded the journal and literary collection *Poétique* at Editions du Seuil; while these editors were 'resistant' to the new theoretical works by contemporaries such as Sollers and

Kristeva, they did support the work of Derrida, Lacoue-Labarthe, and Nancy,[5] and in his essay 'Principles of Pure Criticism' Genette clearly expresses a debt to Derrida's work on 'grammatology'.[6]

Genette's essays written during the 1960s were initially published in leading critical journals in France, such as *Critique* and *Tel Quel*; significant articles by Genette published in *Tel Quel* include those on structuralist poetics (1961), Robbe-Grillet (1962), Mallarmé (1962), Proust 'Palimpsest' (1963), and Flaubert (1963). The collection and publication of eighteen of Genette's essays in book form was a major event in the field of narratology, starting with *Figures I* in 1966, followed by *Figures II* in 1969 and *Figures III* in 1972 (translated into English as *Narrative Discourse*, 1980). *Figures I* and *II* are in many respects Genette's structuralist mapping of the narratological domain. In his 'Structuralism and Literary Criticism' (1964) he begins with Claude Lévi-Strauss's concept of 'bricolage' – or, the act of utilizing the tools at hand – to argue that criticism functions by using 'the same materials – writing – as the works with which it is concerned';[7] the significance of this observation is that criticism has the capacity not just to be a metalanguage (a language higher than the object that it comments upon) but also a metaliterature – that is, a form of writing that no longer separates the critical and the creative. The dissolving of the space between literary-object and critical-metalanguage leads to what Roland Barthes would call in 1968 'the death of the author' and the concomitant birth of the writer. For Genette, this is a moment of celebration, a recognition that structuralist criticism could be a form of 'critical poetry', or, a 'poetry of *bricolage*'.[8] In the essay 'Figures' he sketches out one way of achieving such a mode of writing, defining a figure not in the narrow sense of tropes or figures-of-speech, but more amorphously as the limits of the space existing between 'real' (or poetic/literary) language and 'virtual' language (the same utterance translated into everyday speech). Rather than starting with a figure as a presence in the conventional sense of a particular trope, by calling figures a 'gap' that exists in language-use, Genette makes the poststructuralist move to a theory of absence and dispersal. This switch from a positive to a networked, differential theory of figures is also apparent in the switch from a positive to a 'negative' notion of narrative; in the essay 'Frontiers of Narrative' Genette rejects the conventional approach of narrative as something that is a natural, sequential self-telling in favour of lessons learnt from modernity, that narrative questions, disturbs and contests the very conditions of its own possibility. What this means is that the critic needs to work at the 'negative limits of narrative'[9] examining and deconstructing the binary oppositions that constitute it: diegesis and mimesis; narration and description; and narrative and discourse. The popularity and influence of *Narrative Discourse* means that the deconstructive brilliance of *Figures I* and *II* is sometimes overlooked; in 'Frontiers of Narrative' the diegesis/mimesis opposition is first reversed, with Genette arguing that so-called dramatic mimesis is actually a production or constitutive rather than being a secondary representation, and that furthermore, such 'poetic fiction' is thus not a simulacrum, but a production via language. Narrative creates what Genette calls 'the verbal equivalent of non-verbal events' or, representation.[10] This leads him to the second deconstructive move, going beyond the first reversal, to argue that mimesis 'is' diegesis. Similarly, instead of holding in strict opposition description and narration, Genette argues that description is subsumed into 'the general economy of narrative',[11] whereas Émile Benveniste's opposition of narrative and discourse cannot be maintained, as close analysis reveals the way in which the two interpenetrate and contaminate one another.

Awareness of this deconstructive approach to narrative prepares the reader for *Figures III*, particularly the essay 'Discours du récit' translated into English as *Narrative Discourse* in 1980, almost a decade after its first publication. While *Narrative Discourse* undoubtedly provides the conceptual framework for the ensuing narratological field, it also continues to deconstruct common perceptions concerning narrative per se, by focusing on ambiguity and narrative as a relational discourse, i.e. the relationships between narrative (the text) and story (the content or events), narrative and narrating (the mode or producing of the story), and story and narrating. Genette's classificatory system, drawing upon Todorov, is broken down into five main narratological aspects: order, duration, frequency, mood and voice. Order deals with comparisons between the order of events as narrated on the page, and the order of succession these same events have in the story-world; duration is the relationship between the passing of time and the amount of text devoted to it; frequency is the number of times an event is narrated; mood, which used to be called point-of-view, is the regulation of narrative information; and voice is the type of narrator (including his or her positioning inside or outside of the story-world). Each of these categories breaks down into sub-categories, examples, and problems, elucidated or at the very least systematically sketched-out via examples from Proust, giving the critic a wealth of tools to work with. Order breaks down into its constituent anachronies (temporal disruptions), such as analepsis (flashback) and prolepsis (flashforwards); duration reveals key changes in speed, called acceleration and deceleration; frequency has a number of sub-sets that all deal with different modes of iteration, converted into formulae, such as 'narrating n times what happened once' or 'nN/1S'; mood deals with distance and different types of discourse; and voice is situated via narrative levels, such as 'intradiegetic' (inside the story-world) or extradiegetic (outside the story-world). Narratology is a powerful tool not just for analysing literary texts, but also other media. In exploring the relationships between literature and film, narratological tools enable critics such as Jakob Lothe to move away from a hierarchy of media, arguing for example that 'as filmic discourse, the beginning of [the film text] *Apocalypse Now* is as complex as that of *Heart of Darkness* [one of its literary 'source' texts]'.[12] Narratology has thus played a key part in the study of popular culture and postmodern multimedia texts.

Genette's next major study – *Mimologiques: Voyage en Cratylie* (1976) – was once his least-known work in the English-speaking world, until translated by Thaïs E. Morgan in 1994 as *Mimologics*.[13] As Morgan summarizes, this massive study explores a variety of responses to the basic question: 'Do the sounds, shapes, and patterns of language imitate the world?.' Even Saussure, who argued that the sign is arbitrary, explored mimologics, the relation between word and thing, in his work on anagrams and in his discussion of onomatopoeia in his *Course in General Linguistics* (Genette calls Saussure's approach a 'graphic mimologics'). The tension between these two overarching and competing versions of sign-systems in Saussure (with the arbitrary sign eventually winning the debate), can also be seen in the overarching positions in *Mimologics* between Plato's Cratylus (perceiving a natural connection between word and thing) and Hermogenes (perceiving an arbitrary connection). A key component in this study is the myriad origin-of-language philosophers, most of whom have anchored their ideas in a theory of 'natural' or mimetic linkage between word and world. Genette followed *Mimologics* with an ambitious, interconnected study of what he calls transtextuality, that is to say, the 'transcendence' or relationships between texts, explored in three volumes: *Introduction à l'architexte* (1979), *Palimpsests* (1982) and *Seuils* (1987). *The Architext* (as the 1992 translation was called) is written like a detective story, where the 'crime' in question is the mis-attribution to Aristotle by countless critics, of the generic division 'drama, epic, lyric'. Why does this matter? Genette reveals that such a poetics derives from Romantic origins, that poetics thus has a ertain historicity, and that genre itself functions by merging 'the phenomena – among others – of nature and of culture'.[14] Examining the persistence of generic divisions, Genette discovers that their reach is projected backwards and forwards beyond the Romantic era, giving such a poetics a certain inviolable quality, whereas his own more radical notion of the architext is that of temporary relations or hyperlinks between texts, which may eventually be dissolved as some other relationship is formed. Exploring this textual transcendence further in *Palimpsests* and *Paratexts* (the 1997 translation of *Seuils*), Genette develops a theory of the hypertext, which grafts itself onto or overwrites the preceding 'hypotext' – a universal literary procedure, but one which is more prevalent in certain novels, for example – and that of the paratext, the threshold or border zone of a text, i.e. that which surrounds a text yet is also its condition of possibility in the world. Examples include 'titles and subtitles, pseudonyms, forewords, dedications, epigraphs, prefaces, intertitles, notes, epilogues, and afterwords'.[15] While the theories of transtextuality put forward by Genette have a system-building quality, an aesthetic turn is apparent in his more recent work, including the narratological essays published as *Fiction et diction* (1991), which explore the aesthetic function that creates or defines literariness. The two-part study *L'oeuvre de l'art* (1994) and *The Aesthetic Relation* (1999), draws upon Nelson Goodman's opposition of autographic and allographic works of art, where the former is regarded as singular and authentic, the latter a work that functions in the realm of the copy, and repetition. This 'turn' to aesthetics may be more accurately conceived of as a foregrounding of concerns that are present in Genette's earliest works, concerns that consistently counter narratological system-building with an openness to contradiction, ambiguity and that which is currently unwritten.

Notes

1 Gérard Genette, *Narrative Discourse Revisited*, trans. Jane E. Lewin, Ithaca, NY: Cornell University Press, 1988, p. 7.
2 Gérard Genette, *Narrative Discourse*, trans. Jane E. Lewin, Oxford: Basil Blackwell, 1980, p. 84.
3 Ibid., p. 85.
4 Gérard Genette, 'Structuralism and Literary Criticism', in *Figures of Literary Discourse*, trans. Alan Sheridan, NY: Columbia University Press, 1982, pp. 3–25; p. 13.
5 See Patrick Ffrench, *The Time of Theory: A History of* Tel Quel (1960–1983), pp. 164–165, footnote 193.
6 Gérard Genette, 'Principles of Pure Criticism', in *Figures of Literary Discourse*, pp. 61–74; p. 69. For a discussion concerning Genette and Derrida, see Geoff Bennington, 'Genette and Deconstruction', *The Oxford Literary Review*, 4.2 (1980): 86.
7 Gérard Genette, *Figures of Literary Discourse*, trans. Alan Sheridan, New York: Columbia University Press, 1982, p. 3.

8 Ibid., p. 6.
9 Ibid., p. 128.
10 Ibid., p. 132.
11 Ibid., p. 134.
12 Jakob Lothe, *Narrative in Fiction and Film: An Introduction*, Oxford: Oxford University Press, 2000, p. 184.
13 See Gerald Prince's foreword to *Mimologics*, trans. Thaïs E. Morgan, Lincoln, NE and London: University of Nebraska Press, 1994.
14 Gérard Genette, *The Architext: An Introduction*, trans. Jane E. Lewin, Berkeley, CA: University of California Press, 1992, p. 69.
15 See Richard Macksey's foreword to *Paratexts: Thresholds of Interpretation*, trans. Jane E. Lewin, Cambridge: Cambridge University Press, 1997, p. xviii.

See also in this book

Booth

Major works

Figures I (1966). Paris: Editions Seuil.
Figures II (1969). Paris: Editions Seuil.
Figures III (1972). Paris: Editions Seuil.
Mimologics (1976). Trans. Thaïs E. Morgan, Lincoln, NE and London: University of Nebraska Press, 1994.
The Architext: An Introduction (1979). Trans. Jane E. Lewin, Berkeley, CA: University of California Press, 1992.
Narrative Discourse (1980). Translation of 'Discours du récit' from *Figures III*, trans. Jane E. Lewin, Oxford: Basil Blackwell.
Figures of Literary Discourse (1982). Translations of selections from *Figures I* and *Figures II*, trans. Alan Sheridan, New York: Columbia University Press.
Palimpsests: Literature in the Second Degree (1982). Trans. Channa Newman and Claude Doubinsky, Lincoln, NE and London: University of Nebraska Press, 1997.
Narrative Discourse Revisited (1983). Trans. Jane E. Lewin, Ithaca, NY: Cornell University Press, 1988.
Paratexts: Thresholds of Interpretation (1987). Trans. Jane E. Lewin, Cambridge: Cambridge University Press, 1997.
Fiction & Diction (1991). Trans. Catherine Porter, Ithaca, NY and London: Cornell University Press, 1993.
The Work of Art: Immanence and Transcendence (1994). Trans. G.M. Goshgarian, Ithaca, NY and London: Cornell University Press, 1997.
The Aesthetic Relation (1999). Trans. G.M. Goshgarian, Ithaca, NY and London: Cornell University Press.

Further reading

Black, David Alan, 'Genette and Film: Narrative Level in Fiction Cinema', *Wide Angle*, 8.3–4 (1986): 19–26.
Diengott, Nilli, 'Narration and Focalization: The Implications for the Issue of Reliability in Narrative', *Journal of Literary Semantics*, 24.1 (1995): 42–49.

Lothe, Jakob, *Narrative in Fiction and Film: An Introduction*, Oxford: Oxford University Press, 2000.

Nelles, William, 'Getting Focalization into Focus', *Poetics Today*, 11.2 (1990): 365–382.

Rimmon-Kenan, Shlomith, *Narrative Fiction: Contemporary Poetics*, London and New York: Methuen, 1983.

Shen, Dan, 'Narrative, Reality, and Narrator as Construct: Reflections on Genette's "Narrating"', *Narrative*, 9.2 (2001): 123–129.

SANDRA MORTOLA GILBERT (1936–)
AND SUSAN DAVID GUBAR (1944–)

Collaborative research has played an important part in the development of feminist literary theory, and 'Gilbert and Gubar' as they are jointly known have played a major part in the development and legitimization of such collaboration. Literary critic Lorraine York notes how '"Gilbert and Gubar" has become a familiar campus literary shorthand' and furthermore, their co-edited *Norton Anthology of Women's Literature* (1985) and other significant authored works have all 'gained canonical status'.[1] How did this collaborative research come about, and why did it lead to such groundbreaking criticism? As Gubar notes in a discussion of the shared writing process of *The Madwoman in the Attic*: 'It was clear that the poets were for Sandra. She's a poet and she was getting the poets.'[2] In fact Gilbert's Ph.D. from Columbia University was on 'The Major Poems of D.H. Lawrence' (1968; published 1973) and she has also published numerous works of her own poetry, whereas Gubar's interests were focused on the novel form, and her Ph.D., from the University of Iowa, was on 'Tudor Romance and 18th Century Fiction' (1972). Both worked at Indiana University where in 1973 they co-taught a course in literature by women, and started to perceive a 'coherence of theme and imagery' in a wide range of otherwise disparate authors, 'from Jane Austen and Charlotte Brontë to Emily Dickinson, Virginia Woolf, and Sylvia Plath'.[3] This shared vision appeared to map out 'a distinctively female literary tradition', one which, at the time of their exploration, lacked critical definition; writing on the opening page of the book that emerged from this study, *The Madwoman in the Attic: The Woman Writer and the Nineteenth-Century Literary Imagination* (1979), they define more precisely these images and themes:

> Images of enclosure and escape, fantasies in which maddened doubles functioned as asocial surrogates for docile selves,

metaphors of physical discomfort manifested in frozen land-
scapes and fiery interiors . . . along with obsessive depictions
of diseases like anorexia, agoraphobia, and claustrophobia.[4]

Overall, there is the trope of imprisonment, and the need and desire
for escape, embodied most provocatively in the figure of Bertha
Mason Rochester, the 'madwoman' in the attic in Charlotte Brontë's
novel *Jane Eyre* (1847). This trope also applies not just to character,
content and theme but also to literary production and expression by
nineteenth-century female authors; as Gilbert and Gubar theorize, this
is a literal and metaphorical *architecture* of confinement, in time and
place, but also in terms of patriarchal aesthetics and poetics, through
which women were expected to produce their own art. Their study
of major female nineteenth-century novelists and poets recognizes
and foregrounds strategic resistances to this overarching trope of
confinement, leading to redefinitions of subjectivity and feminist
literary aesthetics. In critical terms and from a feminist perspective,
Gilbert and Gubar strategically occupy and rework Harold Bloom's
theory of the 'anxiety of influence', creating a chiasmus or crossing
between the experiential generation of literary aesthetics and the ways
in which literature can, in turn, create experience. Fundamental
tropes for this project include those of sexuality and procreation (such
as rejecting the sexist alignment of paternity with creativity), and the
overriding network of images that are created by the ur-image of
nineteenth-century woman as either an 'angel' or a 'monster' in the
house. It is not enough, Gilbert and Gubar assert, to simply follow
authors such as Virginia Woolf in destroying these images, it is also
essential for a feminist literary history and criticism to understand the
'nature and origin of these images'.[5] In other words, one of the points
where Gilbert and Gubar represent an advance is in their notion that
women's own modes of creativity have been contaminated by patriarchal images and tropes; given the relationship between aesthetic
creativity and the construction of subjectivity, the literary-critical
project begins to take on much more serious implications. Gilbert and
Gubar thus deconstruct what they perceive to be Bloom's patriarchal
notion of an anxiety of influence, one where literary 'forefathers'
haunt the tradition in a father-and-son relationship traced back to
Bloom's reading of Freud.

   Gilbert and Gubar ask where does the female writer fit into this
Oedipal drama? 'Deconstruct' is the correct word to use here, because
Gilbert and Gubar recognize, in a brilliant critical move, that Bloom
provides all of the tools for the critique and dismantling of the

patriarchal concept of anxiety that he puts forward himself; in other words, the very fact that he foregrounds the patriarchal basis of literary history is, in itself, a momentous recognition. Instead of being caught up in a non-self-reflexive continuation of literary criticism, Bloom interrupts and brings to consciousness, like Freud, 'assumptions readers and writers do not ordinarily examine'.[6] Gilbert and Gubar thus realize that another model needs to be put forward to answer the question of where women fit into this patriarchal structure and sequential chain of literary production: a model that goes beyond the first phase of deconstruction (a reversal of binary oppositions) to the second phase, a 'revisionary process' that involves redefining precisely the processes of female 'socialization'. Thus, women writers search for precursors, not to engage in a female version of Freud's/Bloom's Oedipal drama (where the son creatively misreads and assimilates the originary literary model of the father), but instead, to align themselves with those who have already rebelled against patriarchal strictures. Drawing upon Elaine Showalter, Gilbert and Gubar also acknowledge the importance of a distinctive, separate, female literary subculture that is not only 'exhilarating' but one that is charged with a creative actuality which, they suggest, is equivalent to a new renaissance; in comparison, Gilbert and Gubar regard male literary production as one that doesn't just proceed via anxiety and a feeling of belatedness, but is also fundamentally exhausted. While this assertion does not tie-in with the spectacular rise of contemporary male authors in the post-colonial field, for example, the fact that the book was written in the mid- to late 1970s does align it with the 'post-war literature decline' thesis that pervaded much of the literary academy; one that would be overturned in the 1980s and beyond. Furthermore, *The Madwoman in the Attic* has significance for feminist criticism, especially in the thesis that there is an ongoing internalization of oppressive yet formative patriarchal tropes in early writings by female authors. The *division of labour* that brought about this significant collaborative publication was in part brought about by the tenure system in the US; as Lorraine York argues: 'The material conditions of academic life in American post-secondary institutions were also influential. They began work on *Madwoman*, "exactly when Sandra went to Davis [University of California], and we were physically separated by miles and miles of the continent".'[7] There are other factors at play in this university system that militate against collaborative work, such as the need to claim sole authorship or editorship of a major publication to gain credit; yet the importance of support networks for feminist critics working in institutions that themselves have a patriarchal basis, continually leads back to the positive benefits of collaboration. With their next major research project, the writing of the three-volume work *No Man's Land: The Place of the Woman Writer in the Twentieth Century*, Gilbert and Gubar developed 'a more integrative collaborative practice',[8] one that contributed substantially to a re-reading of feminist literary history.

In their preface to the first volume of *No Man's Land* (*The War of the Words*, 1988), Gilbert and Gubar note how they perceived their project to be a sequel to *The Madwoman in the Attic*, one that ballooned from a projected single volume into three parts because of the need to reassess not just literary history, but social history and, indeed, the received wisdom concerning literary modernists in general. As a work of revision, then, *No Man's Land* maps out the modernist terrain of cultural transformation via the central trope of the 'battle of the sexes', traced from the mid-nineteenth century onwards. Gilbert and Gubar are aware that their insistence on access to historical subjects and movements is, in itself, problematized by postmodernism and the rise of new historicism, but they argue that such 'challenges to history and authorship, radically antipatriarchal as they may seem, ultimately erase the reality of gendered human experience'.[9] While history may be perceived as 'chaos', for Gilbert and Gubar, it is precisely the narratives of 'gender strife' that emerge from this chaos in a coherent, yet heterogeneous, fashion. This agonistic theory of gender relations provides both plot and literary-historical topology, starting with Victorian literature and preceding to contemporary writers of the twentieth-century. As in *The Madwoman in the Attic*, Bloom and Freud once again provide psychosexual models of social and literary development; in *No Man's Land* a key term developed from these sources is that of a 'female affiliation complex', that is to say, a more complex 'dynamics of female literary inheritance' than that traced in the nineteenth century. Gilbert and Gubar argue that in the twentieth century, the affiliation complex is created by women's multiple, dialogic, engagement with the past, an engagement that takes place not just in the private room-of-one's-own, but also in the newly accessible public sphere: 'When we apply the model that we have been calling the affiliation complex to women's literary history, therefore, we inevitably find women writers oscillating between their matrilineage and their patrilineage in an arduous process of self-definition.'[10] 'Affiliation' becomes a strategic replacement for words such as 'influence' and 'authorship', overthrowing the Bloomian overtones and implications; 'affiliation' represents the choice that women authors can make, not just a choice of specific authors or other individuals, but a choice of building a new feminist genealogy. In Volumes Two (*Sexchanges*, 1989) and Three (*Letters From The Front*, 1994) of *No Man's Land*, Gilbert and Gubar offer their own affiliative choices to continue the mapping of the battle of the sexes; in Volume Two the primary focus is sexual experimentation or the 'changing definitions of sex and sex roles' explored through three main phases, the repudiation/ revision of the Victorian 'ideology of femininity', the 'antiutopian scepticism' towards feminization of writers such as Edith Wharton and Willa Cather, and the 'apocalyptic engendering' of the new which is traced via lesbianism and gender-trauma deriving from the First World War. Future shock is explored in Volume Three, with Gilbert and Gubar engaging with issues of gender impersonation, and combating two new potential threats from their perspective to feminist work: the erasure of gender differences with the rise of post-structuralist theorists such as Jacques Derrida and Judith Butler, and the backlash against feminism from multiple sources, perhaps the most problematic for them being Camille Paglia, rather than other conventional and con-servative male thinkers. Does the third volume 'answer back' to the new wave of feminists and/or critics of feminism? The answer lies in a more nuanced reading of Gilbert and Gubar's work beyond their own canonized books, for example, in the key essay (by Gubar) 'What Ails Feminist Criticism?' published in *Critical Inquiry* (1998)[11] where the divorce between high theory and literary text is regarded as a prob-lematic outcome of the poststructuralist turn. While Gubar worries in this essay about the influence of high theory on a new wave of graduate students, much of the feminist criticism undertaken in the con-temporary humanities remains grounded in the collaborative work of Gilbert and Gubar, regardless of the directions that younger scholars may now take.

Notes

1 Lorraine York, *Rethinking Women's Collaborative Writing*, Toronto: University of Toronto Press, 2002, p. 47.
2 Ibid., p. 48.
3 Sandra M. Gilbert and Susan Gubar, *The Madwoman in the Attic: The Woman Writer and the Nineteenth-Century Literary Imagination*, New Haven, CT and London: Yale University Press, 1979, p. xi.
4 Ibid.
5 Ibid., p. 17.
6 Ibid., p. 47.
7 Lorraine York, *Rethinking Women's Collaborative Writing*, p. 49.
8 Ibid., p. 48.

9 Sandra M. Gilbert and Susan Gubar, *No Man's Land: The Place of the Woman Writer in the Twentieth Century, Volume 1, The War of the Words*, New Haven, CT and London: Yale University Press, 1988, p. xiv.

10 Ibid., p. 169.

11 Susan Gubar, 'What Ails Feminist Criticism?' *Critical Inquiry*, 24 (Summer 1998): 878–902.

See also in this book

Booth, Showalter

Major works

The Madwoman in the Attic: The Woman Writer and the Nineteenth-Century Literary Imagination (1979). New Haven, CT and London: Yale University Press.

Shakespeare's Sisters: Feminist Essays on Women Poets (eds, 1979). Bloomington, IN: Indiana University Press.

The Norton Anthology of Literature by Women (eds, 1985). New York: Norton.

No Man's Land: The Place of the Woman Writer in the Twentieth Century, Volume 1, The War of the Words (1988). New Haven, CT and London: Yale University Press.

No Man's Land: The Place of the Woman Writer in the Twentieth Century, Volume 2, Sexchanges (1989). New Haven, CT and London: Yale University Press.

No Man's Land: The Place of the Woman Writer in the Twentieth Century, Volume 3, Letters from the Front (1994). New Haven, CT and London: Yale University Press.

Further reading

Benstock, Shari, 'From the Editor's Perspective: Women's Literary History: To Be Continued', *Tulsa Studies in Women's Literature*, 5.2 (1986): 165–183.

Cain, William E., ed., *Making Feminist History: The Literary Scholarship of Sandra M. Gilbert and Susan Gubar*, New York: Garland, 1994.

Duckworth, Alistair M., 'Jane Austen and the Conflict of Interpretations', *Women and Literature*, 3 (1983): 39–52.

McDayter, Ghislaine, '"Consuming the Sublime": Gothic Pleasure and the Construction of Identity', *Women's Writing*, 2.1 (1995): 55–75.

Rosdeitcher, Elizabeth, 'An Interview with Sandra M. Gilbert and Susan Gubar', *Critical Texts*, 6.1 (1989): 17–38.

PAUL GILROY (1956–)

It is no mere incidental comment that opens the preface to Paul Gilroy's *The Black Atlantic: Modernity and Double Consciousness* (1993): 'This book was first conceived while I was working at South Bank Polytechnic in London's Elephant and Castle.'[1] The South London location is highly symbolic and overdetermined: site of the former Polytechnic, which facilitated access to higher education for ethnic minorities among many other marginalized groups, and later in the 1990s, the location for the Stephen Lawrence Inquiry, the official investigation into the failed police prosecution of the men accused of the racist murder of a young black architecture student, Stephen Lawrence. Kent Constabulary's separate investigation into the failed prosecution, undertaken for the Police Complaints Authority, concluded that there was 'institutional racism' within the Metropolitan Police Service, such a notion being long vocalized by Britain's black community. The official language of a police inquiry could be recoded using the title of Gilroy's earlier book: 'There Ain't No Black in the Union Jack' (1987), a text which, as Houston A. Baker, Jr, notes in the preface, examines the 'moral panic' (using Stuart Hall's term) of 1960s and 1970s Britain, with the state of crisis that accompanied Britain's postcolonial decline and revealed varieties of racist nationalisms at work in the State and society. Gilroy's exploration of Britain's recent nationalist and racist history is rooted in personal experience and study: born in London, England, to English and Guyanese parents, Gilroy has long had a personal and professional interest in the myriad manifestations of black British culture, with special focus on Afro-Caribbean music. Gilroy was educated at the University of Birmingham, where he completed his doctorate in 1986, and played a major part in the development of a new leftist critique of Britain as part of the work initiated by Birmingham's Centre for Cultural Studies. As Houston A. Baker, Jr, asserts:

> If Stuart Hall was a major voice of the Center, then Paul Gilroy and his colleagues who collaborated during the early 1980s to produce The Empire Strikes Back: Race and Racism in 70s Britain were brilliant disciples who carried a master voice to new resonance.[2]

After a number of academic posts at The University of Birmingham, The University of Essex and South Bank Polytechnic, London (now London South Bank University), Gilroy moved to Goldsmith's College, University of London, where he worked until 1998 as a lecturer in Sociology. Moving to the US, Gilroy became a professor of sociology and African-American studies in 1998 at Yale University, followed in 2005 by the prestigious post of Anthony Giddens Professorship of Social Theory, at The London School of Economics, England.

Publication in 1987 of *'There Ain't No Black In The Union Jack': The Cultural Politics of Race and Nation*, was a major event in the critical exploration of race and ethnicity in British society and culture. Gilroy managed to neatly and compellingly synthesize a Marxist/Cultural Studies approach with the 'grass roots' of political activism and contemporary black British culture. Exploring the formation of racism in British society, Gilroy contends that racism defined via the 'black problem' (or blacks as victims) is a way of actively excluding race from history:

> Seeing racism in this way [as an external phenomenon], as something peripheral, marginal to the essential patterns of social and political life can, in its worse manifestations, simply endorse the view of blacks as an external problem, an alien presence visited on Britain from the outside.[3]

While reversing this image, and re-introducing black British figures and concepts into an historical awareness, Gilroy also does something far more fundamental: he remaps the Cultural Studies approach, arguing that an awareness of race and racism is essential and integral, for example, with the reworking of questions of, and the relationship between, race and class in the first main chapter of the book. Gilroy's approach can be thought of as 'syncretist' a word deriving from 'syncretism', which literally means 'a joining of forces'. Originally used in theological writing, but also in secular theatre criticism, the transfer of the term to postcolonial literature and theory is viewed with some suspicion.[4] Ashcroft, Griffiths and Tiffin, define the term as one 'sometimes used to avoid the problems some critics have associated with the idea of hybridity in identifying the fusion of two distinct traditions to produce a new and distinctive whole'.[5] Gilroy reveals how the term is apt, because his bringing together of different cultural forces in his book, say Rastafarian, Afro-Caribbean, or Afro-American, is one that retains a sharp edge of oppositional politics, as well as an assertion of autonomy. In other words, re-inserting black British subjects into the nation forces the British to examine some uncomfortable truths concerning their treatment of diverse British subjects. Nowhere in Gilroy's book is this more apparent than in his brilliant and evocative traversing of 'the expressive culture of black Britain'[6] in the fifth chapter, 'Diaspora, utopia and the critique of capitalism'. Gilroy argues that the exclusionary effects of racism cannot be sustained because the essentialist foundations of such a production of 'black alterity' are, themselves, 'precarious constructions' and 'discursive figures', that is to say, they are not only artificial constructs but also elements in a wider struggle for identity formation. Emerging in that struggle is the oppositional practice of black expressive cultures that themselves draw sustenance from the black diaspora:

> In particular, the culture and politics of black America and the Caribbean have become raw materials for creative processes which redefine what it means to be black, adapting to distinctively British experiences and meanings. Black culture is actively made and re-made.[7]

This dynamic process of black cultural production would lead to an even wider theory of black subjectivity and history, in Gilroy's *The Black Atlantic: Modernity and Double Consciousness* (1993) a groundbreaking study that Gilroy modestly calls 'an essay about the inescapable hybridity and intermixture of ideas'.[8]

Locating black British identity in a transitional and transnational space – that of the Black Atlantic, the routes between Africa, the Americas, and the UK – allows Gilroy to posit a diasporic and dynamic theory of identity, rather than one rooted in essentialism and racism. 'Diaspora' means dispersal: 'the voluntary or forcible movement of peoples from their homelands into new regions ... a central historical fact of colonization'.[9] Gilroy is aware of the links between his use of diaspora and that of Jewish history: 'The themes of escape and suffering, tradition, temporality, and the social organization of memory have a special significance in the history of Jewish responses to modernity.'[10] Where Gilroy applies a radical re-reading of black diaspora in his study, is in relation to modernity: arguing that scholars of modernity excluded the role of black artists, Gilroy contends that black cultural expression is a 'counter-culture' of modernity, that is to say, not something excluded from, or separate from modernity, but a force that 'reveals the hidden internal fissures in the concept of modernity'.[11] As McLeod summarizes: 'This makes a nonsense *both* of a sense of the West as ethnically and racially homogenous, and of ideas concerning an essentialised, common "black" community separated from Western influence.'[12] In other words, the 'double consciousness' of the Black Atlantic, allows for identity *and* difference, and is both constitutive and critical of modernity. Gilroy's study has wide historical scope, and includes analysis of diverse figures such as Martin Robison Delany, Frederick Douglass, W.E.B. Du Bois, and Richard Wright, to name just some of the central black artists and intellectuals who are returned to and examined as part of the journeys – or more accurately, crossings – of black modernity. As Charles Piot asserts, Gilroy

> rereads black expressive forms and the works of North American black intellectuals in a transoceanic, transnational perspective. Thus he shows how African American music, from that of the Fisk University Jubilee Singers in the nineteenth century to contemporary hip-hop, is a hybrid transcultural product, and how the work of Martin Delaney, W.E.B. Du Bois, and Richard Wright . . . were deeply influenced by their travels in Europe and their encounters with Enlightenment culture.[13]

While Gilroy's approach has received criticism from key black scholars such as George Eliot Clarke (who argues that Gilroy has ignored the role of African Canadians in his theories), the fact remains that his concept of the Black Atlantic has brought about a fundamental re-examination of the history and politics of modernity, alongside a more nuanced and sophisticated notion of black Western culture.

Notes

1 Paul Gilroy, *The Black Atlantic: Modernity and Double Consciousness*, Cambridge, MA: Harvard University Press, 1993, p. viii.
2 Paul Gilroy, *'There Ain't No Black In The Union Jack': The Cultural Politics of Race and Nation*, Chicago, IL: University of Chicago Press, 1991 (first published 1987), foreword by Houston A. Baker, Jr, p. 4.
3 Ibid., p. 11.
4 Bill Ashcroft, Gareth Griffiths and Helen Tiffin, *Key Concepts in Post-Colonial Studies*, London and New York: Routledge, 1999, p. 229.
5 Ibid.
6 Paul Gilroy, *'There Ain't No Black In The Union Jack': The Cultural Politics of Race and Nation*, p. 13.
7 Ibid., p. 154.
8 Paul Gilroy, *The Black Atlantic: Modernity and Double Consciousness*, p. xi.
9 Ibid., pp. 68–69.
10 Ibid., p. 205.
11 Ibid., p. 38.
12 John McLeod, *Beginning Postcolonialism*, Manchester: Manchester University Press, 2000, p. 229.
13 Charles Piot, 'Atlantic Aporias: Africa and Gilroy's Black Atlantic', *South Atlantic Quarterly*, 100.1 (Winter 2001): 155–170; p. 158.

See also in this book

Baker, Bhabha, Gates

Major works

The Empire Strikes Back: Race and Racism in 70s Britain (ed., *et al.*, 1982).
London: Hutchinson/The Centre for Contemporary Cultural Studies,
University of Birmingham.
'There Ain't No Black In The Union Jack': The Cultural Politics of Race and Nation
(1987). Chicago, IL: University of Chicago Press, 1991.
The Black Atlantic: Modernity and Double Consciousness (1993). Cambridge,
MA: Harvard University Press.
Against Race: Imagining Political Culture Beyond the Color Line (2000).
Cambridge, MA: Belknap Press of Harvard University Press.
After Empire: Melancholia or Convivial Culture? (2004). London and New York:
Routledge.

Further reading

Chrisman, Laura, 'Rethinking Black Atlanticism', *Black Scholar*, 30.3–4
(2000): 12–17.
Clarke, George Elliott, 'Must All Blackness Be American? Locating Canada
in Borden's "Tightrope Time," or Nationalizing Gilroy's *The Black
Atlantic*', *Canadian Ethnic Studies*, 28.3 (1996): 56–71.
Dayan, Joan, 'Paul Gilroy's Slaves, Ships, and Routes: The Middle Passage as
Metaphor', *Research in African Literatures*, 27.4 (Winter 1996): 7–14.
Gunning, Dave, 'Anti-Racism, The Nation-State and Contemporary Black
British Literature', *Journal of Commonwealth Literature*, 39.2 (2004): 29–43.
Piot, Charles, 'Atlantic Aporias: Africa and Gilroy's Black Atlantic', *South
Atlantic Quarterly*, 100.1 (2001): 155–171.

STEPHEN GREENBLATT (1943–)

Reminiscing about his encounter with the historians of literature at
Yale in the 1960s, Greenblatt sketches a tired and demoralized
methodology that had suffered from the exigencies of the New
Critics, content to recreate and convey the 'literary spirit of each age'.
What did the progressive connection of age to age leave out in this
approach? As Greenblatt notes: 'Leaps in time were discouraged, let
alone radical discontinuities, anomalies, and eccentric illuminations.'
Further, close-readings of texts were 'detached from extratextual or
intertextual causality'.[1] In other words, some of the key procedures
of what would come to be known as the 'new historicism' were resol-
utely off-limits. Greenblatt was born in Cambridge, Massachusetts,
and was educated at Yale University and Pembroke College,
University of Cambridge. At Yale he completed his BA in 1964, and
then studied as a Fulbright Scholar at Cambridge for two years before
returning to Yale to do postgraduate research, switching from his

interest in the twentieth century to the Renaissance, writing a dissertation on Sir Walter Raleigh. Greenblatt made good use of his student
research, publishing his undergraduate work as *Three Modern Satirists:
Waugh, Orwell, and Huxley* (1965) and his dissertation as *Sir Walter
Ralegh: The Renaissance Man and his Roles* (1973). Greenblatt spent
much of his academic career at the University of California, Berkeley
(1969–1997), where he also attended seminars with visiting scholar
Michel Foucault. In 1997 Greenblatt became the Harry Levin
Professor of Literature at Harvard University, and in 2000 he became
the John Cogan Professor of Humanities.

With the publication of *Renaissance Self-Fashioning: From More to
Shakespeare* (1980), Greenblatt's role as a leading new historicist was
consolidated. While the term 'new historicism' had been in circulation since the early 1970s, it was the theoretical sophistication that
Greenblatt and his colleagues brought to its application that meant
that it was now distinguished as an emerging methodology. What is
new historicism? Rejecting the isolation of texts – and the privileging
of canonical works – by the New Critics and then the Structuralists,
new historicists seek to read texts as part of a diverse, and at times
contradictory, social and ideological network of power-knowledge
relations. This involves reading not just canonical, but also marginal,
fragmentary and seemingly inconsequential texts, that have previously
been ignored or simply passed over by literary historians. Another key
process for new historicists is boundary blurring or crossing, as previously stabilized, quarantined knowledge domains are deconstructed
via the recognition of new discursive formations. In the introduction
to *Renaissance Self-Fashioning*, Greenblatt argues that this is the case
with the blurring of the boundaries between literature and social life,
thus self-fashioning 'invariably crosses the boundaries between the
creation of literary characters, the shaping of one's own identity,
the experience of being molded by forces outside one's control, [and]
the attempt to fashion other selves'.[2] As Greenblatt continues:

> Such boundaries may, to be sure, be strictly observed in criti-
> cism, just as we may distinguish between literary and behav-
> ioral styles, but in doing so we pay a high price, for we begin
> to lose a sense of the complex interactions of meaning in a
> given culture.[3]

Using Clifford Geertz's concept of culture being a 'set of control
mechanisms' that govern human behaviour, Greenblatt argues that

Renaissance self-fashioning – or the construction of the self – is, in the transition from 'abstract potential' to actual 'concrete historical embodiment', its equivalent. Where is literature in this process? Greenblatt argues that literature functions here in three interlinked ways: (1) as a manifestation of the concrete behaviour of its particular author; (2) as itself the expression of the codes by which behaviour is shaped; and (3) as a reflection upon those codes.[4] This list, from a new historicist perspective, represents different facets, not isolatable instances. Thus a critical approach that isolates one way of perceiving literature will lead to reductiveness and error. Isolating the first approach leads to reductive biographical criticism, whereas the second leads to a crude Marxism, and the third strips away literature's materiality and impact. Greenblatt advocates a cultural/anthropological approach, invoking critics such as Clifford Geertz, James Boon, Mary Douglas, Jean Duvignaud, Paul Rabinow and Victor Turner. Thus, literature is not to be perceived as a system of signs, since the latter, according to Greenblatt, is constitutive of culture, not a mere abstract expression or reflection. New historicism becomes here a 'poetics of culture'.[5] Even with the distance from 'crude' Marxism, such a poetics maintains a dialectical structure, which can be seen at work in *Renaissance Self-Fashioning*: the triads are the figures of More and Tyndale 'reconceived' by Wyatt, whereas Spencer and Marlow are 'reconceived' by Shakespeare. In schematic terms, Greenblatt sets out these triads as: the two modes of power being (i) the shift from Church, to book, to the absolutist State; and (ii) the shift from celebration, to rebellion, to subversive submission; and the literary mode being 'a shift from absorption by community, religious faith, or diplomacy toward the establishment of literary creation as a profession in its own right'.[6]

Greenblatt's most controversial forays into literary history have inevitably involved the study of Shakespeare, in *Shakespearian Negotiations: The Circulation of Social Energy in Renaissance England* (1988) and, more recently, in his more biographical *Will in the World: How Shakespeare Became Shakespeare* (2004). Shakespeare is shown to be embedded in myriad discursive formations, although critics have been sceptical concerning the creative historical speculation of the more recent book. Greenblatt's essays, published as *Learning to Curse: Essays in Early Modern Culture* (1990), set out the new historicist project in some detail, including work that explores 'new world' encounters, covered in great detail in *Marvelous Possessions: The Wonder of the New World* (1991). Reflecting upon the controversy surrounding the 1992 quincentennial anniversary of Columbus's 'discovery' of America, Greenblatt ponders the ways in which new historicist scholarship is in tune with the rejection of a simplistic nationalism in favour of 'the vision of the vanquished' to use Nathan Wachtel's phrase.[7] As Greenblatt notes:

> There is a growing sense of alternative histories, competing accounts, and muffled voices. Much current writing attempts in a variety of ways to register the powerful presence of otherness – not an abstract, quasi-allegorical figure of the Other, whether brute or victim, but a diverse range of cultures and representations and individuals with whom the Europeans were forced to interact.[8]

The attraction of new historicism has been in large part its flexibility and dynamic ability to explore the voice, or the texts, of the Other, and to re-think literary critical and historical traditions and systems from this new perspective.

Notes

1 Stephen Greenblatt, 'What is the History of Literature?', *Critical Inquiry*, 23 (Spring 1997): 460–481; p. 474.
2 Stephen Greenblatt, *Renaissance Self-Fashioning*, Chicago, IL and London: The University of Chicago Press, 1980, p. 3.
3 Ibid.
4 Ibid., p. 4; quotation modified by Lane.
5 Ibid., p. 5.
6 Ibid., p. 8.
7 Stephen Greenblatt, 'Columbus Runs Aground: Christmas Eve, 1492', in *The Sheila Carmel Lectures: 1988–1993*, ed., Hana Wirth-Nesher, Tel Aviv: Tel Aviv University, 1995, pp. 127–147; p. 128.
8 Ibid.

See also in this book

Booth, de Man

Major works

Three Modern Satirists: Waugh, Orwell, and Huxley (1965). New Haven, CT: Yale University Press.
Sir Walter Ralegh: The Renaissance Man and his Roles (1973). New Haven, CT: Yale University Press.
Renaissance Self-Fashioning: From More to Shakespeare (1980). Chicago, IL and London: University of Chicago Press, 2005, reprinted with new preface.

The Forms of Power and the Power of Forms in the Renaissance (1982). Norman, OK: Pilgrim Books.

Shakespearean Negotiations: The Circulation of Social Energy in Renaissance England (1988). Berkeley, CA: University of California Press.

Learning to Curse: Essays in Early Modern Culture (1990). New York and London: Routledge.

Marvelous Possessions: The Wonder of the New World (1991). Chicago, IL and London: University of Chicago Press.

Racial Memory and the Performance of Culture (with Catherine Gallagher, 1999). Eugene, OR: University of Oregon Press.

Practicing New Historicism (2000). Chicago, IL and London: University of Chicago Press.

Hamlet in Purgatory (2001). Princeton, NJ: Princeton University Press.

Will in the World: How Shakespeare Became Shakespeare (2004). New York: W.W. Norton.

The Greenblatt Reader (edited by Michael Payne, 2005). Oxford and Malden, MA: Blackwell Publishing.

Further reading

Bellamy, Elizabeth Jane, 'Desires and Disavowals: Speculations on the Aftermath of Stephen Greenblatt's "Psychoanalysis and Renaissance Culture"', *Clio*, 34.3 (2005): 297–315.

Ellis, David, 'Biographical Uncertainty and Shakespeare', *Essays in Criticism*, 55.3 (2005): 193–208.

Gauntlett, Mark, 'The Interests of the Theatre: Stephen Greenblatt on Shakespeare's Stage', *Essays in Theatre*, 16.1 (1997): 53–66.

Pieters, Jurgen, ed., *Critical Self-Fashioning: Stephen Greenblatt and the New Historicism*, Frankfurt am Main: Peter Lang, 1999.

Pieters, Jurgen, *Moments of Negotiation: The New Historicism of Stephen Greenblatt*, Amsterdam: Amsterdam University Press, 2002.

DONNA J. HARAWAY (1944–)

International heroine of Cyberpunk, Donna Haraway's work delights and infuriates critics in equal measure. Her most famous publication, 'Manifesto for cyborgs' (1985)[1] has become the classic text in the field, and is an essential starting place for a new realm of transcultural and transdisciplinary studies, where science, science fiction, cybernetics and feminist theory intersect. Born in Denver, Haraway was initially educated at Colorado College, a private liberal arts and sciences college in Colorado Springs, gaining her BA in Zoology and Philosophy in 1966, as well as fulfilling the BA English major requirements. She held a Boettcher Foundation Scholarship while at Colorado College, and won a Paris Fulbright Scholarship to study the history and philosophy of science at the Faculté des Sciences,

Université de Paris, during 1966–1967. After a summer spent at the Marine Biological Laboratory, Woods Hole, Massachusetts, Haraway did graduate research at Yale University's Department of Biology, gaining her M.Phil. in 1969, and her Ph.D. in 1972, for interdisciplinary research. After working as an Assistant Professor at New College, University of Hawaii, Haraway moved to the Department of History of Science at Johns Hopkins University (1974–1980); she moved to the University of California, Santa Cruz as an Associate Professor in 1980, working in the History of Consciousness Board of Studies, and Women's Studies. She has also worked as a department member in Anthropology (1990) and Environmental Studies (1996). She has held numerous distinguished visiting professorships and awards, including the Gustav Meyers Human Rights Award (1990), the Robert K. Merton Award, American Sociological Association, Science, Knowledge and Technology Section (1992), the Ludwik Fleck Book Prize, Society of Social Studies of Science, Best Book in the Field, Annual Prize (1999) and the J.D. Bernal Award, Society for Social Studies of Science, for lifetime contributions to the field (2000). Early publications by Haraway include essays on the history of Socialist thought in Science, animal sociology and sociobiology, primatology and cybernetics. But it was her 'Manifesto for cyborgs', first published in the *Socialist Review*, with numerous translations and reprints since, that touched a nerve. Haraway's socialist-feminist critique of science was here given a powerful twist: unlike many of her precursors, she does not reject technology, or promote a utopian 'organicist' or 'redemptive concept of nature'.[2] As critic Kate Soper argues, for Haraway:

> cyber-technology is not simply [an] oppressive product of the military–industrial complex, but [the] potential asset of emancipation insofar as it continually destabilizes and revises existing conceptual boundaries and identities. It is in this context that she insisted on the power of the 'cyborg' to reconfigure and advance a progressive politics, and it is this hybrid entity and its beneficent properties which are in part theorized, in part celebrated, in her most influential and contested text, the 'Manifesto for Cyborgs'.[3]

How does Haraway define the entity that she calls a 'cyborg'? And how has her work developed from this key essay?

Haraway calls a cyborg a 'cybernetic organism', that is to say: 'a hybrid of machine and organism, a creature of social reality as well as a creature of fiction'.[4] In this aphoristic definition, we can see how not only is the cyborg a 'mixture' or synthesis of artificial machine and natural being, but it is also a hybrid entity philosophically speaking, drawn from ideas concerning how people want the world to be (speculative literature and theory), as much as any entity already in existence. This latter notion is important if we are to grasp Haraway's mode of thinking: her writing works as a map of social and bodily realities and as 'an imaginative resource' for developing further ideas. Haraway asserts that twentieth-century people are cyborgs, and that as such they reject all of the previous grand narratives of religion, capitalism, sexism and racism; for Haraway, the cyborg is 'post-gender' and leads, in a Deleuzian fashion, to new bondings, couplings and machinic entities, such as that between human beings and animals, or, the blurred boundaries in modern science and technology between the organic and the machinic. How is the latter different from pre-cyborg hybrid entities? Haraway argues that pre-cyborg hybrids were always dependent upon a 'ghost in the machine', be it spirit, or a soul, or the human side of the entity; cyborgs, however, are not part living and part dead (machine), instead, the boundaries between these two definitions have blurred to such an extent that machines now appear living and autonomous while organic beings can appear death-like, static and inert. In the film *Bladerunner*, for example, the androids or replicants are more beautiful and accomplished than humans, who in turn are run down and sickly, like broken or defective machines. It is essential to note that for Haraway the cyborg is a revolutionary entity, one that has rejected the search for organic, social or political wholeness, remaining open to future definition and socio-political relations. Instead of regarding cyborgs as a manifestation of a military-technological society, Haraway argues that as transgressive force, cyborgs can also be thought of, simultaneously, as resistors, activists, action and affinity groups. That is to say, any transgressive but temporary resisting group creates a cyborg society. From this, and contemporary feminist rejection of ever-splintering but still-essentialist categories of 'woman', Haraway posits an alternative 'cyborg feminism': 'Cyborg feminists have to argue that "we" do not want any more natural matrix of unity and that no construction is whole.'[5] This involves moving from a hierarchical world to one of new networks which Haraway calls 'the informatics of domination'.[6] Haraway provides a chart of the radically transformed realm of these new networks in her manifesto, the left column representing the hierarchical world, the right column the polymorphous world of information systems:

Representation	Simulation
Bourgeois novel, realism	Science fiction, postmodernism
Organism	Biotic component
Depth, integrity	Surface, boundary
Heat	Noise
Biology as critical practice	Biology as inscription
Physiology	Communications engineering
Small group	Subsystem
Perfection	Optimization
Eugenics	Population control
Decadence, *Magic Mountain*	Obsolescence, *Future Shock*
Hygiene	Stress management
Microbiology, tuberculosis	Immunology, AIDS
Organic division of labour	Ergonomics/cybernetics of labour
Functional specialization	Modular construction
Reproduction	Replication
Organic sex role specialization	Optimal genetic strategies
Biological determinism	Evolutionary inertia, constraints
Community ecology	Ecosystem
Racial chain of being	Neo-imperialism, United Nations humanism
Scientific management in home/factory	Global factory/Electronic cottage
Family/Market/Factory	Women in the integrated circuit
Family wage	Comparable worth
Public/Private	Cyborg citizenship
Nature/Culture	Fields of difference
Co-operation	Communications enhancement
Freud	Lacan
Sex	Genetic engineering
Labour	Robotics
Mind	Artificial intelligence
Second World War	Star Wars
White Capitalist Patriarchy	Informatics of Domination[7]

Haraway regards the transition from the left-hand side to the right-hand side of this list as irreversible: the 'natural' hierarchy encoded on the left, for example, natural reproduction, is replaced for Haraway in this instance by replication (as perhaps, a *strategy*). Another related example is that of the transition from 'Sex' to 'Genetic engineering'. In both of these transitions, the irreversibility is created by an awareness that what was posited on the left-hand side as 'natural' has now, in a cyborg universe, been revealed to be an artificial construct. There is no going back, and this includes 'going back' to creation or origin stories; as Haraway says: 'The cyborg would not recognize the Garden of Eden; it is not made of mud and cannot dream of returning to dust.'[8] Nature essentialism is replaced in the transition from hierarchical epoch to cybernetic epoch by design, and of course this includes the design (assembly and disassembly) of people. What does this mean for feminism? For a start, organic and hierarchical dualisms must be abandoned in favour of the cyborg feminism that analyses and interposes itself into the 'actual situation of women' in the 'world system of production/reproduction and communication'.[9] Instead of science and technology being oppressive systems of domination, cyborg feminists need to re-code these very domains, and utilize previously oppressive technological tools for their own ends. Haraway also applies her new theory of cyborgs to race and ethnicity, formulating, at times tortuously, but always provocatively and productively, a new matrix for the empowering and re-telling of the stories of women of colour.

Haraway's work has been developed in myriad directions since she published her manifesto in 1985; the manifesto itself now constitutes chapter eight of a much larger study and collection of essays, *Simians, Cyborgs, and Women: The Reinvention of Nature* (1991), a text that explores new ways of perceiving the world, new ontologies, from a cyborg feminist perspective; Haraway's focus in the first part of the book is the science and sociology of primates, while the second part examines contested notions of 'nature' and 'experience'; part three of her study introduces the cyborg, feminism and medical discourses, among other issues. What is clear is that this volume of essays presents a coherent response to societal and technological change; as Patricia Clough puts it in relation to Haraway's contributions as a whole: 'the changes in the conception of matter and materiality also require that we rethink family, nations, bodies, machines, nature, technology, and the disciplines'.[10] In fact Haraway's contributions in these areas predates her most popular volume with the key works *Crystals, Fabrics and Fields: Metaphors of Organicism in Twentieth-Century Developmental Biology* (1976) and *Primate Visions: Gender, Race, and Nature in the World of Modern Science* (1989). More recent work includes the book *Modest_Witness@Second_Millennium. FemaleMan©MeetsOncoMouse™: Feminism and Technoscience* (1997). Haraway's work has had considerable influence on an entire generation of cyberpunk writers and activists, as well as feminists, literary theorists and sociologists; as

Steve Pile and Nigel Thrift argue, her work has enabled theorists 'to produce a new materialism based around rethinking the subject's bodily roots, where the body stands for the radical materiality of the subject'; in other words, 'Haraway wants us to think about what new kinds of bodies are being constructed in the modern scientific world . . . what new kinds of gender systems are being produced'.[11] And to give the last word to Patricia Clough: 'No other cultural critic has had more influence than Haraway in bringing forward difficult questions that point to the ways scientific work and knowledge are interimplicated with a wide range of global and local practices of exploitation and domination.'[12]

Notes

1 Donna J. Haraway, 'Manifesto for Cyborgs: Science, Technology, and Socialist Feminism in the 1980s', *Socialist Review*, 80 (1985): 65–108; reprinted as 'A Cyborg Manifesto: Science, Technology, and Socialist-Feminism in the Late Twentieth Century' in Donna J. Haraway, *Simians, Cyborgs, and Women: The Reinvention of Nature*, London and New York: Routledge, 1991, Chapter 8.
2 Kate Soper, 'Of OncoMice and FemaleMen: Donna Haraway on Cyborg Ontology', *Women: A Cultural Review*, 10.2 (1999): 167–172; p. 167.
3 Ibid., pp. 167–168.
4 Donna J. Haraway, *Simians, Cyborgs, and Women: The Reinvention of Nature*, p. 149.
5 Ibid., p. 157.
6 Ibid., p. 161.
7 Ibid., pp. 161–162.
8 Ibid., p. 151.
9 Ibid., p. 163.
10 Patricia Clough, 'The Work of Donna Haraway: Its Contribution to Social Theory', *Found Object*, 8 (2000): 125–139; p. 134.
11 Steve Pile and Nigel Thrift, 'Mapping the Subject', in Steve Pile and Nigel Thrift, eds, *Mapping the Subject: Geographies of Cultural Transformation*, London and New York: Routledge, 1995, pp. 13–51; p. 18.
12 Patricia Clough, 'The Work of Donna Haraway: Its Contribution to Social Theory', p. 133.

See also in this book

Deleuze and Guattari

Major works

Crystals, Fabrics and Fields: Metaphors of Organicism in Twentieth-Century Developmental Biology (1976). New Haven, CT: Yale University Press.
Primate Visions: Gender, Race, and Nature in the World of Modern Science (1989). London and New York: Routledge.

Simians, Cyborgs, and Women: The Reinvention of Nature (1991). London and New York: Routledge.

Modest_Witness@Second_Millennium. FemaleMan©MeetsOncoMouse™: Feminism and Technoscience (1997). London and New York: Routledge.

Further reading

Campbell, Kirsten, 'The Promise of Feminist Reflexivities: Developing Donna Haraway's Project for Feminist Science Studies', *Hypatia*, 19.1 (2004): 162–182.

Clough, Patricia Ticineto, 'The Work of Donna Harraway: Its Contribution to Social Theory', *Found Object*, 8 (2000): 125–139.

Csicery-Ronay, Istvan, Jr, 'The SF of Theory: Baudrillard and Haraway', *Science Fiction Studies*, 18.3 (1991): 387–404.

Schneider, Joseph, *Donna Haraway: Live Theory*, London: Continuum, 2005.

Soper, Kate, 'Of OncoMice and FemaleMen: Donna Haraway on Cyborg Ontology', *Women: A Cultural Review*, 10.2 (1999): 167–172.

Sundén, Jenny, 'What Happened to Difference in Cyberspace? The (Re)Turn of the She-Cyborg', *Feminist Media Studies*, 1.2 (2001): 215–232.

GEOFFREY H. HARTMAN (1929–)

It is no coincidence that of all Jacques Derrida's books that he could have explicated, Geoffrey Hartman chose the one that most insistently interweaves literature and philosophy: Derrida's *Glas* thus found its most creative and intelligent reader upon publication of Hartman's *Saving the Text: Literature, Derrida, Philosophy* (1981).[1] While Hartman's readers may have previously been more familiar with his groundbreaking work on Wordsworth, his interest in the literary-critical field in general was more than apparent from the beginning of his academic career. Hartman was born in Frankfurt-am-main, Germany in 1929, and he emigrated to the US in 1946. Educated at Yale University, Hartman also made Yale his home, working there as an instructor and then assistant professor from 1955 to 1962, then moving to the University of Iowa where he took the post of Associate Professor of English. Hartman was made full professor in 1964, then moved to Cornell University in 1965; finally, in 1967 he returned to Yale where he became Professor of English and comparative literature, Karl Young Professor in 1974, and Sterling Professor in 1994. The scale of Hartman's critical vision was immediately apparent from the publication of his first book, *The Unmediated Vision: An Interpretation of Wordsworth, Hopkins, Rilke, and Valery* (1954). In this book, Hartman set out his critical stall: recognizing that literature was 'more than an organic creation, a social pastime, a religious trope, an emotional outlet, a flower of civilization, more even than an exemplary stage for ideal probabilities', Hartman argued that literature had been recognized as an autonomous institution, a mode of knowledge, with laws and a moral force.[2] Rejecting the notion that criticism has become absolutely heterogeneous in 'approach', Hartman sets out on a quest for 'a method universal in its appeal, a method of interpretation which could reaffirm the radical unity of human knowledge'.[3] This is one that respects the autonomy of the aesthetic object, yet still manages to present 'a principle of synthesis' that will be universally applicable.[4] Does Hartman achieve this? With his theory of a post-Cartesian literary or poetic 'unmediated' consciousness or vision, that is to say, one that rejects transcendent authority or mediation in favour of the texts of Nature, the body or human consciousness,[5] the answer, given the concomitant direction of contemporary theory, tends towards the affirmative. Even with his traditional subject matter – Wordsworth, Hopkins, Rilke and Valery – it is apparent that Hartman's textual field of study will eventually dovetail with that of the poststructuralists. For the moment, the fact that in *The Unmediated Vision* it is Wordsworth who is called the 'turning point' and a poet who expresses 'full consciousness', is of significance for Hartman's own critical development, *The Unmediated Vision* being followed in 1964 with his *Wordworth's Poetry: 1787–1814.*

Seen as an event in Wordsworth criticism, *Wordsworth's Poetry* offers a powerful reading of poetic self-consciousness, developed in the first chapter on 'The Solitary Reaper'. Hartman tracks the ways in which emotional minutiae are capable of triggering profound and potentially overwhelming imaginative responses in Wordsworth in a 'dialectic between nature and the imagination';[6] such triggering does not necessarily occur instantaneously, and this temporal delay is indicative of the precariousness of such self-awareness. Heightened imagination in Wordsworth is interpreted by Hartman to be '*consciousness of self raised to apocalyptic* [or its highest] *pitch*'.[7] In the foreword to Hartman's collection of essays called *The Unremarkable Wordsworth* (1987), Donald G. Marshall argues that:

> The appearance twenty-five years ago of *Wordsworth's Poetry* marked an epoch in the study of that poet and of romanticism generally. . . . Hartman's essays on Wordsworth written in the intervening quarter century and gathered here are once again revolutionary, though their character and importance are much less likely to be perceived and absorbed. This difference tells us a great deal about the evolution of criticism,

about Hartman's own career, and perhaps something also about Hartman.[8]

Hartman puts it another way: he regards the decline of hermeneutics and the rise of high theory to be as much about the rejection of the originary–secondary divide as anything else; as he puts it in 'The Interpreter', which appeared in *The Fate of Reading, and Other Essays* (1975), we are now interested in Derrida on Rousseau almost as much as reading Rousseau in the first place. In another essay in the same volume, 'The Fate of Reading', Hartman meditates upon literary criticism, dividing it into two main functions: construction of *metalanguage* (an 'abstract reordering of terms') or the construction of a *paralanguage* (subordinating 'abstract concepts by playing them off against the specificity of texts').[9] While he retains the option of a 'variable style', that is to say, a mixture of the two functions, Hartman's own methodology remains faithful to the event of each individual textual encounter because of his ability to create a paralanguage, an echo or a mimetic extension and recreation of textual rhythms, forms and sounds. Paralanguage is a responsive experiencing of a text, not the production of a text's 'grammar' or structural integrity which can so often be a distancing between reader and literary object; 'This is a book of experiences', says Hartman in the opening sentence to his *Criticism in the Wilderness: The Study of Literature Today* (1980).

One of the reasons for the success of *Criticism in the Wilderness* is that Hartman rejects the notion of criticism as a parasitic enterprise, regarding it instead as *symbiotic* with literature, and, even more radically, but still in the tradition of Benjamin and others, criticism is *immanent* to literature (without this notion leading back to the old idea of criticism as a secondary form). Hartman ponders the different historical and social theoretical movements that had solidified during the second half of the twentieth century, aware that certain key texts created isolated canons; he asks, is it possible to mediate between the critical traditions? One key question is whether philosophy is viewed as literary text? Just as Eliot criticized Arnold for perceiving rigid boundaries between the critical and the creative before drawing back from the dangers that then accrued, so Hartman perceives contemporary criticism as becoming a fusion of the critical and the creative. This, in turn, creates a demand: criticism should not merely review a work, or be considered a mere supplement to the primary text; criticism becomes a testing of limits, of aesthetics and knowledge. This is where Hartman finds a coincidence between Anglo-American and French 'waves' of theory: the repudiation of metaphysics and the replacement of Hegel's concept of absolute knowledge with 'a textual infinite, an interminable web of texts or interpretations'.[10] Derrida's *Glas* is a prime example of this notion:

> It is not only hard to say whether *Glas* is 'criticism' or 'philosophy' or 'literature,' it is hard to affirm it is a book. *Glas* raises the specter of texts so tangled, contaminated, displaced, deceptive that the idea of a single or original author fades.[11]

What makes Hartman's work so intriguing, however, is that his intellectual project is also one that accounts for the impact of texts upon human being: 'Books have their own fate; and I am sufficiently convinced that *Glas*, like *Finnegan's Wake*, introduces our consciousness to a dimension it will not forget.'[12] One year after Hartman's *Criticism in the Wilderness*, these comments on *Glas* appeared in expanded form in his *Saving the Text: Literature/Derrida/Philosophy* (1981). Hartman's focus on the poetics of Derrida's *Glas* confirmed his own status as one of the American Yale School critics, a group that had arisen in the 1970s, with the inaugural work of Paul de Man; the Yale School registered strongly the linguistic and rhetorical playfulness of deconstruction, as well as the notion that philosophy and literature were fundamentally interpenetrated. *Saving the Text* starts by investigating the chiasmus between the Genet-Hegel columns of *Glas*, at multiple textual, rhetorical, rhythmic and musical levels; the chiastic structure of *Glas* also becomes Hartman's passage through Derridean thought. Hartman's own word for his study of Derrida is 'translation', although in the final chapter of the book, 'Words and Wounds', Hartman offers a 'counterstatement' to Derrida, questioning his insistence on anti-representational thinking, i.e. the primacy of the play of the signifier in literature and philosophy. The openness of endless play is replaced with a therapeutic enclosure where 'the affective power of the word itself is what is enclosed by the literary work'.[13]

A major blow to the Yale School of criticism was the discovery of Paul de Man's European, collaborationist, wartime journalism, utilized by many critics in America to attack the general project of deconstruction. In *Minor Prophecies: The Literary Essay in the Culture Wars* (1991), Hartman responded to this attack, mindful not only of his own status of refugee from Nazi Germany but also his Jewish background. Registering de Man's anti-Semitism, and the complicity of his thought with the rise of Fascism, Hartman is also shocked by the contemporary collapsing of all literary theory into some kind of tainted history because of de Man's activities; Hartman argues for, and provides, a more thoughtful and subtle meditation on the parallels between early and late de Man, as well as advocating for a more ethical stance from contemporary theory, clarifying its role and potentialities. Hartman's role as Director of the Video Archive for Holocaust Testimonies at Yale University has been central to this ethical turn. Responding to President Ronald Reagan's visit to a German cemetery in 1985 where Nazi soldiers had been buried, Hartman edited the collection *Bitburg in Moral and Political Perspective* (1986); in the same year, Hartman co-edited with Sanford Budick a major new collection on Biblical interpretation called *Midrash and Literature*. Judaic studies and memorialization of the Shoah continued to be a major concern for Hartman in the 1990s, with publication of *Holocaust Remembrance: The Shapes of Memory* (ed., 1994) and *The Longest Shadow: In the Aftermath of the Holocaust* (1996). Biblical text and interpretation has always informed Hartman's readings of literature, philosophy and critical theory; this apparent 'turn' towards the Shoah should not efface the memories that Hartman has kept alive from the very beginnings of his career.

Notes

1 See my brief discussion of Hartman and Derrida in my *Functions of the Derrida Archive: Philosophical Receptions*, Budapest: Akadémiai Kiadó, 2003, pp. 104–107.
2 Geoffrey H. Hartman, *The Unmediated Vision: An Interpretation of Wordsworth, Hopkins, Rilke, and Valery*, New York: Harcourt, Brace, 1966, pp. ix–x.
3 Ibid., p. x.
4 Ibid.
5 Ibid., p. 154.
6 Donald G. Marshall, 'Foreword: Wordsworth and Post-Enlightenment Culture', in Geoffrey H. Hartman, *The Unremarkable Wordsworth*, Minneapolis, MN: University of Minnesota Press, 1987, pp. vii–xxiii; p. vii.
7 Geoffrey H. Hartman, *Wordsworth's Poetry: 1787–1814*, New Haven, CT and London: Yale University Press, 1964, p. 17.
8 Donald G. Marshall, 'Foreword: Wordsworth and Post-Enlightenment Culture', in Geoffrey H. Hartman, *The Unremarkable Wordsworth*, p. vii.
9 Geoffrey H. Hartman, *The Fate of Reading, and Other Essays*, Chicago, IL and London: The University of Chicago Press, 1975, p. 268.
10 Geoffrey H. Hartman, *Criticism in the Wilderness: The Study of Literature Today*, New Haven, CT and London: Yale University Press, 1980, p. 202.
11 Ibid., p. 204.
12 Ibid.
13 Geoffrey H. Hartman, *Saving the Text: Literature/Derrida/Philosophy*, Baltimore, MD and London: The Johns Hopkins University Press, 1981, p. 150.

See also in this book

Bloom, de Man, Derrida

Major works

The Unmediated Vision: An Interpretation of Wordsworth, Hopkins, Rilke, and Valery (1954). New Haven, CT and London: Yale University Press.
André Malraux (1960). London: Bowes and Bowes (Studies in Modern European Literature and Thought).
Wordsworth's Poetry: 1787–1814 (1964). New Haven, CT and London: Yale University Press.
Hopkins: A Collection of Critical Essays (ed., 1966). Englewood Cliffs, NJ: Prentice-Hall (Twentieth Century Views).
Beyond Formalism: Literary Essays, 1958–1970 (1970). New Haven, CT and London: Yale University Press.
Romanticism: Vistas, Instances, Continuities (ed. with David Thorburn, 1973). Ithaca, NY: Cornell University Press.
The Fate of Reading, and Other Essays (1975). Chicago, IL and London: The University of Chicago Press.
Psychoanalysis and the Question of the Text (ed., 1978). Baltimore, MD and London: The Johns Hopkins University Press.
Criticism in the Wilderness: The Study of Literature Today (1980). New Haven, CT and London: Yale University Press.
Saving the Text: Literature/Derrida/Philosophy (1981). Baltimore, MD and London: The Johns Hopkins University Press.
Easy Pieces (1985). New York: Columbia University Press.
Shakespeare and the Question of Theory (ed. with Patricia Barker, 1985). London: Methuen.
Bitburg in Moral and Political Perspective (ed., 1986). Bloomington, IN: Indiana University Press.
Midrash and Literature (ed. with Sanford Budick, 1986). New Haven, CT and London: Yale University Press.
The Unremarkable Wordsworth (1987). Minneapolis, MN: University of Minnesota Press.
Minor Prophecies: The Literary Essay in the Culture Wars (1991). Cambridge, MA: Harvard University Press.
Holocaust Remembrance: The Shapes of Memory (ed., 1994). London: Blackwell.
The Longest Shadow: In the Aftermath of the Holocaust (1996). Bloomington, IN: Indiana University Press.
The Fateful Question of Culture (1997). New York: Columbia University Press.

Further reading

Arac, Jonathan, Godzich, Wlad and Martin, Wallace, eds, *The Yale Critics: Deconstruction in America*, Minneapolis, MN: University of Minnesota Press, 1983.
Atkins, George Douglas, *Geoffrey Hartman: Criticism As Answerable Style*, London and New York: Routledge, 1990.
Elam, Helen Regueiro, ed. and introduction, 'Essays in Honor of Geoffrey H. Hartman', Special Issue of *Studies in Romanticism*, 35.4 (1996): 491–652.

Marshall, Donald G., 'Geoffrey Hartman, Wordsworth, and the Inter-
pretation of Modernity', in Kenneth R. Johnston, *et al.*, eds, *Romantic
Revolutions: Criticism and Theory*, Bloomington, IN: Indiana University
Press, 1990; pp. 78–97.
Whitehead, Anne, 'Geoffrey Hartman and the Ethics of Place: Landscape,
Memory, Trauma', *European Journal of English Studies*, 7.3 (2003): 275–292.

LINDA HUTCHEON (1947–)

Integral to Linda Hutcheon's vision of the politics and poetics of postmodernism is a third perspective: that of Canada and Canadian literature. Hutcheon's major surveys of postmodernism for which she is
internationally renowned – *A Poetics of Postmodernism: History, Theory,
Fiction* (1988) and *The Politics of Postmodernism* (1989) – are thus inter-
twined with another text that enriches and completes this particular
trilogy: *The Canadian Postmodern: A Study of Contemporary English-
Canadian Fiction* (1989). Born into an Italian family in Toronto,
Ontario, Hutcheon gained her BA in 1969 from The University of
Toronto, and did graduate work in Italian at Cornell University (MA,
1971) and then in comparative literature back at The University of
Toronto (Ph.D., 1975). Working initially at McMaster University
(1976–1988), Hutcheon became involved in 1980 with the Centre for
Comparative Literature at The University of Toronto, as an adjunct
professor; in 1988 she moved to Toronto permanently as Professor of
English and Comparative Literature. She has held numerous awards,
honorary degrees and fellowships, and in 2000 she was named
President of the Modern Language Association of America. Initial
publications include a translation of Felix Leclerc's *Allegro* (1974) and
monographs on *Narcissistic Narrative: The Metafictional Paradox* (1980),
Formalism and the Freudian Aesthetic: The Example of Charles Mauron
(1984), and *A Theory of Parody: The Teachings of Twentieth-Century Art
Forms* (1985). While these books made significant contributions to literary critical studies, it was her postmodernism trilogy that gained
Hutcheon international acclaim.

In an essay called 'A Crypto-Ethnic Confession' Hutcheon re-
counts how her Italian heritage, 'hidden' beneath her married name,
is one of the factors that encouraged her 'paradoxical desire to blend
into the majority Anglo culture while still retaining my ethnic difference'.[1] Hutcheon's 'crypto-ethnic' identity and her associated work
in comparative literature, is the perfect background for approaching
such an open, diverse and at times contradictory form as postmodernism, since as Hutcheon argues:

Postmodern representational practices that refuse to stay neatly within accepted conventions and traditions and that deploy hybrid forms and seemingly mutually contradictory strategies frustrate critical attempts (including this one) to systematize them, to order them with an eye to control and mastery – that is, to totalize.[2]

A non-totalizing account of a genre and cultural movement that resists academic summary and survey is one of Hutcheon's finest achievements. Yet the impetus to study some of the postmodern materials came out of a 'surveying' task: the research for the chapter 'The Novel 1972–84' for Volume Four of the *Literary History of Canada*. Hutcheon situates her approach to literary materials as occurring at a time when liberal humanism was being replaced in humanities departments with a more nuanced notion of multiple perspectives, ethnicities and awareness of gender constructs and stereotypes. Specifically, Hutcheon regards the lessons of feminism as being key in this move towards a more open approach to literary texts. Her *Canadian Postmodernism*, therefore, emerged from a task that revealed not uniform literary order and progression, but instead 'a set of challenges' and 'different experiences with language and life': 'The "great tradition" of novelists has been dissolving; the supposedly universal culture and values in which it was based were found to be rooted in a particular place, time, class, and possibly, even sex.'[3] What Hutcheon offers, given this shift in intellectual engagement under way in the humanities with the rise of theory, is a trilogy that approaches postmodernism from three main directions: that of poetics ('a flexible conceptual structure that could at once constitute and contain postmodern culture and our discourses both about it and adjacent to it');[4] that of nation and cultural history ('Another consequence of the postmodern valuing of the different and the diverse in opposition to the uniform and the unified is perhaps more particularly Canadian');[5] and that of politics ('politics and the postmodernism have made curious, if inevitable, bedfellows').[6] Hutcheon's approach is firmly anchored in knowledge of a wide range of theoretical and creative texts; in the process of her close reading, she avoids making grand statements that fail to recognize the reality of aesthetic practice: thus she is deeply suspicious of neat binary oppositions that create a divide between modernism and postmodernism. As she argues, postmodernism's relation to modernism is not one of a radical break, and neither does it represent a simplistic progression. Hutcheon also utilizes major critical tools with a critical awareness of their potential limitations, for example, being cautious when it comes to Foucault's 'transhistorical essentializing' of the concept of power, when his project is ostensibly 'anti-totalizing and anti-essentializing'.[7] One of the most important threads that interweaves Hutcheon's postmodern trilogy is that of postmodernism and feminisms, to utilize the title of chapter six from *The Politics of Postmodernism*; in each volume, key feminist theoreticians and authors permeate the text, triggering a multiplicity of perspectives on contemporary cultural and critical positions. Without wishing to conflate feminism and postmodernism, Hutcheon argues 'for the powerful impact of feminist practices on postmodernism'.[8] Hutcheon explores the parallel practices of feminism and postmodernism, arguing not only for points of contact, but also differences, for example, the shared interest in the politics of representation, and the challenge to traditional notions of desire; but in terms of differences, the argument for Hutcheon is that postmodernism often suffers from 'its double encoding as both complicity and critique' while feminism escapes this problem by asserting a position in relation to the production and articulation of gender.[9]

It would be a mistake to reduce Hutcheon's work to her postmodernism trilogy, even given the impact of these particular texts. Apart from the chapter on the 'early postmodernism' of Leonard Cohen in *The Canadian Postmodern*, Hutcheon also published in 1989 a book-length study of Cohen's work; during the early 1990s, Hutcheon explored questions of Canadian identity and ethnicity in a co-edited collection of short-stories and interviews (with Marion Richmond, 1990) and the 'ironies' of ethnicity and race are the subject of chapter two of *Splitting Images: Contemporary Canadian Ironies* (1991), the latter book emerging from Hutcheon's year spent as John P. Robarts Professor of Canadian Studies at York University, Toronto. Hutcheon's work on postcolonialism and feminism includes coverage and insightful analysis of film and photography, and she has also focused more closely on the aesthetics and politics of Canadian photography. In 1991 she co-authored, with Mark A. Cheetham, *Remembering Postmodernism: Trends in Recent Canadian Art*, and the following year she edited *Double-Talking: Essays on Verbal and Visual Ironies in Canadian Art and Literature*. An intriguing collaborative approach with partner Michael Hutcheon has led to a trilogy on opera and medical discourses and history: *Opera: Desire, Disease, Death* (1996), *Bodily Charm: Living Opera* (2000) and *Opera: The Art of Dying* (2004). The hybrid collaborative approach, i.e. between that of a professor of medicine and a professor of literature, aligns with the hybrid nature of opera itself: a complex performative 'musical-theatrical experience'.[10] *A Theory of*

Adaptation (2006) emerges from Hutcheon's multimedia, transdisciplinary experiences of adaptations: resisting the orthodox approach that denigrates adaptation, Hutcheon once again rejects the too-easy approach to 'secondary' forms; instead, deriving theory from practice, she challenges this negative reading from multiple methodological perspectives, arguing that the product and process of adaptations needs to be recognized not just formally, but experientially. After addressing the current theories of adaptation, Hutcheon goes on to explore 'adapters' themselves, audiences, and the 'migration' of adaptations, the transculturation of stories across cultures, languages and history.[11]

Hutcheon's research into parody, irony, historiographic metafiction, postmodernism, opera, adaptations, postcolonialism, poststructuralism, feminism and myriad diverse cultural outputs in Canada and beyond – including publication of over two hundred book chapters and articles and delivering over three hundred and fifty public lectures – has led to her position as a leading cultural commentator. It therefore comes as no surprise that Canadian literary critic Sherrill Grace argues that Hutcheon 'has been instrumental in advancing the interdisciplinary study of literature . . . [Hutcheon has shown us why] in this era of globalization, Humanists need to think outside their disciplinary boxes to embrace wider views of culture and cultural production'.[12]

Notes

1 Linda Hutcheon, 'A Crypto-Ethnic Confession', www.athabascau.ca/cll/writers/hutcheon_essay.html, accessed 2 August 2005.
2 Linda Hutcheon, *The Politics of Postmodernism*, London and New York: Routledge, 2002, p. 35.
3 Linda Hutcheon, *The Canadian Postmodern: A Study of Contemporary English-Canadian Fiction*, Toronto: Oxford University Press, 1988, appendix, p. 188.
4 Linda Hutcheon, *A Poetics of Postmodernism: History, Theory, Fiction*, London and New York: Routledge, 1988, p. ix.
5 Linda Hutcheon, *The Canadian Postmodern: A Study of Contemporary English-Canadian Fiction*, p. 19.
6 Linda Hutcheon, *The Politics of Postmodernism*, p. 2.
7 Linda Hutcheon, *A Poetics of Postmodernism: History, Theory, Fiction*, p. 189.
8 Linda Hutcheon, *The Politics of Postmodernism*, p. 138.
9 Ibid., p. 149.
10 Linda Hutcheon and Michael Hutcheon, *Opera: Desire, Disease, Death*, Lincoln, NE and London: University of Nebraska Press, 1996, p. xvi.
11 I am grateful to Linda Hutcheon for pre-publication access to this book.
12 Sherrill Grace to Richard J. Lane, email, 27 July 2005.

See also in this book

Foucault, Lyotard

Major works:

Narcissistic Narrative: The Metafictional Paradox (1980). Waterloo: Wilfrid Laurier University Press. New edition, London and New York: Methuen, 1984.

Formalism and the Freudian Aesthetic: The Example of Charles Mauron (1984). London and New York: Cambridge University Press.

A Theory of Parody: The Teachings of Twentieth-Century Art Forms (1985). London and New York: Methuen.

A Poetics of Postmodernism: History, Theory, Fiction (1988). London and New York: Routledge.

The Canadian Postmodern: A Study of Contemporary English-Canadian Fiction (1988). Toronto: Oxford University Press.

Leonard Cohen and his Writing (1989). Toronto: ECW Press.

The Politics of Postmodernism (1989). London and New York: Routledge.

Other Solitudes: Canadian Multicultural Fictions (ed. with M. Richmond, 1990). Toronto: Oxford University Press.

Splitting Images: Contemporary Canadian Ironies (1991). Toronto: Oxford University Press.

Double-Talking: Essays on Verbal and Visual Ironies in Contemporary Canadian Art and Literature (1992). Toronto: ECW Press.

A Postmodern Reader (ed. with J. Natoli, 1993). Albany, NY: State University of New York Press.

Irony's Edge: The Theory and Politics of Irony (1994). London and New York: Routledge.

Opera: Desire, Disease, Death (with Michael Hutcheon, 1996). Lincoln, NE: Nebraska University Press.

Bodily Charm: Living Opera (With Michael Hutcheon, 2000). Lincoln, NE: Nebraska University Press.

Opera: The Art of Dying (2004). Harvard University Press.

A Theory of Adaptation (2006). London and New York: Routledge.

Further reading

Baena, Rosalía, 'Critical Perspectives on Writing Ethnicity: Linda Hutcheon', in Rocío G. Davis and Rosalía Baena, eds, *Tricks with a Glass: Writing Ethnicity in Canada*, Amsterdam: Rodopi, 2000; pp. 287–298.

Duvall, John N., 'Troping History: Modernist Residue in Fredric Jameson's Pastiche and Linda Hutcheon's Parody', *Style*, 33.3 (1999): 372–390.

McCance, Dawn, '"Bodily Charm": An Interview with Linda Hutcheon and Michael Hutcheon', *Mosaic*, 34.3 (2001): 159–177.

O'Grady, Kathleen, '*Theorizing* – Feminism and Postmodernity: A Conversation with Linda Hutcheon', *Rampike*, 9.2 (1998): 20–22.

LUCE IRIGARAY (1934–)

In the preface to her *Key Writings*, Luce Irigaray describes her project as the rendering possible of a philosophy and culture of two subjects, within the context of a patriarchal Western philosophy that has 'forgotten' the existence of 'subjectivity in the feminine'.[1] That this project has been influential is undoubted, especially given the impact of Irigaray's first major critique of the patriarchal foundation and structure of psychoanalysis in her doctoral thesis *Speculum of the Other Woman* (1974) which led not only to her being expelled from the École Freudienne but also the loss of her teaching position at the Université de Paris VIII-Vincennes. Irigaray was born in Belgium, achieving her *Licence en philosophie et lettres* in 1954, and her MA in philosophy and literature from the University of Louvain in 1955, with a thesis on Paul Valéry. After teaching in Brussels, she moved into the psychoanalytical field via the Université de Paris where she gained her *Licence de psychologie* in 1961, and then through the Institut de Psychologie de Paris, where she gained a diploma in 1962. Doctoral studies reveal Irigaray's two major areas of focus – with her thesis in linguistics from Université de Paris X at Nanterre in 1968, and a thesis in philosophy from the Université de Paris VIII-Vincennes in 1974, subsequently published and translated in 1985. To understand why Irigaray's second doctoral thesis caused such a furore, it is worth briefly considering her route into psychoanalytical studies. Working initially at the FNRS (Belgian Scientific Research) she moved to the CNRS (National Centre for Scientific Research), as a research assistant specializing in neurolinguistics; Irigaray also partook of Jacques Lacan's infamous seminars and became part of Lacan's École Freudienne de Paris, an institution that Lacan had set up after he had been 'excommunicated' from the IPA (International Psychoanalytical Association) in 1963. But why was *Speculum of the Other Woman* a text that led to Irigaray's expulsion and her own 'excommunication'? As Margaret Whitford argues:

> What is interesting about Irigaray's critique is that it is a critique from within psychoanalysis. She uses psychoanalytic theory against itself to put forward a coherent explanation for theoretical bias in terms of unconscious fantasy, splitting, resistance and defences in the discourses of psychoanalysis.[2]

The key to Irigaray's approach is thus her adoption of *deconstructive* strategies, her working 'from within', in particular with her critique of Freud's patriarchal account of the development of female sexuality. Irigaray is also scathing when it comes to the phallocentric basis of Lacanian re-readings of Freud, critiquing 'the primacy of the phallus' and his mirror stage theory.[3] In a powerfully written essay called 'The Poverty of Psychoanalysis', Irigaray also attacks Lacanians for being ahistorical, unaware or unwilling to become aware of the founding tropes of their notion of psychoanalytical theory and practice. In a process of role-reversal, parody, and a searing use of psychoanalytical logic, Irigaray analyses the members of the École Freudienne de Paris utilizing their own Lacanian terminology to reveal how they are self-protective of their existing order:

> [they are] the agents or servants of repression and censorship ensuring that this order subsists as though it were the only possible order, that there can be no imaginable speech, desire or language other than those which have already taken place, no culture authorized by you other than the monocratism of patriarchal discourse.[4]

Irigaray's transgression, then, was to tackle the new orthodoxy of Lacanianism, and worse still, to point out that this group had in itself become blind to questions concerning gender and sexuality. The 'Selfsame' subject, to use Irigaray's term, is the result of the new orthodoxy, a human being of either sex whose sexual development is predicated upon Freud's theories of castration and *male* sexuality, as well as Lacan's mirror stage. In replacement, Irigaray offers the 'speculum' or, a mirror of interiority as an alternative trope of sexuation.

The speculum represents an alternative economy of knowledge concerning two subjects rather than one (male and female), and a rejection of the patriarchal notion of the singular subject produced via the mirror stage; Irigaray is also playing with the homonymic connections between speculum and the word *spéculer* [speculate], whereby Western knowledge of gender difference has traditionally been reductive: 'The other must therefore speculate [*spéculer*] the (male or female) one, reduplicating what man supposedly already knows as the place of (his) production.'[5] If there is occasionally an assertion of gender difference in the Freudian/Lacanian patriarchal scenario, there are multiple routes that Western knowledge takes to collapse difference and reduce multiplicity; in the process, Irigaray asserts: '"She" must be no more than the path, the method, the theory, the *mirror* for the "subject" that leads back, via a process of repetition, to re-cognition of the unity of (his) origin.'[6] From a positive perspective, Irigaray asserts that: '*The/A woman is never closed/shut (up) in one volume.*'[7] As Margaret Whitford notes:

> Playing on the idea of the mirror . . . [Irigaray] points out that Lacan's mirror can only see women's bodies as lacking, as a 'hole'; to see what is specific to women, he would have needed a mirror that could look inside. The mirror, of course, is the mirror of theory or discourse, and although Lacan is not named, *Speculum* is as much a challenge to Lacan as it is to Freud and to western philosophy.[8]

The feminist project of *Speculum of the Other Woman*, therefore, involves a re-reading of the foundational texts of Western speculative thought; Irigaray calls philosophy a 'discourse on discourse' (i.e. a meta-discourse or one commenting on systems of knowledge at a higher level), which indicates its importance in terms of power: 'the power of its systematicity, the force of its cohesion, the resourcefulness of its strategies, the general applicability of its law and its value'.[9] In other words, Irigaray will chart the defining factors that lead to philosophy's 'mastery'. What are these defining factors? One especially important process for the production and maintenance of this mastery is the reduction of difference, of otherness, to the Selfsame, including the 'difference between the sexes'.[10]

How has Irigaray's project developed since *Speculum of the Other Woman*? How has she mapped out an alternative speculation concerning the two subjects? In 'The Power of Discourse' Irigaray speaks of

> the necessity of 'reopening' the figures of philosophical discourse – idea, substance, subject, transcendental subjectivity, absolute knowledge – in order to pry out of them what they have borrowed that is feminine, from the feminine, to make them 'render up' and give back what they owe the feminine.[11]

The other pathway that Irigaray has taken, has been the continuation and development of her work in neurolinguistics, which she first published in 1973 with her thesis *Le langage des déments*, more recently focusing on empirical research into differences in gender and language use. Her deconstructive, feminist critique of philosophy has involved a significant number of essays and book publications, key texts being *This Sex Which Is Not One* (1977, trans. 1985), *The Marine Lover of Friedrich Nietzsche* (1980, trans. 1991), *Elemental Passions* (1982, trans.

1992), *The Forgetting of Air in Martin Heidegger* (1983, trans. 1999), and *To Be Two* (1997, trans. 1999). In the essay 'This Sex Which Is Not One', Irigaray counteracts male-centric notions of sexuality with woman's autoeroticism; philosophy and sexuality converge with her notion that male pleasure is always supplemented and mediated, whereas female autoeroticism does not necessarily need mediation. This convergence of the material (the body) and the metaphysical (philosophy, the economy of psychoanalysis, etc.) is one of the conditions for Irigaray's escape from accusations of essentialism: read only as a writer concerned with physiological differences, she *appears* essentialist, but when the material and the metaphysical are seen to combine in her work, a much more profound critical landscape emerges, one that rejects the male fantasy of woman's sexuality, in favour of a 'different language' that has been 'submerged' by the logic of the entire tradition of Western metaphysics. Utilizing an alternative, deconstructive logic, Irigaray sketches out an economy of form (male) versus formlessness/absence (female), an economy that she explicitly rejects by proposing that woman is to be reduced neither to one (an absence, a hole), nor, doubled (the sex which is not one). Further, the Oedipal drama is also rejected as 'perpetuating the authoritarian discourse of fathers'.[12] Irigaray celebrates instead a disseminated, diversified female pleasure, which is also a comment on the 'female imaginary', open to multiple differences. The challenge to patriarchy, then, is the questioning of 'all prevailing economies';[13] what this should lead to is not a simplistic reversal of patriarchy, but a more subtle return to the modes of oppression, the conditions of possibility of phallocentric economies, be they conceptual or material. As Irigaray puts it in *The Marine Lover of Friedrich Nietzsche*: 'she [woman] does not oppose a feminine truth to the masculine truth. Because this would once again amount to playing the – man's – game of castration.'[14] The concept and role of castration is, in the same book, regarded as 'the "absolute" spot in the economy of signs'[15] an unrepresentable moment in phallocentric systems of thought.

Irigaray's contributions to feminism, linguistics and philosophy, while considerable, are still undergoing evaluation in the West, especially as more translations of her work become available. Her engagement with major Western philosophers are written in a particularly fluid and dialogic form, requiring of the average reader familiarity and in-depth knowledge of primary texts. Having said this, however, to genuinely think the 'two subjects' of metaphysics may require *beginning* with Irigaray's interrogations of philosophy, combining such a new beginning with her understanding of language, gender and sex differences, and above all, the role of psychoanalysis in modern thought.

Notes

1 *Luce Irigaray: Key Writings*, ed. Luce Irigaray, London and New York: Continuum, 2004, p. vii.
2 Margaret Whitford, ed., *The Irigaray Reader*, Oxford: Basil Blackwell, 1991, p. 5.
3 Ibid., p. 6.
4 Luce Irigaray, 'The Poverty of Psychoanalysis', in Margaret Whitford, ed., *The Irigaray Reader*, p. 82, quotation modified by Lane.
5 Luce Irigaray, 'Volume Without Contours', in Margaret Whitford, ed., *The Irigaray Reader*, p. 65.
6 Ibid.
7 Ibid.
8 Margaret Whitford, ed., *The Irigaray Reader*, p. 7.
9 Luce Irigaray, 'The Power of Discourse and the Subordination of the Feminine', in Margaret Whitford, ed., *The Irigaray Reader*, p. 123.
10 Ibid.
11 Ibid.
12 Luce Irigaray, 'This Sex Which Is Not One', in Robyn R. Warhol and Diane Price Herndl, eds, *Feminisms: An Anthology of Literary Theory and Criticism*, New Brunswick, NJ: Rutgers University Press, 1997, pp. 363–369; p. 365.
13 Ibid., p. 368.
14 Luce Irigaray, *The Marine Lover of Friedrich Nietzsche*, trans. Gillian C. Gill, New York: Columbia University Press, 1991, p. 86.
15 Ibid., p. 83.

See also in this book

Butler, Lacan

Major works

Le langage des déments (1973). The Hague: Mouton.
Speculum of the Other Woman (1974). Trans. Gillian C. Gill, Ithaca, NY: Cornell University Press, 1985.
This Sex Which Is Not One (1977). Trans. Catherine Porter, Ithaca, NY: Cornell University Press, 1985.
The Marine Lover of Friedrich Nietzsche (1980) Trans. Gillian C. Gill, New York: Columbia University Press, 1991.
Elemental Passions (1982). Trans. Joanne Collie and Judith Still, London: Athlone Press, 1993.
The Forgetting of Air in Martin Heidegger (1983). Trans. Mary Beth Mader, London: Athlone Press, 1999.
To Speak is Never Neutral (1985). Trans. Gail Schwab, London and New York: Routledge, 2002.
The Irigaray Reader (1991). Ed. Margaret Whitford, Oxford: Basil Blackwell.
To Be Two (1997). Trans. Mary Beth Mader, London: Athlone Press, 1999.

Further reading

Caldwell, Anne, 'Transforming Sacrifice: Irigaray and the Politics of Sexual Difference', *Hypatia*, 17.4 (2002): 16–38.

Cooper, Sarah, 'Luce Irigaray: Reading and Writing the Body', in Julia Prest and Hannah Thompson, eds, *Corporeal Practices: (Re)figuring the Body in French Studies*, Amsterdam: Peter Lang, 2000; pp. 135–151.

Krier, Theresa M. and Harvey, Elizabeth D., eds, *Luce Irigaray and Premodern Culture: Thresholds of History*, London and New York: Routledge, 2005.

Lorraine, Tamsin, *Irigaray & Deleuze: Experiments in Visceral Philosophy*, Ithaca, NY: Cornell University Press, 1999.

Stone, Alison, 'The Sex of Nature: A Reinterpretation of Irigaray's Metaphysics and Political Thought', *Hypatia*, 18.3 (2003): 60–84.

Ziarek, Ewa Plonowska, 'Toward a Radical Female Imaginary: Temporality and Embodiment in Irigaray's Ethics', *Diacritics*, 28.1 (1998): 60–75.

WOLFGANG ISER (1926–)

While structuralists and poststructuralists have remained focused on texts as objects, be they regarded as organized networks or decentred, differential networks, Wolfgang Iser has contributed significantly to the development of a competing tradition: that of meaning being generated in the *processes* and *experiences* of reading; in other words, meaning is not perceived as residing in a separate autonomous artefact but in the virtual space of convergence between text and reader. The opposing views of these two traditions has in many respects kept them worlds apart, although there is the occasional critical skirmish and cross-border attempts at dialogue. But Reader Response, as it has become known, remains a powerful alternative to the high theory that largely came out of France; Reader Response, or as Iser developed it and more accurately speaking, *Aesthetic Response*, has its origins in the development of new ways of approaching literary and aesthetic texts that took place in Germany. Iser was born in Marienberg, Germany in 1926, and educated at the University of Heidelberg where he was awarded his Ph.D., and is now a Fellow of the Academy of Arts and Sciences. He holds numerous fellowships and doctoral awards, and is renowned for his work at the University of Constance (1967–) – where he is a leading member of the Constance School of Reception Aesthetics – and for his work at the University of California, Irvine (1978–). A formative early text, translated and reprinted many times, is Iser's inaugural lecture at the University of Constance, 'Indeterminacy and the Reader's Response in Prose Fiction'. Iser draws upon a range of German critics and philosophers to develop his ideas, including Gadamer, Hegel, Husserl and

Ingarden, and it is through Iser that phenomenology in particular has been given a literary-critical application.

Two key texts by Iser that continue to interest critics are *The Implied Reader: Patterns of Communication in Prose Fiction from Bunyan to Beckett* (1972), and *The Act of Reading: A Theory of Aesthetic Response* (1976). What does Iser mean by the 'implied reader'? He argues that the 'term incorporates both the prestructuring of the potential meaning by the text, and the reader's actualization of this potential through the reading process'.[1] Iser suggests that between the norms of society and everyday life and the experience of reading a literary text, there is a gap that triggers an aesthetic response, structured by temporary freedom from restricted everyday experience and the exercising of emotional and cognitive faculties. Iser's central term here is 'discovery': the implied reader *discovers* the gap between actual and fictional worlds, and this process while endlessly re-occurring, does have historical specificity. The text thus replaces the familiar with the unfamiliar, and the reader has to work to fill in the interstices of meaning:

> The role of the reader as incorporated in the novel must be seen as something potential and not actual. His [*sic*] reactions are not set out for him, but he is simply offered a frame of possible decisions, and when he has made his choice, then he will fill in the picture accordingly.[2]

In a sense, the implied reader works upon a text first through a series of negations (the 'discoveries') and then through constructive, positive interpretive choices which are offered to him or her by the text. In chapter eleven of *The Implied Reader*, Iser elaborates on the 'phenomenological' impetus of his theory of reading, building on Roman Ingarden's notion of 'realization' whereby different 'schematized views' of the text are brought to light. Iser suggests that the text created by the author be called the 'artistic text' and that text realized by the implied reader be called the 'aesthetic': the 'literary text' is that which exists somewhere between the two in the virtual realm that is actualized by the *intersection* of the artistic and the aesthetic. It is this 'virtuality' that Iser suggests leads to a dynamic situation, provoking the reader to explore new textual avenues, which in turn realizes more complexity in the text; rather than this being a vicious circle, it is instead portrayed as a dynamic process of 'unfolding' meaning via the creative capacities of text and reader. As Iser says: 'A literary text must . . . be conceived in such a way that it will engage the reader's imagination in the task of working things out for himself, for reading is only a pleasure when it is active and creative.'[3] Drawing upon Sterne's *Tristram Shandy*, a text's boundaries are now redrawn in relation not to a set number of inherent components, but rather, *experientially*: at one end of the scale lies the boundary of 'boredom' and at the other end the boundary of 'overstrain'. This begs the question as to where exactly on this scale comes the reader's intelligence, but Iser turns to Virginia Woolf to explore the text's stimulating properties, and her observations that the 'trivial' in Jane Austen stimulates and triggers 'enduring form' in the reader's mind. Iser thus argues that 'unwritten' and 'unspoken' aspects of the text draw in the reader, who in turn outlines what is only presented textually in ghostly form, yet nonetheless, is still controlled by the text's schemata.

For Iser, the next question is whether this process can be adequately described, and to answer this he suggests that a 'phenomenological' approach is needed. Why 'phenomenological'? Iser wants to move away from psychoanalytical models of reading, which he believes are too pre-determined and restrictive; with 'phenomenological' analysis, Iser is able to examine textual/readerly processes via the construction of autonomous 'worlds' presented or performed by literary works. He does this with reference to Ingarden's analysis of 'intentional sentence correlatives' and Husserl's observation that 'every originally constructive process is inspired by pre-intentions, which construct and collect the seed of what is to come, as such, and bring it to fruition'.[4] What joins these together is the phenomenological interest in time: literary sentences do not simply function as statements of fact, they foreshadow or indicate something that will follow, and thereby create an 'expectation'. Iser argues that the most successful literary texts do not simply fulfil such expectations in a didactic and simplistic manner, rather, they continually modify them. Where is the reader in this? She is drawn into the text experientially as the text continually produces or 'opens up' a horizon of possibility, which will be modified or changed as the text proceeds; but this is not a passive process – the reader responds creatively via memory and changed circumstances, through a feeling of involvement in the text's performativity and world-creating in the virtual 'reality' of the intersection of text and reader. Contra Ingarden, however, Iser is not concerned with disruption of the otherwise smooth flow of the coming into being of the virtual 'reality' of the literary text; instead, the interruptions and blockages to the continual temporal modification of anticipatory reading desires, actually realizes a further space for the reader's creative capacity: put simply, the space to then fill in the gaps. We can thus see that the 'phenomenological' approach addresses the temporality, spatiality, and lived-experiences of literary texts. When the implied reader fills in the gaps, she may create a new temporality, a new realization which is also a new *'gestalt'* (or 'consistent interpretation').[5] Thus, repeated readings of a text create new time sequences: not just new insights, as such, but new ways of mapping and experiencing the time and space of the virtual 'reality' of the reading process.

Iser's *The Implied Reader* and its slightly more theoretical companion text, *The Act of Reading*, have generated a wealth of critical research into the role of the reader, including some strong-spirited criticisms of his position from theorists such as Stanley Fish.[6] More recent texts by Iser, beginning with the publication of his *Prospecting: From Reader Response to Literary Anthropology* (1989), lead to a more abstract realm of theorizing, investigating 'the nature and purpose of interpretation/hermeneutics'.[7] But Iser continues to appeal to many critics who are looking for a rigorous alternative to high theory, while wishing to accommodate and incorporate notions of performativity and dynamic text-reader interactions.

Notes

1 Wolfgang Iser, *The Implied Reader: Patterns of Communication in Prose Fiction from Bunyan to Beckett*, Baltimore, MD and London: Johns Hopkins University Press, 1974, p. xii.
2 Ibid., p. 55.
3 Ibid., p. 275.
4 Ibid., p. 277.
5 Zoltán Schwáb, 'Mind the Gap: The Impact of Wolfgang Iser's Reader-Response Criticism on Biblical Studies – A Critical Assessment', *Literature and Theology*, 17.2 (June 2003): 170–181; p. 171.
6 See, for example, Stanley Fish, 'Why No One's Afraid of Wolfgang Iser', *Diacritics*, 11.1 (1981): 2–13.
7 Zoltán Schwáb, 'Mind the Gap: The Impact of Wolfgang Iser's Reader-Response Criticism on Biblical Studies – A Critical Assessment', p. 176.

Major works

Die Weltanschauung Henry Fieldings (1952). Bd. Tübingen: Niemeyer.
Walter Pater: The Aesthetic Moment (1960). Trans. David Henry Wilson, Cambridge and New York: Cambridge University Press, 1987.
'Indeterminacy and the Reader's Response in Prose Fiction' (1970). In J. Hillis Miller, ed., *Aspects of Narrative: Selected Papers from the English Institute*, London and New York: Columbia University Press, 1971, pp. 1–45.
The Implied Reader: Patterns of Communication in Prose Fiction from Bunyan to Beckett (1972). Baltimore, MD and London: Johns Hopkins University Press, 1974.

The Act of Reading: A Theory of Aesthetic Response (1976). Baltimore, MD: Johns Hopkins University Press; London and Henley: Routledge & Kegan Paul, 1978.

Laurence Sterne: Tristram Shandy (1987). Trans. David Henry Wilson, Cambridge and New York: Cambridge University Press, 1988.

Staging Politics: The Lasting Impact of Shakespeare's Historical Plays (1988). Trans. David Henry Wilson, New York: Columbia University Press, 1993.

Prospecting: From Reader Response to Literary Anthropology (1989). Baltimore, MD: Johns Hopkins University Press.

The Fictive and the Imaginary: Charting Literary Anthropology (1991). Trans. David Henry Wilson and Wolfgang Iser, Baltimore, MD: Johns Hopkins University Press, 1993.

The Range of Interpretation (2000). New York: Columbia University Press.

Further reading

Allen, Robert Clyde, 'Reader-Oriented Criticism and Television', in Robert Clyde Allen, ed., *Channels of Discourse: Television and Contemporary Criticism*, Chapel Hill, NC: University of North Carolina Press, 1987; pp. 74–112.

Armstrong, Paul B., 'The Politics of Play: The Social Implications of Iser's Aesthetic Theory', *New Literary History*, 31.1 (2000): 211–223.

Rimmon-Kenan, Shlomith, 'A "Figure" in Iser's "Carpet"', *New Literary History*, 31.1 (2000): 91–104.

Shaffer, Elinor, 'Circling the Reader: The Reception of Wolfgang Iser in the U.K. 1970–2003', *Comparative Critical Studies*, 1.1–2 (2004): 27–43.

Theisen, Bianca, 'The Four Sides of Reading: Paradox, Play, and Autobiographical Fiction in Iser and Rilke', *New Literary History*, 31.1 (2000): 105–128.

Tompkins, Jane P., *Reader Response Criticism: From Formalism to Post-Structuralism*, Baltimore, MD: Johns Hopkins University Press, 1981.

Wilson, David Henry, 'Working with Wolfgang', *Comparative Critical Studies*, 1.1–2 (2004): 19–25.

ROMAN OSIPOVISCH JAKOBSON (1896–1982)

Known among literary theorists primarily for his work on the 'Two Aspects of Language' – that is, the arrangement of signs through processes known as combination and selection – Jakobson's remarkable career encompassed far more than this: he was an accomplished linguist, folklorist, literary critic, expert in Slavic cultures and mythology, medievalist, and film and theatre critic. In all of these areas Jakobson made significant contributions and discoveries, preparing the way for other scholars who followed. The life challenges that Jakobson faced, with the enormous social and political upheavals taking place, especially the Russian Revolution, and the two world wars, also contributed to his involvement in a wide range of languages, cultures and literatures. Born in Moscow, Jakobson studied at the Lazarev Institute of Oriental Languages, entering Moscow University in 1914 where he engaged in Slavic studies in the Philological Faculty. Prior to graduating with an MA in 1918, Jakobson also studied Sanskrit at Petersburg University.[1] Initially working as a research assistant at Moscow University, years of upheaval were soon to follow due to the political climate in Russia. Nonetheless, in 1915 Jakobson and six others founded the Moscow Linguistic Circle, which engaged in the study of language as a system, rejecting the historical approach to the study of language change and development. Jakobson moved to Czechoslovakia in 1920, receiving his doctorate from Prague University in 1930, taking up a post at Masaryk University, Brno. During this period, Jakobson and others founded the Prague Linguistic Circle, another key organization in the development of linguistic studies. However, the Nazi occupation led to Jakobson's flight from Czechoslovakia to Scandinavia (1939), and then emigration to the US (1941). Jakobson's reception in the US was mixed, with his initial university position (1942–1946) being held at the European university in exile called the École Libre des Hautes Études, gaining also a visiting professorship in General Linguistics at Columbia University, where he became T.G. Masaryk Professor of Czechoslovak Studies in 1946. Jakobson became the Samuel Hazard Cross Professor of Slavic Languages and Literature at Harvard University in 1949, and in 1957 he became an Institute Professor at the Massachusetts Institute of Technology.

While Jakobson is most often discussed in introductory accounts in the West in relation to the linguist Ferdinand de Saussure, scholars of Slavic Studies point out that the influences and sources of Jakobson's work are far more complex. In Russia Jakobson had drawn many of his ideas from the reconstruction of the medieval Igor Tale, as well as his discussions with the members of the Moscow Linguistic Circle; in Czechoslovakia he developed not only the bulk of his linguistic and critical theories, but also the phonological theory of language; in Scandinavia he worked on neurolinguistics and developed his theories based upon speech aphasia; in his Polish studies he drew deeply upon the Polish linguists Baudouin and Kruszewski who, Jakobson argued, preceded Saussure, and in America he studied and championed the work of the philosopher Charles Sanders Peirce. As early as his period as a research associate at Moscow University, Jakobson was developing key components of his linguistic theory; drawing upon the experimental poetry and arts of the period was a key process; influences include Stéphane Mallarmé, the Italian Futurist Marinetti, and Russian Futurist poetry. As Jakobson writes:

In 1912, Russian Futurist poetry, or more generally speaking, avant-garde poetry, was beginning to take hold. . . . This blossoming of modern Russian poetry followed the remarkable developments of modern painting, in particular French postimpressionism and its crowning achievement, Cubism. Both were widely disseminated in prewar Moscow.[2]

From this rich cultural milieu, Jakobson would develop his ideas in linguistics that would later have a profound impact upon the subject as a whole.

The two fundamental aspects of language, for Jakobson, were metaphor and metonymy. In his 'Two Aspects of Language and Two Types of Aphasic Disturbances', Jakobson develops this assertion via neurolinguistics. Examining the breakdown of communication in people suffering from aphasia, Jakobson argued that the disintegration of sound patterns also needed supplementing with that of grammatical system. Word choice involves two processes: concurrence and concatenation, which in Saussurian terms is synchrony and diachrony. Put more simply, there is word choice or selection, and there is word combination or the building of more or less complex units through time. Through studying the linguistic challenges of aphasiacs Jakobson was brought to the assertion of the underlying metaphoric and metonymic poles in all language systems: 'Metaphor is alien to the similarity disorder, and metonymy to the contiguity disorder.'[3] Jakobson notes, however, that even in normal situations, these two poles may have a different level of dominance:

> In aphasia one or other of these two processes is restricted or totally blocked – an effect which makes the study of aphasia particularly illuminating for the linguist. In normal verbal behaviour both processes are continually operative, but careful observation will reveal that under the influence of a cultural pattern, personality, and verbal style, preference is given to one of the two processes over the other.[4]

What is the significance of this? Jakobson argues that literature and the visual arts are also analysable via these two poles; in Romanticism and Symbolism there is the primacy of the metaphoric process, while in Realism, the metonymic dominates; in Cubism metonymy rules ('the object is transformed into a set of synecdoches'), whereas in Surrealism, the metaphoric is key. Jakobson also sees this opposition at work in film, regarding certain techniques (close-ups, multiple perspective that goes beyond the fixed perspectives of theatre) as metonymic, whereas others (montage, dissolves) are metaphoric. As Jakobson asserts: 'The dichotomy discussed here appears to be of primal significance and consequence for all verbal behaviour and for human behaviour in general.'[5]

Another key early essay for literary critical studies is 'Linguistics and Poetics', where Jakobson argues that there is a close correspondence between linguistics and poetics, where the 'poetic function' ultimately defines the literary, that is, the projection of *the principle of equivalence from the axis of selection into the axis of combination*.[6] Critic Richard D. Cureton summarizes:

> In our best poetry, linguistic form itself is thematized, and therefore language itself becomes the aesthetic center of the work. Paradigmatic choices (e.g., linguistic categories, slots, relations, functions, meanings, etc.) are selected, arranged, and concentrated into distinctive linguistic textures, and these linguistic textures are the work's central artistic accomplishment.[7]

Jakobson's ideas have permeated virtually all aspects of literary criticism; this is perhaps most marked in his founding of the Moscow Linguistic Circle and the Prague Linguistic Circle. The Moscow Linguistic Circle also exchanged ideas with another key group, the Petrograd Society for the Study of Poetic Language (OPOIAZ), which was founded in 1916; these two groups are known as the Russian Formalists, and their combined search for the basic structures or devices of poetic meaning is regarded as a key moment in literary-critical and linguistic history. For Jakobson, the differences between everyday, communicative, and poetic, self-foregrounding, language was essential, whereby the poetic is distinguished by its drawing attention to language use itself. In its contemporary manifestation, while much of Jakobson's linguistics has been accepted as the framework upon which semiotic and structuralist-based approaches were developed, becoming part of a normative understanding, it is the work of Jacques Lacan and his followers that still utilizes basic Jakobsonian insights. In essays such as 'The Agency of the Letter in the Unconscious or Reason Since Freud' and 'The Subversion of the Subject and the Dialectic of Desire in the Freudian Unconscious', the fundamental insight that the unconscious is structured like a language is heavily influenced by Jakobson.

Notes

1 Krystyna Pomorska, 'Roman Jakobson (October 11, 1896–July 18, 1982)', *The Polish Review*, 29.1–2 (1984): 43–56; p. 43.
2 Roman Jakobson and Krystyna Pomorska, *Dialogues*, Cambridge, MA: The MIT Press, 1988, pp. 6–7.
3 Roman Jakobson, *Language in Literature*, ed. Krystyna Pomorska and Stephen Rudy, Cambridge, MA and London: The Belknap Press of Harvard University Press, 1987, p. 109.
4 Ibid., p. 110.
5 Ibid., p. 112.
6 Ibid., p. 71; Jakobson's italics.
7 Richard D. Cureton, 'Jakobson Revisited: Poetics, Subjectivity, and Temporality', *Journal of English Linguistics*, 28.4 (2000): 354–392; p. 355.

See also in this book

Lacan

Major works

Selected Writings (seven volumes, 1962–1985). Paris: Mouton.
The Framework of Language (1980). Ann Arbor, MI: Michigan Studies in the Humanities.
Verbal Art, Verbal Sign, Verbal Time (1985). Eds Krystyna Pomorska and Stephen Rudy, with Brent Vine, Minneapolis, MN: University of Minnesota Press.
Language in Literature (1987). Eds Krystyna Pomorska and Stephen Rudy, Cambridge, MA and London: The Belknap Press of Harvard University Press.

Further reading

Cureton, Richard D., 'Jakobson Revisited: Poetics, Subjectivity, and Temporality', *Journal of English Linguistics*, 28.4 (2000): 354–392.
Donnelly, Linda, 'Jakobson's Model of Communication: Its Application to the Analysis of the Literary Text', in Piotr Fast and Waclaw Osadnik Osadnik, eds, *From Kievan Prayers to Avantgarde: Papers in Comparative Literature*, Warsaw, Poland: Wydawnictwo Energeia, 1999; pp. 19–32.
Falk, Julia S., 'Roman Jakobson and the History of Saussurean Concepts in North American Linguistics', *Historiographia Linguistica*, 12.3 (1995): 335–367.
Waugh, Linda R., 'Semiotics and Language: The Work of Roman Jakobson', in Roberta Kevelson, ed., *Hi-Fives: A Trip to Semiotics*, New York: Peter Lang, 1998.

FREDRIC R. JAMESON (1934–)

One of the strangest moments in Marxist criticism must surely be the Marxist cultural and literary critic Fredric Jameson exploring the Westin Bonaventure Hotel in downtown Los Angeles, as a way of elucidating the social and architectural space of postmodernity.[1] Dialectical reasoning is applied to the baffling feelings of dislocation experienced while attempting to walk through a postmodern hyperspace, one in which entrances and exits, elevators and escalators, all serve to disrupt the normal human expectations of form and function. For Jameson, the Bonaventure Hotel aspires to be a total space or world, if not a 'miniature city', one in which sense-making processes, such as the passage through architectural form as narrative or personal and public story, are fundamentally disturbed, leading to a 'dialectical intensification' where the meaning of the place is itself, not some wider relationship with or expression of history or community outside of the building. Like Charlie in the Chocolate Factory, Jameson is both appalled and delighted by the disorientation caused by the radical realignment of spatial hotel coordinates, leading to such statements as 'escalator and elevator are also . . . dialectical opposites' while the elevator gondolas become a 'dialectical compensation'.[2] Jameson concludes his visit by arguing that 'postmodern hyperspace' thus transcends 'the capacities of the individual human body to locate itself, to organize its immediate surroundings perceptually, and to map cognitively its position in a mappable external world'.[3] And yet, for all this, Jameson *does* brilliantly and amusingly map postmodern hyperspace by constantly moving his observations from the sublime to the ridiculous, and by parodying postmodernity with a clear subtext: that a comparison can be made with the spaces of human interaction and sociality that do still exist, somewhere, outside of late capitalist hyperreal hotels. If anyone has clarified the relations between postmodernism and economic and ideological factors, it is Jameson, far more so than those who hyperbolically celebrate, or simply critique, postmodernism per se. Born in Cleveland, Ohio, Jameson was educated at Haverford College, gaining his BA in 1954, followed by an MA (1956) and Ph.D. (1960) from Yale. Jameson initially worked at Harvard, followed by just under a decade teaching at The University of California at San Diego in French and Comparative Literature (1967–1976). After work at Yale and the University of California at Santa Cruz, Jameson was appointed William A. Lane, Jr, Professor of Comparative Literature at Duke University (1986). Jameson has received numerous prestigious awards and fellowships, including two

Guggenheim Fellowships; his publications during this period have included some of the key commentaries on Marxist and structuralist thinkers – such as his *Marxism and Form* (1971), *The Prison House of Language: A Critical Account of Structuralism and Russian Formalism* (1972) and *The Political Unconscious: Narrative as a Socially Symbolic Act* (1981), as well as insightful analyses of postmodern culture collected in *The Cultural Turn: Selected Writings on the Postmodern, 1983–1998* (1998).

The immense diversity of Jameson's critical canon – its wide philosophical, political and aesthetic range – can be situated in relation to a short passage in the concluding chapter ('Towards Dialectical Criticism') of *Marxism and Form*, where Jameson defends Marxism as a critical philosophy and asserts that his own approach will involve 'a coordination of Hegelian and Marxist conceptual operations'.[4] Jameson emphasizes the importance of the anti-systematic force of dialectical thinking, and notes that Marxism can be thought of as an inner 'permanent revolution' that rejects any possibility of a position 'outside' of history, such as the methodology of speculative thought or metaphysics, thus:

> Marx's thought represents an advance over that of Hegel, who reserved a single position outside of history for the philosopher of history himself, and was to that extent unable to grasp the notion of being-in-situation in its most paradoxical dimensions.[5]

Jameson's Marxism, then, seeks to remain a critical rather than a systematic philosophy, one that remains 'in-situation' and attempts to proceed by dialectical 'rectification'. In correcting or 'rectifying' critical misunderstanding of Hegelian idealism, Jameson notes that his work will be in opposition to 'Anglo-American empirical realism', a mode of thinking that Jameson argues is 'a check on social consciousness: allowing legal and ethical answers to be given to economic questions, substituting the language of political equality for that of economic inequality and considerations about freedom for doubts about capitalism itself'.[6] Jameson argues that such thinking leads to compartmentalization and fragmentation, leading to an inability to see the totality at work. In a sense, his literary critical project has been an ongoing puncturing of such compartments, a flooding of discrete categories with that of dialectical insight. In *Marxism and Form*, dialectical insights are raided from the works of Adorno, Benjamin, Marcuse, Bloch, Lukács and Sartre (in order of study), through a series of vignettes that culminate in a meditation on a future Marxist literary-critical methodology that rejects the exaltation of criticism to 'the level of literary creation' (a reference to 'French' high theory) and instead offers what Jameson calls a more 'honest' dialectical approach, that is to say, one that responds to historical change.[7] Marxist literary criticism, in this rendering of its capacities, goes beyond Anglo-American philosophy in its insights, but doesn't transcend history in the sense of the new French theory, and may in its interpretative abilities lead to the future replacement of the abstract with the concrete.

In *The Prison-House of Language*, Jameson engages with the formalist and structuralist work that had fed into the new poststructuralist theory that would be one of the main competitors of Marxist literary criticism. Jameson takes a number of interesting strategic positions: locating the rise of formalist and structuralist thought in relation to Marxist thinking, and also examining closely the synchronic/diachronic axes in Saussurian linguistics, given that the rejection of the diachronic can be figured as a rejection of the significance of historical change. The basic Saussurian insight, that language functions synchronically as a system of differences, is anathema to a materialist philosophy, but Jameson performs a number of recuperative manoeuvres, to bring Saussure's followers – in the shape of the *Tel Quel* group and others – back into the dialectical fold. Thus *Tel Quel* are praised for their *rejection* of the transcendental signifier, or, 'ultimate substantialized dimension of meaning or absolute presence' which is evident in their 'militant atheism'.[8] Jameson even manages to recuperate Derrida's concept of the trace as a potentially Marxist insight, and history reappears, regardless of structuralist and poststructuralist assertions, in 'the smallest differential event' of Derrida's *différance*.[9] The prison-house of language, or, the linguistic turn, is thus broken open by the eruption of the temporal. Does Jameson provide an alternative to his massive critique/recuperation of structuralism and its variations? The answer is found in *The Political Unconscious*, Jameson's Marxist *tour de force* of narrative interpretation, which asserts Marxism as an 'untranscendable horizon' that can perceive the totality that all other interpretive methods fail to fully engage with. Jameson's work on 'strategies of containment' or, the illusion that other interpretive codes give a total explanation, allows him to compare, test, and 'measure' the outcome of Marxist interpretation. This distance from other critical methodologies – 'the ethical, the psychoanalytic, the myth-critical, the semiotic, the structural, and the theological'[10] – allows not only for some powerful readings of Balzac, Gissing and

Conrad, but also in *Late Marxism: Adorno, or, The Persistence of the Dialectic* (1990), a wresting back from the postmodernists of Adorno's 'old-fashioned dialectical discourse',[11] and in *Brecht and Method* (1998), a careful recovery of 'praxis' from Barthes' linguistic readings of Brecht. Thus, Jameson ends *Late Marxism* with the hope that even given the birth of an entirely postmodern society, the 'thing itself' or 'objective experience of social reality' will always emerge.[12]

Notes

1 Fredric Jameson, *The Cultural Turn: Selected Writings on the Postmodern, 1983–1998*, London and New York: Verso, 1998, p. 11.
2 Ibid., p. 14.
3 Ibid., p. 16.
4 Fredric Jameson, *Marxism and Form: Twentieth-Century Dialectical Theories of Literature*, Princeton, NJ: Princeton University Press, 1971, p. 361.
5 Ibid., p. 365.
6 Ibid., p. 367.
7 Ibid., p. 415.
8 Fredric Jameson, *The Prison-House of Language: A Critical Account of Structuralism and Russian Formalism*, Princeton, NJ: Princeton University Press, 1972, p. 182.
9 Ibid., p. 187.
10 Fredric Jameson, *The Political Unconscious: Narrative as a Socially Symbolic Act*, London: Methuen, 1981, p. 10.
11 Fredric Jameson, *Late Marxism: Adorno, or, The Persistence of the Dialectic*, London and New York: Verso, 1990, p. 5.
12 Ibid., p. 251.

See also in this book

Eagleton

Major works

Sartre: The Origins of a Style (1961). New Haven, CT: Yale University Press.
Marxism and Form: Twentieth-Century Dialectical Theories of Literature (1971). Princeton, NJ: Princeton University Press.
The Prison-House of Language: A Critical Account of Structuralism and Russian Formalism (1972). Princeton, NJ: Princeton University Press.
Fables of Aggression: Wyndham Lewis, the Modernist as Fascist (1979). Berkeley, CA: University of California Press.
The Political Unconscious: Narrative as a Socially Symbolic Act (1981). London: Methuen.
The Ideologies of Theory: Essays 1971–1986 (1988). *Volume 1, Situations of Theory; Volume 2, Syntax of History*, London and New York: Routledge.
Late Marxism: Adorno, or, The Persistence of the Dialectic (1990). London and New York: Verso.
Brecht and Method (1998). London and New York: Verso.

The Cultural Turn: Selected Writings on the Postmodern, 1983–1998 (1998). London and New York: Verso.

Further reading

Anderson, Perry, *The Origins of Postmodernity*, London: Verso, 1998.

Homer, Sean, *Fredric Jameson: Marxism, Hermeneutics, Postmodernism*, London and New York: Routledge, 1998.

Kellner, Douglas and Homer, Sean, eds, *Fredric Jameson: A Critical Reader*, Basingstoke: Palgrave, 2004.

Miklaucic, Shawn, 'Jameson and Form: Spatial Representation in the Texts of Fredric Jameson', *Mediations*, 21 (1998): 36–54.

Roberts, Adam, *Fredric Jameson*, London and New York: Routledge, 2000.

Simons, Jon, 'Postmodern Paranoia? Pynchon and Jameson', *Paragraph*, 23.2 (2000): 207–221.

(SIR) FRANK KERMODE (1919–)

Defender of the canon, defender of the faith in literature, and the insider's insider, Frank Kermode has been reading, reviewing and interpreting literature for over six decades; in his skirmishes with literary theorists, he has paved the way for the introduction of a more theoretical approach to literary studies, even if that was not the desired effect. Born in England, in 1919, Kermode was educated at Liverpool University, where he gained his BA in English in 1940, and his MA (with a thesis on the poet Abraham Cowley) in 1947; he served in the Royal Navy during 1940–1946. Kermode's first academic posts were at Kings College Newcastle (1947–1949), and The University of Reading (1949–1958), during which time he published his first book, called *Romantic Image* (1957). In 1958, Kermode was appointed as the John Edward Taylor Chair of English Literature at The University of Manchester, and the Winterstoke Professor of English at The University of Bristol in 1965. Two more highly distinguished posts were to follow: in 1967 Kermode became the Lord Northcliffe Professor of Modern English Literature at University College London, and in 1974 he became the King Edward Professor of English Literature at Cambridge. Visiting professorships included Harvard University (1961) and Columbia University (1983 and 1985). What such a list of prestigious titles and positions does not tell the reader is the extensive service Kermode has performed for the world of letters, in his reviews and editorial roles. Kermode has published hundreds of review articles in journals and magazines such as *The Listener*, *Encounter*, the *New York Review of Books*, the *New York Times Book Review* and *The London Review of Books*.[1] Key edited anthologies and other texts include *English Pastoral Poetry: From the Beginnings to Marvell* (1952), *Five Centuries of Shakespeare Criticism* (1965), *The Oxford Anthology of English Literature* (with John Hollander, 1973) and *The Literary Guide to the Bible* (with Robert Alter, 1987), to name but a few.

While Kermode has not promulgated any particular theory, or developed a school of followers, his critical writings may be mapped according to two main phases: his publications up to and including *The Sense of an Ending* (1967), and his following shift, via exploration of the new French theory (especially Roland Barthes), to a more meta-textual approach apparent in texts such as *The Genesis of Secrecy* (1979) and *The Art of Telling* (1983). The early publications include *Romantic Image* (1957), *John Donne* (1957), the formative and influential *Wallace Stevens* (1960), *William Shakespeare: The Final Plays* (1963) and *D.H. Lawrence* (1973). Kermode's essential humanism is given commanding force with his celebration of the poet and the importance of poetry in human life; in a lecture on Shakespeare given at the Center For Advanced Studies, Wesleyan University, in 1964, Kermode argues against the notion that Shakespeare's genius is 'natural', not by advocating a 'learned' Shakespeare in his place, but rather one of great intellect expressed through the intensity and 'perversity' of Shakespeare the poet.[2] Thus, Kermode advocates a more comprehensive historical and textual understanding of Shakespeare, while still maintaining the priority of his *literary* identity and expression.

After the publication of *The Sense of an Ending*, Kermode starts to comment more substantially on literary theory. Nowhere is this shift more apparent than in his comments concerning 'the canon', comments that are also indicative of a humanist approach. How does Kermode define the canon, and why is he so keen to defend it? In an essay published in 1988 based on a lecture delivered that year at the Free University, Amsterdam, Kermode opposes the 'mnemonic' notion of canon with that of the 'regulative' notion. In this opposition, cultural preservation and memorialization is opposed to that of a power-based notion of canon; with the former, Kermode insists that canon is a mnemonic device for handling information in the face of an 'overwhelming mass of data';[3] in other words, something is worth selecting and preserving from the 'mass' cultural matrix. Shifting to Christian history, Kermode points out that canon initially meant 'the rule of faith or truth' and then this same sense was applied to the Scriptures; the point being obliquely made is that canon becomes normative, but also an expression of *institutional* rules that are worth following. While Kermode thus concedes that those opposed to canons are justified in connecting them with expressions of *institutional* power, he does not accept that such attackers are being truthful, in that he suggests that rather than destroy canons, they would rather take them over. Further, Kermode argues that the canon is not brought into existence by any one 'party in power', rather, it comes into existence through time, and through informed consent.[4] Why must the canon be defended? To understand this, the role of the critic must be brought into the equation; as Christopher J. Knight argues: 'The critic, for Kermode, is a facilitator who helps the work find and hold an audience, principally by pointing to those places within it where value . . . may be found.'[5] The critic is thus a secondary figure commenting upon the primary literary text that has been produced by an artist of great insight or genius. The humanist task, then, becomes sorting the wheat from the chaff (reviewing) and maintaining the modernity or relevance of the canon (interpretation). Who is attacking the canon? Kermode suggests that it is 'minorities': feminists, African-Americans, postmodernists, postcolonialists, and so on. Kermode's position here is complex: he argues that those who regard canon as no more than an expression of power also do not wish to 'remember the past in any orderly way'.[6] The key word here is 'orderly' suggesting that the canon brings order, while its dismantling will bring chaos. For Kermode, a canon is a coherent 'totality' and those who recognize this and cherish this have a duty to protect the canon through expressing to others precisely *why* they value canon. So Kermode perceives the attackers of canon to be inconsistent and contradictory in their demands: they wish to expand the canon at the same time as they wish to entirely dismantle it; they bemoan the exclusion of minority writers, while arguing that the canon was responsible for holding back minorities from writing in the first place; they wish to gain canonical status for minority writing without gaining the concomitant institutional power-knowledge status that they were previously suspicious of, and so on. Responding in *An Appetite for Poetry* (1989) to criticisms made of Kermode's position on canon by the deconstructionist Jonathan Culler, Kermode offers five elucidating criticisms of Culler's approach that help with an overall understanding of the subject:

> First, despite wishes to the contrary, 'canons are formed by exclusions as well as inclusions' . . . Second, 'canons are not . . . enclosures full of static monuments' (AP, 15). Rather, they are texts plus commentary, giving 'the contents of the canon

a perpetual modernity' (ibid.). Third, 'without canon there would be no tradition ensuring what can be thought of as the special forms of attention elicited by canonical texts' . . . Fourth, 'there is, indeed, no . . . necessary association between canons and political oppression'. . . [and Fifth] it is not true that canons are predicated on the notion of aesthetic totality. The relation of a text 'to a totality of texts' is always a problematic matter, and this 'is why interpretation is endless – why it can make sense to speak of texts as inexhaustible, and of the 'great' texts as calling for continual institutional inquiry (AP, 18).[7]

Perhaps ironically, it is the very theories produced by those Kermode calls 'minorities' that are providing new ways of interpreting canonical texts. However, this still leaves the underlying fact that the founding contract between canon and critic – that the latter values, defends and therefore maintains the 'perpetual modernity' of the former – has now been broken.

Even though Kermode has not founded a school of criticism, he has still contributed greatly to critical thinking in Anglo-American literary criticism. Commentators sometimes call Kermode a 'religious' or 'theological' thinker, which he has, perhaps disingenuously, denied. In an essay called 'Institutional Control of Interpretation' (1979), for example, Kermode speaks 'about the institution of literary and critical scholarship' via 'analogy with ecclesiastical and other institutions'.[8] In this essay, Kermode's analogy between Church and secular school, merely foregrounds a pattern and a relationship that critics perceive in his work as a whole. For Kermode, in a post-Christendom world, the arts are where true value now resides; yet the canon, being 'texts plus commentaries', needs not just defence per se, i.e. defence of the *list* of great books or the books themselves, but also *regulation* of those who are permitted into the institution of literary criticism to write the commentaries in the first place: in other words, the 'licensed' exegetes or insiders, who can access the 'latent' meaning of aesthetic texts. Observing an MLA program, Kermode calls the manifestation of feminist and black studies 'marginal innovation and unrest' describing this as a 'total license in regard to canon' which will necessarily be ameliorated and controlled.[9] In other words, the institution – the MLA – allows for a temporary carnivalesque, a letting-off steam, but in the process maintains previously held values, standards and order. Since Kermode wrote these words, it has become apparent that the carnivalesque in some ways now reigns. In *The*

Genesis of Secrecy: On the Interpretation of Narrative (1979), Kermode traces the authority of interpretive insiders to no less a figure than Jesus Christ, in Mark 4:11–12, summarized with the statement 'Only the insiders can have access to the true sense of these stories.'[10] Insiders are in this schema 'good' readers, while outsiders are beyond the pale, and need guidance and education by the insiders. Kermode is a canny reader, it goes without saying, and he tempers this hard-and-fast distinction or binary opposition with an aside that this Scriptural statement occurs when Jesus is frustrated by the inability of his disciples (the ultimate insiders) to understand that which they should already know. The opposition is thus not set in stone, and a controlled chiasmus is how the binary actually functions in Kermode's work. In *The Genesis of Secrecy*, Kermode is the insider par excellence with his new reading of Henry Green's *Party Going*, but he is an outsider when it comes to his readings of the New Testament. These readings are knowledgeable, intriguing and quite brilliant: in the process, while still not being a theologian, Kermode crosses from outside to inside, having in a sense authorized his own passage (the book is now standard reading on many religious studies courses or courses that study religion and literature). Kermode's theory of reading can also be seen most clearly in *The Genesis of Secrecy* where interpretive insight is akin to Dilthey's 'impression-point', that is to say, a moment of perception that 'gives sense and structure to the whole'[11] be that whole life, or a text or a canon. Such a moment Kermode calls 'divination' and a text may have several such divinations in its total *gestalt*. Digging around in texts in search of these moments of divination, thus uncovering the latent meaning, may sound analogous to psychoanalytical methodologies, and indeed in his prologue to *The Art of Telling: Essays on Fiction* (1983), Kermode argues that our 'era of interpretation might be said . . . to have begun when Freud published *The Interpretation of Dreams*'.[12] But even more tellingly, Kermode ends his prologue not with the implications of Freud, but rather the notion of earning as critics 'the privilege of access to that kingdom of the larger existence which is in our time the secular surrogate of another Kingdom whose horizon is no longer within our range'.[13]

Notes

1 Christopher J. Knight, *Uncommon Readers: Denis Donoghue, Frank Kermode, George Steiner, and the Tradition of the Common Reader*, Toronto: University of Toronto Press, 2003, p. 162.
2 Frank Kermode, *On Shakespeare's Learning*, Middletown, CT: Wesleyan University Press, 1965, p. 22.

3 Frank Kermode, 'Canons', *Dutch Quarterly Review of Anglo-American Letters*, 18.4 (1988): 258–270; p. 258.
4 Ibid., p. 265.
5 Christopher J. Knight, *Uncommon Readers: Denis Donoghue, Frank Kermode, George Steiner, and the Tradition of the Common Reader*, p. 161.
6 Frank Kermode, 'Canons', p. 268.
7 Christopher J. Knight, *Uncommon Readers: Denis Donoghue, Frank Kermode, George Steiner, and the Tradition of the Common Reader*, p. 200.
8 Frank Kermode, 'Institutional Control of Interpretation', *Salmagundi*, 43 (1979): 72–86; p. 84.
9 Ibid., p. 82.
10 Frank Kermode, *The Genesis of Secrecy: On the Interpretation of Narrative*, Cambridge, MA: Harvard University Press, 1979, p. 2.
11 Ibid., p. 16.
12 Ibid., p. 30.
13 Ibid., pp. 31–32.

Major works

John Donne (1957). London and New York: Longmans, Green & Co.
Romantic Image (1957). London: Routledge & Kegan Paul.
The Living Milton (1960). London: Routledge & Kegan Paul.
Wallace Stevens (1960). Edinburgh: Oliver & Boyd.
William Shakespeare: The Final Plays (1963). London: Longmans, Green & Co.
The Patience of Shakespeare (1964). New York: Harcourt, Brace & World.
On Shakespeare's Learning (1965). Middletown, CT: Wesleyan University Press.
The Sense of an Ending: Studies in the Theory of Fiction (1967). Oxford and New York: Oxford University Press.
Continuities (1968). London: Routledge & Kegan Paul.
Shakespeare, Spenser, Donne: Renaissance Essays (1971). London: Routledge & Kegan Paul.
D.H. Lawrence (1973). London: Fontana.
The Oxford Anthology of English Literature (ed. with John Hollander, 1973). Oxford and New York: Oxford University Press.
The Classic: Literary Images of Permanence and Change (1975). New York: Viking.
The Genesis of Secrecy: On the Interpretation of Narrative (1979). Cambridge, MA: Harvard University Press.
Essays on Fiction: 1971–1982 (1983). London: Routledge & Kegan Paul.
Forms of Attention (1985). Chicago, IL: University of Chicago Press.
The Literary Guide to the Bible (ed. with Robert Alter, 1987). Cambridge, MA: Harvard University Press.
History and Value (1988). Oxford: Clarendon Press.
An Appetite for Poetry (1989). Cambridge, MA: Harvard University Press.
Poetry, Narrative, History (1990). Oxford: Basil Blackwell.
The Uses of Error (1990). London: Collins.

Further reading

Browning, Logan D., 'A Conversation with Sir Frank Kermode', *Studies in English Literature*, 45.2 (2005): 461–479.

Gillespie, Gerald, 'New Apocalypse for Old: Kermode's Theory of Modernism', *Boundary 2*, 3.2 (1975): 307–323.

Gorak, Jan, *Critic of Crisis: A Study of Frank Kermode*, Columbia: University of Missouri Press, 1987.

Kerrigan, William, 'Shakespeare and Kermode', *Raritan*, 20.3 (2001): 141–146.

Knight, Christopher J., *Uncommon Readers: Denis Donoghue, Frank Kermode, George Steiner, and the Tradition of the Common Reader*, Toronto: University of Toronto Press, 2003.

Tudeau-Clayton, Margaret and Warner, Martin, eds, *Addressing Frank Kermode: Essays in Criticism and Interpretation*, Urbana, IL: University of Illinois Press, 1991.

JULIA KRISTEVA (1941–)

A confluence of the new radical French thinkers took place in the 1960s, their mouthpiece being the journal *Tel Quel* (1960–1983). One of the most exciting contributors to the journal was Julia Kristeva, whose re-readings of semiotics, structuralism, linguistics and Lacanian psychoanalysis transformed the thought of her contemporaries. Born in Bulgaria in 1941, Kristeva was educated at the University of Sofia, and emigrated to France in 1965, studying at The University of Paris VII. In Paris she was soon immersed in the heady world of theory, attending seminars by Roland Barthes, Lucien Goldmann and Jacques Lacan. She defended her thesis in 1973, published the following year as *La Révolution du langage poétique: L'Avant-garde à la fin du XIXe siècle* (translated a decade later as *Revolution in Poetic Language*, 1984). Kristeva already had a significant presence among the Parisian intelligentsia: prior to her thesis defence she had published many critical essays in academic journals and two books, *Séméiotiké: Recherches pour une sémanalyse* (1969) and *Le Texte du roman: Approche sémiologique d'une structure discursive transformationelle* (1970). She became Professor of Linguistics at Paris VII in 1974, and in addition to this post became a practising psychoanalyst.

Séméiotiké: Recherches pour une sémanalyse is a crucial book in the development of semiotics, expanded upon significantly in *La Révolution du langage poétique: L'Avant-garde à la fin du XIXe siècle*. In these texts Kristeva advances a number of key concepts: *sémanalyse*, the *geno-text* and *pheno-text*, *paragram*, *chora* and *intertextuality*. *Sémanalyse* is a critique of the scientific basis of structuralist linguistics, in particular, the notion that poetic or literary texts can be reduced to (or explained by) language itself; in other words, *Sémanalyse* rejects the approach that argues that the tools used for linguistic analysis are also the very words under study. Kristeva argues instead that poetic texts function translinguistically, that is to say 'across' the relations and spaces of literature.[1] Translinguistic traversal suggests an 'outside' that structuralist linguistics cannot account for, be this 'outside' the pre–Oedipal subject or a pre–linguistic realm (see Lacan entry). A concrete example can be found in Kristeva's work in *Tel Quel* on Saussure's anagrams; an anagram is a word or a phrase that can be rearranged using the same letters to form another word or phrase. Saussure's study of Roman poetry had potentially subversive import: the notion that poetic language, as Baudrillard puts it is 'beyond the laws, axioms and finalities assigned it by linguistics'.[2] However, for Kristeva, the importance of Saussure's work in this field is indicated by the temporal shift between 'ana-' and 'para-' in the words anagram and paragram, the former ('ana-') implying a hidden anterior meaning within a word that the poetic reveals in its supplementarity (the poetic always supplements functional or communicative language), the latter ('para-') implying that the poetic is a deconstructive dissemination or dispersal 'across' a textual field. In other words, Kristeva adopts the term 'paragram' to resist regarding the poetic as a mere supplement of 'normal' communicative language; instead, the poetic works in relation with and *alongside* communicative language.

Kristeva develops the terms *geno-text* and *pheno-text*, or, the translinguistic and the communicative (i.e. everyday material language), which expands upon this traversal. The *geno-text* and *pheno-text* do not exist in isolation: they are co–constitutive and are always in process. An example drawn from Kristeva's work is the poetic phrase that Baudelaire invents '*meubles voluptueux*' ('voluptuous furniture'). The two individual words that are juxtaposed belong to denotative, communicative language, yet the poetic act of juxtaposing them is *not* a supplementary addition of poetic value, rather it is a 'short-circuit' of the two.[3] Thus, the words 'voluptuous' and 'furniture' belong to the *pheno-text* and the short–circuiting is the action or the drive of the *geno-text*. In psychoanalytical terms, the *geno-text* belongs to the worlds of the affects, and it is generative of the *pheno-text*, while always exceeding the latter (i.e. it cannot be explained by the text that 'results'). It is the task of *sémanalyse* to understand the relations between the *geno-text* and *pheno-text*.

In *La Révolution du langage poétique: L'Avant-garde à la fin du XIXe siècle*, Kristeva expands upon the notion of the *geno-text* in relation to the space that she calls the *chora*, that is, a pre–linguistic space and/or phase. The word *chora* is derived from Plato's *Timaeus*, and literally means 'a receptacle' but Kristeva radically modifies the term in two main ways: first, utilizing Lacanian psychoanalytical discourse, she theorizes the *chora* as a pre-linguistic 'maternal' space that precedes the mirror-stage (see Lacan entry), a space without name (it is pre-symbolic); second, she equates *chora* with her notion of the semiotic, that is, the signifying practices that always exceed the realm of the symbolic. In *Powers of Horror* (1980), in a section concerning the clean and the unclean in Biblical narrative, Kristeva argues that the foundational separation of monotheism (one God) from polytheism (many gods) was also a separation of monotheism from 'the phantasmatic power of the mother', i.e. the *chora* described here as constituting in each person 'the abyss that must be established as an autonomous . . . *place* and *distinct* object, meaning a *signifiable* one, so that such a person might learn to speak'.[4] In other words, here the *chora* is necessarily excluded from the law of the father and the symbolic, but is nonetheless an essential interiority through which the subject comes to formation. During this phase of her work, Kristeva also developed the concept of *intertextuality* to argue against the closed systems of structuralism in favour of the open systems of poststructuralism. In the development of this concept, Kristeva builds upon the theories of Mikhail Bakhtin, in particular his notion of polyphonic utterances, that is to say, a free play of at times contesting voices in a single text, such as a novel. In *Le Texte du roman* the notion of speech utterance is replaced by that of textuality and the micrological unit known as the *ideologeme*, the smallest ideological component in a system. Kristeva argues that the *ideologeme* coordinates the connectivity of texts to form an intertextual network of meaning (e.g. the coordination of semiotic and symbolic systems). The act of reading/writing becomes a transformative reorganization of the socio-historical intertextual network. In what way then is the structuralist system perceived to be closed? In arguing for a science of signs, early practitioners of structuralism and semiotics treated texts as exhaustible, in other words a finite set of interpretative tools, drawn from the text itself, could be used to delimit and map *all* of the text's functional components. Kristeva, however, argues that there are components that in some ways precede and exceed the *pheno-text* that traditional structuralism and semiotics operates with and upon; another way of formulating this process is to think about exactly *how* a system may be exceeded but not transcended (i.e. the desire is not to lapse back into a metaphysical way of thinking). Kristeva utilizes a mathematical discourse and the term 'transfinite' to explain the non-metaphysical 'outside' of a system. The transfinite (drawn from the work of mathematician Georg Cantor, 1845–1918) is the paradoxical 'last' number in an infinite set of numbers, that is to say, the last term of one set which is the first term of the next infinite set; in other words, it is a number that is neither inside nor outside of the infinite number set. The important point is that the number exists, it is neither imaginary nor transcendent. As Ffrench puts it:

> The transfinite point is 'just outside' what is already there, a point at the limit, right on it, *à même*. Literature, and literary theory, is read in *Tel Quel* as a transformation of the phenomenal, of language, from this point. The task of semiology or analysis is to analyse the finite in relation to the transfinite.[5]

Kristeva's concept of *intertextuality* is thus one component in a wider theory of text as 'productivity' where there is always a subject-in-process spoken and situated by the relations between sign systems.

The incredibly complex and dense theorizing of Kristeva's work was opened up by a shift into a more accessible style of writing in her next wave of books (including a major translation into English of some of her earlier essays in *Desire in Language: A Semiotic Approach to Literature and Art*, 1980). In 1980, the feminist force and components of Kristeva's earlier work were brought into focus with her *Powers of Horror: An Essay on Abjection*. The 'abject' is the cast-away, the expulsed or rejected Other, something that cannot be assimilated. Kristeva ties in her analysis of the abject (in psychoanalysis, Biblical narrative, and literature, especially the work of Céline) with the separation and denial of the 'feminine' (especially the role of the mother), from Western symbolic systems. Abstract systems of thought are now reworked via analysis of the 'abjected' female body and those patriarchal signifying practices that have a psychical impact via regulation. Rejecting the Freudian and Lacanian law of the father, Kristeva posits a process that shatters repression and removes the subject from ego-psychology: the abject returns the ego to 'a source in the non-ego, drive, and death'.[6] In other words, the processes of abjection are both explanatory of patriarchal exclusion and effacement of women/the maternal and once more revealing of a new productivity. This feminist and psychoanalytical work continues in different form with the advocating of maternal discourses in *Tales of Love* (1983) and the work on the sacred and religion is continued and expanded in the book *In the Beginning was Love: Psychoanalysis and Faith* (1985). The emphasis on love via melancholy and estrangement is found in *Black Sun: Depression and Melancholy* (1987) and *Strangers to Ourselves* (1988). More recent work includes a novel, called *The Samurai* (1990) that is based upon the Parisian intellectual scene that Kristeva experienced during the 1960s, and significant studies of Proust (1993) and Hannah Arendt (1999). Kristeva's work has been enormously influential in theoretical studies, especially in relation to feminist approaches to the concept of the *chora* and the maternal, experiential aspects of the pre-symbolic *geno-text*.

Notes

1 Patrick Ffrench, *The Time of Theory: A History of* Tel Quel *(1960–1983)*, Oxford: Clarendon Press, 1995, p. 164.
2 Jean Baudrillard, *Symbolic Exchange and Death*, London: Sage, 1998, p. 195.
3 Ibid., p. 222; Kristeva is developing this idea from Lacan.
4 Julia Kristeva, *Powers of Horror: An Essay on Abjection*, trans. Leon Roudiez, NY: Columbia University Press, 1982, p. 100.
5 Patrick Ffrench, *The Time of Theory: A History of* Tel Quel (1960–1983), p. 169.
6 Julia Kristeva, *Powers of Horror: An Essay on Abjection*, p. 15.

See also in this book

Bakhtin, Derrida

Major works

Séméiotiké: Recherches pour une sémanalyse (1969). Paris: Seuil.
Le Texte du roman: Approche sémiologique d'une structure discursive transforma-tionelle (1970). The Hague/Paris: Mouton.
About Chinese Women (1974). Trans. Anita Barrow, NY: Marion Boyars, 1977.
Revolution in Poetic Language (1974). Trans. Margaret Waller, NY: Columbia University Press, 1984.
Desire in Language: A Semiotic Approach to Literature and Art (1980). Ed. Leon Roudiez, trans. Thomas Gora, Alice Jardine, Leon Roudiez, New York: Columbia University Press.
Powers of Horror: An Essay on Abjection (1980). Trans. Leon Roudiez, NY: Columbia University Press, 1982.
Tales of Love (1983). Trans. Leon Roudiez, NY: Columbia University Press, 1987.
In the Beginning was Love: Psychoanalysis and Faith (1985). Trans. Arthur Goldhammer, New York: Columbia University Press, 1987.
Black Sun: Depression and Melancholy (1987). Trans. Leon Roudiez, New York: Columbia University Press, 1989.
Strangers to Ourselves (1988). Trans. Leon Roudiez, New York: Columbia University Press, 1991.
The Samurai (1990). Trans. Barbara Bray, New York: Columbia University Press, 1992.
Les Nouvelles maladies de l'âme (1993). Paris: Fayard.
Proust and the Sense of Time (1993). Trans. Stephen Bann, New York: Columbia University Press.

The Portable Kristeva (1997). Ed. Kelly Oliver, New York: Columbia University Press.
Hannah Arendt (1999). Trans. Ross Guberman, New York: Columbia University Press, 2001.

Further reading

Baudrillard, Jean, *Symbolic Exchange and Death*, London: Sage, 1998.
Ffrench, Patrick, *The Time of Theory: A History of* Tel Quel *(1960–1983)*, Oxford: Clarendon Press, 1995.
Fletcher, John and Benjamin, Andrew, eds, *Abjection, Melancholia, and Love: The Work of Julia Kristeva*, London and New York: Routledge, 1990.
Huntington, Patricia, *Ecstatic Subjects, Utopia and the Recognition: Kristeva, Heidegger, Irigaray*, Albany, NY: State University of New York Press, 1998.
Ives, Kelly, *Cixous, Irigaray, Kristeva: The Jouissance of French Feminism*, Kidderminster: Crescent Moon, 1996.
Lechete, John, *Julia Kristeva*, London and New York: Routledge, 1990.
Oliver, Kelly, *Ethics, Politics and Difference in Julia Kristeva's Writing*, New York: Routledge, 1993.
Smith, Anne-Marie, *Julia Kristeva: Speaking the Unspeakable*, London: Pluto Press, 1998.

JACQUES-MARIE EMILE LACAN (1901–1981)

The linguistic turn in psychoanalysis was brought about by Lacan, in particular with his idea that the unconscious is structured like a language. Many of the terms developed by Lacan in his radical reworking of Freud – such as the 'mirror stage' in a child's development – have passed into everyday critical parlance. Lacan initially studied clinical medicine at the Hôpital Sainte-Anne (1927–1931), gaining his *diplôme de médicine légiste* in 1931; he then moved to the *Special Infirmary of the Préfecture de Police* and did his doctoral research at the Henri Roussele hospital, gaining his *doctorat d'état* in forensic medicine in 1932, his thesis being published the same year (*De la psychose paranoïaque dans ses rapports avec la personnalité*). Lacan's thesis on paranoia was a groundbreaking synthesis of clinical psychiatry, Freud and surrealism, and it marks his shift from psychiatry to psychoanalysis – he was also profoundly influenced in his work by his readings of Bergson, Husserl, Jaspers, Nietzsche and Spinoza.[1] More problematically, as Elisabeth Roudinesco points out, his thesis is most directly based upon a case study and appropriation of one woman's life-story: Marguerite Pantaine. Lacan's early lectures following publication of his thesis did *not* gain acceptance from the official psychoanalytical organizations of the day, especially that of the IPA, the International Psychoanalytical Association. Lacan's delivery of his groundbreaking 'Le stade du miroir' at the 14th International Congress of the IPA in 1936, was rudely cut short by the president, Ernest Jones. The paper was subsequently not submitted by Lacan for publication, and a reworked version would not be delivered until the 16th IPA in Zurich in 1949. This updated and expanded version was eventually published in the *Revue français de psychanalyse* (no. 4, 1949). Lacan's philosophical development was plain to see with this paper: he had been studying Saussure, and had been attending Kojève's seminars on Hegel's *Phenomenology of Spirit* (seminars that inaugurated a return to Hegel in France), as well as mixing with diverse intellectuals and thinkers, from Georges Bataille to Claude Lévi-Strauss. Lacan's fame increased exponentially with his 'Seminar' held from 1951 to 1980 at the Hôpital Sainte-Anne, the École Normale Supérieure and finally at the Faculté de droit du Panthéon under the auspices of the École Pratique des Hautes Études. Major essays, lectures and unpublished papers were published in 1966 and 1977 as *Ecrits I* and *II*, with nine of the essays being translated into English in 1977 as *Écrits: A Selection*. Book XI of the Seminar was also translated into English and published in 1977 as *The Four Fundamental Concepts of Psychoanalysis*.

The mirror stage is the most widely known Lacanian concept that explains in part the early formation of the subject. Drawing upon Henri Wallon's *Les Origines du caractère chez l'enfant* (1934), Lacan argued that the central component of the mirror stage is that of reflection, whereby a pre-lingustic, pre-Oedipal infant, whose subjectivity is formless, shapeless and otherwise fragmented identifies with her self-reflection and in the process gains an idealized image of self-unity. Whereas before the mirror stage (which happens at age six to eighteen months) 'perception and bodily experience are mutual correlatives',[2] or are indissociable, after the mirror stage the infant thinks of herself as a separate being in a world of objects. She also identifies with another main image that she sees: that of her Mother; from being a child immersed in a formless world, she is now aware of difference and delimitation, self and (m)Other (a combination of the Other and this early and central image of the Mother).[3] The advantages to this process – an awareness of separate objects and beings, demarcated boundaries and differences – can also lead to future difficulties, with subjectivity always being defined by some exterior image or separate object. From this stage on subjectivity necessarily becomes intersubjectivity. The mirror stage also charts the movement from the realm of the Imaginary, to that of the Symbolic: for Lacan, the Imaginary is pre-linguistic and image-based whereas the Symbolic is linguistic and cultural. The transition between the Imaginary and the Symbolic depends in large part upon a shift in identification from the (m)Other to the law of the father. Once the subject has been born into language by making the transition to the Symbolic, this does not mean that the Imaginary no longer exists or is left behind. There are three main co-constitutive or permanently interrelated orders in Lacan's theory: the Imaginary, the Symbolic and the Real (later he adds a possible fourth order of the Symptom). The Imaginary is structured by needs and image-identifications; the Symbolic is structured by language and the law; the Real is that which can neither be pictured nor articulated through language. Importantly, all three orders work in conjunction in the adult individual, although Lacan places differing emphases upon them in his lectures and publications.

The Symbolic order is explored in Lacan's seminar from 1955 on Edgar Allan Poe's short story *The Purloined Letter* (1844). Lacan focuses on the story's structural repetitions in two main scenes or sequences: first, a letter that is visibly troubling the Queen is stolen in her and the King's presence by their Minister (he replaces the letter with a copy; the Queen does not object as she does not want to draw the King's attention to the letter's contents); second, the letter is searched for by the police in the Minister's office, and initially it cannot be found, so the detective Dupin is called for – he sees the letter in the office and surreptitiously replaces it with a duplicate. Lacan argues that there are 'three glances' of interest here: first, the glance that sees nothing (King, police), second, the glance that sees the first glance and is deluded into thinking that the letter is hidden (Queen, Minister), third, the glance that sees that the first two glances allow what should remain hidden to become exposed (Minister, Dupin). What has all this to do with the Symbolic? Lacan calls the letter in this story a 'pure signifier': radicalizing Saussure, he argues that the 'pure signifier' is one that only ever refers to other signifiers in an endless deferral of meaning, i.e. it is detached from the signified, barred from having a fixed connection with the concept or idea. The subject is represented, in the seminar, by the intersubjective relationships that are coordinated by the play of the pure signifier.[4] Lacan calls this play a 'signifying chain' modifying insights derived from Freud, Saussure and Roman Jakobson. From Freud, Lacan inherits and modifies the theory of repetition compulsion and the death instinct, replacing Freud's notion of the need to master neuroses with the idea that 'the symptom is a metaphor for the human condition'.[5] Freud perceived the repetition compulsion as being open to correction via analytical acts of remembrance; Lacan contra Freud argued that repetition was always the interpretation of difference, not a recovery of the same. In other words, repetition is not about recalling some past event that has been cast into the Freudian unconscious, because Lacan has a different model of the *formation* and situation of the unconscious: the Lacanian unconscious is structural and linguistic. Another way to think the latter two is to say that the split of subjectivity (conscious–unconscious) becomes folded and projected in all conscious *and* all unconscious activity. This occurs for Lacan at the entry into the Symbolic, where the desire for the (m)Other is replaced by the law of the father: to speak is to always re-negotiate the unfulfilled desires of the Imaginary and the non-negotiable impact of the Real. The unconscious is formed with the transition to symbolization: instead of the unconscious being a topographically defined place, as in Freudian pyschoanalysis, in Lacan it functions as a discourse.

Lacan has recourse to Jakobson in mapping out this discursive production: the tropes of metaphor and metonymy are aligned in Jakobson's researches on aphasia (different forms of language-use and speech impairment), which in turn draws once more on Saussurian linguistics. Thus, the subject suffering from 'similarity disorder' cannot utilize word substitutions (metaphor) and the subject suffering from 'contiguity disorder' cannot utilize adjacent words (metonymy). Jakobson proposed that the tropes of metaphor and metonymy functioned along the two Saussurian *synchronic* (selective and associative) and *diachronic* (combinative and syntagmatic/sequential) axes. These two fundamental functional dimensions of the sign not only produce Symbolic speech but also articulate unconscious utterance. Lacan asserted that Freud had long since articulated his own version of the two axes in the *Interpretation of Dreams* with the concepts of condensation and displacement. Lacan, rejecting regulative order in all of the superimposed theories on the two axes, argues for a radical undermining of self-certainty or straightforward analytical 'access', recovery or interpretation of the psyche. Rather, the two axes represent a fundamental eccentricity of subjectivity. In his essay 'The Agency of the Letter in the Unconscious or Reason Since Freud', Lacan infamously replaces Descarte's *cogito ergo sum* – I think therefore I am – with the eccentric subject: 'I am not wherever I am the plaything of my thought; I think of what I am where I do not think to think.'[6] The two axes or polarities of the two tropes do not *centre* the subject – the subject is *displaced* by them. Returning to the seminar on Poe's *The Purloined Letter*, we can see the eccentric subject being worked upon by the attempt to possess and conceal the 'pure signifier' of the letter. In replicating the position of the Queen in his attempt to possess the letter, the Minister and then Dupin, are both feminized according to Lacan. The eccentric subject performs gender, for Lacan, always in relation to a lack, one traversed via the castration complex and the 'missing' phallus. Finally, then, the 'meaning' of the purloined letter is not its content or its 'signified' as such, rather, it is the fact that it acts upon the subjects involved in its passage through the text that matters for Lacan. The seminar on *The Purloined Letter* has generated much literary-theoretical debate, including an essay by Jacques Derrida called 'The Purveyor of Truth' (1975, the English version published in 1987 as a section of *The Post Card: From Socrates to Freud and Beyond*), as well as other major essays collected in *The Purloined Poe: Lacan, Derrida, and Psychoanalytic Reading* (1988). The gendered subjects revealed by Lacan's reading also suggest ways in which Lacanian psychoanalysis is of use to feminist critics, but also – with his theories of castration and lack – re-inscribe a patriarchal phallocentric system of thought.

With his increasing reliance on diagrams (such as his long-used *Möbius strip*) and mathematical formulae utilized in the process of mapping psychoanalytical concepts and processes, Lacan's thought developed in ever more complex and murky ways. Considering that his texts always operated playfully at the level of language and in many respects 'deconstructively' (even given the differences between Lacan and Derrida), it is quite a feat to have become even more difficult to understand and translate. In part, as Roudinesco suggests, this increasingly Beckettian discourse was caused by a self-reflexive critical re-examination of his own published texts, which had taken on symbolic weight as official Lacanian doctrine: the results were his theories of the *matheme* (resistance to the incomprehensible and a transmission of this ineffable 'knowledge') and the *Borromean knot* (a mathematical process). These final attempts to reformulate his own thinking are considered largely unsuccessful; however, the impact Lacan had on many of the new French theorists, such as Kristeva and Lyotard, and more recently upon Slavoj Žižek, has meant that Lacanian concepts have become a fundamental part of literary theoretical discourse. Ongoing feminist critique and development of Lacanianism have, perhaps, been the most fruitful lines of inquiry.

Notes

1   Elisabeth Roudinesco, *Jacques Lacan: An Outline of a Life and a History of a System of Thought*, trans. Barbara Bray, Cambridge: Polity, 1997, p. 32.
2   Ellie Ragland-Sullivan, *Jacques Lacan and the Philosophy of Psychoanalysis*, Urbana and Chicago, IL: University of Illinois Press, 1987, p. 19.

3 Ibid., p. 16 and p. 25.
4 John P. Muller and William J. Richardson, eds, *The Purloined Poe: Lacan, Derrida, and Psychoanalytic Reading*, Baltimore, MD and London: The Johns Hopkins University Press, 1988, p. 62.
5 Ellie Ragland-Sullivan, *Jacques Lacan and the Philosophy of Psychoanalysis*, p. 110.
6 Jacques Lacan, *Écrits: A Selection*, trans. Alan Sheridan, London: Tavistock, 1977, p. 166.

See also in this book

Butler, Freud, Kristeva

Major works

De la psychose paranoïaque dans ses rapports avec la personnalité (1932). Paris: Le François.
'La famille' (1938). *Encyclopédie française*, Paris: Larousse.
'The Mirror Stage as Formative of the Function of the I as Revealed in Psychoanalytic Experience' (1949). *Revue français de psychanalyse* (no. 4); reprinted in *Écrits*, Paris: Seuil, 1966; trans. in *Écrits: A Selection*, London: Tavistock, 1977.
Écrits I & II (1966). Paris: Seuil.
Television: A Challenge to the Psychoanalytic Establishment (1974). Interview with Jacques-Alain Miller, Paris: Seuil; trans. Denis Hollier, Rosalind Krauss and Annette Michelson, New York: Norton, 1990.
Écrits: A Selection (1977). Trans. Alan Sheridan, London: Tavistock.

Lacan's Seminar – translations

The Four Fundamental Concepts of Psychoanalysis (1973). Trans. Alan Sheridan, London: Hogarth, 1977.
Freud's Papers on Technique: 1953–1954 (1975). Trans. John Forrester, New York: Norton, 1988.
The Seminar of Jacques Lacan/Encore (1975). Ed. Jacques-Alain Miller (*Seminar*), New York: Cambridge University Press, 1988; trans. Bruce Fink (*Encore*), New York: Norton, 1998.
The Ego in Freud's Theory and in the Technique of Psychoanalysis: 1954–1955 (1977). Trans. Sylvana Tomaselli, New York: Norton, 1988.
The Psychoses (1981; corrected edition 1983). Trans. Russell Grigg, New York: Norton, 1993.
The Ethics of Psychoanalysis (1986). Trans. Dennis Porter, New York: Norton, 1992.

Further reading

Fink, Bruce, *The Lacanian Subject: Between Language and Jouissance*, Princeton, NJ: Princeton University Press, 1995.
Grosz, Elisabeth, *Jacques Lacan: A Feminist Introduction*, London and New York: Routledge, 1990.

Homer, Sean, *Jacques Lacan*, London and New York: Routledge, 2005.

Muller, John P. and William J. Richardson, eds, *The Purloined Poe: Lacan, Derrida, and Psychoanalytic Reading*, Baltimore, MD and London: The Johns Hopkins University Press, 1988.

Ragland-Sullivan, Ellie, *Jacques Lacan and the Philosophy of Psychoanalysis*, Urbana and Chicago, IL: University of Illinois Press, 1987.

Roudinesco, Elisabeth, *Jacques Lacan: An Outline of a Life and a History of a System of Thought*, trans. Barbara Bray, Cambridge: Polity, 1997.

Wright, Elizabeth, *Psychoanalytic Criticism: Theory in Practice*, London and New York: Methuen, 1984.

Žižek, Slavoj, *Looking Awry: An Introduction to Jacques Lacan through Popular Culture*, Cambridge, MA: The MIT Press, 1991.

FRANK RAYMOND LEAVIS (1895–1978)

A sense of crisis pervades the work of F.R. Leavis, one that reflected the shift in Britain during his lifetime from a hierarchical society to one dominated by the values of mass-culture. Ironically, while Leavis is best known as a critic who wanted to uphold specific aesthetic and cultural values as a buffer against commodity culture, his continual championing of modern English literature as the essential mode of study in the university system, encouraged younger critics to move more firmly into the direction of popular or contemporary mass-cultural literary forms. Leavis's lifelong outspoken views led in part to his own personal struggle with the Oxbridge faculty system: after receiving his BA in English from Emmanuel College, Cambridge, in 1921, and his Ph.D. on the relationship between journalism and literature in 1924, Leavis became a probationary lecturer at Emmanuel, a post that was not renewed, ending in 1931. During the early 1930s Leavis had a part-time post of Supervisor at Downing College which turned into the position of Director of Studies; he gained a teaching post once more in 1936; subsequent promotions included a readership (1959–1962) and Fellowship of Downing College (1962–1964). What such a condensed biographical sketch fails to reveal, is the enormous impact Leavis had on the world of English literature, at the levels of teaching and research. Leavis's crusade to maintain the cultural health of Britain involved an intense suspicion and at times rigorous analysis of the discourses of advertising, journalism, film and the worlds of industry and science; this crusade was given most powerful manifestation in pedagogic projects and the literary critical essays published in the journal *Scrutiny*, which Leavis and his cohort had founded in 1932. The most important intellectual companion in Leavis's life, closely involved in shared critical projects, was his wife

Queenie Dorothy; known as Q.D. Leavis, her own groundbreaking study of mass-culture, popular fiction and the novel form – *Fiction and the Reading Public* – was published in 1932.[1] Between F.R. and Q.D., the Leavis's were a formidable and influential critical force.

Leavis's critical works read like manifestos; this is simultaneously their strength and their weakness because it gives them a vitality and a force, but also a sense of dogmatic and egotistical self-certainty. The manifesto mode is needed when the writer believes that he or she is on a crusade to change something in the world, here, the way in which literary aesthetics are perceived as a way of combating social decline; this is not as far-fetched as it might sound, given the predilection of the contemporary humanities towards strong ethical and ideological readings of texts, readings that largely critique the traditional values of Western colonialism, and Eurocentric culture and society. In his pamphlet *Mass Civilisation and Minority Culture* (1930), Leavis argues that the minority values of the cultural guardians of society are being undermined by industrialization and new media such as film. As Chris Baldick argues, for Leavis:

> what was new and threatening in the post-war world was precisely that the 'mass' was beginning actively to challenge the status of the minority, creating an oppositional language subversive of cultural authority. The appearance of the word 'high-brow' is identified by Leavis as the most alarming evidence of this trend.[2]

In other words, the once respected cultural elite – or the guardians of high culture – are now placed under suspicion, 'high-brow' being a derogatory term for someone who is 'elitist' in the pejorative sense that the word now carries. How does Leavis define this cultural 'minority' or elite? In an amazing piece of literary-critical eugenics, he defines them as constituting 'the consciousness of the race' and keeping 'alive the subtlest and most perishable parts of tradition'; they are also the guardians of 'the implicit standards that order the finer living of an age' as well as the language 'upon which fine living depends'.[3] In no way does Leavis qualify or define further such a series of sweeping statements, as those who form part of this cultural elite should already instinctively or intuitively know what he is talking about. While 'eugenics' may appear too strong a word to use in this context, it must be acknowledged that Leavis's works are produced using a series of key terms that are clustered around notions of critical and societal 'health', 'strength' and the opposite, i.e. 'decline', terms which are, in part, derived from Ezra Pound, for example his *How to Read* (1931): 'Has literature a function in the state, in the aggregation of humans, in the republic . . .? . . . It has to do with maintaining the very cleanliness of the tools, the health of the very matter of thought itself.'[4] As with most manifesto writers, Leavis needed a new outlet or vehicle for his ideas: in 1932, this took two forms, first, the publication of Leavis's *New Bearings in English Poetry*, and second, with the formation of a new critical journal called *Scrutiny*. In *New Bearings in English Poetry*, Leavis asserts that the great poets of the age are 'more alive than other people, more alive in his [*sic*] own age' as well as constituting part of the healthy cultural elite; the poet 'is unusually sensitive, unusually aware, more sincere and more himself than the ordinary man can be'.[5] In arguing that it is impossible to convince those who are not already converted to this argument of the veracity of such widespread assertions of superiority, Leavis makes another argumentative leap to suggest that the lack of interest in poetry among 'the intelligent' means that something has gone wrong with modern society. Who are these great poets? Leavis argues that they are T.S. Eliot, Ezra Pound and Gerard Manley Hopkins (in a later list, one that opens Leavis's *The Great Tradition* (1948) the great novelists are added to the new canon: Jane Austen, George Eliot, Henry James and Joseph Conrad). What is it that causes Leavis to anoint these poets with such high praise? They are each, in their own ways, 'more aware of the general plight than his contemporaries, and more articulate' with Eliot transcending all to make himself 'the consciousness of his age'.[6] Concomitantly, as this holy trinity of poets reach such profound insight into the age, the 'ordinary cultivated reader is ceasing to be able to read poetry' because of a deluge of mass-media texts, a 'perpetual avalanche of print' that is incapacitating.[7] What is to be done? The answer was *Scrutiny*.

F.R. and Q.D. Leavis launched *Scrutiny* with the help of a group of followers in 1932; the journal would go on to exert an enormous influence on the study of English literature in Britain and elsewhere. In his essay 'Under Which King, Bezonian?', Leavis responded to George Santayana and others, who had asked for an expanded definition of the journal's underlying philosophy. Refusing to pin himself down to finding salvation in a single formula or creed, such as Marxism, Leavis did provide an elegiac narrative or vision of a pre-industrial England, where the arts were in accord with the everyday 'real' lives of the common folk; deliberately and provocatively couching his argument in a Marxist discourse, Leavis suggests that this accord was an art of living, involving codes, developed in ages of continuous experience, of relations between man and man, and man and the environment in its seasonal rhythm. This culture the progress of the nineteenth century destroyed, in country and town; it destroyed (to repeat a phrase that has been used in *Scrutiny* before, and will be, no doubt, again) the organic community. And what survives of cultural tradition in any important sense survives in spite of the rapidly changing 'means of production'.[8]

For Leavis, industrialization was a process of ongoing abstraction and separation of the high arts from the real, or the concrete; even though the utopian 'organic community' had been transformed by the dystopia of modernity, it was essential to still maintain a 'living relation' or mediation between high culture and the masses. *Scrutiny*'s task was, therefore, to be 'vigilant and scrupulous' concerning this mediation, its primary, but not exclusive, vehicle being literary criticism and its 'special educational interest'.[9] True to his word, Leavis produced a number of texts that provided a framework for educationalists at all levels, including: *How to Teach Reading: A Primer for Ezra Pound* (1932), *Culture and Environment: The Training of Critical Awareness* (with Denys Thompson, 1933) and *Education and the University: A Sketch for an 'English School'* (1943). The restorative pedagogic project involves repairing the damage to traditional cultural values and standards caused by the chaos and crisis of modernity via the study of select authors; Leavis's list of 'positive suggestions' in *How to Teach Reading* includes: the training of sensitivity rather than technique; reading lots of 'good criticism' (such as the critical essays of T.S. Eliot and presumably anything published in *Scrutiny*); reading Shakespeare properly; gaining a knowledge of literary and social history; and above all reading the literature of the present. Leavis suggests that: 'Out of a School of English that provided the training suggested here might come, not only a real literary criticism of Shakespeare, but a beginning in the criticism of the novel.'[10] Once more, proclamation was followed by serious critical output, with two groundbreaking books: *The Great Tradition: George Eliot, Henry James, Joseph Conrad* (1948) and *D.H. Lawrence: Novelist* (1955). For Leavis, these novelists are *the* modern tradition, making one aware of 'the possibilities of life', expressing their genius through prose fiction, and in Lawrence's case in particular, writing a profound 'study of contemporary civilization'.[11] Leavis continued to interrelate literary criticism with a wider ideological and pedagogic programme, widened to include a stronger critique of science and technology, in publications such as *Two Cultures? The Significance of C.P. Snow* (1962), *English Literature in Our Time and the University* (1967) and *The Living Principle: 'English' as a Discipline of Thought* (1975). Leavis's collected essays and posthumous publications also added to an immense output. In retrospect, while critical trends have long left behind the 'Leavisite' approach, the word itself has become part of the English language, although it is often creatively misused. The standing of English as a discipline has long since lost ground to the very scientific and technological society that Leavis abhorred, but the subject itself stands firmly upon the critical foundations that Q.D. and F.R. Leavis developed.

Notes

1 Q.D. Leavis, *Fiction and the Reading Public* (first published 1932 by Chatto & Windus), London: Bellew, 1990.
2 Chris Baldick, *The Social Mission of English Criticism: 1848–1932*, Oxford: Clarendon Press, 1987, p. 163.
3 F.R. Leavis, *For Continuity*, Cambridge, 1933, quoted in Baldick, pp. 164–165.
4 Quoted in F.R. Leavis, *For Continuity*, quoted in Baldick, p. 167.
5 F.R. Leavis, *New Bearings in English Poetry: A Study of the Contemporary Situation*, London: Chatto & Windus, 1932, p. 13.
6 Ibid., p. 196.
7 Ibid., p. 213.
8 F.R. Leavis, 'Under Which King, Bezonian?', reprinted in *A Selection from Scrutiny: Compiled by F.R. Leavis*, Cambridge: Cambridge University Press, 1968, pp. 166–174; p. 169.
9 Ibid., p. 174.
10 F.R. Leavis, *Education & The University: A Sketch for an 'English School'*, London: Chatto & Windus, 1961 (first published 1943), p. 126.
11 F.R. Leavis, *D.H. Lawrence: Novelist*, Middlesex: Penguin, 1985 (first published 1955), p. 120.

See also in this book

Empson, Richards

Major works

Mass Civilisation and Minority Culture (1930). Cambridge: Minority Press/ Gordon Fraser.
D.H. Lawrence: Novelist (pamphlet 1930; revised edition 1955). London: Chatto & Windus.
How to Teach Reading: A Primer for Ezra Pound (1932). Cambridge: Gordon Fraser.
New Bearings in English Poetry: A Study of the Contemporary Situation (1932). London: Chatto & Windus.

Culture and Environment: The Training of Critical Awareness (with Denys Thompson, 1933). London: Chatto & Windus.
For Continuity (1933). Cambridge: Minority Press.
Revaluation: Tradition and Development in English Poetry (1936). London: Chatto & Windus.
Education and the University: A Sketch for an 'English School' (1943). London: Chatto & Windus.
The Great Tradition: George Eliot, Henry James, and Joseph Conrad (1948). London: Chatto & Windus.
The Common Pursuit (1952). London: Chatto & Windus.
Two Cultures? The Significance of C.P. Snow (1962). London: Chatto & Windus.
'Anna Karenina' and Other Essays (1968). London: Chatto & Windus.
Scrutiny (compiled by F.R. Leavis, 1968). Cambridge: Cambridge University Press.
Lectures in America (with Q.D. Leavis, 1969). London: Chatto & Windus.
English Literature in Our Time and the University (1969). London: Chatto & Windus.
Dickens the Novelist (with Q.D. Leavis, 1970). London: Chatto & Windus.
Nor Shall My Sword: Discourses on Pluralism, Compassion, and Social Hope (1972). New York: Barnes and Noble.
Letters in Criticism (ed. John Tasker, 1974). London: Chatto & Windus.
The Living Principle: 'English' as a Discipline of Thought (1975). Oxford: Oxford University Press.
Thought, Words and Creativity: Art and Thought in Lawrence (ed. G. Singh, 1976). London: Chatto & Windus.
F.R. Leavis's Recent Uncollected Lectures (ed. Abdel-Azim Suwailem, 1976). London: Anglo-Egyptian Bookshop.
The Critic as Anti-Philosopher: Essays and Papers (ed. G. Singh, 1982). London: Chatto & Windus.
The Common Pursuit (1984). London: The Hogarth Press.
Valuation in Criticism and Other Essays (ed. G. Singh, 1986). Cambridge: Cambridge University Press.

Further reading

Baldick, Chris, The Social Mission of English Criticism: 1848–1932, Oxford: Clarendon Press, 1987.
Bilan, R.P., The Literary Criticism of F.R. Leavis, Cambridge: Cambridge University Press, 1979.
Leavis, Q.D., Fiction and the Reading Public (first published 1932 by Chatto & Windus), London: Bellew, 1990.
Mulhern, Francis, The Moment of 'Scrutiny', London: New Left Books, 1979.
Walsh, William, F.R. Leavis, London: Chatto & Windus, 1980.

GEORG (GYÖRGY) LUKÁCS (1885–1971)

The Hungarian Marxist Georg Lukács wrote his key works during a time of great political upheaval and revolution in Europe: the sweeping literary critical statements of his major works in this area, such as *Theory of the Novel* (1916), *History and Class Consciousness: Studies in Marxist Dialectics* (1923) and *The Historical Novel* (1937), are reflective of the ongoing crisis and transformation of political and social life during the first half of the twentieth century. Lukács was born in Budapest, Hungary, and was educated at the University of Budapest where he gained his Ph.D. in 1906. A theatre enthusiast from an early age, writing plays, being involved in dramatic groups and working as a theatre reviewer for local arts journals, Lukács shifted his critical approach at university with his study of German philosophy. He travelled to the universities of Berlin and Heidelberg during his studies, and came under the influence of the thinkers Simmel, Weber and Bloch. The major intellectual influence on Lukács, however, was that of the German philosopher Hegel and the revolutionary economic and political thinker Karl Marx. Lukács held a number of diverse posts, including Peoples commissar for culture and Red Army political commissar during the Bela Kun communist regime in Hungary in 1919, and, after a period of exile in Vienna, Berlin, and then Moscow (where he was a member of the Marx-Engels Institute in the 1930s), Professor of Philosophy at the University of Budapest (1945–1956). In 1956, Lukács once more became a minister, this time under the government of Imre Nagy, but this political transformation in Hungary was soon brought to an end by the Soviets, leading to a brief period of exile for Lukács and then a return to Hungary, where he would live for the rest of his life.

It was in Vienna, during his period of exile, that Lukács turned to a more serious study of Marx, or, as he puts it, his exile was the time 'when I really studied Marx properly'.[1] In his notes towards an autobiography, he expands, somewhat aphoristically, on this shift in emphasis: 'Philosophy of Marx: rejecting all forms of Revisionism (Kant, etc.): Hegel. General direction: unified philosophical foundations of Marxism . . . Revolution the essential element of Marxism.'[2] Lukács had already written his books *Soul and Form* (1911) and *Theory of the Novel*, but now, with the Marxist shift, came his major work *History and Class Consciousness*. As critic Almási Miklós notes: 'The most enduring discovery of this book was the reconstruction . . . of Marxian alienation; [and] his description of the phenomena of reification and fetishization.'[3] These insights would be of great importance for the Frankfurt School, and for leading critics who continue their programme, such as Jürgen Habermas.[4] Terry Eagleton argues that 'no other work of Marxist philosophy has proved so richly influential' as that of *History and Class Consciousness*.[5] What leads Eagleton to make such an assessment? From the opening essay, 'What is Orthodox Marxsim?', Lukács involves the reader in an intense exploration of *method*; thus 'orthodox' Marxism, is not the uncritical or hypercritical attachment to Marx as sacred text (arguing which of Marx's theses should have canonical status, and so on):

> On the contrary, orthodoxy refers exclusively to *method*. It is the scientific conviction that dialectical materialism is the road to truth and that its methods can be developed, expanded and deepened only along the lines laid down by its founders.[6]

Lukács' understanding of the dialectical 'conception of totality'[7] is key; expressions of difference, says Lukács, can only be comprehended via social relations as they themselves evolve historically. The endpoint, here, is not Hegelian, rather, social contradictions are perceived as necessary, as 'arising out of the antagonisms of this [capitalist] system of production'.[8] The totality, then, is the perspective that facilitates understanding of reality as a social process, and for Lukács, only this perspective enables us to see through the illusion of capitalistic fetishistic commodity forms.

In *The Historical Novel*, the centrality of social relations and historical progression is foregrounded with the analysis of the works of Sir Walter Scott. Lukács argues that the French Revolution made 'history' a mass experience, one that brought about a shift in consciousness whereby what might have once appeared 'natural' is now clearly an outcome of political upheaval: 'Hence the concrete possibilities for men to comprehend their own existence as something historically conditioned, for them to see in history something which deeply affects their daily lives and immediately concerns them.'[9] The masses, in other words, are awoken from their slumber. How do these experiences manifest themselves in literary form? Lukács regards the transformation of society as a total phenomenon: not just material, experiential change, but also change at the level of consciousness. Such a transformation forms the basis for Sir Walter Scott's historical novels, where the 'middling' protagonists are regarded not as a failure of imagination, but precisely the opposite. Thus Scott's historical novel is regarded as a 'renunciation' of Romanticism, where the middling protagonist is merely the centre in a network of social relations, all of which is 'subject to the event'.[10] Instead of the Romantic genius, or, the Romantic hero, being idealized, Scott's leading figures represent historical change or an abstract principle, while the lived social-relations of the surrounding characters give the 'many-sided picture' of reality. Thus, Lukács summarizes: 'What matters therefore in the historical novel is not the re-telling of great historical events, but the poetic awakening of the people who figured in those events.'[11] The historical novel, in other words, demonstrates via its aesthetics actual historical change as it impacts lived communities in the world.

Notes

1 Georg Lukács, *Record of a Life: An Autobiographical Sketch*, trans. Rodney Livingstone, London and New York: Verso, 1983, p. 159.
2 Ibid.
3 Miklós Almási, 'György Lukács and the Crisis of European Culture', in *Hungary and European Civilization*, ed., György Ránki, Indiana University Studies on Hungary 3, Budapest: Akadémiai Kiadó, 1989, pp. 467–480; p. 472.
4 Ibid., p. 473.
5 Terry Eagleton, *Figures of Dissent: Critical Essays on Fish, Spivak, Žižek and Others*, London and New York: Verso, 2003, p. 91.
6 Georg Lukács, *History and Class Consciousness: Studies in Marxist Dialectics*, trans. Rodney Livingstone, Cambridge, MA: MIT Press, 1990, p. 1.
7 Ibid., p. 10.
8 Ibid.
9 Georg Lukács, *The Historical Novel*, trans. Hannah and Stanley Mitchell, Atlantic Highlands, NJ: Humanities Press, 1978, p. 24.
10 Ibid., p. 35, quoting the Russian critic Belinsky.
11 Ibid., p. 42.

See also in this book

Eagleton

Major works

Soul and Form (1911). Trans. Anna Bostock, Cambridge, MA: MIT Press, 1974.
Theory of the Novel (1916). Trans. Anna Bostock, Cambridge, MA: MIT Press, 1971.
History and Class Consciousness: Studies in Marxist Dialectics (1923). Trans. Rodney Livingstone, Cambridge, MA: MIT Press, 1990.
The Historical Novel (1937). Trans. Hannah and Stanley Mitchell, Atlantic Highlands, NJ: Humanities Press, 1978.
The Young Hegel: Studies in the Relation Between Dialectics and Economics (1948). Trans. Rodney Livingstone, London: Merlin Press, 1975.
Essays on Realism (1971). Ed. Rodney Livingstone, trans. David Fernbach, Cambridge, MA: MIT Press, 1980.

Further reading

Gluck, Mary, *Georg Lukács and his Generation, 1900–1918*, Cambridge, MA: Harvard University Press, 1985.

Lunn, Eugene, *Marxism and Modernism: An Historical Study of Lukács, Brecht, Benjamin, and Adorno*, Berkeley, CA: University of California Press, 1982.

Miklós, Almási, 'György Lukács and the Crisis of European Culture', in György Ránki, ed., *Hungary and European Civilization*, Indiana University Studies on Hungary 3, Budapest: Akadémiai Kiadó, 1989; pp. 467–480.

Pizer, John, 'Narration vs. Description in Georg Lukács's *History and Class Consciousness*', *Intertexts*, 6.2 (2002): 145–164.

Tihanov, Galin, 'Revising Hegel's Phenomenology on the Left: Lukács, Kojève, Hyppolite', *Comparative Criticism*, 25 (2004): 67–95.

Žižek, Slavoj, 'From *History and Class Consciousness* to *The Dialectic of Enlightenment* . . . and Back', *New German Critique*, 81 (2000): 107–123.

JEAN-FRANÇOIS LYOTARD (1924–1998)

It may appear ironic that one of the leading prophets of postmodernism emerged from a revolutionary Marxist background: instead of presenting a vision of workers rising up against the late capitalist state, Lyotard's most famous book, *The Postmodern Condition: A Report on Knowledge* (1979) – commissioned by the Conseil des Universités of the government of Quebec – maps out a world of performative knowledge and truth, systems theory and cybernetics, asserting the importance of game-playing theory and practice. Lyotard was born in Versailles in France in 1924, eventually becoming a teacher of philosophy, including two years spent teaching in Constantine, Algeria, where he became involved in the anti-colonial struggles. Between 1954 and 1966 he was also involved in the *Socialisme ou Barbarie* group (Socialism or Barbarism), which had been set up by the Chaulieu-Montal Tendency, a group of political dissidents organized by Cornelius Castoriadis and Claude Lefort, who had broken from the Fourth International in 1948, and had set up a journal in 1949. *Socialisme ou Barbarie* attempted to develop a fluid political organization that would not solidify and rigidify into top-heavy layers of bureaucracy and hierarchy, as had happened with Stalin's government. While Lyotard was involved with the May 1968 protests in Paris, and the journal *Socialisme ou Barbarie* was itself rediscovered by the students as an important intellectual and revolutionary tool, Lyotard eventually moved away from Marxism, in the process developing his new theories of libidinal economy. Lyotard also moved from school teaching to the Sorbonne in 1959, and then to the University of Paris X, Nanterre in 1966, followed by a move to the Centre National de la Recherche Scientifique and then the University of Paris VIII, Vincennes. Through his increasing fame, due largely to the positive reception to his publications and the high quality of his teaching, Lyotard gained a number of international posts, including the role of Distinguished Professor at the University of California, Irvine and Visiting Professor at Yale University; he also was the founding Director of the Collège International de Philosophie in Paris.

While Lyotard had published a thoughtful study of Husserl and Merleau-Ponty in 1954, called *Phenomenology*, it was his second major publication in 1971 – *Discours, figure* – that really brought Lyotard to prominence. *Discours, figure* is a complex deconstruction of structuralism and Lyotard's own earlier thought – this self-reflexive critique and rejection of an earlier work, as Geoffrey Bennington has pointed out, is a recurring feature for Lyotard, partly as a way of constantly disrupting potential closure in dynamic and open systems of thought. What does Lyotard so strongly object to in the work of Saussure and Lacan? In both cases he objects to the separation of 'discourse' and 'figure' in the development of structuralist linguistics and a linguistic psychoanalysis (i.e. Lacan), arguing that both 'discourse' and 'figure' are interlinked from the beginning – texts have visual attributes that precede and exceed the purely semiotic *and* rhetorical analyses of them. So, where Saussure posits a sign as only having differential value (i.e. it is not any of the other signs that could have been used), Lyotard argues that signs also occupy and function via figurative space. The same argument is made in modified form with his analysis of Lacan's use of Jakobson and Freud: the visualization of the Freudian dreamwork is foregrounded in opposition to Lacan's notion that the unconscious is structured like a language. In *Des dispositifs pulsionnels*, Lyotard develops his previous reading to argue that there is a force of fluctuating intensities that completely precedes sign-systems: drawing upon the early Freud (and Nietzsche) he calls this force the libido developing the idea in *Libidinal Economy* (1974). Lyotard charts libidinal intensities that necessarily fluctuate in time and space: he uses a complex terminology: the libidinal band (prior to representation, with a free flow of desire), the disjunctive bar (the separation of domains/terms/ neutral space which creates the distinctive surface of the band as a conceptuality), the theatrical space of representation as 'a particular modification of libido or primary process',[1] and the theatrical set-up or *dispositif*, which is utilized to examine the theatrical space of the political. In arguing that, for example, Marx's discourse was founded on (i.e. is) a libidinal economy, Lyotard reveals the intensities in an otherwise cold system:[2] it also lost Lyotard a lot of Marxist friends.

Libidinal Economy re-reads Marx in relation to economies of desire and pleasure, opening up a space of comprehension of capitalism that is otherwise lacking in classical Marxist analyses of production. This 'space' of comprehension is often called quite simply 'the post-modern' implying a radically different set of interpretative parameters to previous modes of analysis. Lyotard defines the postmodern quite simply in his introduction to *The Postmodern Condition* as 'an incredulity toward metanarratives'.[3] What does he mean by this? First, Lyotard argues that *all* knowledge, including scientific knowledge, is discursive, reliant upon legitimating rules, and expressed as moves in 'language games' (the term is derived from Wittgenstein's later phil-osophy). Metanarratives are those narratives that *legitimate* knowledge production: e.g. grand narratives that assert progress towards a pre-defined goal, be it absolute knowledge (Hegel) or total freedom (the progression toward total liberty). Lyotard argues that metanarratives belong to the modern period, whereas the 'incredulity' towards them is a marker of postmodernity. Where does this 'incredulity' derive from? Lyotard gives a series of possibilities, such as the interrelation between capitalist investment and desired research outcomes, the blur-ring of knowledge domain boundaries (traditional modes of research are broken down and sometimes radically implode), the rise of new technologies that are fundamentally information–manipulation based (computing, cybernetics, etc.), and major historical events that funda-mentally question the search for universal reason (such as the Holocaust). The grand narratives of knowledge being produced as 'truth' are replaced by performativity where knowledge is considered as an expression of power:

> The State and/or company must abandon the idealist and humanist narratives of legitimation in order to justify the new goal: in the discourse of today's financial backers of research, the only credible goal is power. Scientists, technicians, and instruments are purchased not to find truth, but to augment power.[4]

The example of genetically modified (GM) food can help here: when a farmer plants GM seeds, he or she is merely licensed to grow the seeds for a particular harvest. The farmer is not allowed to grow some of the crop to produce more seeds that he or she would then own and plant in subsequent years. Instead, the farmer must buy a new batch of GM seeds each year. GM seeds are thus modified via manip-ulation of genetic code for a higher yield or 'performance', but the code can only be licensed, not owned, by the user: the parent company thus has the power to control all of the major aspects of a food production cycle. Arguments about potential environmental impact with the use of GM seeds are countered by arguments concerning performativity: they produce more crop (i.e. they make more profit), therefore they must be 'better'. Is this system open to resistance and change? Lyotard suggests that radically new conceptual developments have the potential to dramatically disrupt, oppose and modify the system. Drawing upon the work of Thomas Kuhn, Lyotard argues that new moves in a language game *can* powerfully contradict existing rules; however, if these new moves offer a performative gain the system will eventually modify itself to function according to a new set of rules. Kuhn calls such a modification a paradigm shift; Lyotard calls the new move 'paralogy'. Paralogical moves are essentially unpredictable, destabilizing and potentially subversive. The shift from Newtonian science to Quantum mechanics is often given as an example of paralogical thought; however, the criterion of performativity then produces an interesting outcome, since experiments are still produced 'in' one or the other of these systems (i.e. are understood via these systems), even though they are contradictory. Why? Because each system still works and still gets results, even if they do contradict one another. In summary, Lyotard is saying that within any particular system, there is a potential move in a language-game that exceeds the understanding of that system: in his perhaps most philosophical work, *The Differend: Phrases in Dispute* (1983), this 'exceeding the system' is a potential attribute of the 'phrase'.

The term 'phrase' can be thought of as an interaction and relationship in a particular expression, which may or may not be linguistic – e.g. silence can constitute a phrase. Lyotard says that each phrase has a referent (what it is about, its 'case'), a sense (what is being said about the referent or the case), an addressor (who expressed the phrase), and an addressee (the person to whom the phrase was addressed). The combination of these four coordinates can be further complicated, thus: 'A phrase may entail several referents, several senses, several addresses, several addressors.'[5] Lyotard adopts the term 'phrase' to explore the events known as 'a differend', that is, a conflict between two or more parties that cannot be resolved 'for lack of a rule of judgment applicable to both arguments'.[6] In other words, if a judgement is made, one party will be wronged, since both parties appear to have a legitimate case. As Lyotard puts it: 'One side's legitimacy does not imply the other's lack of legitimacy.'[7] *The Differend: Phrases in Dispute* examines the articulation of conjoined phrases from different phrase regimens (different sets of rules that generate and constitute phrases); Lyotard argues that when heterogeneous phrases are linked, a differend results, but this linkage brings into play 'thought, cognition, ethics, politics, history or being'.[8] The most controversial example of a differend is Holocaust denial, in this case with the specific example of 'Auschwitz' – the infamous Nazi concentration camp. Apart from the differend of Holocaust denial itself, i.e. imposing a set of interpretive requirements that the denier knows in advance cannot be met (e.g. demanding direct evidence from those murdered in the death camps, which of course they cannot provide), the Holocaust is in itself a foundering of Western reason and marks a major differend of ethical thought, that is, an obligation to reconceptualize what has followed in relation to this event, to find new idioms to express what appears to be inexpressible. A large amount of Lyotard's work is about the 'inexpressible' as a dynamic or force that can lead to a reconceptualization of the political via aesthetics; examples of the inexpressible – or the unpresentable – in his work include the sublime and the 'inhuman'. In *The Inhuman: Reflections on Time* (1988), Lyotard defines two competing notions of the 'inhuman': the first, the technologically produced and reduced subject, and the second, the childlike being that exists in an unpredictable and uncanny way, breaking the boundaries of preprogrammed systems in uncanny ways. At the close of *The Postmodern Condition*, Lyotard had advocated waging a war on 'totality': 'let us be witnesses to the unpresentable, let us activate the differences'.[9] Lyotard's major impact on contemporary theory, especially as it pertains to literary studies, has been in this waging of war on totality; Lyotard's work on postmodernism, the sublime, the differend and the inhuman, has played a major part in mapping out the postmodern condition and has been richly suggestive of new approaches to aesthetics, ethics and contemporary politics.

Notes

1   Geoffrey Bennington, *Lyotard: Writing the Event*, Manchester: Manchester University Press, 1988, p. 27.
2   Ibid., p. 35.
3   Jean-François Lyotard, *The Postmodern Condition*, trans. Geoffrey Bennington and Brian Massumi, Minneapolis, MN: Minnesota University Press and Manchester: Manchester University Press, 1984, p. xxiv.
4   Ibid., p. 46.
5   Jean-François Lyotard, *The Differend: Phrases in Dispute*, trans. Georges van den Abeele, Minneapolis, MN: Minnesota University Press and Manchester: Manchester University Press, 1986, p. 14.

6   Ibid., p. xi.
7   Ibid.
8   Ibid., p. xii.
9   Jean-François Lyotard, *The Postmodern Condition*, p. 82.

See also in this book

Baudrillard, Hutcheon, Jameson

Major works

Phenomenology (1954). Trans. Brian Beakley, New York: SUNY Press, 1991.
Discours, figure (1971). Paris: Klincksieck.
Dérive à partir de Marx et Freud (1973). Paris: UGE.
Des dispositifs pulsionnels (1973). Paris: UGE.
Libidinal Economy (1974). Trans. Iain Hamilton Grant, Bloomington, IN: Indiana University Press, 1993.
Instructions païennes (1977). Paris: Galilée.
Duchamp's TRANS/formers (1977). Venice, CA: Lapis P.
Just Gaming (with Jean-Loup Thébaud, 1979). Trans. Wlad Godzich, Minneapolis, MN: Minnesota University Press and Manchester: Manchester University Press, 1984.
The Postmodern Condition (1979). Trans. Geoffrey Bennington and Brian Massumi, Minneapolis, MN: Minnesota University Press and Manchester: Manchester University Press, 1984.
The Differend: Phrases in Dispute (1983). Trans. Georges van den Abeele, Minneapolis, MN: Minnesota University Press and Manchester: Manchester University Press, 1986.
The Assassination of Experience by Painting (1984). Trans. Rachel Bowlby, London: Black Dog.
L'Enthusiasme: la critique kantienne de l'histoire (1986). Paris: Galilée.
Peregrinations: Law, Form, Event. (1988). New York: Columbia University Press.
Heidegger and 'the jews' (1988). Trans. Andreas Michel and Mark Roberts, Minneapolis, MN: University of Minnesota Press, 1990.
The Inhuman: Reflections on Time (1988). Trans. Geoffrey Bennington and Rachel Bowlby, Cambridge: Polity, 1991.
The Postmodern Explained: Correspondence 1982–1985 (1988). Trans. Don Barry, Bernadette Maher, Julian Pefanis, Virginia Spate and Morgan Thomas, Minneapolis, MN: University of Minnesota Press, 1992.
The Lyotard Reader (1989). Ed. Andrew Benjamin, Oxford: Oxford University Press.
Lessons on the Analytic of the Sublime (1991). Trans. Elizabeth Rottenberg, Stanford, CA: Stanford University Press, 1994.
Political Writings (1993). Trans. Bill Readings and Kevin Paul Geiman, London: UCL Press.
Postmodern Fables (1993). Trans. Georges van den Abeele, Minneapolis, MN: Minnesota University Press, 1997.
Signed, Malraux (1996). Trans. Robert Harvey, Minneapolis, MN: Minnesota University Press, 1999.

The Confessions of Augustine (1998). Trans. Richard Beardsworth, Stanford, CA: Stanford University Press, 2000.

Further reading

Bennington, Geoffrey, *Lyotard: Writing the Event*, Manchester: Manchester University Press, 1988.
Browning, Gary, *Lyotard and the End of Grand Narratives*, Cardiff: University of Wales Press, 2000.
Carrol, David, *Paraesthetics: Foucault, Lyotard, Derrida*, London and New York: Methuen, 1987.
Gibson, Andrew, *Postmodernity, Ethics and the Novel*, London and New York: Routledge, 1999.
Malpas, Simon, *Jean-François Lyotard*, London and New York: Routledge, 2003.
Readings, Bill, *Introducing Lyotard: Art and Politics*, London and New York: Routledge, 1991.
Williams, James, *Lyotard and the Political*, London and New York: Routledge, 2000.

HERBERT MARSHALL McLUHAN (1911–1980)

Punning that one of his books was a 'collide-oscope of interfaced situations',[1] the Canadian literary critic and internationally renowned media theorist, Marshall McLuhan, also hints at how his conceptual terrain needs to be viewed: through multiple lenses that bring different views of his life and work into collision and contrast. McLuhan's most infamous phrase – 'the medium is the message' – is viewed again, from the perspective of the media working 'us over completely',[2] to become 'the medium is the massage'. Technology, which has so often been perceived as a fundamental threat to human existence, is explored from another perspective by McLuhan, as the 'extensions' of humanity, prefiguring much current thought concerning cybernetics and robotics. McLuhan's stock rises and falls with each wave of literary and media theorists who rediscover and critique his work, revealing a process of McLuhanesque eternal return, the point being that McLuhan's insights into the modern media-based world remain more relevant for a wide range of consumers, than other passing theoretical trends. In other words, McLuhan's sound-bites remain in circulation and are variously and voraciously recycled. McLuhan's insights are rooted in what at first appears to be an entirely different world: that of a broad humanist learning and a background of personal Catholic belief. Born in Edmonton, McLuhan studied at The University of Manitoba, where he completed a BA in 1933, and an MA with a thesis

213

on George Meredith in 1934, before moving to The University of Cambridge, where he studied with F.R. Leavis and I.A. Richards, and gained his next BA in 1936. McLuhan began teaching at St Louis University in 1937, the same year that he converted to Catholicism; the significance of this conversion is apparent in the media theorist Arthur Kroker's assessment that 'McLuhan's mind represents one of the best syntheses yet achieved of the Catholic legacy'.[3] During his time at St Louis, McLuhan was working on his doctorate on Nashe, called *The Place of Thomas Nashe in the Learning of His Time*, completed and awarded by the University of Cambridge in 1943. Moving to Windsor, Ontario, in 1944, McLuhan worked at Assumption College before gaining a post at St Michael's College, The University of Toronto, in 1946, where he was to remain for the rest of his academic life.

It may seem bizarre to today's technophiles to learn that McLuhan's thought is rooted in the trivium, the lower division of the medieval liberal arts: grammar, rhetoric and logic (the higher division, the quadrivium, consists of arithmetic, geometry, astronomy and music). 'Trivium' is latin for a crossroads where three streets intersect: in 1967, over two decades after his doctoral thesis, McLuhan would write of a new type of crossroads, one that transgressed barriers, since: 'Our time is a time for crossing barriers, for erasing old categories – for probing around.'[4] The crossroads can be traced elsewhere in McLuhan's thought: in his interest in the modernism of Ezra Pound and Wyndham Lewis, as well as T.S. Eliot and James Joyce, and in the French *symbolists* of Baudelaire, Rimbaud, Laforgue, Mallarmé and Valéry, which crossed with his interests in New Criticism and Catholic thought.[5] During this time, McLuhan was also reading the Canadian 'technological realist'[6] Harold Innis, and this influence would be felt in McLuhan's first major publication, *The Mechanical Bride: Folklore of Industrial Man* (1951), a series of pithy analyses of North American advertisements, which 'figure the mechanization and fragmentation of all aspects of intellectual and emotional life, including the libidinal'.[7] It was his publication of *The Gutenberg Galaxy: The Making of Typographic Man* (1962), however, that announced McLuhan's presence on the international cultural scene. Once again, Innis's influence could be perceived, alongside that of J.C. Carothers, in McLuhan's argument that the development of typography led to a visual realm of culture, one where the psychodynamics of print is making way for that of the auditory spaces of the new electronic media. What is revolutionary about this? For McLuhan print culture facilitated the organization of a spatial continuum through linear progression, whereas the new electronic, auditory culture, in effect, *abolishes* the space-time continuum because of its instantaneity and simultaneity: 'electric technology is instant and omni-present and creates multiple centres-without-margins'.[8] In *Understanding Media: The Extensions of Man* (1964), such a revolutionary mode of thinking is explored in the realms of clothing, housing, money, photography, advertising, games and television, to list just some of the chapters. In his introduction to the MIT Press Edition of *Understanding Media*, Lewis H. Lapham lists the 'leitmotifs' of McLuhan's book. The items in the left-hand column belong to the world of print-based culture, those in the right-hand column to the electronic world where 'the medium is the message', in other words, McLuhan's prophetic charting of postmodernity:

Print	*Electronic Media*
visual	tactile
mechanical	organic
sequence	simultaneity
composition	improvisation
eye	ear
active	reactive
expansion	contraction
complete	incomplete
soliloquy	chorus
classification	pattern recognition
center	margin
continuous	discontinuous
syntax	mosaic
self-expression	group therapy
Typographic man	Graphic man[9]

McLuhan developed the terms 'hot' and 'cool' medium to describe these two realms: a hot medium is one that is data rich, a cool one being of low definition and data poor; hot media do most of the work for the audience, whereas cool media demand audience work and what McLuhan calls 'participation'. Contrary to many commentators on television, McLuhan regards TV as a cool medium, whereas print, in its fomenting of nationalism and religious unrest, is a hot medium. McLuhan warns against comparing television with film or photography, since with television, the viewer, bombarded with light, is the screen.[10] Film and photography have exceptionally high-definition images; for McLuhan, the low-definition televisual image is not deficient or substandard, rather, it is instead a fundamental difference: that of a mosaic pattern, unconsciously reconfigured by the viewer to create an abstract, sculptural and iconic form. McLuhan takes this a step further, to argue that there is a difference between visual and mosaic space; the latter involves 'imaginative reorganization' or a paradigm shift:

> The nonvisual mosaic structures of modern art, like those of modern physics and electric-information patterns, permit little detachment. The mosaic form of the TV image demands participation and involvement in depth of the whole being, as does the sense of touch.[11]

The world of literacy extended visual power in terms of information organization but also led to detachment and 'noninvolvement'; visual power is isolating and isolated in its modes of representation, whereas the mosaic is an instantaneous synesthesia of all the senses, and is primarily a non-representational 'extension of the sense of touch'[12] (in other words, it is a production). McLuhan ponders what this means for the young people in his time who have grown up with the TV image as their primary orienting mode of interacting with the world; again, he rejects the argument that 'low-quality' TV programmes could be replaced with 'high' cultural content to improve the viewer's mind, and instead he argues that, from an existential perspective, TV's mosaic image is a powerful 'total involvement in all-inclusive *nowness*'[13] that has transformed the subject's relationship with his or her social environment. No longer wanting specialism, for example, in the professions, the children of television instead want *involvement*. As an example of this total involvement, McLuhan uses the example of the televised funeral of the assassinated American President J.F. Kennedy; a more contemporary example is the funeral of the British Princess Diana. In both cases, the argument is that TV has the power to involve an entire population in ritual, but as a cool medium: 'It involves us in moving depth, but it does not excite, agitate or arouse.'[14] A hot medium, such as radio or print culture, could have agitated or aroused the people following such political and personal tragedies, leading to unrest and possible anarchy, but a cool medium, in its total absorption and involvement of the people in a ritualistic mourning of which they fully partake, also *calms* the people in an act of catharsis or psychic massaging. Hot media arouse people to perform or at the least desire cathartic acts in the future, such as political insurrection, whereas cool media fulfil people in the here-and-now in a constant succession of immediate occurrences.

One of the side-effects of the simultaneity and instantaneity of electronic modes of being (the extension of the central nervous system into 'a global embrace'),[15] is that of the 'global village', where all subjects participate in the consequences of every action. For McLuhan, this is also a shift from the concept of the private individual to that of the publicly exposed being, a shift also from control of content, to 'instant sensory awareness of the whole'[16] where the medium is the message (and the massage). Structure and configuration are now key, and in his exploration of these ideas, McLuhan's texts function at the surface level to create a *gestalt*. *The Medium is the Massage: An Inventory of Effects* (1967), is a text where graphic space and design massively disrupt the linearity of print culture, mainly through the techniques of close-up and magnification/blow-up. Other effects abound, including the fact that the original printing of the book was done in two different formats, leading to a doubling that as Richard Cavell points out 'identifies the residual role of tactility within the visual'.[17] Pages in the book are printed upside down, text is treated as graphic image free from the linearity of type (through rotation, blow-up and so on), advertisements, cartoons and iconic images from popular culture overpower more conventional pictures, image repetitions overpower fragmented phrases and sentences, and quotations become more important than conventional notions of 'primary' text. The text simultaneously has a modernity and a slightly 'sixties' feel about it; it also may have lost much of its shock value due to the multitude of imitations that have since followed. Nonetheless, some of the book's more radical ideas have become gnomic statements: short, pithy truths that most media-savvy people would probably now agree with, recognizing McLuhan as a prophetic voice from the past. The eternal return to McLuhan begins with such a recognition, and various virtual McLuhans repeatedly surface in today's digital domain as different groups reinvent themselves electronically through such leading media gurus. The 'tribalism' that results from the creation of the electronic global village is also an ethical responsibility; as McLuhan argues, minority groups can no longer be ignored, and through the commitment and participation of electronic media 'we have become irrevocably involved with, and responsible for, each other'.[18]

Notes

1 Marshall McLuhan and Quentin Fiore, *The Medium is the Massage: An Inventory of Effects*, produced by Jerome Agel, Toronto: Penguin, 2003, p. 10.
2 Ibid., p. 26.
3 Arthur Kroker, *Technology and the Canadian Mind: Innis/McLuhan/Grant*, Montréal: New World Perspectives, 1996, p. 68.
4 Marshall McLuhan and Quentin Fiore, *The Medium is the Massage: An Inventory of Effects*, p. 10.

5 Donald F. Theall, 'Who/What Is Marshall McLuhan?' in, Hart Cohen, ed., *Revisiting McLuhan, Media International Australia: Culture & Policy*, 94 (February 2000): 13–27, p. 24.
6 Arthur Kroker, *Technology and the Canadian Mind: Innis/McLuhan/Grant*, p. 99.
7 Richard Cavell, *McLuhan in Space: A Cultural Geography*, Toronto: University of Toronto Press, 2003, p. 32.
8 Paul Jones, '"McLuhanist" Societal Projections and Social Theory: Some Reflections' in Hart Cohen, ed., *Revisiting McLuhan, Media International Australia: Culture and Policy*, (2000) 94: 39–55, p. 44.
9 Lewis H. Lapham, Introduction to Marshall McLuhan, *Understanding Media: The Extensions of Man*, Cambridge, MA and London: The MIT Press, 1994, pp. xii–xiii.
10 Marshall McLuhan, *Understanding Media: The Extensions of Man*, p. 313.
11 Ibid., p. 334.
12 Ibid.
13 Ibid., p. 335.
14 Ibid., p. 337.
15 Ibid., p. 3.
16 Ibid., p. 13.
17 Richard Cavell, *McLuhan in Space: A Cultural Geography*, p. 128.
18 Marshall McLuhan and Quentin Fiore, *The Medium is the Massage: An Inventory of Effects*, p. 24.

See also in this book

Haraway

Major works

The Mechanical Bride: Folklore of Industrial Man (1951). New York: Vanguard.
The Gutenberg Galaxy: The Making of Typographic Man (1962). Toronto: University of Toronto Press.
Understanding Media: The Extensions of Man (1964). New York: McGraw-Hill; Cambridge, MA and London: The MIT Press, 1994.
The Medium is the Massage: An Inventory of Effects (with Quentin Fiore, 1967). Produced by Jerome Agel, New York: Bantam & Random House; Toronto: Penguin, 2003.
Verbi-Voco-Visual Explorations (1967). New York: Something Else Press.
Counterblast (1968). New York: Harcourt, Brace and World.
War and Peace in the Global Village (with Quentin Fiore, 1968). Produced by Jerome Agel, New York: Bantam.
The Interior Landscape: The Literary Criticism of Marshall McLuhan 1943–1962 (ed. Eugene McNamara, 1969). New York: McGraw-Hill.
Culture is Our Business (1970). New York: McGraw-Hill.

Further reading

Cavell, Richard, *McLuhan in Space: A Cultural Geography*, Toronto: University of Toronto Press, 2003.

Gerrie, James, 'Innis, McLuhan and Grant and the Challenge of Tech-nological Dependence', *Arachne*, 6.2 (1999): 87–100.

Heim, Michael, 'The Computer as Component: Heidegger and McLuhan', 16.2 (1992): 304–319.

Kroker, Arthur, *Technology and the Canadian Mind: Innis/McLuhan/Grant*, Montréal: New World Perspectives, 1996.

Marvin, Carolyn, 'Innis, McLuhan and Marx', *Visible Language*, 20.3 (1986): 355–359.

Schafer, R. Murray, 'McLuhan and Acoustic Space', *The Antigonish Review*, 62–63 (1985): 105–113.

Theall, Donald F., 'Who/What Is Marshall McLuhan?' in Hart Cohen, ed., *Revisiting McLuhan, Media International Australia: Culture & Policy*, (February 2000) 94: 13–27.

VLADIMIR IAKOVLEVICH PROPP (1895–1970)

One of the great ironies of Vladimir Propp's life is the fact that each of his major publications was out-of-synch with the changing politi-cal climate of Russia, where he lived and worked: given that in the West he is most famous for a single, groundbreaking work called *Morphology of the Folktale* (1928; trans. 1958) – a work in which time is replaced with timeless permutations of narrative sequences and char-acters – then it is even more remarkable that history, or epochal trans-formations, kept intervening so powerfully in his daily existence. Propp was born in St Petersburg, and studied Russian and German philology at The University of St Petersburg, graduating in 1918. After working as a teacher of languages, Propp became a college instructor of German, and then progressed to the faculty of Leningrad University in 1932. After specializing once more in languages, Propp eventually focused on folklore, becoming the Chair of the Depart-ment of Folklore. Propp's first and, for the West, most important study was a morphological account of the Russian fairytale or wondertale, which was published in 1928 with a modified title, *Morphology of the Folktale*. Many people in the West remained unaware of the trials and tribulations that Propp endured in Soviet Russia: *Morphology of the Folktale* was seen by the communist authorities as a 'deviation from socialist realism', while Propp's next book, *Historical Roots of the Wondertale* (1946), was similarly condemned but this time as an exam-ple of a failure to be Russian enough:

> *Historical Roots* was used as a flagrant example of 'sycophancy' (owing to its predominantly foreign bibliographical apparatus), and neither the fact that Propp's main texts were Russian tales

nor the Marxist protestations scattered generously in the introductory chapter saved him from condemnation.[1]

Propp was made to publicly recant his erroneous ways, but his problems did not end there: the publication of his patriotic third book, *Russian Heroic Epic Poetry* (1955), coincided with yet another change in the political climate in Russia, and the book subsequently received a poor reception. Two more extensive studies were yet to come: Propp's *Russian Agrarian Festivals* (1963) and the posthumous *Problems of Laughter and the Comic* (1976).

How did Propp's *Morphology of the Folktale* come to have such a large, international following? The answer involves briefly examining the route that this book took into the critical debates occurring in the West in the late 1950s, when Propp's book was translated into English. In America, the importance of *Morphology of the Folktale* was made clear by Alan Dundes (1934–2005), the anthropologist and folklorist who applied Propp's ideas in *The Morphology of North American Indian Folktales* (1964); in France, the structuralist anthropologist Claude Lévi-Strauss published an analysis and review of Propp called 'Structure and Form: Reflections on a Work by Vladimir Propp' (1960). This essay triggered interest in, and wider debate concerning, Propp's work, as well as a strongly worded response from Propp. Felix J. Oinas notes that interest in Propp's book

> assumed proportions that hardly any work in folklore has had since the heyday of Max Müller, with the possible exception of Sir James Frazer's *The Golden Bough*. The English translation, greatly revised in 1968, was followed by translations into Italian (1966); Polish (abbreviated ed., 1968); German; and Rumanian . . . The enthusiasm manifested in the West for the *Morphology* also caused the Soviet leaders and folklorists to revise their stand.[2]

So what was Propp's breakthrough in his study? Propp was a morphologist, someone who looks for meaning in patterns and structures (the overall methodology is derived from Goethe), and he initially studied a series of wondertales or fairy tales to ascertain precisely such patterns: the results of his research indicated that regardless of the particular fairytale examined, certain essential actions are repeated, and always in the same sequence, so again, regardless of the actual manifestation of these actions/sequences, Propp intuited that they fulfilled basic 'functions'; thus the overarching thesis that all folktales have plots with *identical* functions. Propp discovered that these actions took place in definable segments of text, and that their function was to progress the narrative in a certain direction: he argued that there were thirty-one functions in total, although not all of them would be present in every fairytale (he never specified a minimum number of functions at work in a text). A selection of functions gives the idea:

1   one of the members of the family absents himself from home (definition = absentation)
2   an interdiction is addressed to the hero (definition = interdiction)
3   the interdiction is violated (definition = violation)
4   the villain makes an attempt at reconnaissance (definition = reconnaissance)
5   the villain receives information about his victim (definition = delivery)
6   the villain attempts to deceive his victim in order to take possession of him or of his belongings (definition = trickery)
    etc.[3]

Is every action in a narrative a function? Propp answered this question by arguing that: 'Function . . . denotes the action of the character from the point of view of its significance for the progress of the narrative.'[4] He gives the wonderful example of a hero jumping to a princess's window on horseback, as being not about *that* particular action (jumping on horseback), but instead, abstracting further, the *function* of 'performing a difficult task as part of courtship'.[5] So, multiple episodes, are reduced or abstracted to the thirty-one functions, and similarly, multiple characters, are reduced or abstracted to a smaller series of 'types': the villain, the donor, the helper, the princess (the sought-for person) and her father, the dispatcher, the hero, and the false hero.[6] The potential of this methodology is immediately apparent: students of literature are often overwhelmed by the vast number of literary narratives that have been published since the invention of writing and especially with techniques of mass reproduction via the printing press, but a critic taking Propp's approach is not to be daunted by such quantity (or apparent diversity): the morphological analysis of folktales provides a type of Rosetta Stone whereby *all* narratives can now be understood in their pared-down but nonetheless powerful, architectonic and functional structure. It is clear why such a methodology would appeal to those involved with the development of structuralist anthropology, although Claude Lévi-Strauss was critical in his initial reception of Propp, and went on to define his own related but distinctive methodology in his study of myth. Is it possible to mediate between Propp's literary-critical approach, and Lévi-Strauss's anthropological/philosophical approach (in that he wanted to understand the meaning of myth, not just map-out myth patterns)? One potential mediating device might be Propp's fascination with the 'single source' of all given folktales:

> He considers such a source the tale type relating to the abduction of a maiden by a dragon and the subsequent combat with the dragon. The author's predilection for this tale cycle is already obvious in *The Morphology of the Folktale*.[7]

In making a case that this type of fairy tale is the most widespread and complete from a Proppian perspective (i.e. the most number of functions, etc.) and therefore the fairy tale par excellence, the point at which a mythological story turns into this fairytale may also be the mediating moment with what is called the 'basic myth' bridging also the differences of opinion and approach between Propp and Lévi-Strauss.[8] Regardless of this possibility, it is true to say that Propp's first book continues to have an impact upon literary-critical studies today, via a series of structuralist, linguistic and other theoretical explorations based upon his methodology; while debates still continue over the placing of Propp – i.e. was he a formalist or a morphological thinker? – and even though his later books have been generally less well received, Propp continues to be taught as an exemplary figure of the 'structural' or 'formal(ist)' approaches to narrative.

Notes

1   Anatoly Liberman, 'Introduction' to Vladimir Propp, *Theory and History of Folklore*, Anatoly Liberman, ed., trans. Ariadna Y. Martin, Richard P. Martin and others, Minneapolis, MN: University of Minnesota Press, 1984, pp. xii–xiii.
2   Felix J. Oinas, 'V. Ja. Propp (1895–1970)', *Journal of American Folklore*, 84 (1971): 338–340; p. 338.
3   Vladimir Propp, *Morphology of the Folktale*, extracts from the second edition (trans. Laurence Scott, 1968) in Julie Rivkin and Michael Ryan, *Literary Theory: An Anthology*, Oxford: Blackwell, 1998, pp. 28–31, quotation modified by Lane.
4   Quoted in Anatoly Liberman, 'Introduction' to Vladimir Propp, *Theory and History of Folklore*, p. xxx.
5   Ibid.
6   Ibid.
7   V.N. Toporov, 'A Few Remarks on Propp's *Morphology of the Folktale*', in Robert Louis Jackson and Stephen Rudy, eds, *Russian Formalism:*

A Retrospective Glance, New Haven, CT: Yale Center for International and Area Studies, 1985, pp. 252–270; p. 262.
8   Ibid., pp. 262–264.

Major works

Morphology of the Folktale (1928). Ed., Svatava Pirkova-Jakobson, trans. Laurence Scott, Bloomington, IN: Indiana University Research Center in Anthropology, Folklore, and Linguistics, Publication 10, 1958. Second edition revised and edited with a preface by Louis A. Wagner, and new introduction by Alana Dundes, Austin, TX and London: University of Texas Press, 1968.
Historical Roots of the Wondertale (1946). Leningrad: Leningradskij gosudarstvennyj universitet.
Russian Heroic Epic Poetry (1955). Leningrad: Leningradskij gosudarstvennyj universitet.
Russian Agrarian Festivals (1963). Leningrad: Leningradskij gosudarstvennyj universitet.
Problems of Laughter and the Comic (1976). Moscow: Iskusstvo.

Further reading

Dundes, Alan, 'Binary Opposition in Myth: The Propp/Lévi-Strauss Debate', *Western Folklore*, 56.1 (1997): 39–48.
Matejka, Ladislav and Pomorska, Krystyna, eds, *Readings in Russian Poetics: Formalist and Structuralist Views*, Cambridge, MA: The MIT Press, 1971.
Seitel, Peter, 'Theorizing Genres – Interpreting Works', *New Literary History*, 34.2 (2003): 275–297.
Warner, Elizabeth A., *Vladimir Propp, 1895–1970: The Study of Russian Folklore and Theory*, Hull: Hull University Press, 1999.

IVOR ARMSTRONG RICHARDS (1893–1979)

One of the founders of modern criticism, Richards also performed the most infamous pedagogical 'experiment' in the history of literary studies, when he asked a group of students at Cambridge to analyse some poems, without letting them know their titles, their dates, or even the names of the poets who had written them. The responses or misreadings, for Richards, were indicative of a failure of the imagination whereby the students used habitualized modes of thought to investigate texts that did unfamiliar things with language. Was this indicative of some wider problem in the thought processes of the general public? Richards clearly believed that this was so, and thus his key works that followed his experiment – *Principles of Literary Criticism* (1924), *Science and Poetry* (1926) and *Practical Criticism* (1929) – were perceived to have more than literary-critical implications.

Richards was born in Cheshire, England, and studied at Magdalene College, University of Cambridge, where he gained his BA in 1914, and his MA in 1918, working as a lecturer in English and Moral Sciences from 1922. During 1929–1930 Richards worked as a visiting professor at Tsing Hua University in Peking, followed by his return to Magdalene, where he received his Litt.D. in 1932. Made a fellow of Magdalene in 1925, Richards went on to become a visiting lecturer at Harvard University in 1931, eventually settling there at the end of the decade, becoming Professor of English.

How did Richards come to have such an influence on the subject of literary criticism? The neo-positivist atmosphere of Cambridge after the First World War provides part of the answer, with its hostility to metaphysical or speculative philosophy and its concomitant eagerness to produce analytical accounts of the world and its aesthetic objects.[1] Richards' first book, co-written with James Wood and C.K. Ogden, called *The Foundations of Aesthetics* (1922), was a sweeping-clean of most of the previous generation's notions of aesthetics and value, positing instead the theory of 'synaesthesis'; as a bold modernist statement, *The Foundations of Aesthetics* paved the way to a new approach to 'doing English', one that was in tune with the demands and desires of returning First World War veterans. With the theory of 'synaesthesis' Richards *et al.* argued that the harmonizing of different or opposite impulses leads to beauty and the experience of such an aesthetic object allows the perceiver to realize the 'full richness' and 'complexity' of one's environment. Working again with C.K. Ogden, Richards produced *The Meaning of Meaning* (1923), an attempt to define the differences between scientific (referential or prose) and emotive uses of language. However, it was publication of his *Principles of Literary Criticism* that would create shock waves throughout the academic community. In this text Richards reveals a concern for intellectual and aesthetic values in a world which, he suggests, is in danger of being destroyed by mass or popular culture; interestingly, he is responding in part to the dangers of wartime propaganda techniques being transferred to peacetime activities. As he argues:

> For many reasons standards are much more in need of defence than they used to be. It is perhaps premature to envisage a collapse of values, a transvaluation by which popular taste replaces trained discrimination. Yet commercialism has done stranger things: we have not yet fathomed the more sinister potentialities of the cinema and the loudspeaker.[2]

As Chris Baldick argues, the new communication technologies were regarded as a threat by Richards, to the trained elite who had the 'correct' sensitivities and complex minds, and who could appreciate high art and great literature. Performing his poetry experiment on his students, Richards was shocked, however, to discover that they did not appear to share this training, and instead they merely brought 'stock responses' to the appreciation (or in this instance 'misreading') of the literary text. What was the solution? A therapeutic course in 'practical criticism', eventually published in book form. As Douglas-Fairhurst notes:

> Practical Criticism is a self-help manual as well as a sociological survey. We read poetry . . . [Richards] argues, to discover models of orderly response: a poem preserves feelings which we recognize as our own, but could not have formulated on our own. Since the problem with poor reading is that it fails to exercise the mind . . . the exercises he [Richards] goes on to recommend are intended to work as a form of mental aerobics, improving our critical agility, flexibility and stamina.[3]

Richards had already advocated poetry as a redemptive form in an age of mass culture and propaganda; Practical Criticism was to be the training manual for how one attuned one's mind to such an expressive form, plunging deeply into the poetic, yet always reminding the reader that this is a personal commitment and experience. Richards' book had a great effect on the study and teaching of English literature, one that was to be international in scope and long-lasting. In a paper written in 1987, critic John Bowen notes that Practical Criticism

> is still compulsory at Cambridge and other universities, and is well-established, sixty years on, at 'A' Level [a British high school exam]. It involved the placing of unattributed poems (although later it was to include extracts of prose and drama) in front of students who were called upon to produce 'responses' in the form of 'protocols' which Richards then collated and assessed.[4]

The factors that made such an approach desirable and productive, such as the stripping away of biographical and historical context, were also those that made the approach problematic for interpreters who wish to understand the ideologies of textual production and consumption. Yet if Richards' project was one of maintaining the 'health' of the nation, then the pared-down aesthetic text or object can function as a *psychological test* of mental health. A poem by Hopkins, for example, rather than expressing deep metaphysical or religious experiences, becomes akin to a Rorschach test. Richards lists the ten principal critical mistakes that readers make in flunking their tests, and then suggests that readers avoid these in future tests. They include: (1) mnemonic irrelevance (memories); (2) stock responses; (3) sentimentality; (4) inhibition; and (5) doctrinal adhesions.[5] Critics have noted how the easy transition of Practical Criticism from English department to State practice reveals a regulative function at work in testing students in this particular way; Richards himself argued that he wished to regulate minds at a time of the rise of science and mass culture, and the fact that his methodologies would influence the rise of New Criticism in the US is thus indicative of the power of his specific approach.

Richards is generally considered to have changed course with the publication of his *Coleridge on Imagination* (1934), where insights in Coleridge's writings are said to 'anticipate' modern psychological systems of thought. However, while Richards does eventually shift to what he calls his 'Basic English' project, the more complex approach to literary criticism contained in *Coleridge on Imagination* has rarely been explored in much depth, although it does form the subject of a major chapter in Jerome P. Schiller's study *I.A. Richards' Theory of Literature*. Critics generally regard Richards as having shifted from an atomistic to a contextual theory of literature, but many contradictions and problems remain. It is fair to say, however, that after the fame of Practical Criticism, Richards' Basic English project remains forever attached to his name. Developed by Charles K. Ogden and published as *Basic English: A General Introduction with Rules and Grammar* (1930), the Basic English project reduces the complexities of the English language to 850 words for ease of learning and understanding. In *Basic English and Its Uses* (1943), Richards' turn to another redemptive form is apparent: no longer that of poetry, now it is global communication: 'No one who knows Central Europe doubts that a common secondary language of discussion – free from partisan charges – would aid immensely in ironing out boundary tensions', Richards writes in his preface. Communication technologies will lead after the Second World War, Richards argues, to an immense 'mixing' of peoples, which he perceives as a negative fact, unless the communication of 'universal' truths can be established. There is no doubt that in some countries that still utilize Basic English as a pedagogy, the project has been a great success; the wider redemptive ideals are no doubt subject to a healthy dose of scepticism. Nonetheless, it is no mean feat to have influenced not only the direction of literary criticism and State education for many decades, but also the global interest in, and learning of, a compact yet rigorous communication device, even if Basic English is very dull.

Notes

1 Martin Hilsky, 'Some Notes on I.A. Richards's Theory of Literature', *Prague Studies in English*, XV (1973): 19–35; p. 20.
2 Quoted in Chris Baldick, *The Social Mission of English Criticism, 1848–1932*, Oxford: Oxford University Press, 1987, p. 138.
3 Robert Douglas-Fairhurst, 'I.A. Richards's *Practical Criticism*', *Essays in Criticism*, 54.4 (2004): 373–389; p. 380.
4 John Bowen, 'Practical Criticism, Critical Practice: I.A. Richards and the Discipline of English', *Literature and History*, 13.1 (1987): 77–94; p. 85.
5 Ibid., p. 86.

See also in this book

Empson, Leavis

Major works

The Foundations of Aesthetics (with Charles K. Ogden and James Wood, 1922). London: Allen & Unwin.
The Meaning of Meaning: A Study of the Influence of Language upon Thought and of the Science of Symbolism (with C.K. Ogden, 1923). London: Kegan, Paul, Trench & Trubner.
Principles of Literary Criticism (1924). London: Kegan, Paul, Trench & Trubner.
Science and Poetry (1926). London: Kegan, Paul, Trench & Trubner.
Practical Criticism: A Study of Literary Judgment (1929). London: Kegan, Paul, Trench & Trubner.
Mencius on the Mind: Experiments in Multiple Definition (1932). London: Kegan, Paul, Trench & Trubner.
Basic Rules of Reason (1933). London: Kegan, Paul, Trench & Trubner.
Coleridge on Imagination (1934). London: Kegan, Paul, Trench & Trubner.
Basic in Teaching: East and West (1935). London: Kegan, Paul, Trench & Trubner.
The Philosophy of Rhetoric (1936). New York: Oxford University Press.
Interpretation in Teaching (1938). New York: Harcourt.
How to Read a Page: A Course in Effective Teaching, with an Introduction to a Hundred Great Words (1942). New York: Norton.
Basic English and its Uses (1943). New York: Norton.
Speculative Instruments (1955). Chicago, IL: University of Chicago Press.
The Philosophy of Rhetoric (1965). New York: Oxford University Press.
Complementarities: Uncollected Essays and Reviews (1976). Cambridge, MA: Harvard University Press.

Richards on Rhetoric: Selected Essays, 1929–1974 (1990). New York: Oxford University Press.

Further reading

Berthoff, Ann E., 'The World, the Text, and the Reader: I.A. Richards's Hermeneutics', *Modern Philology*, 88.2 (1990): 166–173.

Bowen, John, 'Practical Criticism, Critical Practice: I.A. Richards and the Discipline of "English"', *Literature and History*, 13.1 (1987): 77–94.

Douglas-Fairhurst, Robert, 'I.A. Richards's *Practical Criticism*', *Essays in Criticism*, 54.4 (2004): 373–389.

Russo, John Paul, *I.A. Richards: His Life and Work*, Baltimore, MD and London: The Johns Hopkins University Press, 1989.

Schiller, Jerome P., *I.A. Richards' Theory of Literature*, New Haven, CT: Yale University Press, 1969.

West, David, 'Language, Thought and Reality: a Comparison of Ferdinand de Saussure's *Course in General Linguistics* with C.K. Ogden and I.A. Richards' *The Meaning of Meaning*', *Changing English: Studies in Culture and Education*, 12.2 (2005): 327–336.

PAUL RICOEUR (1913–)

Two different traditions in the study of language and philosophy come together magisterially in Paul Ricoeur's study *The Rule of Metaphor* (1975; trans. 1977), with Anglo-American and 'French' approaches thereby brought into dialogue.[1] While there is much talk of transdisciplinary research in the humanities today, authentic examples are few and far between: with the work of Ricoeur, one of the most wide-ranging transdisciplinary encounters between 'code' (theory) and 'meaning' (hermeneutics) takes place. Ricoeur was born in Valence, France, and soon lost both parents, his mother dying shortly after his birth, and his father in the First World War; Ricoeur subsequently moved to Rennes where he lived with his older sister, an aunt, and his paternal grandparents. The twin poles of Protestantism and an early study of critical philosophy were formative in his youth, as well as the influence of a teacher, Roland Dalbiez ('the first French philosopher to write on Freud and psychoanalysis')[2] and the 'double encounter', after getting his *Licencié ès Lettres* from the University of Rennes in 1933, with the philosophers Gabriel Marcel and Edmund Husserl at the University of Paris in 1934–1935. Interned for five years during the Second World War, Ricoeur credits his reading of Karl Jaspers, especially the three-volume *Philosophy* (1932), 'for having placed my admiration for German thinking outside the reach of all the negative aspects of our surroundings and of the "terror of history"'.[3] During this period, Ricoeur also worked on a translation of Husserl's *Ideen I*. What are the early indicators of Ricoeur's importance to the study of literature? He suggests that his interest in Jaspers' existential philosophy brought together the two poles of metaphysical transcendence and poetics, just as later, with the work for his study *The Symbolism of Evil* (1960), he argues that he had to move away from a Husserlian immediacy of the thinking subject, to one that only knows 'itself' indirectly through signs and narrative. *The Symbolism of Evil* presents the reader with Ricoeur's first definition of hermeneutics, where 'the symbol sets us thinking'.[4] By this point in his career, Ricoeur had worked as Professor of the History of Philosophy at The University of Strasbourg (1948–1956), and then as Professor of Philosophy at the Sorbonne, where he continued until 1967, co-teaching along the way a seminar in phenomenology with Jacques Derrida. A number of events and new movements in France began to affect Ricoeur much as they did all of the major thinkers of this period: the student uprisings in 1968 and the shift in intellectual thought to structuralist methodologies. All of the 'philosophies of the subject' including existentialism now came under attack, and there was a major shift within French theory in the reading of Heidegger's *Being and Time*. Ricoeur had already moved in 1967 to the site of the initial student uprising – Nanterre – where he became Dean of the School of Letters. Ironically, this change of location was brought about by Ricoeur's worries concerning the unbridled expansion of French higher education, and he attributes the militant student leaders with targeting Nanterre in 1968 as a 'weak link' in the chain of Paris universities.

Ricoeur began his own shift away from phenomenology and towards hermeneutics with his study of Freud, published in translation as *Freud and Philosophy: An Essay on Interpretation* (1965; trans. 1970). Ricoeur describes the 'idealist' version of phenomenology, which

> claimed a radical position of ultimate foundation, based upon an intellectual intuition immanent to consciousness . . . At the same time, this final justification contained a fundamentally ethical situation, inasmuch as the fundamental theoretical act expressed the ultimate self-responsibility of the philosophical subject.[5]

Ricoeur's shift to a poststructuralist hermeneutics implies a desire to maintain ethical responsibility, while being aware of the mediated relationships between text and reader. To put this another way, the structuralist notion of the autonomously functioning differential sign had to be overcome. Moving on from the books that encompassed and explored philosophies of the will[6] – namely *Freedom and Nature: The Voluntary and the Involuntary, Fallible Man* and *The Symbolism of Evil* – as well as the study of complex indirect consciousness in the works of Freud, Ricoeur focused more intensely on language and literature, especially with the essential *rejection* of the differential sign in favour of the unit of the sentence; this focus found its most profound expression in *The Rule of Metaphor* and the three-volume study *Time and Narrative*. In his 'Intellectual Autobiography' Ricoeur sketches out the structuralist background to his rejection of the differential sign, mentioning Saussure, Barthes, Greimas, Genette and Lévi-Strauss, as being the main players in this confining of energies to the text, or, 'objectifying abstraction' of semiotics, whereby 'language was reduced to the functioning of a system of signs without any anchor in a subject'.[7] In other words, Ricoeur rejects the Saussurian notion of signification being generated internally to the system or text in favour of signification being generated through relations to other objects and subjects. The key conceptual move is made via Benveniste's observation that 'the primary unit of meaning in actual language is not the lexical sign, but the sentence, which he called the "instance of discourse"'.[8] Ricoeur thus opposes semiotics and semantics, where the latter implies intersubjectivity and a communicative model of meaning.

In chapter seven of *The Rule of Metaphor*, 'Metaphor and Reference', Ricoeur expands significantly on the semiotics/semantics opposition, using the terminology from the philosopher Frege of 'sense' and 'reference' (*Bedeutung*): 'The sense is *what* the proposition states; the reference or denotation is *that about which* the sense is stated.'[9] This is an opposition that deconstructionists will pull apart, but which its defenders suggest is functional in an imperfect language world, where the correspondence between sense and reference is often out of joint. From the latter perspective, it is the internal machinations of a semiotic system divorced from human beings that reaches 'purity'. 'Reference', to use a term from the early Wittgenstein, can be thought of as the 'state of affairs', but when the literary text enters this discussion, a work that produces its own world, then the sense/reference binary appears to be suspended without the help of deconstruction. Ricoeur explains that the text is a more 'complex entity of discourse whose characteristics do not reduce to those of the unit of discourse, or the sentence'.[10] The connotative forces a re-reading of Frege's opposition and takes Ricoeur back to metaphor. Metaphor, to use Mario J. Valdes' phrase, is 'a paradigm', in *The Rule of Metaphor*, 'for all creativity through language'.[11] Critics such as Valdes regard the philosophy of language developed by Ricoeur in *The Rule of Metaphor*, as offering a sophisticated alternative to post-structuralist theories of the text. How can this be the case, given that metaphor is a rhetorical device? In *The Rule of Metaphor*, Ricoeur surveys the history and philosophy of metaphor in Western thought, rejecting the notion that metaphor is mere rhetorical ornament that produces nothing new, and the notion that metaphor is a transference of meaning.[12] By introducing the notion of an 'extra-linguistic reality' as seen above, Ricoeur argues that metaphor actually redescribes reality. The shift to a hermeneutic point of view reveals that metaphor is a 'strategy of discourse', as Ricoeur puts it, one which preserves and develops 'the creative power of language, preserves and develops the *heuristic* power wielded by *fiction*'.[13] Three main components of this theory are those of discourse, tension and mediation, where *discourse* is a large linguistic unit that involves a speaker, a hearer and a world, *tension* is at the heart of all of the theories of how metaphors work or function, and *mediation* is in effect what metaphor *does* as it produces new meaning.[14] As Masako K. Hiraga puts it:

> Ricoeur claims that metaphorical discourse itself has a reference under the condition of the suspension (*epoché*) of a literal reference. This metaphorical reference is the intentional direction toward the world and the reflective direction toward self. In other words, metaphorical discourse speaks of a possible world and a possible way of orienting oneself in this world, and thereby mediates man [*sic*] and the world, man [*sic*] and self, in a novel manner.[15]

Ricoeur develops his hermeneutical approach in *Time and Narrative*, one of the key twentieth-century studies of narrative and philosophy. Literary theorists have focused most carefully on the third part of Ricoeur's study (which begins in the second volume of the English translation) where he explores the 'fictive experience of time' and the text's 'transcendence within immanence'. Ricoeur's fundamental thesis that time cannot be directly spoken of, but must be instead mediated by the indirect discourse of narration (see his concluding remarks), is given full expression through close analysis of literary authors such as Mann, Proust and Woolf. In three corresponding literary works, Ricoeur reveals the ways in which they refigure time 'itself' in the experience of reading them, and as such go beyond Husserl's *Phenomenology of Internal Time-Consciousness* and Heidegger's *Being and Time*, the two works that pervade the overall study.

Ricoeur's oeuvre can barely be contained in short summary form: across his lifetime he has explored phenomenology, ethics, evil, theology, the linguistic turn in contemporary philosophy and theory, analytical philosophy, semiotics and semantics, metaphor, narrative and temporality, and many aspects of existentialist thought not touched upon here. Ricoeur's impact upon literary-critical thought has been immense, yet there are many aspects of his work that have fallen out of favour given the ongoing dominance of poststructuralist thought. Nonetheless, Ricoeur continues to offer a 'semantic' alternative to 'semiotic' thought, one that may eventually be perceived to be of more relevance as the 'post-theory' era develops.

Notes

1 See, for example, Domenico Jervolino's reading of Ricoeur in his *The Cogito and Hermeneutics: The Question of the Subject in Ricoeur*, trans. Gordon Poole, Dordrecht, Boston, MA and London: Kluwer Academic Publishers, 1990, especially chapter 3, p. 106.

2 Paul Ricoeur, 'Intellectual Autobiography', in Lewis Edwin Hahn, ed., *The Philosophy of Paul Ricoeur*, The Library of the Living Philosophers Volume XXII, Chicago and La Salle, IL: Open Court, 1995, pp. 3–53; p. 4.

3 Ibid., p. 9.

4 Ibid., p. 17.

5 Ibid., p. 34.

6 See Bernard P. Dauenhauer's opening sketch of his *Paul Ricoeur: The Promise and Risk of Politics*, Lanham, MD and Oxford: Rowman and Littlefield, 1998.

7 Paul Ricoeur, 'Intellectual Autobiography', p. 22.

8 Ibid.

9 Paul Ricoeur, *The Rule of Metaphor: Multi-Disciplinary Studies in the Creation of Meaning in Language*, trans. Robert Czerny with Kathleen McLaughlin and John Costello, S. J., London: Routledge and Kegan Paul 1978, p. 217.

10 Ibid., p. 219.

11 Mario Valdés, ed., *A Ricoeur Reader: Reflection and Imagination*, Toronto: University of Toronto Press, 1991, p. 12.

12 Masako K. Hiraga, 'On Paul Ricoeur's Theory of Metaphor', *Poetica: An International Journal of Linguistic-Literary Studies*, 20.91 (Jan. 1983): 91–99; pp. 91–92.

13 Paul Ricoeur, *The Rule of Metaphor: Multi-Disciplinary Studies in the Creation of Meaning in Language*, p. 6.

14 Ibid., pp. 92–93.

15 Ibid., p. 94.

See also in this book

Gadamer

Major works

Gabriel Marcel and Karl Jaspers. Philosophie du mystère et philosophie du paradoxe (1948). Paris: Temps Present.

Freedom and Nature: The Voluntary and the Involuntary (1950). Trans. Erazim Kohak, Evanston, IL: Northwestern University Press, 1966.

History and Truth (1955). Trans. Charles A. Kelbley, Evanston, IL: Northwestern University Press, 1965.

Fallible Man (1960). Trans. Walter J. Lowe, New York: Fordham University Press, 1986.

The Symbolism of Evil (1960). Trans. Emerson Buchanan, New York: Harper and Row, 1967.

Freud and Philosophy: An Essay on Interpretation (1965). Trans. Denis Savage, New Haven, CT: Yale University Press, 1970.

The Conflict of Interpretations: Essays in Hermeneutics (ed. Don Ihde, 1969). Trans. Willis Domingo *et al.*, Evanston, IL: Northwestern University Press, 1974.

The Rule of Metaphor: Multi-Disciplinary Studies in the Creation of Meaning in Language (1975). Trans. Robert Czerny with Kathleen McLaughlin and John Costello, S. J., London: Routledge & Kegan Paul, 1978.

Interpretation Theory: Discourse and the Surplus of Meaning (1976). Fort Worth, TX: Texas Christian Press.

The Philosophy of Paul Ricoeur: An Anthology of his Work (Charles E. Reagan and David Stewart, eds, 1978). Boston, MA: Beacon Press.

Hermeneutics and the Human Sciences: Essays on Language, Action and Interpretation (1981). Trans. John B. Thompson, Cambridge: Cambridge University Press.

Time and Narrative (1983, 1984, 1985). Three vols, trans. Kathleen McLaughlin and David Pellauer, Chicago, IL: University of Chicago Press, 1984, 1985, 1988.

Lectures on Ideology and Utopia (1985). Trans. George H. Taylor, New York: Columbia University Press.

From Text to Action: Essays in Hermeneutics II (1986). Trans. Kathleen Blamey and John B. Thompson, Evanston, IL: Northwestern University Press, 1991.

Oneself as Another (1990). Trans. Kathleen Blamey, Chicago, IL: University of Chicago Press, 1992.

A Ricoeur Reader: Reflection and Imagination (Mario J. Valdes, ed., 1991). Toronto: University of Toronto Press.

Lectures I: Autour du politique (1991). Paris: Seuil.

Lectures II: La Contrée des philosophes (1992). Paris: Seuil.

Lectures III: Aux frontières de la philosophie (1994). Paris: Seuil.

Critique and Conviction (1995). Trans. Kathleen Blamey, New York: Columbia University Press, 1998.

The Just (1995). Trans. David Pellauer, Chicago, IL: University of Chicago Press, 2000.

Further reading

Kaplan, David M., *Ricoeur's Critical Theory*, New York: State University of New York Press, 2003.

Kearney, Richard, ed., *Paul Ricoeur: The Hermeneutics of Action*, London: Sage, 1996.

Kemp, T. Peter and Rasmussen, David, eds, *The Narrative Path: The Later Works of Paul Ricoeur*, Cambridge, MA: The MIT Press, 1989.

Simms, Karl, *Paul Ricoeur*, London and New York: Routledge, 2002.

Valdés, Mario, ed., *A Ricoeur Reader: Reflection and Imagination*, Toronto: University of Toronto Press, 1991.

Wood, David, ed., *On Paul Ricoeur: Narrative and Interpretation*, London and New York: Routledge, 1991.

EDWARD WADIE SAID (1935–2003)

One of the most significant postcolonial literary critics of the twentieth century, and a leading commentator on Palestinian culture and politics, Said began his academic career with two books on modern *Western* literature and culture. This crossover between cultures comes as no surprise given Said's beginnings in British-ruled Palestine where he was born in 1935. Colonial-style education in Cairo was followed by a move to Mount Hermon school, Massachusetts, and then Princeton and Harvard, where he completed his doctoral thesis in 1964 on Conrad, published as *Joseph Conrad and the Fiction of Autobiography* (1966). Said was eventually made the Parr Professor of English and Comparative Literature at Columbia University, New York, where he spent most of his academic life. Alongside his commitment to literary-critical studies was a re-engagement with Palestinian political and social issues; in 1977 Said was elected to the Palestine National Council with which he worked closely to develop the projected two-state solution to the Israel–Palestine conflict.

Said's early major contribution to critical thought was to introduce and critique the French poststructuralists, and their precursors (such as Nietzsche). In his *Beginnings: Intention and Method* (1975), Said contrasts the concept of the 'beginning' with the metaphysical concept of the 'origin'. These two concepts represent two different ways of thinking and of producing knowledge; the metaphysical 'origin' is privileged, mythical and transcendent, asserting a point of universal truth, whereas the secular 'beginning' is contingent, ceaselessly re-examined (and re-begun), re-structuring and animating new ways of conceiving the world. Said calls the 'beginning' not an achieved result (as with the 'origin') but a task and a search.[1] Based upon Foucault's concept of 'genealogy' – that is, the examination of knowledge not as a progressive system, but as a series of ruptures and discontinuities – Said also argues for intentionality in the act of beginning, which is also the creation of a necessary fiction. Most of Said's literary examples are modern canonical texts, while the theory he examines in *Beginnings* is poststructuralist and postmodern. Said accounts for this disjunction in his preface to the 1985 edition of *Beginnings*, arguing that modernism was a response to the crisis of what he calls 'filiation' (familial or natural connections) leading to the counter-crisis of affiliation (chosen interconnections that may be non-familial or arbitrarily constructed). The French theory used to explore these crises is thus grounded by Said in the liberal humanist and new critical traditions, and the tensions between these two modes of thought remained throughout his career. In a later collection of essays, *The World, The Text And The Critic* (1983), Said argues that French theory has led to 'a maddening new critical shorthand' whereby close-reading appears to have been abandoned in favour of studying a text's 'function' and formal operations, rather than its materiality, i.e. its formation in a socio-political context.[2] As Said says: 'By "material" . . . I mean the ways, for example, in which the text is a monument, a cultural object sought after, fought over, possessed, rejected, or achieved in time. The text's materiality also includes the range of its authority.'[3] Said's rejection of Derridean deconstruction and his own affiliation with Foucault can be read in this statement; we can also see the commitment to the struggles *from which* texts emerge, and/or *about which* texts comment upon. This awkward relationship of text and context creates many of the dilemmas and contradictions upon which Said's most well-known work, *Orientalism* (1978), is built.

Orientalism is a synthesis of Antonio Gramsci's theories of hegemony and Foucault's theories of discourse. Both Gramsci and Foucault sought to understand the mechanisms whereby power structures within society were maintained and replicated. Both rejected the 'top-down' model of power being forcibly expressed as a simplistic subjugation of others. Gramsci developed the insight that material conditions of subjugation were also matched by ideological conditions, i.e. the institutions and instruments that maintain an *idea* of society and its hierarchical relations. *Hegemony* is the practice of the material *and* the ideological reproduction of values. Foucault's approach to power involves in part the study of discursive formations, that is to say, the mechanism via which knowledge is produced and delimited as a practice. So, in the practice of psychiatry, for example, certain human beings are classified via the production of knowledge as being 'insane' or in other ways outside of the norm; Foucault reveals how such discursive formations change over time, not in a progressive sense, but through violent and sudden ruptures and breaks. Power, for Foucault, is dispersed *across* a discursive formation. Said's synthesis of Gramsci and Foucault reveals a discursive formation called 'Orientalism', that is, a productive hegemonic transdisciplinary body of Western knowledge that constructs and subjugates the 'Orient'. This construction is not all directed one way, as Said argues from the beginning of his study:

> the Orient has helped to define Europe (or the West) as its contrasting image, idea, personality, experience. The Orient is an integral part of European *material* civilization and culture. Orientalism expresses and represents that part culturally and even ideologically as a mode of discourse with supporting institutions, vocabulary, scholarship, imagery, doctrines, even colonial bureaucracies and colonial styles.[4]

Consequently, Said studies a vast range of *colonial* literary and non-literary texts that, he argues, form both a relatively uniform continuum and at the same time reveal differences of opinion. This apparent contradiction leads to the necessity to distinguish between *latent* and *manifest* Orientalism, which although having a Freudian ring to them, can also be thought of as being analogous to the structuralist concepts of *langue* and *parole*. Latent Orientalism, which Said calls an 'unconscious positivity' is the underlying, unconscious continuum of thought that belongs to the entire Orientalist community (it is a shared value system and set of signs, the 'language' and dreamworld of Orientalism); manifest Orientalism is the historically conditioned individual differences of Orientalist expression or utterance, constituted by latent Orientalism, but given individual form. Said calls manifest Orientalism 'the various stated views about Oriental society, languages, literatures, history, sociology, and so forth'.[5] While Said's study has been in many ways foundational for the postcolonial critics who have followed, it must be stressed that it is a work of *colonial discourse analysis*, making sense of the latent Orientalism through close-reading of individual Orientalist utterances or texts. Said asserts that the body of Orientalist knowledge was overall *effective*, it produces subjects and subjugation, it manages people for profit. One of the simplest mechanisms utilized here is the hierarchy of value created via a series of binary oppositions: the Oriental is produced discursively as irrational, depraved, childlike, different, uncomprehending, degenerate, feminine; the European, in contrast, is produced discursively as rational, virtuous, mature, normal, masculine and so on. In the nineteenth century, such a hierarchy was given a so-called 'scientific' basis with theories of eugenics, evolution and notions of 'advanced and backward' races.[6] All such theories are examples of what Said calls the 'radically real', that is, once an Orientalist statement is made, no matter if based on fantasy or prejudice, it creates a 'reality', i.e. is received as a statement of truth. One of the problems encountered in *Orientalism*, however, is the lack of attention paid to those indigenous writers and activists who rejected, resisted and countered the production of colonial discourse. Put another way, Said's continual focus on the producers of colonial discourse leaves very little room for those individuals who actively refused to be claimed by this body of gendered and racialized power-knowledge. Much of the criticism produced by critics after *Orientalism* is involved with reclaiming and recovering the work of such individuals.

At the close of *Orientalism* Said gives a concrete example of contemporary Orientalist discourse production with the imbalanced relationship between the US and the 'Arab world' as he puts it, focusing mainly on comparisons of intellectual work and scholarship. In a series of books following *Orientalism*, however, a new focus is apparent: the Israel–Palestine conflict. In texts such as *The Question of Palestine* (1979), *Covering Islam: How the Media and the Experts Determine How We See the Rest of the World* (1981), *After the Last Sky* (1986) and *Blaming the Victims* (1988), Said radically shifted to become a spokesperson for Palestine, linked most obviously with his in-depth encounters and discussions during fourteen years of involvement with the Palestine National Council (from 1977 to 1991). Said occupied complex political territory, voicing criticism of Yasser Arafat and the Palestine Liberation Organisation as well as severe ongoing criticism of Israel. But Said had not abandoned his study of canonical Western aesthetics: during this period he continued with his interests in music (he was a skilled classical pianist) publishing *Musical Elaborations* (1991) and then a collection of lectures and essays called *Culture and Imperialism* (1993). Ironically, given his many publications on Palestine, it is *Culture and Imperialism* that has received the most critical attention, although this may simply be because it is regarded as a companion volume to the groundbreaking *Orientalism*. In his introduction Said responds to his critics, acknowledging that he had left out of *Orientalism* those activists and intellectuals responsible in part for decolonization, for example in Algeria, Ireland and Indonesia; he stresses that indigenous peoples were not in reality as constructed and perceived by Orientalists and that active resistance to colonialism was invariably successful. Said mentions by name activists and intellectuals such as Frantz Fanon, Amilcar Cabral, C.L.R. James and Walter Rodney, and the authors Chinua Achebe, Ngugi wa Thiongo, Wole Soyinka, Salman Rushdie and Gabriel Garcia Márquez. While all of these figures inform *Culture and Imperialism*, explored in detail in the third chapter, 'Resistance and Opposition', the book as a whole examines Western, 'Imperialist' discursive formations, including the contemporary role played by the US. Important Western authors include Jane Austen, Joseph Conrad, T.S. Eliot and W.B. Yeats. Said coordinates his readings by returning to his concept of affiliation, developing this further via a musical term, *counterpoint*, where

> various themes play off one another, with only a provisional privilege being given to any particular one . . . in the resulting polyphony there is concert and order, an organized interplay that derives from the themes, not from a rigorous melodic or formal principle outside the work.[7]

The result is *contrapuntal* reading, that is a resistance to reinscribing the binary oppositions of Orientalism, and a mode of analysis with no fixed ideological or methodological centre or ground. Contrapuntal reading wrenches texts from their apparently natural filiative situations, to reveal instead their complex colonial or historical *affiliations*; this involves a reorientation of canonical Western texts in general. Said's main example of contrapuntal reading is his analysis of Austen's *Mansfield Park* (1814). What may at first appear marginal in *Mansfield Park* – the Antigua 'plantations' that need to be visited by Sir Thomas to fix some unspecified problems – become, via contrapuntal reading, the key affiliation of the novel and its position within colonial history. Said makes a grand claim for this contrapuntal reading, which summarizes his entire colonial-postcolonial analytical project:

> Having read *Mansfield Park* as part of the structure of an expanding imperialist venture, one cannot simply restore it to the canon of 'great literary masterpieces' . . . Rather, I think, the novel steadily, if unobtrusively, opens up a broad expanse of domestic imperialist culture without which Britain's subsequent acquisition of territory would not have been possible.[8]

Contrapuntal readings cross boundaries, expose interconnections that are barely apparent, and reveal that colonial discourse production is enabling and oppressive, ongoing yet open to resistance and critique.

Said's legacy to colonial, postcolonial and literary–critical studies is immense and, even though it has been thoroughly critiqued and modified, still generates important theoretical research.

Notes

1 Edward W. Said, *Beginnings: Intention and Method*, New York: Columbia University Press, Morningside Edition, 1985, p. 380.
2 Edward W. Said, *The World, the Text and the Critic*, Cambridge, MA: Harvard University Press, 1983, p. 143.
3 Ibid., p. 150.
4 Edward W. Said, *Orientalism*, New York: Pantheon/Random House, 1978, pp. 1–2.
5 Ibid., p. 206.
6 Ibid.
7 Edward W. Said, *Culture and Imperialism*, London: Chatto & Windus, 1993, pp. 59–60.
8 Ibid., p. 114.

See also in this book

Bhabha, Fanon, Spivak

Major works

Joseph Conrad and the Fiction of Autobiography (1966). Cambridge, MA: Harvard University Press.
Beginnings: Intention and Method (1975). New York: Basic Books. New York: Columbia University Press, Morningside Edition, 1985.
Orientalism (1978). New York: Pantheon/Random House.
The Question of Palestine (1979). New York: New York Times Books.
The Palestine Question and the American Context (1979). Beirut: Institute for Palestine Studies.
Covering Islam: How the Media and the Experts Determine How We See the Rest of the World (1981). New York: Pantheon. Updated and revised edition, New York: Vintage, 1997.
The World, The Text And The Critic (1983). Cambridge, MA: Harvard University Press.
After the Last Sky: Palestinian Lives (1986). New York: Pantheon.
Blaming the Victims: Spurious Scholarship & the Palestinian Question (1988). London: Verso.
Musical Elaborations (1991). New York: Columbia University Press.
Culture and Imperialism (1993). London: Chatto & Windus.
Politics of Dispossession: The Struggle for Palestinian Self-Determination, 1969–1994 (1994). New York: Pantheon.
Peace and Its Discontents: Essays on Palestine in the Middle East Peace Process (1995). New York: Vintage.
Out of Place: A Memoir (1999). New York: Knopf.

The Edward Said Reader (2000). Eds, Moustafa Bayoumi and Andrew Rubin, New York: Vintage.

Further reading

Ansell-Pearson, Keith, Parry, Benita and Squires, Judith, eds, *Cultural Readings of Imperialism: Edward Said and the Gravity of History*, London: Lawrence & Wishart, 1996; New York: St Martin's Press, 1997.

Ashcroft, Bill and Ahluwalia, Pal, eds, *Edward Said: The Paradox of Identity*, London and New York: Routledge, 1996.

Bhabha, Homi and Mitchell, W.J.T., 'Edward Said: Continuing the Conversation', Special Issue of *Critical Inquiry*, 31.2 (2005).

Bové, Paul, ed., *Edward Said and the Work of the Critic: Speaking Truth to Power*, Durham and London: Duke University Press, 2000.

Conteh, Morgan, ed., 'Edward Said, Africa, and Cultural Criticism', Special Issue of *Research in African Literatures*, 36.3 (2005).

Hart, William D., *Edward Said and the Religious Effects of Culture*, Cambridge and New York: Cambridge University Press, 2000.

Herman, David, 'Edward Said (1935–2003)', *Salmagundi*, 143 (2004): 76–88.

Hutcheon, Linda, 'In Memory of Edward W. Said (1935–2003)', *University of Toronto Quarterly*, 73.2 (2004): 805–806.

ELAINE SHOWALTER (1941–)

The feminist critic Elaine Showalter has continually confounded her supporters and her detractors with her productive and creative shifts in intellectual stance. Perhaps most famous for the development of a literary-critical feminist methodology called 'gynocriticism', Showalter was one of the first academics to publish a study of feminist literature with a major university press.[1] Her work on 'hysteria' was groundbreaking, leading to new approaches to the analysis of medical discourses and medical history via the study of gender. More recently, Showalter has become a controversial figure, with her outspoken comments on the need for American doctoral students to prepare for a world without enough academic jobs, as well as other provocative comments concerning her love of fashion and popular culture.[2] Showalter was born in Cambridge, Massachusetts, and attended Bryn Mawr College, where she received her BA in 1962; she gained her MA from Brandeis University in 1964 and her Ph.D. on Victorian women writers from the University of California in Davis, in 1970. After teaching at Rutgers University, Showalter moved to Princeton where she became Professor of English in 1984. Awards include the Avalon Foundation Professor of Humanities at Princeton, a Guggenheim Fellowship (1977–1978), a Rockefeller Humanities Fellowship (1981–1982), and a National Endowment for the Humanities Fellowship (1988–1989), among many others. It was Showalter's first book – *A Literature of Their Own: British Women Novelists from Brontë to Lessing* (1977) – that prepared the groundwork for many critics who followed. *A Literature of Their Own* emerged from Showalter's Ph.D. thesis called 'The Double Standard: Criticism of Women Writers in Victorian Periodicals, 1845–1880', a study that Showalter called 'a hybrid, an attempt to write about women in an outmoded and inadequate critical vocabulary'.[3] While Showalter had the primary texts as a welcome resource, the literary-critical discourses available at the time of her study were mainly liberal humanist and patriarchal; Showalter had then to develop a new theory of reading:

> As the issues in my work and my life took on a new meaning in the light of feminism, I began to envisage a much bolder critical undertaking than my thesis, and to imagine a literary criticism that would do for the history of women's writing what Northrop Frye had done for Canadian literature.[4]

Drawing her title from a statement by John Stuart Mill (not Virginia Woolf as some critics have mistakenly thought), *A Literature of Their Own* was precisely that 'bolder critical undertaking'. Adopting a sweeping historical perspective, Showalter argues that there are three phases or stages of professional women's writing in British literature, which she terms *Feminine, Feminist* and *Female*. The *Feminine* phase is that of the pseudonymous female writers from the 1840s to 1880; the *Feminist* phase extends from 1880 to 1920, when women won the right in England to vote; the *Female* phase is 1920 to 'the present' with emphasis upon the political and sexually revolutionary developments that took place in the 1960s. Why was this schema so important to early feminists? Because it moved away from the notion that there was only a minority of truly 'great' women novelists (Jane Austen, the Brontës, George Eliot and Virginia Woolf), which in turn meant that the bulk of literary-critical theorizing concerning women novelists was being developed based upon the concerns of this group. Showalter argues that this distorts the bigger picture by ignoring vast numbers of women authors. In retrospect, with numerous anthologies of women's writing and biographical materials now available, it is difficult to imagine or recreate the excitement that Showalter's approach generated; nonetheless, this schema did facilitate a great deal of critical work and other interest in a wider range of women authors.

What do Showalter's three categories signify from her critical and historical perspective? Reminiscent of Fanon's three main phases of cultural reception and production, the first phase is, for Showalter, one of imitation and internalization of patriarchal notions and modes of artistic production, standards and values; the second phase is one of protest and rejection of those very same modes, standards and values; and the third phase is regarded as one free of the preceding tensions, in a liberatory 'turning inward'. Showalter regards the second and third phases as being not just historically different, but in some senses choices that face women writers: the second phase sacrifices aesthetics for politics, whereas the third phase is regarded as more 'authentic' because of the inward 'self exploration' of female subjectivity that in turn produces autonomous art. The notion of three interrelated historical phases is important for constructing a coherent 'female tradition', one with continuity and complexity; if later feminists critique such an overarching unified view, especially with more theoretical approaches to history following the work of Michel Foucault, they do so with the luxury of new 'subcultural' canons, to use Showalter's phrase. Showalter regards the first two phases of women's writing (imitation and protest) as being forms of dependency; controversially, the early 'female' artists in the formal part of the third phase, such as Dorothy Richardson and Virginia Woolf, come under a fairly sustained attack. Such an approach – critiquing two highly revered modernist and feminist authors – has meant that Showalter herself has received some considerable criticism, most notably from Toril Moi in her *Sexual/Textual Politics* (1985). Moi also attacked Showalter for her lack of theoretical sophistication (meaning lack of French theory), although this misses the point that Showalter was developing new critical approaches and opening up new areas of feminist literary exploration at a time when French theory was largely unknown in English-speaking universities (and Showalter herself would be one of the key editors who brought together early, more theoretical feminist work in book collections such as *The New Feminist Criticism: Essays on Women, Literature, Theory* (1985)). In an influential essay called 'Toward a Feminist Poetics' (1979), Showalter sketched a 'taxonomy' or poetics of feminist criticism:

> in the hope that it will serve as an introduction to a body of work which needs to be considered both as a major contribution to English studies and as part of an interdisciplinary effort to reconstruct the social, political, and cultural experience of women.[5]

Dividing feminist criticism into two 'varieties', Showalter argued that the first concerns 'woman as reader' and the second 'woman as writer';

the first variety is that of *feminist critique*, whereby texts by men are mined by women who go on to reveal their ideological and sexual codes that lead to a new 'apprehension' of textuality in general. *Feminist critique* in Showalter's sense is the important work of examining the 'images and stereotypes of women' produced within literary texts, as well as the mechanisms of representation and omission/effacement in relation to audience, popular cultural forms and semiotics.[6] The second variety of feminist criticism demands new terminology, and Showalter coins the term 'gynocritics' (most commonly called after the publication of this essay 'gynocriticism'). Why does she need this neologism? Because she argues that women as writers/producers of signification are creating new territory: 'Its subjects include the psychodynamics of female creativity; linguistics and the problem of a female language; the trajectory of the individual or collective female literary career; literary history; and, of course, studies of particular writers and works.'[7] As with the previous notion of three phases of literary production, the shift from feminist critique to that of *gynocritics* is one that moves from the essentially political to the 'self-contained and experimental'.[8] Rather than reversing a hierarchy (the opposition of women as consumers or imitators, and men as producers or initiators being reversed), the shift to women as 'producers' of an autonomous aesthetic is a strategic rejection of hierarchical division in the first place. Thus gynocritics map the terrain of female experience and build a critical framework from this starting point, rather than adapting the critical tools that are already in place. This definition does lead to a strange sense of anxiety that pervades Showalter's essay concerning 'high' theory, based upon the notion that the new (at the time) structuralist theory is a masculinist, pseudo-scientific enterprise in which women will only ever be imitators or obscure practitioners and 'Feminists writing in these modes, such as Hélène Cixous and the women contributors to *Diacritics*, risk being allotted the symbolic ghettos of the special issue or the back of the book for their essays.'[9]

Showalter's own major study of gynocritics – *The Female Malady: Women, Madness and English Culture, 1830–1980* – takes the form of a feminist study of the history of psychiatry and a 'cultural history' of madness or 'the female malady'. Divided into three main parts, the book examines: (1) Psychiatric Victorianism (1830–1870); (2) Psychiatric Darwinism (1870–1920); and (3) Psychiatric Modernism (1920–1980). Showalter's underlying thesis is that there is an asserted connection revealed in the history of psychiatric discourses between women and madness; in other words, the prevailing, patriarchal view is that women 'stand for irrationality in general'.[10] Showalter examines many literary examples in her study, including Brontë's *Jane Eyre* and the character of Bertha Mason, the infamous 'madwoman in the attic', and Charlotte Perkins Gilman's short-story 'The Yellow Wallpaper'.[11] She also traces the genealogy of the concept of 'hysteria' and other methods of constraining female identity and sexuality, such as the use of clitoridectomies in Victorian England. As such, and given the scope of her account, Showalter was once again breaking new ground; as Emily Eakin argues: 'Although Foucault's *Madness and Civilization* (1961) had produced a surge of academic interest in insanity during the 1970s, few scholars had attempted a history of modern psychiatry, let alone a history that took gender as its guiding principle.'[12] Showalter followed *The Female Malady* with two further related studies: *Sexual Anarchy: Gender and Culture at the Fin de siècle* (1990) and a collection of essays based in part upon her Oxford University Clarendon Lectures (1989) called *Sister's Choice: Tradition and Change in American Women's Writing* (1991). *Sexual Anarchy* is a lively romp through the narratives and images of sexual crisis and apocalypse that proliferated at the close of the nineteenth and twentieth centuries. The book is fast-paced, and wittily written, while mapping out quite seriously the terrain of *fin de siècle* gender destabilization. The style of *Sexual Anarchy* marks a more publicly accessible mode of writing, developed in Showalter's more recent publications: *Hystories: Epidemics and Modern Culture* (1997), *Inventing Herself: Claiming a Feminist Intellectual Heritage* (2001) and *Faculty Towers: The Academic Novel and its Discontents* (2005). *Hystories* caused controversy with Showalter's apparent reversal of her earlier research: instead of the 'hysteric' being a repressive concept utilized by patriarchy, Showalter re-appropriates the term to examine what she calls the hysterical epidemics in America of alien abduction, chronic fatigue syndrome, Gulf War syndrome, multiple personalities, recovered memories and satanic ritual abuse. All of these 'conditions' or 'syndromes' are charted as a coping mechanism for modern-day American society. In *Inventing Herself* and *Faculty Towers* Showalter takes two related approaches to university personae: first, through a series of accounts of feminist icons, and second, through study of the campus novel. Both books have an understandably North American focus, and both are self-reflexive; as Showalter says in *Inventing Herself*, although it could apply to *Faculty Towers* as well: 'I have put some of my own history into this book, in places where it intersects with the history of feminism in our time.'[13] Whether this is seen as self-indulgent or a strategic feminist move hardly matters: Showalter's poetics of feminist criticism and personae is an important legacy in the history of Anglo-American feminist thought.

Notes

1 As Emily Eakin points out, while Kate Millet had published her *Sexual Politics* in 1970, the study focused exclusively on male modernists; Gilbert and Gubar's *The Madwoman in the Attic: The Woman Writer and the Nineteenth-Century Literary Imagination* would follow Showalter's work in 1979. See Eakin, 'Who's Afraid of Elaine Showalter? The MLA President Incites Mass Hysteria', *Lingua Franca: The Review of Academic Life*, 8.6 (1 September 1998): 28–36.
2 Ibid.
3 Elaine Showalter, 'Introduction, Twenty Years On: *A Literature of Their Own* Revisited', in *A Literature of Their Own: British Women Novelists from Brontë to Lessing*, expanded edition, Princeton, NJ: Princeton University Press, 1999, p. xi.
4 Ibid., p. xii.
5 Ibid., p. 128.
6 Ibid.
7 Ibid.
8 Ibid., p. 129.
9 Ibid., p. 140.
10 Elaine Showalter, *The Female Malady: Women, Madness and English Culture, 1830–1980*, New York: Pantheon, 1985, p. 4.
11 For a more in-depth summary, see Michael P. Spikes, *Understanding Contemporary American Literary Theory*, Columbia, SC: University of South Carolina Press, 1997.
12 Emily Eakin, 'Who's Afraid of Elaine Showalter? The MLA President Incites Mass Hysteria', p. 33.
13 Elaine Showalter, *Inventing Herself: Claiming a Feminist Intellectual Heritage*, New York: Scribner, 2001, p. 17.

See also in this book

Gilbert and Gubar

Major works

A Literature of Their Own: British Women Novelists from Brontë to Lessing (1977). Princeton, NJ: Princeton University Press.
The Female Malady: Women, Madness and English Culture, 1830–1980 (1985). New York: Pantheon.
The New Feminist Criticism: Essays on Women, Literature, Theory (ed., 1985). New York: Pantheon.
Speaking of Gender (1989). London and New York: Routledge.
Sexual Anarchy: Gender and Culture at the Fin de siècle (1990). New York: Viking.
Sister's Choice: Tradition and Change in American Women's Writing (1991). Oxford: Clarendon Press.
Inventing Herself: Claiming a Feminist Intellectual Heritage (2001). New York: Scribner.
Faculty Towers: The Academic Novel and its Discontents (2005). Oxford: Oxford University Press.

Further reading

Eakin, Emily, 'Who's Afraid of Elaine Showalter? The MLA President Incites Mass Hysteria', *Lingua Franca: The Review of Academic Life*, 8.6 (1 September 1998): 28–36.

Fraiman, Susan, 'An Interview with Elaine Showalter: Princeton University: September 3, 1986', *Critical Texts*, 4.2 (1987): 7–17.

Jacobus, Mary, 'Reading Woman (Reading)', in Robyn R. Warhol and Diane Price Herndl, eds, *Feminisms: An Anthology of Literary Theory and Criticism*, New Brunswick, NJ: Rutgers University Press, 1997, pp. 1029–1045.

Kwon, Seokwoo, 'Dual Discourses and Two Versions of *To the Lighthouse*: Showalter-Moi Controversy and the Use of Textual Feminism', *Feminist Studies in English Literature*, 8.2 (2001): 155–181.

GAYATRI CHAKRAVORTY SPIVAK (1942–)

A focus on Spivak's education and intellectual trajectory reveals a life-long commitment to literary-critical studies alongside genuine political engagement. Spivak was born in Calcutta, India in 1942; she later attended Presidency College at the University of Calcutta. After graduating in English in 1959 she spent two more years in Calcutta as a graduate student, before moving to the US to complete her MA and Ph.D. in comparative literature at Cornell University, with the supervision of Paul de Man. Her first book was based on her doctoral thesis on W.B. Yeats' poetry, a study that as noted appears in retrospect quite different from her later postcolonial research, but which adopts a critical stance of English rule in Ireland. Thus, even though in this biographical and critical book Spivak takes a quite descriptive approach to Yeats, she is already engaging with the effects of colonization and the imposition of alien values upon indigenous cultures. Spivak's career after receiving her doctorate has continued with great success, with the awarding of numerous academic posts, titles and honours, including the Andrew W. Mellon Professorship of English at Pittsburgh University (1987) and the Avalon Foundation Professorship in the Humanities at Columbia University (1991). Among many Fellowships Spivak has held the Tagore Fellowship at Maharaja Sayajirao University of Baroda, India.

The highly theoretical approach to postcolonial studies taken by Spivak can be traced to her second major publication, her translation in 1976 of Jacques Derrida's *Of Grammatology* (originally published in French, 1967), which includes a substantial introduction or preface to Derrida's work. This preface maps Spivak's interest in Derrida and deconstruction, especially the concept of 'writing under erasure', that is to say, crossing out an 'inaccurate' or problematic word, but allowing it to remain readable because it is still needed to make sense of a particular system of thought ('writing under erasure' is linked below to Spivak's use of the Lacanian term 'foreclosure'). The preface is also a substantial self-contained essay on Derrida, the essay form being deliberately chosen as one that is both provisional and a potential simulacrum of the book that follows (leading Spivak to theorize, after Derrida, that the book form itself may be nothing but a simulacrum, rather than a stable originary point of meaning). Spivak adopts and substantially adapts the critical essay form with much of her initial postcolonial research, bringing deconstruction and postcolonial theory into conjunction, her first major set of essays being collected as the book *In Other Worlds: Essays in Cultural Politics* (1987).

Why does Spivak use the critical essay as a strategic tool? One answer is that she continually attempts to resist the essentialist positioning of Third World subjects; in her work on Feminism, Marxism and Subaltern Studies, for example, Spivak is careful to articulate the perspective *from which* she writes in relation to the subjects she writes about. The Subaltern Studies historians in India addressed this primary question of subjectivity, arguing that colonial socio-political hierarchies are reproduced in the postcolonial era, and that subaltern subjects – those non-elite peoples denied access to power – had no genuine non-distorting representation or self-expressed voice. The recovery of subaltern voices is thus one of the primary aims of these historians. In 'Can the Subaltern Speak?' (1988) Spivak critiques the essentialist underpinnings of Subaltern Studies, where the marginalized subaltern subject is always defined via his or her difference from the elites. Spivak asserts that the subaltern subject is heterogeneous and, by examining the mechanisms of the supposed 'recovery' of their voice, instead an ongoing displacement and effacement is revealed. The key subject position disentangled by Spivak is that of the female subaltern and the practice of *sati* or widow immolation. In *sati* the widow is burnt to death on her husband's funeral pyre: she is defined solely through the identity of her husband, and is therefore considered to have no identity worth continuing after his death. Furthermore, two competing interpretive narratives intersect here, leading to what Spivak calls a 'double displacement': the Indian patriarchal customs in which the practice of *sati* is embedded, and British colonial law (i.e. law made in the *absence* of any Indian women) during the period of colonial rule. In both interpretive narratives, gender is constructed via fundamentally patriarchal law. Loomba argues that Spivak's analysis needs to be supplemented 'by concentrating not just on the widow who died but also on some of those widows who survived to tell the tale'.[1] In her wider argument, Spivak points to an aporia or unresolvable contradiction in the process of analysing the subaltern subject: postcolonial critical discourse may, in itself, lead to an essentialist displacement of Third World women, while at the same time, it is still necessary to continue with the analysis of colonial oppression of the subaltern. This means that 'interpretative violence' is a necessity that can lead to a strategic methodology (i.e. one that produces results from what appears to be a problematic approach), even if all the critic produces are 'necessary fictions'. There are other strategies that Spivak adopts in relation to this central essay: she has also translated short stories by the Bengali author Mahasweta Devi, and writes about her in 'A Literary Representation of the Subaltern: A Woman's Text from the Third World' (see section three of *In Other Worlds*). Further translations by Spivak of Devi's work are published as *Imaginary Maps: Three Stories by Mahasweta Devi* (1995). Close attention to feminist analyses of Third World women also contributes to Spivak's strategic mode of writing. A key essay, originally published in 1981, is 'French Feminism in an International Frame' where Spivak attacks Kristeva's portrayal from a Western perspective of Chinese women (see Kristeva's *About Chinese Women*, 1977). At stake is the way in which a universal definition of the female subject is constructed via a Western Orientalist vision of the Other, in this case, Kristeva's vision of the Chinese, and also the need for a recognition of the cultural specificity out of which Kristeva's misreadings arose. That is to say, an awareness of the 'French theory' scene reveals the Orientalist assumptions underpinning otherwise apparently valuable feminist work; Spivak argues that the feminist work needs to continue by learning from Third World subjects, not by imposing false interpretive models upon them. A more literary approach is taken in 'Three Women's Texts and a Critique of Imperialism' (1985) – looking at *Jane Eyre*, *Wide Sargasso Sea* and *Frankenstein* – where feminist readings are re-examined by Spivak.

Spivak has a reputation for writing ferociously dense theoretical texts; her supporters argue that the provisional 'unfinished' qualities of her writing represent a strategic resistance to essentialism, closure and to totalizing thought (i.e. thought which claims to know the Other prior to any encounter with a different culture or individual). Spivak's detractors argue that her writing style leads at times to confusion and error, and that this outweighs any strategic gain. It is undoubtedly true that Spivak draws on and develops in unique ways the works of many of the key theorists and philosophers of the twentieth century, nowhere more so than in her book *A Critique of Postcolonial Reason: Toward a History of the Vanishing Present* (1999). The book is arranged into four main sections: (1) Philosophy, (2) Literature, (3) History, (4) Culture, with an essay on Deconstruction in the appendix (the third section also contains a revised version of 'Can the Subaltern Speak?'). The 'Philosophy' section immediately provides an insight into Spivak's development of theoretical concepts and tools in the service of political/postcolonial analysis, in this case with her adoption and adaptation of the Lacanian term 'foreclosure' in the context of the 'native informant'. Rejecting the notion of 'a fully self-present voice-consciousness' (see Spivak's preface to Derrida's *Of Grammatology*), Spivak argues that the native informant is placed under erasure by Western thought, but, in the process is revealed to be the condition of possibility of the Western discursive field of articulation. How does this work, and what does this mean? The mechanism whereby this deconstructive act of erasure or crossing-out (but remaining legible) occurs is 'foreclosure', a term used in diverse ways by Sigmund Freud, but stabilized and redefined by Jacques Lacan. In a Lacanian sense, foreclosure is the 'expulsion of a fundamental "signifier" . . . from the subject's symbolic universe'.[2] Lacan believed that this mechanism explained psychotic phenomena in a way distinctive from Freud's notion of repression; Laplanche and Pontalis point out that foreclosed signifiers are not integrated in the subject's unconscious and that they return not from some inner realm of subjectivity but emerge in (the Lacanian concept of) the Real. What is this Real? It is a synthesis of Freud's notion of a simulacrum of reality (that is a reality composed of unconscious desire and fantasies) supplemented by Lacan's borrowings from Bataille, whereby that Real is also regarded as a morbid, doomed or accursed part of subjectivity, an inaccessible 'black shadow'.[3] The fact that the Real is a simulacrum, i.e. it competes with or even replaces material reality, is central to Spivak's reading: the Real accounts for actual processes (the expulsion or foreclosure/repudiation of the native informant) yet resists essentialist notions of subjectivity (the Real is a simulacrum). The native informant is not simply cast 'outside' of colonial networks of power-knowledge, but is foreclosed: expulsed, unintegrated, beyond reach but constitutive of the colonial Real; the native informant is thus simultaneously perceived by Spivak here as an oppressed *and* a powerful subject, repeatedly denied, but always haunting and through the mechanism sketched above, constitutive of the discursive reasoning of the West.

Resistance to homogenization has been a key aspect of Spivak's approach to literary studies. The essay and interview are significant modes of delivery for her because of their provisional status and openness to revision: thus the multiple versions of her essay 'Can the Subaltern Speak?' and the interview collection *The Postcolonial Critic: Interviews, Strategies, Dialogues* (1990). After working so thoroughly with Western theory and philosophy, Spivak has been working towards alternative non-Western conceptual frameworks, such as Hindu *dharma* as an alternative to Western notions of ideology, and new psychoanalytical perspectives developed via the concept of *sati*.[4] In *Death of a Discipline* (2003), Spivak takes her project further as a modified manifestation of comparative literature, one that reorients the entire study of the humanities within a genuinely global perspective.

Notes

1 Ania Loomba, *Colonialism/Postcolonialism*, London and New York: Routledge, 1998, p. 236.
2 Jean Laplanche and J.-B. Pontalis, *The Language of Psycho-Analysis*, trans. Donald Nicholson-Smith, New York: Norton, 1973, p. 166.
3 Elisabeth Roudinesco, *Jacques Lacan: An Outline of a Life and a History of a System of Thought*, trans. Barbara Bray, Cambridge: Polity, 1997, pp. 216–217.
4 Bart Moore-Gilbert, *Postcolonial Theory: Contexts, Practices, Politics*, London and New York: Verso, 1997, p. 98.

See also in this book

Bhabha, Derrida, Said

Major works

Myself I Must Remake: The Life and Poetry of W.B. Yeats (1974). New York: Crowell.
Translation of Jacques Derrida, *Of Grammatology* (1976). Baltimore, MD: Johns Hopkins University Press.
'Three Women's Texts and a Critique of Imperialism' (1985). *Critical Inquiry*, 12.1: 243–261.
In Other Worlds: Essays in Cultural Politics (1987). London: Methuen.
'Can the Subaltern Speak?' (1988). In Cary Nelson and Lawrence Grossberg, eds, *Marx and the Interpretation of Culture*, Urbana, IL: University of Illinois Press.
Selected Subaltern Studies (ed. with Ranajit Guha, 1988). Oxford and New York: Oxford University Press.
The Postcolonial Critic: Interviews, Strategies, Dialogues (1990). Ed. Sarah Harasym, London and New York: Routledge.
Outside in the Teaching Machine (1993). London and New York: Routledge, 1993.
Imaginary Maps: Three Stories (1995). Trans. and intro. by Gayatri Spivak, London and New York: Routledge.

The Spivak Reader (1996). Donna Landry and Gerald MacLean, eds, London and New York: Routledge.
A Critique of Postcolonial Reason: Toward a History of the Vanishing Present (1999). Cambridge, MA: Harvard University Press.
Death of a Discipline (2003). New York: Columbia University Press.

Further reading

Ashcroft, Bill, Griffiths, Gareth and Tiffin, Helen, *Key Concepts in Post-Colonial Studies*, London and New York: Routledge, 1997.
Laplanche, Jean and Pontalis, J.-B., *The Language of Psycho-Analysis*, trans. Donald Nicholson-Smith, New York: Norton, 1973.
Loomba, Ania, *Colonialism/Postcolonialism*, London and New York: Routledge, 1998.
McLeod, John, *Beginning Postcolonialism*, Manchester and New York: Manchester University Press, 2000.
Moore-Gilbert, Bart, *Postcolonial Theory: Contexts, Practices, Politics*, London and New York: Verso, 1997.
Parry, Benita, 'Problems in Current Theories of Colonial Discourse', *Oxford Literary Review*, 9.1–2 (1987): 27–58.
Roudinesco, Elisabeth, *Jacques Lacan: An Outline of a Life and a History of a System of Thought*, trans. Barbara Bray, Cambridge: Polity, 1997.
Young, Robert, *White Mythologies: Writing History and the West*, London and New York: Routledge, 1990.

LIONEL TRILLING (1905–1975)

A writer of significance in the history of American letters, even at the height of his fame Lionel Trilling was considered 'a critic without portfolio'.[1] What this means for the contemporary reader, used to critical categories, theories and factional groups, is that a historical understanding of Trilling's role is as necessary as an intellectual one. Born in New York to a Jewish immigrant family, Trilling studied for his BA at Columbia College, which he gained in 1925, followed by his MA, completed in 1926. Trilling taught at The University of Wisconsin (1926–1927), and back in New York, at Hunter College (1928–1934); he was awarded a fellowship and the position of instructor at Columbia in 1932, a position that was ended in 1936, galvanizing Trilling into action (he argued for renewal of his post and then completed his dissertation, which was published in 1939). Appointed assistant professor at Columbia in 1939, Trilling became a full professor in 1948, George Edward Woodberry Professor of Literature and Criticism in 1965, and University Professor in 1970.[2] This academic biography only provides a partial view, as Mark Krupnick argues:

[Trilling] ... was also involved in radical politics, as a communist fellow traveler in 1932–33 and as a member of the anti-Stalinist left for the remainder of the decade. For Trilling there existed social institutions apart from the English department. There were a variety of left-wing committees and political groups, and there was the world of New York literary journalism, itself energized by the political crisis of these years.[3]

So while Trilling was lecturing and working on his dissertation, he was also intervening in political debates via his journal publications, including 'thirty reviews for the *Nation* between 1930 and 1936, and eleven more essays for the *New Republic* and *Partisan Review* during the last three years of the decade'.[4]

Trilling's first book, his dissertation on Matthew Arnold, expresses both his interest in British culture and that of the wider cultural and critical picture in America. Arnold wrote at what he perceived to be a time of crisis, and Trilling transposed his thoughts on nineteenth-century Britain into an American context. There are four important principal themes in Trilling's study of Arnold: (1) Arnold's relating literature to wider social concerns; (2) Arnold's 'disinterestedness', or, preference for critical observation and thinking rather than immediate action; (3) Arnold's synthesis of reason and faith as expressed via culture; and (4) Arnold's historical/dialectical method.[5] These themes also map the schema that Trilling would apply in his own readings of literature and culture: rarely a close-reader of specific texts, Trilling transformed reading into a process of ethical and political reflection. Trilling followed *Matthew Arnold* with *E.M. Forster* (1943), a study of the British author whose reputation soared throughout the latter half of the twentieth century, especially in relation to his novels *Howards End* and *A Passage to India*. Trilling's study of Forster is balanced, yet critical, and while he argues that T.S. Eliot offers a more powerful theory of reading, he concludes that Forster's approach is essentially more human because of his overriding faith in the moral realism of art. The importance of such an observation is found in the occasional aside in Trilling's book, such as the throwaway remark that Forster's 'impressionist' criticism, which follows the law of 'personality' rather than an 'architectonic' is preferable after 'the long dull battle over Marxist criticism'.[6]

Trilling worked through many of his ethical, existential and political positions in his novel of ideas, *The Middle of the Journey* (1947), which was well received; however, it was his collection of essays that were initially published between 1940 and 1949 – called *The Liberal*

Imagination: Essays on Literature and Society (1950) – that essentially made his name. Key essays in the volume include 'Freud and Literature', 'The Princess Casamassima', 'Manners, Morals, and the Novel', and 'The Meaning of a Literary Idea', among others. *The Liberal Imagination* is a post-war reaction to what Trilling perceived as the stultifying lack of creative and intellectual will in the Cold War period; he countered this lack with another force: that of art.[7] Manifested most clearly for Trilling in the novel form, art expresses two modes of 'will': the positive (mainly found in the nineteenth-century novel) and the negative (mainly occurring in modernist form, or, in overly political systems of thought and expression). However, rather than expressing a main thesis, *The Liberal Imagination* can be thought of as a testing ground for the dominant intellectual force in America at the time of its writing: that of liberalism.[8] Ever since, critics have been divided over the results of this extended test, and even the meaning of the word 'liberalism' in the first place. The collection as a whole may make more sense for contemporary readers when they position Trilling as someone born into an immigrant family, profoundly aware of his Jewish yet Anglophile (on his mother's side) background, and endowed with a liberal education and upbringing, yet tending towards conservatism in thought and action as a reaction against extreme left-wing thought in America and Europe. This was an academic who would powerfully and publicly favour Freud over Marx during the early years of the Cold War, facilitating shifts in attitude and methodology in the humanities. In his essay 'Freud and Literature', Trilling explores the connection between Freud and the 'Romanticist' tradition, arguing that 'psychoanalysis is one of the culminations of the Romanticist literature of the nineteenth century'.[9] After tracing the aesthetic and philosophical roots of Freud's thinking, as well as the progressively superior literary-critical applications of his thought by Freud and others, Trilling concludes that Freud's psychoanalytical system presents the poetic as constitutive of mind. In other words, literature is no longer secondary, but primary in a formative sense, being a method of thought that is also, as with psychoanalysis, 'a science of tropes'.[10] In sketching out some key aspects from Freud, such as the importance of the 'repetition compulsion', Trilling was prophetically mapping much future humanities research. Trilling returned to Freud throughout his career, with many important contributions such as his Freud Anniversary Lecture presented at the New York Psychoanalytic Institute and Society called *Freud and the Crisis of Our Culture* (1955); in this essay Trilling argues among many other things, that literature is fundamentally subversive, since its function is to make us aware not only of human particularity, but also ethical *authority* when combating cultural and societal stultification. Trilling addresses these concerns in another key essay, 'On the Teaching of Modern Literature' (1961) where he suggests that after all of the technical analyses of literature are performed, there is still the question of 'bearing personal testimony', which means the exposure of the self in judging a work true or false.[11] Of course, what Trilling is doing is opposing a Freudian 'moral' approach to that of the Marxist approach which Trilling now fundamentally opposed. This opposition is also useful in clarifying the role of cultural criticism that Trilling practised: as contemporary literary theory turns in some respects full circle back to the ethical demand, rather than analytical close-reading or speculative flights of fancy of high theory, Trilling's championing of an ethical stance, one predicated upon human freedom that is often at odds with the state or society in general, gains new relevance.

Notes

1 Thomas M. Leitch, *Lionel Trilling: An Annotated Bibliography*, New York and London: Garland, 1993, p. xxi.
2 Stephen L. Tanner, *Lionel Trilling*, Boston, MA: Twayne, 1988, p. 19.
3 Mark Krupnick, *Lionel Trilling and the Fate of Cultural Criticism*, Evanston, IL: Northwestern University Press, 1986, pp. 36–37.
4 Ibid., p. 37.
5 Stephen L. Tanner, *Lionel Trilling*, summarizing and modifying pp. 34–37.
6 Lionel Trilling, *E.M. Forster*, Binghampton, NY: New Directions, 1964, p. 165.
7 William M. Chace, *Lionel Trilling: Criticism and Politics*, Stanford, CA: Stanford University Press, 1980, pp. 82–83.
8 Stephen L. Tanner, *Lionel Trilling*, p. 86.
9 Lionel Trilling, *The Liberal Imagination: Essays on Literature and Society*, Garden City, NY: Doubleday/Anchor Books, 1953, p. 33.
10 Ibid., p. 50.
11 Lionel Trilling, *Beyond Culture: Essays on Literature and Learning*, New York: Viking, 1965, p. 9.

Major works

Matthew Arnold (1939). New York: Norton; Second Edition, with new preface, New York: Columbia University Press.
E.M. Forster (1943). New York: New Directions.
The Middle of the Journey [novel of ideas] (1947). New York: Viking.
The Liberal Imagination: Essays on Literature and Society (1950). New York: Viking.

Freud and the Crisis of Our Culture (1955). Boston, MA: Beacon.
The Opposing Self: Nine Essays in Criticism (1955). New York: Viking.
Beyond Culture: Essays on Literature and Learning (1965). New York: Viking.
Sincerity and Authenticity (1972). Cambridge, MA: Harvard University Press.
Mind in the Modern World (1973). New York: Viking.
Prefaces to the Experience of Literature (1979). New York: Harcourt, Brace, Jovanovich.
Speaking of Literature and Society (1980). New York: Harcourt, Brace, Jovanovich.

Further reading

Bender, Thomas, 'Lionel Trilling and American Culture', *American Quarterly*, 42.2 (1990): 324–347.
Chace, William M., *Lionel Trilling: Criticism and Politics*, Stanford, CA: Stanford University Press, 1980.
Krupnick, Mark, *Lionel Trilling and the Fate of Cultural Criticism*, Evanston, IL: Northwestern University Press, 1986.
Leitch, Thomas M., *Lionel Trilling: An Annotated Bibliography*, New York and London: Garland, 1993.
Nowlin, Michael E., 'Lionel Trilling and the Institutionalization of Humanism', *Journal of American Studies*, 25.1 (1991): 23–38.
Tanner, Stephen L., *Lionel Trilling*, Boston, MA: Twayne, 1988.

SLAVOJ ŽIŽEK (1949–)

The Slovenian Lacanian Hegelian[1] Slavoj Žižek is the contemporary dialectician par excellence; the mapping of his identity via the three descriptors that open this sentence, which can be variously positioned and re-positioned, is one way of temporarily locating him. Born in Ljubljana in the former Yugoslavia, during the period of Communist rule, Žižek studied for a degree in philosophy and sociology at the University of Ljubljana, which he was awarded in 1971, followed by postgraduate study in philosophy, and work as a translator. He gained his second doctorate from the Université de Paris, in 1985, writing on the philosopher Hegel and the psychoanalyst Jacques Lacan. Žižek's major foray into politics culminated in an unsuccessful attempt to become a pro-reform presidential candidate, on a shared platform, in the 1990 Slovenian elections. Žižek next concentrated on his academic research, with his post at the Institute for Social Studies at The University of Ljubljana and a number of visiting professorships at American universities. Žižek currently holds a post at Birkbeck, University of London, where he is the International Director of The Birkbeck Institute for the Humanities.

It was two books based upon his Paris doctorate and published in English translation, that first rudely awoke the world to Žižekian discourse: *The Sublime Object of Ideology* (1989) and *For They Know Not What They Do: Enjoyment as a Political Factor* (1990). Another key early text in the English speaking world is *The Žižek Reader* (1999), edited by Elizabeth Wright and Edmond Wright. Turning to Žižek's exhilarating prose also leads to an associated problem for many beginning readers: the mélange therein of Lacanian discourse and Hegelian methodology – which alternately are 'illuminated' by reference to popular culture, or 'illuminate' popular culture by reference to psychoanalysis/philosophy – induces some anxiety and stress. The cure may be to not worry and to enjoy one's symptom; this involves realizing two things: (1) that Žižek writes dialectically, which means that any particular point in one of his arguments is a temporary stage that will eventually be transformed via its opposing argument (proceeding therefore via Hegelian *negation*), and (2) that Žižek is part of the Slovene Lacanian School, which operates at a level of intellectual intensity rarely glimpsed in the West. But Žižek's work is not impenetrable, rather, one simply needs to learn a few key Lacanian terms, watch a few Hitchcock movies, and then sit back and enjoy the Hegelian ride. Perhaps the key term to approach the Žižekian rollercoaster equipped with, is the 'Real'. This is a Lacanian term that the editors of *The Žižek Reader* describe as 'that which is both inside and outside the subject, resisting the Symbolic's endeavours to contain it'.[2] This definition begs the question: what is the Symbolic? All Lacanian terms are understandable as part of a process of subject formation: sticking with simply the main coordinates, there are three relevant interrelated terms, the pre-linguistic *Imaginary*, the cultural and linguistic *Symbolic*, and the *Real*; the Imaginary is structured by needs and image-identifications; the Symbolic is structured by language and the law; the Real is that which can neither be pictured nor articulated through language. The Real is *not* reality, existing in opposition to it; it is that which is at the limits of language, and can only be partially and incompletely approached as, or via, trauma, lack or enjoyment.[3] But the Real is constitutive and as such forms a 'hard kernel' at the heart of existence. Much of Žižek's writing is an oblique approach to the Real.

Žižek's Hegelianism is highly self-reflexive and self-explanatory; in a chapter of *The Ticklish Subject: The Absent Centre of Political Ontology* (1999), Žižek asks 'What Is "Negation of Negation"?'. He answers via a range of examples: a 'New Age airport pocketbook' called *From Atlantis to the Sphinx* by Colin Wilson, an academic book called *States of Injury* by Wendy Brown, a brief reference to anthropology, then Marx's *Capital*, and finally the 'experience' of the dissident struggle against Party rule in Slovenia. How does his argument proceed? First he notes the surprisingly Hegelian conclusion to *From Atlantis to the Sphinx*, where the historical transition from intuitive to logical types of knowledge, and the current phase of 'reuniting the two halves', is resolved not via some bland and balanced New Age synthesis of intuition/logic, but through recognition that *it has already happened*; as Žižek says:

> the unavoidable conclusion is that *the moment of the Fall (the forgetting of the ancient wisdom) coincides with its exact opposite, with the longed-for next step in evolution.* Here we have the properly Hegelian matrix of development: the Fall is already *in itself* its own self-sublation; the wound is already in itself its own healing, so that the perception that we are dealing with the Fall is ultimately a misperception, an effect of our skewed perspective – all we have to do is accomplish the move from In-itself to For-Itself: to change our perspective and recognize how the longed-for reversal is already operative in what is going on.[4]

This is a slightly long-winded way of saying that the subject of 'misperception' is in need of Lacanian psychoanalysis. Except, of course, that Žižek does not say this; he instead gives the reader another example, that of a 'misperceived' world devoid of oppressors, where such a perspective fails to realize that it is mediated by the oppressor in the first place. Žižek thus poses two answers to his question that structure this chapter: first, negation of negation is a two-stage process, the first negation leaving the subject inside the symbolic domain she is rejecting, the second negation being that of the symbolic domain itself; this is then recognized by Žižek to be a 'pure repetition'. What is the point of this chapter? First, it reveals that the Hegelian dialect can be exposed or learnt through examples that have a certain narrative form; second, that a really good way of moving from In-itself to For-itself is via psychoanalysis (moving from 'misperception' to recognition); third it reveals how applying Hegel allows a rapid and smooth traversal of anthropological, cultural, political, philosophical and sexual domains of experience and knowledge; and fourth, it enables us to admire Žižek himself, as the grand expositor of Hegel via unusual examples. Žižek himself gets even more unusual with his explication of Christianity, but this must be understood to be part of his wider engagement with important twentieth-century thinkers in the humanities, in this instance the philosopher Alain Badiou. Žižek is interested in Badiou's 'politics of truth' or 'theory of subjectivity as fidelity to the Truth-Event'.[5] This theory is given full expression in Badiou's reading of St Paul, but Žižek also gives minor examples from moments of unexpected and unpredictable political change. In *The Puppet and the Dwarf: The Perverse Core of Christianity* (2003), Žižek's own reading of St Paul hinges on the recognition of a shared question between St Paul and Lacan: is there love beyond law?[6] The answer is that only in the incomplete, imperfectability of subjectivity can there be love, and this elevation of imperfection is the Real of Christianity. Žižek also engages extensively with the feminist and gender theorist Judith Butler. As Sarah Kay argues, in this engagement Žižek's fidelity to Lacan reveals a certain weakness in his earlier theorizing of 'woman', a weakness that Butler is aware of; further, by charting Žižek's reading of a single film – *The Crying Game* – his movement through multiple perspectives is revealed, thus Žižek moves

> from occupying a 'heterosexist normative' position condemned by Butler, via a 'queer' position that is quite Butlerian, to adroitly contending that it is, in reality, *Butler* who confers a content on sexual difference and thus normalizes it in a way Žižek would reject.[7]

Žižek switches from the entire Oedipal scene of conflict to a new notion, drawn from Lacan, whereby sexual difference is constituted via a struggle with the death drive: Butler, in this instance, remains rooted in an orthodox notion of gender, with the logical impasse of positing gender identification and misidentification at a stage in subjective formation prior to the Symbolic – in other words, before there is such a thing as gender differentiation. It is in Žižek's engagement with Deleuze, however, that he has received the most opprobrium: in this instance, Žižek's shameful act is the book *Organs Without Bodies: On Deleuze and Consequences* (2004), which Žižek calls 'an *encounter* between two incompatible fields'.[8] This encounter creates Lacanian and Hegelian equivalences to certain key terms, starting on the very first page, where Deleuze's 'excess of the pure flow of becoming' or the reality of the virtual is posited as the Lacanian Real. In other words, there is not just a Lacanian/Hegelian critique of Deleuze at work in this book, but also a recuperation. A more important equivalence is that of Deleuze's 'quasi-cause' with that of

Lacan's '*objet petit a*'; the former is an 'excess' in the emergence of the new, one that cannot be reduced in any way to historical context; Žižek calls the 'quasi-cause' a 'metacause' whereby the effects already exceed the causal explanations. In a Lacanian shift, Žižek postulates that the 'cause' of desire, which is the object and cause of desire at the same time, called '*objet petit a*' functions in the same way as the 'quasi-cause':

> the basic premise of Deleuze's ontology is precisely that corporeal causality is *not* complete. In the emergence of the New, something occurs that *cannot* be properly described at the level of corporal causes and effects. Quasi cause is not the illusory theater of shadows, like a child who thinks he is magically making a toy run, unaware of the mechanic causality that effectively does the work – on the contrary, the quasi cause *fills in the gap of corporeal causality*.[9]

The popular commentator on postmodernism and theory, Steven Shaviro, notes that Deleuze and Guattari foreground this link between their work and Lacan's in a footnote in their *Anti-Oedipus*; Shaviro also sketches one of the 'problems' with Žižek's book for many readers, that the recuperated Deleuze is reduced and constrained by the Lacanian-Hegelianism that charges Žižek's writing.[10] Žižek's oblique approach to the Real, then, causes exhilaration and anxiety, creating simultaneously a feeling of intellectual freedom and oppression; the fact that so many commentators on his work express their own psychological and emotional state, is in itself, perhaps, indicative of a desire to be analysed by Žižek, while simultaneously being horrified by the thought. Perhaps it is a Hegelian desire to move from the In-itself to For-itself, gaining the awareness as Žižek argues in *Organs Without Bodies* that the 'truly New is not simply a new content but the very shift of perspective by means of which the Old appears in a new light'.[11]

Notes

1 Ian Parker, *Slavoj Žižek: A Critical Introduction*, London: Pluto, 2004, p. 5.
2 Elizabeth Wright and Edmond Wright, *The Žižek Reader*, Oxford: Blackwell, 1999, p. 3.
3 Sarah Kay, *Žižek: A Critical Introduction*, Cambridge: Polity, 2003, p. 168.
4 *Slavoj Žižek, The Ticklish Subject: The Absent Centre of Political Ontology*, London and New York: Verso, 1999, p. 71.
5 Ibid., p. 3.

6 Slavoj Žižek, *The Puppet and the Dwarf: The Perverse Core of Christianity*, Cambridge, MA: MIT Press, 2003, p. 114.
7 Ibid., p. 95.
8 Slavoj Žižek, *Organs Without Bodies: Deleuze and Consequences*, London and New York: Routledge, 2004, p. xi.
9 Ibid., p. 27.
10 Steven Shaviro, www.shaviro.com/Blog/?p=229, accessed 21 October 2005.
11 Slavoj Žižek, *Organs Without Bodies: Deleuze and Consequences*, p. 14.

See also in this book

Lacan

Major works

Le Plus Sublime des hystériques: Hegel passe (1988). Paris: Point Hors Ligne.
The Sublime Object of Ideology (1989). London and New York: Verso.
For They Know Not What They Do: Enjoyment as a Political Factor (1991). London and New York: Verso.
Looking Awry: An Introduction to Jacques Lacan through Popular Culture (1991). Cambridge, MA: MIT Press.
Everything You Always Wanted to Know about Lacan (But Were Afraid to Ask Hitchcock) (ed., 1992). London and New York: Verso.
Enjoy Your Symptom! Jacques Lacan in Hollywood and Out (1992). London and New York: Routledge.
Tarrying with the Negative: Kant, Hegel, and the Critique of Ideology (1993). Durham, NC: Duke University Press.
Mapping Ideology (ed., 1994). London and New York: Verso.
The Metastases of Enjoyment: Six Essays on Woman and Causality (1994). London and New York: Verso.
The Indivisible Remainder: An Essay on Schelling and Related Matters (1996). London and New York: Verso.
The Plague of Fantasies (1997). London and New York: Verso.
The Ticklish Subject: The Absent Centre of Political Ontology (1999). London and New York: Verso.
The Art of the Ridiculous Sublime: On David Lynch's Lost Highway (2000). Seattle, WA: University of Washington.
Contingency, Hegemony, Universality: Contemporary Dialogues on the Left (with Judith Butler and Ernesto Laclau, 2000). London and New York: Verso.
The Fragile Absolute – or, Why is the Christian Legacy Worth Fighting For? (2000). London and New York: Verso.
Did Somebody Say Totalitarianism? Five Interventions in the (Mis)Use of a Notion (2001). London and New York: Verso.
The Fright of Real Tears: Krzystof Kieślowski Between Theory and Post-Theory (2001). London: British Film Institute.
On Belief (2001). London and New York: Routledge.
Opera's Second Death (with Mladen Dolar, 2002). London and New York: Routledge.
Revolution at the Gates (ed., 2002). London and New York: Verso.

Welcome to the Desert of the Real: Five Essays on September 11 and Related Dates (2002). London and New York: Verso.
The Puppet and the Dwarf: The Perverse Core of Christianity (2003). Cambridge, MA: MIT Press.
Organs Without Bodies: Deleuze and Consequences (2004). London and New York, Routledge.
Iraq: The Borrowed Kettle (2005). London and New York: Verso.
The Universal Exception (2005). London and New York: Continuum.

Further reading

Baker, Harold D., 'Psychoanalysis and Ideology: Bakhtin, Lacan, and Žižek', *History of European Ideas*, 20.1–3 (1995): 499–504.
Dean, Tim, 'Art as Symptom: Žižek and the Ethics of Psychoanalytical Criticism', *Diacritics*, 32.2 (2002): 21–41.
Eagleton, Terry, 'Enjoy!', *Paragraph*, 24.2 (2001): 40–52.
Kay, Sarah, *Žižek: A Critical Introduction*, Cambridge: Polity, 2003.
Miklitsch, Robert, '"Going through the Fantasy": Screening Slavoj Žižek', *South Atlantic Quarterly*, 97.2 (1998): 475–507.
Parker, Ian, *Slavoj Žižek: A Critical Introduction*, London: Pluto, 2004.

INDEX

Note: **bold** type indicates the main chapter pagination for each theorist; in each chapter there is coverage of each theorist's key texts and concepts. Theoretical concepts are given separate entries in the index to aid in finding them throughout the text.

The Routledge Companion to Critical Theory

Edited by Simon Malpas and Paul Wake

The Routledge Companion to Critical Theory is an indispensable aid for anyone approaching this exciting field of study for the first time.

By exploring ideas from a diverse range of disciplines 'theory' encourages us to develop a deeper understanding of how we approach the written word. This book defines what is generically referred to as 'critical theory', and guides readers through some of the most complex and fundamental concepts in the field, ranging from Historicism to Postmodernism, from Psychoanalytic Criticism to Race and Postcoloniality.

Fully cross referenced throughout, the book encompasses manageable introductions to important ideas followed by a dictionary of terms and thinkers which students are likely to encounter. Further reading is offered to guide students to crucial primary essays and introductory chapters on each concept.

ISBN10: 0–415–33296–6 (pbk)
ISBN10: 0–415–33296–6 (hbk)

ISBN13: 978–0–415–33296–5 (pbk)
ISBN13: 978–0–415–33296–5 (hbk)

Literary Theory: The Basics

Hans Bertens

Part of the successful *Basics* series, this accessible guide provides the ideal first step in understanding literary theory. Hans Bertens:

■ leads students through the major approaches to literature which are signalled by the term 'literary theory'
■ places each critical movement in its historical (and often political) context
■ illustrates theory in practice with examples from much-read texts
■ suggests further reading for different critical approaches
■ shows that theory can make sense and that it can radically change the way we read.

Covering the basics and much more, this is the ideal book for anyone interested in how we read and why that matters.

ISBN10: 0–415–35112–X (pbk)
ISBN13: 978–0–415–35112–6 (pbk)

Available at all good bookshops
For ordering and further information please visit
www.routledge.com

The Routledge Dictionary of Literary Terms

Peter Childs and Roger Fowler

The Routledge Dictionary of Literary Terms is a twenty-first-century
update of Roger Fowler's seminal *Dictionary of Modern Critical
Terms*. Bringing together original entries written by such
celebrated theorists as Terry Eagleton and Malcolm Bradbury
with new definitions of current terms and controversies, this is
the essential reference book for students of literature at all levels.
This book includes:

- New definitions of contemporary critical issues such as
  'Cybercriticism' and 'Globalization'
- An exhaustive range of entries, covering numerous aspects
  to such topics as genre, form, cultural theory and literary
  technique
- Complete coverage of traditional and radical approaches to
  the study and production of literature
- Thorough account of critical terminology and analyses of
  key academic debates
- Full cross-referencing throughout and suggestions for
  further reading.

ISBN10: 0–415–34017–9 (pbk)
ISBN10: 0–415–36117–6 (hbk)

ISBN13: 978–0–415–34017–5 (pbk)
ISBN13: 978–0–415–36117–0 (hbk)

Available at all good bookshops
For ordering and further information please visit
www.routledge.com